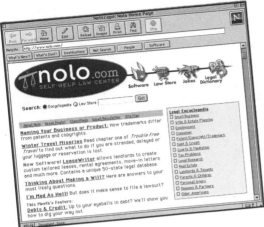

First Edition

Open Your CALIFORNIA BUSINESS

in 24 hours

THE COMPLETE START-UP KIT

By Peri H. Pakroo, J.D.

nolo.com
LAW FOR ALL

YOUR RESPONSIBILITY WHEN USING A SELF-HELP BOOK

We've done our best to give you useful and accurate information in this book. But laws and procedures change frequently and are subject to differing interpretations. If you want legal advice backed by a guarantee, see a lawyer. If you use this book, it's your responsibility to make sure that the facts and general advice contained in it are applicable to your situation.

KEEPING UP TO DATE

To keep its books up to date, Nolo issues new printings and new editions periodically. New printings reflect minor legal changes and technical corrections. New editions contain major legal changes, major text additions or major reorganizations. To find out if a later printing or edition of any Nolo book is available, call Nolo at 510-549-1976 or check our website: www.nolo.com.

To stay current, follow the "Update" service at our website: www.nolo.com. In another effort to help you use Nolo's latest materials, we offer a 35% discount off the purchase of the new edition of your Nolo book when you turn in the cover of an earlier edition. (See the "Special Upgrade Offer" in the back of the book.)

This book was last revised in: August 1999

First Edition	January 1999
Editor	Beth Laurence
Book Design	Linda Wanczyk
Cover Design	Linda Wanczyk
Production	Sarah Toll & Linda Wanczyk
Proofreader	Naomi Leite
Index	Sayre Van Young
Printing	Consolidated Printers

Pakroo, Peri H.
      Open your California business in 24 hours: The complete
start-up kit / by Peri H. Pakroo.
      p. cm.
      Includes index.
      ISBN 0-87337-410-X
      1. New business enterprises -- California -- Handbooks, manuals, etc.
2. Business planning -- California -- Handbooks, manuals, etc. I.
Title.
      HD62.5.P28 1997
      658.1'141'09794--dc21
                               97-37388
                                  CIP

Quantity sales: For information on bulk purchases or corporate premium sales, please contact the Special Sales department. For academic sales or textbook adoptions, ask for Academic Sales. 800-955-4775, Nolo Press, Inc., 950 Parker St., Berkeley, CA 94710.

ACKNOWLEDGMENTS

All authors should be so lucky to have such a swell team of people helping them through the process of writing a book. Thanks to Jake Warner for giving me the inspiration and encouragement to start this book, and to finish it when my mind and fingertips were weary. Major thanks to Beth Laurence for tightening up the information and streamlining it into a finished product. And thanks to the whole editorial staff at Nolo for convincing me I would eventually reach the light at the end of the tunnel with my brain intact.

Thanks to Linda Marie Wanczyk for her creative and clear sense of design. And also to Ely Newman for patiently walking me through the technicalities of putting forms on disk. Sincere thanks to David Rothenberg for lending a CFO's eye to my discussion of small business finances.

Many thanks to all the folks at *The Stranger* and The Paper Formerly Known as *NuCity*—especially Tim Keck and Chris Johnson—for proving to me that it's people and their ideas, not industry rules and standards, that make a small business tick.

Thanks to all my family and friends for their patience and sensitivity in not asking too often "Is your book done yet?"

Most of all, love and thanks to Turtle for keeping my soul happy and free when my mind was not.

DEDICATION

I dedicate this book to my mom and dad, Kay and Reza Pakroo, who for better or worse somehow convinced me I could do anything—even write a book.

ABOUT THE AUTHOR

Before joining the editorial staff at Nolo Press, Peri Pakroo was the editor of two arts and entertainment weeklies—*The Stranger* in Seattle and *NuCity* in Albuquerque—both of which she helped launch with a scrappy crew of expatriates from Wisconsin, her home state. She took a break from publishing to go to law school, and received a law degree from the University of New Mexico in 1995. Bringing together her law and publishing experience, she began editing legal books for Nolo in 1996, specializing in small business issues. She has edited Nolo's *Starting & Running a Successful Newsletter or Magazine, Music Law: How to Run Your Band's Business, Getting Permission: How to License & Clear Copyrighted Materials Online & Off,* and *How to Write a Business Plan,* among other titles. She lives with Juno, Kitty B and Turtle in San Francisco.

TABLE OF CONTENTS

CHAPTER 1

Working for Yourself Is Easier Than You Think

CHAPTER 2

Choosing a Legal Structure

Picking a Winning Business Name That Won't Land You in Court

Choosing a Legal and Lucrative Business Location

Drafting an Effective Business Plan

Federal, State and Local Start-Up Requirements

Insuring Your Business

Getting to Know Your Taxes

CHAPTER 9

Drafting Contracts and Agreements

CHAPTER 10

Bookkeeping, Accounting and Financial Management

C H A P T E R (11)

Your Healthy, Growing Business

C H A P T E R (12)

Getting Professional Help

Government Agencies and Small Business Resources

California County Clerks

Start-up Forms

A P P E N D I X D

How to Use the Forms Disk

Index

Working for Yourself Is Easier Than You Think

You don't have an MBA. Hell, you've never taken a business class. You spent your college years studying literature and art history, and periodically dropping out to travel the world. And now you find yourself thinking about going into business for yourself—maybe restoring antiques, or illustrating books, or running a cafe or selling software. "Me, a businessperson?" you skeptically wonder. You keep trudging to work each morning, but as the hours tick by you find yourself fantasizing more and more about kissing your 9-to-5 job goodbye. You jot down some notes, work out some kinks in your plan and continue to wonder whether it just might fly....

Unfortunately, most people who have toyed with business ideas this way never get to find out whether they would have worked or not. For a variety of practical, financial and psychological reasons, they never make the leap from idea to reality. This is really a shame, since there's nothing that complex or difficult about turning a business idea into an actual working business. Most prospective entrepreneurs would be surprised—and encouraged—to know that the line between "I'm thinking about starting my own business" and "I own and run my own business!" consists of nothing more than a short list of bureaucratic tasks. This book will explain what those tasks are and where to go to complete them.

Stephen Parr,

owner and director of Oddball Film and Video, a stock footage company in San Francisco:

I started making video art in the 1970s. After a while I started collecting all these weird bits of film because it was cheaper than shooting it myself. I gathered all kinds of old, found footage like military training films, educational films, home movies and all kinds of other images and put them together into montages, which I screened in nightclubs as background visuals. I was

showing them all over—clubs in New York, Chicago, San Francisco—and I made some money by selling the tapes to the clubs.

Then I started getting calls from these companies in Silicon Valley who produce industrial videos, like training films and promotional programs for corporate trade shows. Video game companies were calling, too. Companies like Sega, Sun Microsystems and Silicon Graphics wanted to pay me for my footage. The guy I lived with at the time thought I should go into business selling the stock footage I had collected, but at the time, I didn't know if I could make a living doing it. I didn't know anything about the stock footage business. There were a few companies doing it, but they were in New York or L.A., and they seemed really huge.

But since I liked working with images and since the business started to take off on its own, I finally decided to formalize it. I started by picking a company name. I wanted something interesting that conveyed what I did. We came up with Oddball. It's a word that people don't really use anymore, more of a '40s or '50s expression— an oddball is someone kind of weird, unbalanced, or unusual, you know? Well, from there, I just kept compiling more footage, and over the years I started logging it, and buying more.

At the most basic level, my business involves finding, organizing and preserving historical footage. And then distributing it. Our clients include ad agencies; news organizations; documentary and feature film makers; industrial, corporate and music video producers; educational filmmakers; and anyone who needs offbeat and unusual images. In one way we're like a library. We archive and license historical visual information.

These days, I spend most of my time trying to organize and publicize my business. We just launched our Website, and that takes time to maintain. And I spend a lot more time trying to obtain films than actually looking at them. Still, what I do at Oddball is an extension of the work I've been doing all along. I guess it became a business the day I decided I wasn't going to do anything else.

A. 24 Hours? You've Got to Be Kidding!

No, we're not joking or trying to fool you by saying you can start your small business in 24 hours. As long as you've got a business idea that you've developed to a certain degree, all you need to do is visit a few government offices, fill out some forms and pay some fees—and within a day, your idea will have become an actual, legitimate business. Some sole proprietorships and partnerships can be started by registering with just one government office; the simplest corporations have only a couple more registration tasks to complete. You'll see that one business day is plenty of time to finish all your registration tasks, with time to spare for lunch.

Obviously, 24 hours isn't enough time to come up with a brand-new business idea and do all the planning necessary to launch it—but that's not the point of this book. Unlike many other small business guides, we're not going to waste your time quizzing you on whether you have the right personality to be your own boss, or evaluating your business idea, or helping you to identify the personal goals that you hope to achieve by starting a business. If you need more help deciding whether or not you want to start a business or what kind of business you should start, you should probably buy a different book. If, on the other hand, you want a book that cuts to the chase and explains systematically what you need to do to launch a business in California, this book is for you.

But this book is also for those of you who are somewhere in between: fairly certain you want to give your business idea a try but not quite ready to march down to city hall to get your business license. Because, in addition to explaining the official start-up requirements in California, this book also outlines the preliminary work you should do before heading out to file all your official forms. In Chapters 2 through 5, we discuss fundamental tasks such as choosing the right legal structure for your business (sole proprietorship, partnership, LLC or corporation), coming up with a catchy and legally sound business name, and choosing a location that's good for business. We also explain how to draft a business plan that will help you define your business, plan for profitability and attract lenders and investors. If you've already taken care of some or all these tasks, you can either skip these chapters or use them as a guide to evaluate what you've already done.

Finally, to help you all the way through your start-up days, in later chapters we introduce you to a number of basic issues that every ongoing business needs to deal with. These include insurance, taxes, contracts and agreements, and bookkeeping and accounting. Though they're not exactly start-up requirements, they're important to understand in the dawning days of your business so that you'll be able to handle them later when business is fast and furious.

Valerie Hoecke,

owner of Fire Engine Red, a Web development firm:

The legal steps of starting my business weren't really that bad. The hardest thing seemed to be figuring out in which order to do all the steps. My advice to people just starting would be to keep your wits about you; laugh at the fact that maybe you have been standing in the wrong line or made a trip to the wrong office on any particular day. Business owners need to have a sense of humor about their mistakes and be prepared to make errors and backtrack once in a while. Looking back, the start-up process seemed a bit trying at the time, but now I wish that all my business problems were so simple!

Businesses with employees have significant additional responsibilities. In Chapter 11, we offer a general overview of the laws and regulations that govern businesses with employees. If you're thinking about hiring employees, that chapter will help you figure out if you're ready to tackle the many requirements that come with your first hire. It also explains the difference between employees and independent contractors—an important distinction, because using independent contractors does not subject you to most of the laws that apply when you hire employees. If you decide that you need to hire any employees, you'll need to do further reading. An excellent and exhaustive resource is Nolo's *The Employer's Legal Handbook,* by attorney Fred S. Steingold.

B. Making the Decision to Go Official

Some of you may be facing a different question. Instead of wondering whether or not to start a business, you may be trying to decide whether or not to formalize your business—to go the official route and register your business with the appropriate agencies. If you're not sure whether you want to register your business and open it up to the world of government regulations, the information about registration requirements in this book will put you in a better position to make a decision. Chapter 6 walks you through the many governmental requirements that apply to all new businesses, and explains how to go about finding and satisfying any additional requirements that may apply to your specific business.

Generally speaking, any good-sized or otherwise visible business should bite the bullet and complete all necessary registration tasks. Operating under the table can all too easily be exposed, which opens you up to hostile legal action, including fines, penalties and maybe even padlocking the business, simply for operating without the necessary registrations. And if you're making a profit, ignoring the IRS is definitely a bad idea. Besides fines and back taxes, you could even face criminal charges and jail time.

On the other hand, tiny, home-based, hobby-type businesses can often operate for quite some time without meeting registration requirements. If you're braiding hair or holding an occasional junk sale out of your garage, for instance, you could probably get by without formal business registration—at least for a while. Keep in mind, however, that just because it may be possible doesn't mean it's the best option. Often, formally registering your business can benefit you, the owner, as well, since you can then write off business expenses and reduce your personal taxes. In Chapter 4, we discuss hobby businesses in more depth, including how tax laws deal with businesses that continually lose money.

Stephen Parr,

owner and director of Oddball Film and Video, a stock footage company in San Francisco:

> *What a business really is, is you deciding you have a business. It's really nothing more than that.*

C. Business Isn't Brain Surgery

One of the main ideas we want you to take away from this book is that there's nothing mysterious or even terribly complex about the process of starting your own business. Whether you've drafted a highly specific business plan with the help of accountants and consultants or you've scratched it out on a cocktail napkin, the process of turning that idea into a legitimate business is the same. That process is covered in this book.

Choosing a Legal Structure

Even though you may not realize it, chances are you already have a rough idea of the type of legal structure your business will take. That's because in large part, your business's status as a sole proprietorship, partnership or other legal entity depends on how many people will own the business and what type of services or products it will provide—things you've undoubtedly given lots of thought. For instance, if you know that you will be the only owner, then a partnership is obviously not your thing. And if your business will engage in risky activities (for example, repairing roofs), in addition to buying insurance you'll almost surely want to form a corporation or limited liability company, which can shield your personal assets from business liabilities. But in many instances the choice is not that clear-cut.

In California, the basic types of business organization are:

- sole proprietorships
- partnerships
- corporations, and
- limited liability companies (LLCs).

This chapter explains the basic attributes of each business form to help you pick the best one for your business. And yes, we will help you answer the most common question new entrepreneurs ask about choosing a business form: Should I incorporate? As a hint as to what our advice will be, consider that if you focus your energy and money into getting your business off the ground as a sole proprietorship or a partnership, you can always incorporate or form an LLC later.

Incorporated vs. Unincorporated Businesses

One basic distinction that you'll probably hear mentioned lots of times is the difference between incorporated businesses and unincorporated ones. Corporations and LLCs are both, legally speaking, incorporated. Sole proprietorships and partnerships are not.

So what does it mean to be incorporated? Basically, it boils down to being recognized by the law as a business entity that exists separately from its owners. An unincorporated business, by contrast, doesn't have an independent existence. It can't sue, or pay taxes, for example; its owners do those things. It's simply an extension of the sole proprietor or partners who created it.

Perhaps it will help if you think of an incorporated business as a newborn legal baby that will live and grow (and be responsible for its own debts) independently from its owners. An unincorporated business, on the other hand, is simply another earning opportunity of the owner that would no longer exist if the owner didn't want to pursue it (and for which the owner is entirely responsible).

As you read about specific business types in this chapter, you'll see how your decision to incorporate or not will dramatically affect how you run your business. Unincorporated sole proprietorships and partnerships, for example, are simpler to run than corporations (in part because taxes only have to be reported on their owners' returns), but may leave an owner personally vulnerable to business problems such as lawsuits and debts. You'll also see how California's newest business form, the limited liability company, has many of the best characteristics of both incorporated and unincorporated businesses.

A. Sole Proprietorships

Technically, a sole proprietorship is a business that is owned by one person. Sole proprietorships are easy to set up and to maintain—so easy that many people own sole proprietorships and don't even know it! Freelance photographers and writers, craftspeople who take jobs on a contract basis, salespeople who receive only commissions and independent contractors who are not on any employer's regular payroll are all sole proprietors. This is true whether or not you've registered your business with your city or obtained any licenses or permits. And it makes no difference whether you also have a regular day job. As long as you operate a for-profit business on your own (or sometimes with your spouse—see Section 1, below) and have not incorporated or formed a limited liability company, you are a sole proprietor.

Ignoring local registration requirements may get you in trouble. Just because you blunder into starting a business without quite realizing it—for example, you do a little freelance computer programming, which classifies you as a sole proprietorship by default—don't let the fact that you're technically a sole proprietorship or a partnership fool you into thinking that you've satisfied the governmental requirements for starting a business. Most cities in California require businesses—even tiny home-based sole proprietorships—to register with the city and pay at least a minimum tax. And if you do business under a name different from your own, you must register that name—known as a fictitious business name—with your county. In practice, lots of businesses are small enough to get away with ignoring these requirements. But if you are caught, you may be subject to back taxes and other penalties. How to register your business with the necessary government offices is explained in step-by-step detail in Chapter 6.

1. Running a Business With Your Spouse

A married couple can jointly own and operate a business as a sole proprietorship, under certain conditions. For tax purposes, your spouse is allowed to work for your sole proprietorship without being classified as an employee or as a business partner. This setup, sometimes called a husband/wife sole proprietorship, offers some benefits in the taxes you'll owe and the paperwork you need to keep. For one, allowing your spouse to work for you without classifying him as an employee frees you from having to pay payroll tax. That not only saves you money but, if you have no other employees, also allows you to avoid the time-consuming record-keeping involved in being an employer. Similarly, if you choose not to classify your spouse as a partner or an independent contractor, he won't have to pay self-employment taxes and your business won't have to file a partnership tax return. (See Chapter 8 for more detailed information on taxes.)

So if he's not an employee or a partner, then what is your spouse? The answer is: nothing in particular. There's no official title for a person who works for his spouse's sole proprietorship. Just accept the IRS's good graces for allowing his informal status—and don't ask questions.

Husband/wife sole proprietorships aren't for everyone. The IRS's special rule about husband/wife sole proprietorships is designed to give some leeway to a sole proprietor who's married, by allowing the sole proprietor's spouse to work for the business without triggering tax requirements that normally apply to employees or business partners. It's not intended for spouses who want to share business decision-making equally. If you and your spouse want to be active partners in a co-owned business, create a partnership. If your spouse tries to squeak by as a non-classified worker in a husband/wife sole proprietorship when you're really working together as a partnership, if you're audited the IRS might decide for itself that you're a partnership—and sock the spouse with back self-employment taxes.

2. Pass-Through Taxation

In the eyes of the law, a sole proprietorship business is not legally separate from the person who owns it. This is one of the fundamental differences between a sole proprietorship and a corporation or LLC. The fact that a sole proprietorship and its owner are one and the same has two major effects: one related to taxation, and the other to legal liability.

One key feature of sole proprietorships is that at income tax time, you simply report all business income or loss on your personal federal return. The business itself is not taxed. The IRS calls this pass-through status, because business profits are taxed only when they pass through to the business owner. The only difference between reporting income from a business and reporting wages from a job is that along with Form 1040, you'll need to include Schedule C, on which you'll provide your business's profit and loss information. One helpful aspect of this arrangement is that if your business loses money—and, of course, many start-ups do in the first year or two—the business losses can be used to offset any taxable income you have earned from other sources.

Example:

Rob has a day job at a coffee shop at a modest salary. His hobby is collecting obscure records at thrift stores and rummage sales. Contemplating the sad fact that he has no extra money to spend at the flea market on Saturday morning, he decides to sell some of the vinyl gems he's found. Still working his day job, he starts a small sole proprietorship that he calls Rob's Revolving Records.

During his first full year in business, he sees that a key to consistently selling his records is developing connections and trust among record collectors. Unfortunately, while he is concentrating on getting to know potential buyers and others in the business, sales are slow. At year-end he closes out his books and sees that marketing items like business cards, a Website and other incidental supplies have cost him nearly $9,000, while he made only $3,000 in sales. But there is some good news: Rob's loss of $6,000 can be counted against his income from his day job, which will reduce his taxes by about $2,000. That translates into a nice refund check, which he'll put right into the record business.

Be ready for the day you'll owe taxes. Once your business is underway and turning a profit, you'll undoubtedly be more concerned with taxes than in the early days of your business, when you're probably losing money. For detailed information on taxes for the various types of small businesses, be sure to read *Tax Savvy for Small Business*, by attorney Frederick W. Daily (Nolo Press). This book gives exhaustive information on deductions, recordkeeping and audits, which will help you minimize your tax bill and stay out of trouble with the IRS.

3. Personal Liability for Business Debts

Another crucial thing to know about sole proprietorships is that you, as the business owner, can be held personally liable for business-related obligations. This means that if your business doesn't pay a supplier, defaults on a debt, loses a lawsuit or otherwise finds itself in financial hot water, you, personally, will be forced to pay up. No question, this can be a sobering possibility, especially if you own (or soon hope to) a cool house, car or other treasures. Personal liability for business obligations stems from the fundamental legal attribute of being a sole proprietor: you and your business are one and inseparable.

As explained in more detail in Sections C and D of this chapter, the law provides owners of corporations and LLCs (incorporated businesses) with what the law calls "limited personal liability" for business obligations. This means that, unlike sole proprietors, people who use an incorporated business form—and who do not personally guarantee a loan or other obligation—can normally keep their house, investments and other personal property, even if their business fails. If you are engaged in a risky business, you may want to consider forming a corporation or an LLC (although a thorough insurance policy often does the trick).

4. Creating a Sole Proprietorship

Setting up your sole proprietorship is incredibly easy. Unlike an LLC or a corporation, you don't have to file any forms or pay any fees to the state to begin business as a sole proprietor. All that's required is that you declare your business to be a sole proprietorship when completing the general registration requirements that apply to all new businesses, such as registering with your county or city.

For example, when filing for a business tax registration certificate with your city, you'll be asked to declare what kind of business you're starting. In some cities this involves checking the "sole proprietorship" box on a form, while other cities have separate tax registration forms for sole proprietorships. Similarly, other forms you will file, such as those to register a fictitious business name and to obtain a seller's permit, will also ask for this information. (These and other start-up requirements are discussed in detail in Chapter 6.)

Kimberly Torgerson,

owner of *Your Word's Worth*, a freelance editing and writing service:

I like the variety and flexibility of freelancing. Until recently, I tended to take on projects that would enable me to work intensely, then take lots of time off to write, travel or just putter. Recently, though, I bought property—which means I'm not taking much time off these days. I just say YES to new projects. The challenge is setting my course as people's deadlines shift. So far, so good.

B. Partnerships

Add one or more owners to a sole proprietorship, stir gently and—poof!—you've got a partnership. By definition, a partnership is a business that has more than one owner and that is not incorporated.

1. General vs. Limited Partnerships

Usually, when you hear the term "partnership," it means a general partnership. In a general partnership, each owner shares management of the business and liability for the acts of the partnership. There are, however, two special kinds of partnerships, called limited partnerships and registered limited liability partnerships (RLLPs). They operate under very different rules and are relatively uncommon, so we only briefly discuss them below.

A limited partnership requires at least one general partner and at least one limited partner. The general partner has the same role as in a general partnership: he controls the company's day-to-day operations and is personally liable for business debts. The limited partner contributes financially to the business (for example, invests $100,000 in a real estate partnership) but has minimal control over business decisions or operations.

In return for giving up management power, a limited partner gets the benefit of a cap on personal liability. She can lose her investment in the business, but is not liable for anything over that amount. But beware: A limited partner who tires of being passive and starts tinkering under the hood of the business should understand that her liability can quickly become unlimited that way. If a creditor can prove that the limited partner took acts that led the creditor to believe that she was a general partner, she can be held fully and personally liable for the creditor's claims.

One special kind of limited partnership, called a registered limited liability partnership (RLLP), is currently available only to lawyers and accountants. These professionals aren't keen on general partnerships because they don't want to be personally liable for another partner's problems—particularly those involving malpractice claims. Forming a corporation to protect personal assets may be too much trouble, and California won't allow these professionals to form an LLC. The solution is a business form called a registered limited liability partnership (RLLP). This business form protects the partners from debts against the partnership arising from professional malpractice lawsuits against another partner. The partner who loses a malpractice suit, however, doesn't escape liability.

2. Pass-Through Taxation

Like a sole proprietorship, a general partnership is not a separate tax entity from the partners. This means the partnership itself does not pay any income taxes; rather, income passes through the business to each partner, who pays taxes on his share of profit (or deducts his share of losses) on his personal federal tax return (Form 1040, with Schedule E attached). A partnership, however, must file what the IRS calls an "informational return"—Form 1065—to let the government know how much the business earned or lost that year. No tax is paid with this return—just think of it as the feds' way of letting you know they're watching.

3. Personal Liability for Business Debts

Since a partnership is legally inseparable from its owners, just like a sole proprietorship, you'd be right in guessing that partners (with the exception of limited partners) are personally liable for business-related obligations. What's also crucial to understand is that in a general partnership, the business actions of any one partner bind the other partners, who can be held personally liable for those actions. So if your business partner takes out an ill-advised high-interest loan on behalf of the partnership, makes a terrible business deal or gets in some other business mischief without your knowledge, you could be held personally responsible for any debts that result.

Example:

Jamie and Kent are partners in a profitable landscape gardening company. They've been in business for five years and have earned healthy profits, allowing them each to buy a house, decent wheels and even a few luxuries, including Jamie's collection of garden sculptures and Kent's roomful of vintage musical instruments. One day Jamie, without telling Kent, orders a shipment of exotic poppy plants that he is sure will be a big hit with customers. But when the shipment arrives, so do agents of the federal drug enforcement agency who confiscate the plants, claiming they could be turned into narcotics. Soon thereafter criminal charges are filed against Jamie and Kent, resulting in several newspaper stories. Though the partners are ultimately cleared, their attorney fees come to $50,000 and they lose several key accounts, with the result that the business runs up hefty debts. As a general partner, Kent is personally liable for these debts even though he had nothing to do with the ill-fated poppy purchase.

Before you get too worried about business debts, keep in mind that many businesses don't need to worry about personal liability. Being vulnerable to personal liability for business debts can indeed be nerve-wracking, but for many small businesses the chance of having major problems is slim. For instance, if you're engaged in a low-risk enterprise such as freelance editing, landscaping or running a small band that plays weddings and other social events, chances are that your risk of facing a huge lawsuit or a catastrophic debt is pretty small. Don't let a lawyer or other self-interested professional scare you into thinking you must incorporate "just in case...." For low-risk businesses, the costs of incorporating—both in dollars and hours—usually just aren't justified. A good business insurance policy that covers most liability risks is almost always a better investment.

4. Partnership Agreements

By drafting a partnership agreement, you can structure your relationship with your partners pretty much however you want. You and your partners can establish the respective shares of profits (or losses) each partner will receive, what the responsibilities of each partner are, what should happen to the partnership if a partner leaves, and take care of any of a number of other issues. It is not legally necessary for a partnership to have a written agreement—the simple act of two or more people doing business together creates a partnership. But only with a clear written agreement will all partners be sure of the important—and sometimes touchy—details of your business arrangement.

In the absence of a partnership agreement, California's version of the Uniform Partnership Act (UPA) kicks in as a standard, bottom-line guide to the rights and responsibilities of each partner. For example, if you don't have a partnership agreement, then California's UPA states that each partner has an equal share in the business's profits, losses and management power. Similarly, unless you provide otherwise in a written agreement, your partnership won't be able to add a new partner without the consent of all partners, and your partnership will be terminated when one partner leaves, either voluntarily or by death or expulsion.

It's important to understand that many of the legal provisions contained in the Uniform Partnership Act can be overridden if you and your partners have your own written agreement.

What a Partnership Agreement Can't Do

Although a general partnership agreement is an incredibly flexible tool in defining the ownership interests, work responsibilities and other rights of partners, there are some things it can't do. These include

- freeing the partners from personal liability for business debts

- restricting any partner's right to inspect the business books and records

- affecting the rights of third parties in relation to the partnership—for example, a partnership agreement that says a partner has no right to sign contracts won't affect the rights of an outsider who signs a contract with that partner, and

- eliminating or weakening the duty of trust (the fiduciary duty) owed by each partner to other partners.

There's nothing terribly complex about drafting a partnership agreement. They're usually only a few pages long, and cover basic issues that you've probably thought over to some degree already. Partnership agreements typically cover at least the following issues:

- name of partnership and partnership business

- date of partnership creation

- purpose of partnership

- contributions (cash, property and work) of each partner to the partnership

- each partner's share of profits and losses

- salaries and provisions for taking profits (often called partners' draws)

- each partner's management power and duties

- how the partnership will handle departure of a partner, including buy-out terms

- provisions for adding or expelling a partner, and

- dispute resolution procedures.

These and any other terms you include in a partnership agreement can be dealt with in more or less detail. Some partnership agreements cover each topic with a sentence or two; others spend up to a few pages on each provision. Of course, you need an agreement that's appropriate for your business, but it's not a good idea to skimp on your partnership agreement. Take a look at the short sample partnership agreements on the following pages to see how a very basic partnership agreement can be put together. You'll also find a blank partnership agreement in Appendix C and on the CD-ROM that comes with this book. These samples are about as basic as it gets—the bare minimum—and you'll almost surely want to use something more detailed for your business.

Sample 1

Partnership Agreement #1

Alison Shanley and Peder Johnson make the following partnership agreement.

Name and Purpose of Partnership

As of September 22, Alison and Peder are the sole owners and partners of the Vermont Fly-Fishing Company. The Vermont Fly-Fishing Company shall be headquartered in Dunsmuir, California and will sell fly-fishing equipment by mail order.

Contributions to the Partnership

Alison and Peder will make the following contributions to the partnership:

Alison Shanley	$10,000 cash
	desk, miscellaneous office furniture (value: $1,000)
total contribution:	**$11,000**
Peder Johnson	$7,000 cash
	computer system (value: $2,000)
total contribution:	**$9,000**

Profit and Loss Allocation

Alison and Peder will share business profits and losses in the same proportions as their contributions to the business.

Management of Partnership Business

Alison and Peder will have equal management powers and responsibilities.

Departure of a Partner

If either Alison or Peder leaves the partnership for any reason, including voluntary withdrawal, expulsion or death, the remaining partner shall become the sole proprietor of the Vermont Fly-Fishing Company, which shall become a sole proprietorship. The remaining partner shall pay the departing partner, or the deceased departing partner's estate, the fair market value of the departing partner's share of the business as of the date of his or her departure. The partnership's accountant shall determine the fair market value of the departing partner's share of the business according to the partnership's book value.

Mediation of Disputes

Alison and Peder agree to mediate any dispute arising under this agreement with a mutually acceptable mediator.

Amendment of Agreement

This agreement may not be amended without the written consent of both partners.

Alison Shanley	Peder Johnson
_____	_____
Signature	*Signature*
_____	_____
Date	*Date*
_____	_____
Address	*Address*
_____	_____
Social Security #	*Social Security #*

Sample 2

Partnership Agreement #2

Christine Wenc, Simon Romero and Brendan Doherty agree to the terms of the following agreement.

1. **Name of Partnership.** Christine, Simon and Brendan are partners in the Wenc & Romero Partnership. They created the partnership on July 12, 1999.

2. **Partnership Purpose.** The Wenc & Romero Partnership will provide newspaper clipping services to clients.

3. **Contributions to the Partnership.** Christine, Simon and Brendan will contribute the following to the partnership:

   Christine: $1,000 cash; one Macintosh computer (value $1500) and one monitor (value $500).

   Simon: $1,000 cash; one fax machine (value $400); one laser printer (value $1200).

   Brendan: $500 cash; various office equipment (value $500).

4. **Profits and Losses.** Christine, Simon and Brendan shall share profits and losses as follows:

Christine	40%
Simon	40%
Brendan	20%

5. **Partnership Decisions.** Christine, Simon and Brendan will have the following management authority:

Christine	2 votes
Simon	2 votes
Brendan	1 vote

   No partner may accept an assignment without the agreement of the others.

6. **Additional Terms to Be Drafted.** Christine, Simon and Brendan agree that in six months they will sign a formal partnership agreement which covers the items in this agreement in more detail, and the additional following items:

   • each partner's work contributions

   • provisions for adding a partner

   • provisions for the departure of a partner

   • provisions for selling the business.

7. **Amendments.** This agreement may not be amended without the written consent of all partners.

   Christine Wenc

   _____
   Signature   Date

   Simon Romero

   _____
   Signature   Date

   Brendan Doherty

   _____
   Signature   Date

Recommended reading on partnerships. *The Partnership Book,* by attorneys Denis Clifford and Ralph Warner (Nolo Press), is an excellent step-by-step guide to putting together a solid, comprehensive partnership agreement. Also, *How to Create a Buy/Sell Agreement and Control the Destiny of Your Small Business,* by attorneys Bethany Laurence and Anthony Mancuso, explains how to draft terms that will enable you to deal with business ownership transitions.

Publicly traded corporations are a different ball game. This chapter deals with privately held corporations owned by a small group of people who are actively involved in running the business. These corporations are much easier to manage than public corporations, where shares are sold to the public at large. If you want to sell shares of a corporation to the general public, you should consult a lawyer.

Any corporation that sells its stock to the public at large is heavily regulated by state and federal securities laws, while corporations that sell shares without advertising and only to a select group of people who meet specific state requirements are often exempt from many of these laws.

C. Corporations

For many, the term "corporation" conjures up the image of a massive business empire more akin to a nation-state than a small business. In fact, a corporation doesn't have to be huge, and most aren't. Stripped to its essentials, a corporation is simply a specific legal structure that imposes certain legal and tax rules on its owners (also called shareholders). A corporation can be as large as IBM or as small as one person—you.

The most fundamental legal characteristic of a corporation is that it's a separate legal entity from its owners. If you've already read this chapter's sections on sole proprietorships and partnerships, you'll recognize that this is a major difference between those business types and corporations. And as you might suspect, this distinction has important legal implications. The most important of these are that shareholders are normally protected from personal liability for business debts, and that the corporation itself—not just the shareholders—is subject to income tax.

1. Limited Personal Liability

Generally speaking, owners of a corporation are not personally liable for the corporation's debts. (There are some exceptions to this rule, discussed below.) Limited personal liability is probably the biggest reason why owners choose to incorporate their businesses: to protect themselves from legal and financial liability in case their business flounders or loses an expensive lawsuit and can't pay its debts. In those situations, creditors can take all of the corporation's assets (including your investment), but they generally can't get at the personal assets of the shareholders. Losing your business is no picnic, but it's a lot better to lose only what you put into the business than to have to say goodbye to everything you own.

Example:

Tim and Chris publish Tropics Tripping, *a monthly travel magazine with a focus on Latin America. Because they both have significant personal assets, and because the magazine publishing industry is inherently risky, they formed their business as a corporation. A couple of years into business, their subscription and advertising revenue starts to suffer when a recession plus political unrest in several Latin American countries reduces interest in travel to that area. Hoping the situation will* *turn itself around, Tim and Chris forge ahead—and go deeper into debt as it proves impossible to pay printing and other bills on time. Finally, when their printer won't do any more print runs on credit, Tim and Chris are forced to call it quits and declare bankruptcy. Tropics Tripping's debts total $250,000, while business assets are valued at only $90,000—leaving a $160,000 debt to creditors. Thankfully for Tim and Chris, they won't have to use their personal assets to pay the $160,000, because as owners of a corporation, they're shielded from personal liability.*

Forming a corporation to shield yourself from personal liability for business obligations—the main reason that business owners choose to incorporate—provides good, but not total, protection for your personal assets. Here are the principal areas where corporation owners still face personal liability.

- **Personal guarantees.** If you give a personal guarantee on a loan to the corporation, then you are personally liable for the repayment of that loan. Since such a guarantee is often required by banks and other lenders, this is a good reason to be a conservative borrower. Of course, if no personal guarantee is made, then only the corporation—not the shareholder—is liable for the debt.

- **Taxes.** The IRS or the California Franchise Tax Board may go after the personal assets of corporate owners for overdue corporate federal and state tax debts, particularly overdue payroll taxes. This is most likely to happen to owners of small corporations who have an active hand in managing the business, rather than to passive shareholders.

- **Negligent or intentional acts.** A corporate owner who does something negligently (that is, carelessly), or perhaps even intentionally, that ends up hurting someone can't hide behind the corporate barrier to escape personal liability. Shareholders are subject to personal liability for wrongs they commit—such as attacking a customer or leaving a wet floor in a store—that result in injury.

- **Blurring the boundaries between corporation and owners.** When corporate owners ignore corporate formalities and treat the corporation like an unincorporated business, a court may ignore the existence of the corporation (in legal slang, they may "pierce the corporate veil") and rule that the owners are personally liable for business debts and liabilities. To avoid this, it's important for corporate owners not to allow the legal boundary between the corporation and its owners to grow fuzzy. You should scrupulously respect corporate formalities such as holding shareholders' and directors' meetings, keeping attentive minutes, issuing stock certificates and maintaining corporate accounts strictly separate from personal funds.

Don't be fooled into thinking that incorporating will solve all your liability problems. Limited personal liability can prevent you from losing your home, car, bank account and other assets—but it won't protect you from losing your investment in your business. A business can quickly get wiped out if a customer, employee or supplier wins a big lawsuit against it and the business has to be liquidated to cover the debt. In short, even if you incorporate to protect your personal assets, you'll want to purchase appropriate insurance to protect your business assets. (Insurance is discussed in Chapter 11, "Your Healthy and Growing Business.")

2. Corporate Taxation

The words "corporate taxes" raise a lot of fear and loathing in the business world. Fortunately, the reality of corporate taxation is usually less depressing than the hype. Here are the basics—think of it as Corporate Tax Lite. If you decide to incorporate, you'll likely want to consult an accountant or small business lawyer who can fill you in on the fine print.

The first thing you need to know is that for tax purposes, you'll be treated differently depending on whether you operate as a regular corporation (also called a C corporation) or you elect S corporation status for tax purposes. An S corporation is the same as a C corporation in most respects (that's why we haven't already mentioned it). But when it comes to taxes, C and S corporations are very different animals. A regular, or C, corporation is itself subject to taxes, while an S corporation is treated like a partnership for tax purposes and doesn't pay any income taxes itself. Like partnership profits, S corporation profits (and losses) pass through to the shareholders, who report them on their personal returns.

These two types of corporations are explained in more detail below.

a. C Corporations

As a separate tax entity, a regular corporation must pay income taxes on its own return, much like an individual does. After deductions such as employee compensation, fringe benefits, and all other reasonable and necessary business expenses have been subtracted from its earnings, a corporation pays tax on whatever profit remains. Often in small corporations where all the owners of the business are also employees, all the profits are paid out in tax-deductible salaries and fringe benefits—leaving no profit and thus no taxes due by the corporation. (The owner/employees must, of course, pay tax on their salaries on their personal returns.)

Fringes and Perks

In addition to salaries, many fringe benefits are tax-deductible business expenses for corporations. If a corporation pays for benefits such as health and disability insurance for its employees and owner/employees, the cost can usually be deducted from the corporate income, reducing a possible tax bill. (But benefits to an owner/employee of an S corporation who owns 2% or more of the stock don't count as deductible business expenses.) As a general rule, owners of sole proprietorships or partnerships can deduct the cost of providing these benefits for employees, but not for themselves. (Sole proprietors and partners can, however, deduct a portion of medical insurance premiums, though it's technically a deduction for the individual, not a business expense.)

The fact that fringe benefits for owners are deductible for corporations may make incorporating a wise choice. But it's less likely to be a winning strategy for a capital-poor start-up that can't afford to underwrite a benefits package.

Tax Rates for Corporations

Taxable Income	Rate
0 to $50,000	15%
$50,000 to $75,000	25%
$75,000 to $10,000,000	34%
$10,000,000 and up	35%

Income between $100,000 and $335,000 is also charged an additional 5% tax, designed to make up for the tax savings that were enjoyed while the corporation was small.

The fact that initial rates of corporate taxation are comparatively low (15%–25%) means that rather than paying out all profits as salaries and bonuses, many corporations decide to keep some profits in the business from one year to the next. This practice, sometimes called income-splitting, basically involves strategically setting salaries at a level so that money left in the business is taxable only at the 15% or 25% corporate tax rate (up to $50,000 or $75,000). Since any amount of "reasonable" compensation to employees is deductible, corporate owners have lots of leeway in setting salaries to accomplish this.

Example:

Alexis and Matt run Window to the Past, Inc., a glass manufacturing business that specializes in custom work for architectural renovations. Toward the end of the year, they calculate that year's profit to be approximately $145,000. They decide to give themselves each a $50,000 bonus out of the profit (on top of their $40,000 salaries). Because both salaries and bonuses are tax-deductible business expenses, this reduces Window to the Past's taxable income to $45,000. The result is the corporate profits will be taxed at only 15%, the lowest rate. If Alexis and Matt had left all the profits in the business, they would have been taxed at 34%—more than twice what they ended up paying. Of course, their bonuses increase Alexis and Matt's personal income. They'll each be taxed on their personal returns at 31%, rather than 28%.

This income-splitting strategy is available only to shareholders who also work for the corporation. If they're not at least part-time employees, then shareholders won't be in a position to earn salaries or bonuses, and will be able only to take money from the corporation as dividends. This brings us to the vexing problem of double taxation, routinely faced by larger corporations with shareholders who aren't active employees. Unlike salaries and bonuses, dividends paid to shareholders cannot be deducted as business expenses from corporate earnings. Since they're not deducted, any amounts paid as dividends are included in the total corporate profit and taxed. And when the shareholder receives the dividend, it is taxed at the shareholder's individual tax rate as part of his personal income. As you can see, any money paid out as dividends gets taxed twice: once at the corporate level, and once at the individual level.

You can avoid double taxation simply by not paying dividends. This is usually easy if all shareholders are employees, but probably more difficult if some shareholders are passive investors anxious for a reasonable return on their investment.

Tax savings may be less important than protecting your personal assets. Even if you can't avoid double taxation, incorporating still might be your best option if you want to minimize your personal liability. Losing some tax dollars to double taxation may be much easier to swallow than losing your life's savings and work to creditors of your unincorporated business.

b. The Un-Corporation: S Corporations

Unlike a regular corporation, an S corporation does not pay taxes itself. Any profits pass through to the owners, who pay taxes on income as if the business were a sole proprietorship or a partnership. Yet the business is still a corporation. This means, of course, that it is a legally distinct entity from its owners, who are protected from personal liability for business debts, just as shareholders of C corporations are.

Until the relatively recent arrival of the LLC (discussed in Section D), the S corporation was the business form of choice for those who wanted limited liability protection but not the two-tiered tax structure of a C corporation. Today, relatively few businesses are organized as S corporations, since S corporations are subject to many regulations that do not apply to LLCs. For instance, an S corporation may not have more than 75 shareholders, all of whom must be U.S. citizens. And shareholders of an S corporation must allocate profits according to what percentage of stock each owner has. For example, a 25% owner would have to receive 25% of the profits (or losses) even if the other owners wanted a different division.

3. Forming and Running a Corporation

Besides tax complexity, a major drawback to forming a corporation—either a C or an S type—is time and expense. Unlike sole proprietorships and partnerships, you can't clap your hands twice and conjure up a corporation. To incorporate, you must file Articles of Incorporation with California's Secretary of State, along with a filing fee of $100 and a minimum annual franchise tax of $800. You'll have to file a Statement by Domestic Stock Corporation every year, beginning within 90 days of filing your Articles of Incorporation. (These requirements are covered in detail in Chapter 6.) And if you decide to sell shares of the corporation to the public—as opposed to keeping them in the hands of a relatively small number of owners—you'll have to comply with lots of complex federal and state securities laws. Finally, to protect your limited personal liability, you need to act like a corporation, which means adopting bylaws, issuing stock to shareholders and keeping records of various meetings of directors and shareholders.

In other words, the protection afforded by incorporating comes at a price. Figure in the likelihood that you'll have to hire lawyers, accountants and other professionals to keep your corporation in compliance, and it's easy to see how expensive running a corporation can be.

Recommended reading on corporations. For more information on the many complexities of forming a corporation, be sure to read either *How to Form Your Own California Corporation* or *The Corporate Minutes Book,* both by attorney Anthony Mancuso and published by Nolo Press.

D. Limited Liability Companies (LLCs)

Like many business owners just starting out, you might find yourself in this common quandary: On one hand, the thought of having to cope with the risk of personal liability for business misfortunes scares you; on the other, you would rather not deal with the red tape of starting and operating a corporation. Fortunately for you and many other California entrepreneurs, you can avoid these problems by taking advantage of a relatively new form of business called the limited liability company, commonly known as an LLC. LLCs combine the pass-through taxation of a sole proprietorship or partnership (business taxes are paid on each owner's personal federal income tax return) with the same protection against personal liability that corporations offer.

One rule you need to know up front is that California requires LLCs to have at least two members. Although the vast majority of states allow one-person LLCs, California is not one of them. So if you were planning to go it alone, an LLC can't be your cup of tea.

1. How LLCs Are Unique

If the pass-through tax status and limited personal liability of an LLC seem a lot like the features of an S corporation, you're right. But a significant difference between these two types of businesses is that LLCs are not bound by the many regulations that govern S corporations. For instance, certain rules limiting the type and number of owners in an S corporation don't apply to LLCs. Unlike S corporations, LLCs can have more than 75 owners (called members), and they don't need to be U.S. citizens.

Another, and probably more significant, difference between an LLC and an S corporation is that the owners of an LLC may distribute profits (and the tax burden) however they see fit, without regard to each member's ownership share in the company. For instance, a member of an LLC who owns 25% of the business could receive 50% of the profits if the other members agree. In an S corporation, remember, profits must be tied to each shareholder's ownership share.

2. Special Taxes on LLCs

Before you decide the LLC is the best thing since Easy Cheese, you should know there is a dark side. LLCs are subject to a special, annual LLC tax of $800, even if you make no profit or lose money. You'll have to pay this up front when you create your LLC by filing Articles of Organization with California's Secretary of State. There's also a filing fee of $70 just for your paperwork to be processed. Many brand-new business owners aren't in the position to pay this kind of money right out of the starting block, so they start out as partnerships until they bring in enough income to cover these costs.

LLCs have great tax flexibility. One flexible feature of LLCs is that members may choose to have the company taxed like a corporation rather than as a pass-through entity. (In fact, sole proprietorships and partnerships have this option as well.) True, for many LLC owners one of the most popular features of the LLC is pass-through taxation, so you may wonder why any of them would choose to be taxed as a corporation. The answer is that, because of the income-splitting strategy of corporations discussed above in Section C, in some instances LLC members come out ahead by having their business taxed as a separate entity at corporate tax rates.

For example, if the owners become successful enough to keep some profits in the business rather than handing them out as bonuses at the end of the year, the corporate tax rate saves them money. As discussed above, federal income tax rates for corporations (and for LLCs taxed as corporations) start at a lower rate than the rates for individuals. For this reason, many LLCs start out being taxed as partnerships, and when they make enough profits to justify keeping some in the business (rather than doling them out as salaries and bonuses), they opt for corporate-style taxation.

E. So, Which One to Choose?

The differences between the various types of business organizations basically boil down to two legal issues: the personal liability of owners for business debts, and taxes. While these issues can have a huge impact on successful small businesses a few years down the road, business owners who are just starting out on a shoestring often care most about spending as little money as possible on the legal structure of their business. This is certainly an understandable approach; far more new businesses die painful deaths because they don't control costs than because they lose lawsuits. In short, for many new small businesses, incorporating or organizing as an LLC is as unnecessary an expense as a swank downtown office or a gleaming chrome espresso machine in the lunchroom.

That said, owners of larger businesses with a number of investors or of any business engaged in a high-risk activity should always insist on limited personal liability, either with an LLC or a corporation. This is even more true if the business can't find or afford appropriate insurance.

Recommended reading on LLCs. *Form Your Own Limited Liability Company*, by attorney Anthony Mancuso (Nolo Press) gives detailed information on this new business form, including step-by-step instructions and forms for creating one.

Analyzing Your Risks

Sometimes it's easy to tell when your business venture poses financial risks. If you're planning to launch an investment firm or start a hazardous waste management company, there is little doubt that you'll need all the protection you can get, including limited personal liability as well as adequate insurance. Other businesses are not so obviously risk-laden, but still could land you in trouble if fate strikes you a blow. Here are a few red flags to watch for when analyzing how risky your business is:

- using hazardous materials, such as dry cleaning solvents or photographic chemicals, or hazardous processes, such as welding or operating heavy machinery

- manufacturing or selling edible goods

- driving as part of the job

- building or repairing structures or vehicles

- caring for children or animals

- providing or allowing access to alcohol

- allowing activities that may result in injury, such as weightlifting or skateboarding, and

- repairing or working on items of value, such as cars or antiques.

If you've identified one or more risks your business is likely to face, figure out whether business insurance might give enough protection. Some risky activities, such as job-related driving, are good candidates for insurance and don't necessarily warrant incorporating. But if insurance can't cover all of the risks involved in your business, it may be time to incorporate.

Picking a Winning Business Name That Won't Land You in Court

In the previous chapter, we provided information to help you decide on the best legal structure for your business. Here we cover another key start-up issue: naming your business and its products and services. There's a lot of room for personal and professional creativity when picking a business name—but there are also legal requirements and pitfalls that you absolutely need to know. In particular, it's important for all business owners to understand the basics of trademark law, which establishes and protects ownership rights to certain names used in business. Owning a trademark gives certain legal rights to the owner that need to be taken seriously.

If you choose a business name that is too similar to a competitor's name, for instance, you could find yourself accused of violating the competitor's trademark (called "infringing") and could be forced to change your business name. This can be a serious blow to a business that has worked hard to build name recognition among its customers—not to mention the cost of changing signs, stationery, pre-printed invoices and the like.

But suppose you plan to open a local business so small that you don't even expect to compete with businesses in the next county, much less in another state or country. You probably wonder if the arcane world of trademark law really affects you. Just 20 years ago the answer would have been no—you didn't really have to worry too much about name conflicts back then. As long as a quick search of your phone book didn't reveal any obvious local conflicts

and you didn't call your business "Ford" or "IBM," you were fine. But in today's world of the Internet, mail order and rapidly growing national chains, the idea of "local" isn't what it used to be. Even if you open just a tiny bookstore in a small town, if you inadvertently choose the same name as an Internet store that your local customers can access, you may very well find yourself being accused of infringement of its trademark—even if the online store has its headquarters on a different continent.

One good way to figure out how educated and concerned you need to be about trademark law is to consider what the consequences will be if you are forced to change your business name. If a name change would be cheap and easy and wouldn't seriously confuse your customers, then don't lie awake nights worrying about the issue. However, if changing your name would be messy or expensive (changing signs, yellow pages ads and business directory listings, to mention a few possibilities), you'll want to take the time and trouble to be sure the name you want doesn't already belong to someone else.

Have we convinced you that paying attention to the law of business names is important? Good. In this chapter we'll explain how to go about choosing a name that won't land you in legal hot water and, once chosen, how to secure the maximum legal protection for it. We'll also cover some non-legal aspects of the naming process, including tips and advice on how to approach it in the best way for your particular business.

Getting the Terms Straight

One reason the law of business names often seems confusing is that the subject is riddled with lots of arcane and often overlapping legal jargon. For example, local, state and federal agencies often use different terms to describe the same or very similar legal concepts. Here's a brief rundown of the terms you should understand, all of which are discussed in greater detail in the rest of this chapter.

- The term "**legal name**" means the official name of the entity that owns a business. The legal name of a sole proprietorship is simply the full name of the owner. If a general partnership has a written partnership agreement that gives a name to the partnership, then that name is the legal name. Otherwise, the legal name of the general partnership is simply the last names of the owners. And for limited partnerships, LLCs and corporations, the legal name is the name registered with the California Secretary of State.

- A **trade name** is simply the name of the business itself, which may or may not be the same as the legal name of the owner(s). John O'Toole's Classic Cars, Amoeba Records and Nolo Press are examples of trade names. You see trade names on business signs, in the telephone book and on invoices. In many transactions, such as opening a bank account or applying for a loan, you'll need to provide both the legal name of the owner(s) and the trade name of the business.

- The term "**fictitious business name**" is used when the trade name is different from the legal name of the entity (individual(s), partnership, LLC or corporation) that owns the business. For instance, if John O'Toole named his sole proprietorship Turtle's Classic Cars, the name "Turtle's Classic Cars" would be a fictitious business name because it does not contain his last name, "O'Toole." A fictitious business name is sometimes called a DBA name. DBA stands for "doing business as," as in: "John O'Toole, doing business as Turtle's Classic Cars." If your business uses a fictitious business name, you need to register it with your county.

- When a business incorporates, it must choose and register a **corporate name** with the California Secretary of State. Similarly, a limited liability company (LLC) must register an LLC name and a limited partnership must register an LP name with the California Secretary of State. Corporate, LLC and limited partnership names must have the Secretary of State's approval before they will be registered. If a corporation, LLC or limited partnership operates under the same name registered with the Secretary of State, then the corporate, LLC or limited partnership name will be both the legal name and trade name.

- A **trademark** (sometimes called simply a mark) is any word, phrase, design or symbol used to market a product or service. Technically, a mark used to market a service is called a service mark, though the term "trademark" is commonly used for both types of marks. Owners of trademarks have legal rights under both federal and California law which give them the power in some cases to prevent others from using their trademark to market goods or services.

- "**Business name**" tends to be a catch-all term referring to all the names used in business—the name of a business itself, a corporate name, a fictitious business name and the names of a business's products and services. When we use it—or when you see it someplace else—be sure you keep in mind the difference between the various types of business names.

Trademark isn't the only legal issue related to business names. Besides watching out for trademark conflicts, business owners also need to comply with county fictitious business name requirements and state corporate name registration requirements. By state law, if your name qualifies as a fictitious business name, you need to register a Fictitious Business Name statement with your county clerk. And for corporations, LLCs and limited partnerships, the name of the business must be approved by the Secretary of State before it will accept Articles of Incorporation, Organization or a Statement of Limited Partnership. These other legal name requirements are covered in Chapter 6.

A. An Overview of Trademark Law

In a nutshell, trademark law—which is made up of a vast body of statutes, regulations and court decisions—prevents a business from using a name or logo that is likely to be confused with one that a competing business already uses. This general rule applies both to the name of the business as well as to the names of any products or services. Allowing businesses to have exclusive use of certain names helps consumers to identify and recognize goods in the marketplace.

When you buy Racafrax brand of wood glue, for instance, you'll know that it will be similar in quality to the Racafrax glue you bought last time. By contrast, if any company was allowed to call their glue "Racafrax Glue," customers would never know what they were getting. And because customers would never know when they were using the Racafrax company's glue, the Racafrax company wouldn't be able to build customer trust or goodwill, even if its glue was the best available. In this way, customers and businesses alike benefit from trademark protection.

This section will give you a run-down of what's protected by trademark law and how to determine and protect your trademark rights to the names you use. A basic knowledge of this area will help you understand what steps you should take as part of forming your business to avoid infringing others' rights. And it will also give you the legal basics to understand whether your rights are being infringed down the road.

Pick a name with an eye toward avoiding legal trouble—you can't afford a court fight. The main reason to learn the basics of trademark law is not so you can successfully defend your name in court against another business that claims a superior right to use it. Even if you were to win a complex and expensive court fight, you'd be a huge loser when it comes to time, worry and legal fees. Far better to avoid disputes in the first place by choosing a safe name that has a very low likelihood of leading to an infringement lawsuit.

Trademark Protects More Than Names

Because you are in the start-up phase of your business, we talk mostly about how trademark applies to business names in this chapter. But the rules we discuss apply to a lot more—logos, designs, slogans and packaging features can also be protected by trademark. For example, Nike's slogan, "Just Do It," and American Express's mantra, "Don't leave home without it," are protected by the law of trademark. For more information on using trademarks in other aspects of your small business, be sure to read *Trademark: Legal Care for Your Business and Product Name*, by Kate McGrath and Stephen Elias (Nolo Press).

1. What Is a Trademark?

The definition of "trademark" is essentially this simple: any word, phrase, logo or other device that you use to identify your products or services in the marketplace is a trademark. This includes the names of products or services themselves and usually the name of the business that's selling them. Using a name in commerce to identify goods or services for sale is enough to make it a trademark; there's no registration requirement. (Registration will, however, greatly strengthen your power to enforce your rights to the trademark. Registration is covered in Section C.) To use a mark means to use it in public commerce to identify a product or service, not just on internal documents or on product samples that aren't available to the public.

Keep in mind, however, that a key part of the definition of a trademark is that it must be used to identify goods or services *for sale*. If your business name isn't used in public in conjunction with something you're trying to sell, it isn't considered a trademark.

For example, if a software company called ZZP Web Masters markets bookmarking software for the Internet called "WebWorm," then the name WebWorm is a trademark. If the only marketing done for WebWorm is an ad that reads, "Manage your bookmarks with WebWorm," then the business name ZZP Web Masters will not be a trademark because it's not used in public to sell WebWorm. But an ad that reads, "WebWorm: The best bookmarking software on Earth, by ZZP Web Masters," includes two trademarks: the product name WebWorm and the trade name ZZP Web Masters.

The power of a trademark comes from the fact that you may be entitled to exclude others from using the same mark if you used it first. In legal terms, if someone "infringes your trademark" by using it in a way that's likely to confuse customers, you can take them to court and force them to stop using it, and maybe even to pay damages. For example, if ZZP Web Masters had been selling

WebWorm for two years and then another company started selling a similar product, also called WebWorm, ZZP Web Masters could sue the other company and force it to stop using the name. If ZZP Web Masters could prove that their business suffered because of the infringement, they might also be awarded monetary damages.

So far, so good—you're probably even wondering why everyone says trademark issues are such a bear to deal with. Here's why: Just because you own a trademark doesn't mean you can always prevent someone else from using it (and likewise, another owner of a trademark can't always prevent you from using his mark). Unlike a copyright, which generally gives the same level of protection to all owners, a trademark gives widely varying degrees of protection to the owner, depending on a variety of circumstances. So, as we explain in Section 2, below, the key legal point isn't so much whether you own a trademark as whether it qualifies for protection—and if so, how much.

Trademarks vs. Service Marks

You've probably heard the term "trademark," which applies to names, logos and slogans that identify products (such as Chia Pet), a whole lot more than the term "service mark," which is used when a name identifies a service (such as H&R Block Tax Preparation Services). One reason for this is that, since the legal rules for trademarks and service marks are virtually identical, the term "trademark," or sometimes just "mark," is commonly used for both types of marks. But since technically the two terms do refer to different things, you should be aware of the distinction, especially if your businesses will primarily provide services.

Business Names and Trademarks Often Overlap

Many trade names double as trademarks and service marks for products and services of the business. For instance, when McDonald's (trade name) advertises McDonald's french fries, the trade name "McDonald's" also becomes a trademark because it is used to identify the maker (or brand) of french fries. And when the company puts up a sign in front of its restaurant, the term "McDonald's" becomes a service mark, identifying who's providing the fast food service of that restaurant. In other words, any time you use your trade name to identify a product, service or business location, you're using the trade name as a mark—either a trademark or a service mark. As you can see, a name can wear a bunch of different hats: it can be a trade name, a legal name and a trademark (or service mark) all in one.

Legal Name	Trade Name	Trademarks/Service Marks
McDonald's Corporation	McDonald's	McDonald's french fries Big Mac Mayor McCheese Golden arches symbol
Microsoft Corporation	Microsoft	Microsoft Word Windows 95 Internet Explorer "Where do you want to go today?" slogan
Nolo Press/Folk Law, Inc.	Nolo Press	Nolo Press Scales symbol "Law for all" slogan
Trader Joe's Company	Trader Joe's	Trader Joe's Baked Tortilla Chips Trader Giotto's Italian Roast coffee beans Trader Darwin's vitamins
Ronco, Inc.	Ronco	Popeil Pocket Fisherman Dial-O-Matic Food Slicer
Kraft Foods, Inc.	Kraft	JELL-O Gelatin Cheez Whiz Tang Instant Breakfast Drink "It's the cheesiest" slogan for Kraft Macaroni & Cheese "Good to the last drop" slogan for Kraft Maxwell House Coffee

2. When Do Trademarks Conflict?

As you surely know, plenty of businesses share the same name, or at least part of the same name, without violating each other's trademark rights. Examples include United Airlines and United Van Lines; Ford Motor Company and Ford Modeling Agency; and Scott Paper Products and Scott Sunglasses. Legally, that's because trademark infringement occurs only when the use of a mark by two (or more) different businesses is likely to cause customer confusion. (An exception to this rule, called the "dilution" doctrine, is explained in Section 3, below.) If customers aren't likely to be confused, then both businesses may legally use the same mark. But if customer confusion is likely, then the rightful owner of the mark can prohibit the other business from using it, and can sue for damages for any unauthorized use.

This is one of the trickiest bits of trademark law: determining whether two marks legally conflict (in other words, whether customer confusion is likely). You should be aware of a few factors that courts deem particularly important in making this determination:

- how strong the original trademark is
- how much the products or services really compete against one another, and
- how similar the trademarks are in appearance, sound or meaning.

a. Strong vs. Weak Marks

The general rule is that distinctive business names receive the strongest legal trademark protection. A truly distinctive trademark (called a "strong trademark") is one that clearly distinguishes the product or service it represents from others. Memorable, unusual names like Xerox or 3M are good examples of distinctive marks. And the stronger a trademark, the more power a business has to prevent others from using it. While there's no magic formula for what makes a trademark distinctive, strong marks tend to be surprising or fanciful names that often have nothing to do with the business, product or

service. Other examples of distinctive marks are Big Mac, Velcro and Comet (cleanser).

On the flip side, a weak trademark consists of ordinary, descriptive words (but, as we explain below, weak trademarks can become stronger with use). Ordinary words include those that merely describe aspects of the product or business, such as durability ("Sturdy Knapsacks"), location ("The Edge of Town Tavern") or other qualities ("Speedy Dry Cleaners," "Tasty Vegetables"). Personal names used in a trademark are usually considered to be ordinary marks and therefore weak. Weak trademarks don't receive as much protection as strong trademarks because they aren't considered as likely to cause customer confusion. Since weak trademarks are merely descriptive of the product or service, they don't trigger a strong association in customers' minds between the mark and a particular product or service brand.

An additional reason why descriptive trademarks aren't strongly protected is to make sure that competitors aren't unfairly prevented from using common words to describe their own products. For example, a food delivery service company called "Galloping Gourmet" wouldn't be able to monopolize the word "gourmet" and stop a deli from using the name "Tom's Gourmet Sandwiches."

But just because you have a descriptive, weak trademark doesn't mean that you're totally vulnerable to trademark infringement. Because of a legal doctrine called unfair competition, being the first to use a descriptive trademark may offer all the protection you need. Unfair competition law is based on the idea that it's not fair for another business to rip off your business's good reputation. If you've been selling dry cleaning services in Bakersfield under the name Jean's Quick Cleaners, for example, and someone else in the same city opens Jean's Quick Cleaners, you could claim unfair competition and likely have them prevented from using that name. As you can see, unfair competition law can have the same result as trademark law: it can prevent another business from using a name identical or confusingly similar to yours if you used the name first.

Another reason a weak trademark can be valuable is if it grows stronger as it becomes distinctive through use. Called "acquiring a secondary meaning" in legalese, it is particularly likely to occur when a product or service with a weak mark becomes a lasting success, making it far more likely that the public will associate the mark with the product or service. Thus as Jean's Quick Cleaners becomes well-known in the Los Angeles basin for doing an excellent job, the previously weak trademark will become stronger as customers come to associate the ordinary name with the particular service. Examples of the weak-to-strong phenomenon include Spic 'n' Span Cleaners, Tom's Natural Toothpaste, Chap Stick and The Yellow Pages.

b. Do the Products or Services Actually Compete?

If the products or services that share the same trademark are in completely unrelated fields or industries, or if they're sold in non-overlapping geographical regions (and not on the Internet), there's obviously far less chance that customers will be confused by the similar trademarks. In other words, the less products or services actually compete, the less likely it is that there will be a trademark violation. For example, a pizza joint named Rocket Pizza probably won't be confused with a record store named Rocket Records, even if they exist in the same city. And an auto shop named Armadillo Repairs in Portland, Maine most likely won't run into any trademark conflicts with Armadillo Auto Repairs in San Diego. Being so far apart and serving purely local customers, chances are slim that customers would confuse the two.

The Internet and other long-distance marketing techniques are creating millions of new competitors. As we mentioned at the beginning of this chapter, with the arrival and widespread use of the Internet, the fast expansion of mail-order catalog businesses, and ever more frequent travel, the old rule that small, local businesses don't have to worry about trademarks from other geographical regions has largely gone out the window. Today even small, local businesses commonly establish Websites, hundreds of thousands of businesses send out catalogs, and even some local restaurants and hotels seek to reach a national (or even worldwide) pool of tourists. The upshot is that many formerly local businesses that ten years ago never would have been confused with each other are now competitors, which of course increases the likelihood of trademark infringement if their names are similar. Be sure to read Section 4 below on new trademark issues and considerations in today's ever smaller world.

Of course, there are plenty of gray areas where two businesses aren't in head-to-head competition, but use the same marks for products that are similar enough to make a customer stop and think, for example, "Is a Parker calendar made by the same company as Parker pens?" Even though a company with a similar name may not be stealing business from a competitor, it may be ripping off that company's goodwill and getting a free ride from its advertising. The answer as to whether infringement exists in these gray areas often depends on how strong the original trademark is (as we discussed above). Ultimately, it's a combination of these factors—whether a mark is strong or weak and whether the products actually compete—that determine whether customer confusion is likely and a trademark is being infringed.

Factors that Determine Customer Confusion		
	Non-competing products/services	**Directly competing products/services**
Weak trademark	Least likelihood of customer confusion	Some likelihood of customer confusion
Strong trademark	Some likelihood of customer confusion	Most likelihood of customer confusion

c. Sight, Sound and Meaning Test

Obviously, dual use of identical trademarks can cause customer confusion. But what about merely similar trademarks? It is essential to understand that small or superficial differences between two trademarks may not be enough to prevent customer confusion. If two marks that describe a similar product or service look alike, sound alike or have the same meaning, it's likely that they'll be considered to conflict with each other, just as if they were identical. The difference in spelling, for example, does not make the name "Ekzon" sufficiently different from "Exxon" to avoid trademark problems. And even though they're expressed in two different languages, the names "Le Petit Fleur" and "The Little Flower" have the same meaning, which increases the likelihood that some customers would confuse the two.

The following examples illustrate how the rules we've just discussed might apply in some specific situations.

Example 1:

You open an auto lubrication business and name it Jiffy Oil. A few weeks later, you receive a stern letter from the attorneys of Jiffy Lube, a national chain of auto lubrication businesses. The letter informs you that the name "Jiffy Oil" infringes on their rights to the trademark "Jiffy Lube," since customers are likely to confuse the two names because the names are very similar and are used to describe an almost identical service. They demand that you change your business's name or be taken to court. You'd be wise to comply with their demand. Their "Jiffy Lube" trademark, though a descriptive term (for fast lubrication), has become a strong mark over time since customers have come to recognize it as a specific brand

of service. And because your shop is a direct competitor of Jiffy Lube, the chance of customer confusion is high.

Example 2:

Your pet products company begins selling a toy that looks like a cross between a dog and a weasel, which you name the Garden Weasel. Soon after your toy hits the market, the makers of the nationally marketed Garden Weasel 5-in-1 garden tool contact you, claiming that you are infringing their trademark. Though their trademark is distinctive (memorable and unusual) and therefore strong, the products don't compete with one another. Since you feel that the products are unrelated enough to minimize the chance of customer confusion, your first thought is to stick with the Garden Weasel name. Think again. If you are sued—and you well may be—defending the lawsuit is likely to cost you tens or possibly even hundreds of thousands of dollars that you almost surely can't afford. A better approach would probably be to tweak your name a bit, to something like the Lawn Weasel or the Garden Ferret, for instance.

Example 3:

You open a coffee shop in Weed, California and name it Pam's Coffee Stop. A year into your business, you're driving through Barstow, California and notice a small café also named Pam's Coffee Stop. After thinking about it, you decide that there's little chance of a trademark violation by either business. The trademark is ordinary and descriptive and therefore weak, plus your shops are so far away from each other that they're not competitors. But this gets you thinking about trademark laws and you wonder what you'd do if a big national chain started using the name and moved into your area. The answer is, you would retain the right to use the name because you were the first to use it in your area. But the chain could prevent you from expanding into other areas of the country if this ever became your goal.

3.   The Dilution Exception

As we mentioned in Section 2, above, there is a big exception to the rule that says one trademark infringes another only where there is the likelihood of customer confusion. Even when customer confusion is improbable, courts will prohibit a business from using someone else's trademark if the use will diminish—or "dilute"—its distinctiveness. This legal protection occurs only when a mark is so well known that even if you were to use it in a different context than the original trademark, lots of people would think of the original trademark. For example, a court might prohibit a athletic shoe manufacturer from using the trademark Exxon or a gas station from calling itself Nike. Even though customers would not be likely to confuse an oil company with a shoe maker, this sort of copying is a legal no-no, since allowing others to use the very famous trademark can chip away at its distinctiveness and slowly reduce its legal strength.

4.   The Internet Changes the Rules

Particularly if you plan to put your business online, you'll not only have to worry about trademarks of businesses already on the Web, but also those of businesses located anywhere the Web reaches— which, of course, is just about everywhere. Another way of saying this is that if you create a Web page for a small home-based business, your business is no longer local in character—you're essentially launching a worldwide business that will compete with businesses everywhere, whether or not those businesses are online.

For example, if you create a Website for your antique restoration business, Dalliance Designs, you're essentially competing with every antique restoration business in the country. If one of these owns the trademark "Dalliance Designs," the fact that you are now competing with that business opens an ugly can of worms. In short, going online greatly increases the number of potential trademark conflicts your business might face.

But the Web has changed trademark rules for everybody—even businesses that don't go digital. As more and more small businesses launch Websites introducing themselves in a keystroke to consumers all over the globe, your purely local, offline business might find itself in competition with businesses several time zones or even continents away. Although courts are still chewing over many trademark issues raised by online commerce, it is already clear that, in some circumstances at least, a Web business with the same name as yours poses just as much a threat of a trademark lawsuit as does a real-life, bricks-and-steel business across the street.

Example:

Jarrod is a mechanic who opens a small machine shop in a rural area of California. He's lived in the area for 30 years, and knows every business for miles around. Nevertheless, as part of choosing a name for his business, Jarrod carefully checks the phone book and the county register for fictitious business names and ultimately settles on his first choice, Checkers Tool and Die. All goes smoothly for a few months, until a customer compliments Jarrod on his slick-looking Website. This leaves Jarrod totally confused since he hates computers and has only a vague notion of what the Web is. But in talking with his customer about this mysterious Website, Jarrod realizes that a machine shop in Florida is also using the name "Checkers Tool and Die" and sells a number of specialized parts via an online catalogue. This doesn't particularly worry Jarrod until his customer goes on to explain that if the distant business can prove it owns the trademark to "Checkers Tool and Die" and convinces a court that it shares the same market as Jarrod, it might be able to force Jarrod to stop using the name.

Although at least one customer has been confused, Jarrod doesn't really expect the Florida outfit to go after him—after all, his business is small, local, provides primarily repair services (with parts as a sideline) and doesn't sell on the Web. Nevertheless, even the possibility of legal trouble worries him—especially because he'd like to open a retail machine parts shop next to his repair shop. After learning that the Florida outfit has been using the name Checkers Tool and Die for years and seems to be putting lots of energy into expanding their Website, Jarrod decides to be safe and spend the time and money necessary to change the name of his business before he expands.

B. Name Searches

By now you get the picture that a business name dispute is no walk in the park. To avoid potential trademark hassles later on, you need to do some digging before you finally settle on a name for your business. The main way to accomplish this is to conduct a name search to find out whether another business already uses a name that's identical or similar to the one you want to use. As you'll see in the next few pages, the main practical question here is how extensive that search should be in your particular case. The information in this section will help you figure out how to go about researching your chosen name, and what to do once you've found one that's available.

Recommended reading on names and trademark issues. For more help with trademark searching and registration, by far the best source of sophisticated information is *Trademark: Legal Care for Your Business and Product Name*, by Stephen Elias and Kate McGrath (Nolo Press). In addition to explaining in detail how to conduct an extremely thorough trademark search, it also guides you step by step through the process of registering your trademark.

After picking a catchy name for your business, your first step is to look into whether it's already being used by another business. As you should now understand, how thoroughly you should search will depend largely on the size and geographical scope of your business and your plans for its future. If you plan from day one to sell a product nationally—whether via catalog, through retailers or online—you'll obviously need to worry about trademarks across the country. If, on the other hand, you're starting a small home-based service business, don't plan to advertise and are relatively certain you won't expand geographically, a search of names in your county, and perhaps state, could from a practical point of view be enough (though we recommend that you always search widely).

Also keep in mind that the extent of your search isn't only how widely you search geographically, but also how deeply you search—in terms of looking not only for identical names, but also for those that are merely similar or have a slight resemblance to yours. Searching for the exact name (also called a "direct hit" search) is quick and cheap, but risky. A more in-depth search, such as one that looks for names with slight variations in spelling, is safer, but can get quite complicated and expensive.

1. Sources of Name Information

Before you start researching your chosen name, it's important to realize that there is no one place to look. In large part, this is because a business can—and millions do—establish a trademark simply by using it. This means that while checking federal and state trademark registers is useful, you'll also want to check many other sources of information about business names. You should check some or preferably all of the following resources for name conflicts, depending on how extensive a search you need. Methods for searching these databases are discussed below.

a. The World Wide Web

We recommend this one first because it is huge, fast and free. By using several of the Web's search engines, such as Yahoo!, AltaVista, InfoSeek or Excite, you can quickly see whether someone else on the Web is using a specific term and how they are using it. (Addresses for these and other Web resources are in Appendix A.) Search engines are easy to use; simply enter the terms you're looking for (often called a "query") and the engine will scan the Web and retrieve any sites that contain the terms in your query. Consult the "help" area of the particular search engine you're using for more detailed instructions on how to construct your queries.

Valerie Hoecke,
owner of Fire Engine Red, a Web development firm:

With the emergence of Websites as a major part of how many companies market themselves, it may be wise to research the availability of a domain name and reserve one for your business Website at the same time that you begin investigating company names and doing trademark research. Business owners can research name availability and register names at the InterNIC Website, at http:// www.internic.net.

b. Industry Sources

Trade publications and business directories can be great sources of business name information—and they can also give you good ideas for names. You can also call trade associations and chambers of commerce to ask if they can provide lists or directories of businesses in the area.

c. Phone Directories

Don't overlook the phone book as a valuable collection of local name information. If the name you want to use is in your phone book, there's no reason to waste money searching the federal trademark register or other government databases.

d. Federal Trademark Register

Unless you expect your business to stay tiny and local forever, it's a good idea to search the federal trademark register to determine whether the name you've chosen is already being used by a similar business in the United States. Perhaps the most important reason to search the federal register is to avoid being sued for willful infringement. If you use a name already registered at the federal level, you can be sued for knowingly violating someone else's trademark—even if you didn't actually check the federal register and know it was there. Searching the federal register can be complicated, and there are a few different ways to go about it. Search options are discussed below.

e. California Secretary of State Databases

The California Secretary of State maintains databases of registered names of corporations, limited partnerships and LLCs. Be aware, however, that the corporate, limited partnership and LLC name databases do not overlap, even though they're all maintained by the Secretary of State. In other words, you need to check each database separately. To check to see if a name appears in the corporate, LLC or limited partnership database, you can mail in a list of possible names along with $10 per database you want searched. A staff person at the Secretary of State's office will do the search and let you know which ones are in use (as well as reserve for you, for 60 days, the first name on your list that isn't being used).

California Secretary of State Offices	
Sacramento Headquarters	1500 11th St. 916-657-5448
Fresno Branch	2497 West Shaw #101 & 102 209-243-2100
Los Angeles Branch	300 S. Spring 213-897-3062
San Diego Branch	1350 Front St. #2060 619-525-4113
San Francisco Branch	235 Montgomery St., Suite 725 415-439-6959

f. California's Trademark Unit

The California Secretary of State also maintains a state trademark registry at its Trademark Unit. This database is a good one to check, particularly because you can search by phone for free. You're allowed to have two names checked per phone call. Contact California's Trademark Unit at 916-653-4984.

You may also want to check some or all other states' trademark registries. You can check them by calling the state(s) yourself and finding out their individual rules for searching the state trademark register, or you can hire a trademark search firm to do the work for you. Search firms and types of searches are discussed below, in Section 2.

g. County Fictitious Business Name Databases

Each county maintains a database of fictitious business names (FBNs) that have been registered in that county. If you register a fictitious business name statement with your county (discussed in Chapter 6), you'll be asked to first check the county's FBN database to see if any other business in the county has already registered that name. But even if you won't be using an FBN—because you'll use your own name or your corporate, limited partnership or LLC name—it's a good idea to check the FBNs used by other businesses. In all counties these databases can be searched in person for free, or for a small fee (from $5 to $25 or so, depending on the county) you can submit a name by mail and have it checked by a staff person at the county clerk's office. You can check any and all county databases for a name even if you don't plan to register an FBN statement there. A list of California county clerks and contact information appears in Appendix B.

Example:

Tom and Jen, both veterinarians, search their county's fictitious business name database for the name "Critter Care," which they want to use for the animal hospital they're planning to open. They don't find anyone else using the name in their area, so they believe they can use it. But just to be safe, Jen decides to check the California state trademark directory for the name. She finds out that a California corporation has already obtained state trademark protection for the name "Critter Care." Since that corporation was doing business under its own name and not a fictitious one, it didn't have to register with any county fictitious name databases, so even if Tom and Jen had checked fictitious names statewide they wouldn't have found it. (Tom and Jen also would have found the name by checking the Secretary of State's corporate name database.)

Lots of trademarks aren't registered. It's important to remember that just because a name doesn't appear in any of the Secretary of State's files (the state trademark registry or the databases of registered corporate, limited partnership or LLC names) or in any county's fictitious business name database, doesn't mean another business doesn't already own that trademark. Use of the name, not registration, is what creates trademark ownership. Plenty of businesses own trademarks that they have never registered. And many businesses won't bother registering at the state level, but will register a federal trademark. That's one reason why it's often a good idea to do a federal trademark search, too.

Also keep in mind that the free or relatively cheap searches offered by state and county agencies check only for exact matches—and won't tell you whether a similar name is included in that database. If, for example, the county clerk's office tells you that "The Dog House" does not appear in its database, you might be surprised later to find that "The Dawg Haus" has been in business for years. In short, you may have to do a more extensive search than the one provided by the state or county office.

2. Conducting a National Search

Just as there are lots of different databases and registers to search, there are different ways to go about searching them. If, after careful thought, you decide you need only to do a minimal search, then using some of the local databases described above may do the trick.

Others, however, may need to conduct a national search, which basically means searching the database of federally registered trademarks, called the federal register. A large public library or special business and government library near you should carry the register, which contains all federal trademark and service mark names arranged by categories of goods and services. Another option is to hire a search firm to do the work for you. A number of companies, including Sc[i]3, Compu-Mark and Trademark Express, offer trademark search services.

The cheapest and easiest type of national search is a direct-hit search, which will reveal whether another business has registered an identical name with the federal Patent and Trademark Office (PTO). You can often hire one of the companies mentioned above to do a direct-hit search for you for less than $50. While direct-hit searches are quick and cheap, they are not thorough—they usually won't turn up trademarks that are similar, but not identical, to the name you're considering. For example, if you want to name your softball training center "The Strike Zone," a direct-hit search may not turn up a trademark for "The S. Zone." And as discussed above, any mark that looks like, sounds like or means the same as your name could present a trademark conflict.

More extensive national searches take a lot more time and money, but may be necessary if you plan for your business to reach a wide audience. For an in-depth search, it may make the most sense to hire a search firm. For more information on national searches, see *Trademark: Legal Care for Your Business and Product Name*, by Stephen Elias and Kate McGrath (Nolo Press).

3. Analyzing Your Search Results

If, after your search, you determine that the name you've chosen does not already belong to someone else, you can go ahead and use it. Assuming you really are the first user of the name in your type of business, you'll own the trademark, which will give you the right to stop others from using it in certain situations. But since registering a trademark conveys important additional rights and protections, you may want to register your name in California and with the federal government. The basics of trademark registration are discussed below in Section C.

But what if your search turned up an identical or similar name to the one you want to use? If the name has been registered for official trademark protection, especially at the federal level, you should take that as a huge "No Trespassing" sign that should be taken seriously. Even if you feel certain that your business is different enough from that of the trademark owner to allow you to use the name, you should proceed only with lots and lots of caution. If your search shows that the name is being used but isn't registered, then you might have a bit more leeway—but not much more. Since use, not registration, conveys trademark rights, you still need to be very careful not to infringe that owner's rights.

That being said, there are a few instances when taking a name that is already being used by someone else might be a marginally okay idea. As we mentioned above, if the name is being used for a company that provides a very different product or service than the one you plan to sell, then you may have good reason to move forward with your plans to use the name. This is especially true if the two businesses serve only local markets and are hundreds of miles apart. For example, just because a tiny clothing store in Newport Beach calls itself Nature's Calling doesn't mean that you, in Humboldt County, can't use Nature's Calling for your plumbing business. But if you wanted to start a clothing store called Nature's Calling, then you really should consider choosing a different name. Even if the company using the name seems like a local outfit in a far away place, it could have plans to expand its territory.

In short, if a company is registered with the state or federal trademark office, you may want to start thinking of a new name. If, on the other hand, you think the businesses are different enough for your use of the trademark to be safe, consider hiring an attorney specializing in trademark law for the sole purpose of helping you decide if the two names are too close for comfort.

C. Trademark Registration

Registering your trademark with the federal or state government will strengthen your rights to it and make it easier to protect the name in case of a dispute. Registration is simply a process of notifying the state or, more commonly, the U.S. government that you're using a particular trademark. When registration is complete, the trademark gets placed on an official list of registered names commonly called a trademark register. The U.S. Patent and Trademark Office maintains two registers, the Principal Register and the Supplemental Register. California's Trademark Unit has just one.

When people refer to a federally registered trademark, they're generally talking about marks on the Principal Register. Trademarks that appear on the Principal Register get the most protection, and the penalties can be harsh for those who use a name that appears on it. The Supplemental Register, on the other hand, is reserved for weaker, less distinctive trademarks that don't qualify for the Principal Register. The main function of the Supplemental Register is to provide notice of a mark's current use to anyone who does a trademark search. After five years on the Supplemental Register a mark may qualify to be moved to the Principal Register if it's been in continuous use during that period.

California (and most other states) maintain just one register for all trademarks. State registration doesn't give as many benefits as federal registration, so it generally makes most sense to register federally for the widest scope of protection. Some trademarks, however, don't qualify for federal registration because they aren't used in national, international or territorial commerce—in other words, they're only used within the state. These marks can only be registered at the state level. Although use of a trademark on the Internet almost guarantees the right to apply for federal registration, if you truly are only using the mark within California, state registration may be the only option.

The Patent and Trademark Office—the office that administers federal trademarks—provides forms and instructions which are available from a number of sources, including the PTO's Website at http://www.uspto.gov. For simple trademarks such as business names (as opposed to trademarks for special packaging or product design—called "trade dress" in the biz), the instructions should be easy enough to follow. If you have online access, you can fill in the form online and either submit it electronically, or print out a completed copy and snail-mail it to the PTO. For more detailed information on registering your federal trademark, see *Trademark: Legal Care for Your Business & Product Name*, by Stephen Elias and Kate McGrath (Nolo Press).

The process of registering a trademark with the state of California is similar to the federal system's procedure. State trademark registration forms are available from the Trademark Unit of California's Secretary of State, or you can download them from the Web at http://www.ss.ca.gov/business/ts/ts_formsfees.htm. Contact California's Trademark Unit at 916-653-4984 for more information.

D. Winning Names for Your Business, Products and Services

Now that you have a general idea of the legal hurdles you need to clear and the snags and traps to watch out for, let the naming begin! Despite the hassles involved in learning a little trademark law, choosing names for your business and its products or services remains one of the more fun parts of starting your business. It gives you a chance to use your creative juices to come up with a name that is both marketable and infused with your individual personality (or the collective personalities of your business partners). A business name can help you establish the overall vibe of your business, from strictly professional to downright funky to a dozen things in between.

Besides legal restrictions and personal preferences, the traditions and realities of your particular industry or business will probably have a lot to do with what kind of business name you choose. Good, memorable business and product names range from the clever (SuperFantastic Bubble Plastic, Netscape Navigator, Liquid Paper) to the straightforward (24-Hour Fitness, Fruit Roll-Ups, Jenny Craig Weight Loss Centres) to sometimes even the cryptic (Yahoo!, Chia Pet, Floam). In part because there really are so many different kinds of businesses and so many approaches to choosing a distinctive name, it's impossible to give any kind of specific name advice. There are, however, a few things that are helpful to keep in mind when choosing your business names.

• Sometimes straightforward, informative names work better than fancy ones. For example, if you plan to open a shop selling aquarium supplies and tropical fish in Oakland, East Bay Aquariums & Fish may be a far more effective name than The Lure of the Ocean. Also, since humble, descriptive names qualify for less trademark protection (unless they are already famous; see Section A2, above), choosing an ordinary name—especially one with a geographic identifier—will likely simplify your trademark search.

• Think about how your customers will locate your business and your products. If you don't expect customers to seek out or remember your company as a whole, but only its products, it's silly to focus much attention on the business name. For instance, while millions of people know the product The Clapper and its commercial jingle ("Clap on! Clap off! The Clapper!"), few know or care who its makers are.

• Before you finally commit to a name, get some feedback from potential customers, suppliers and others in your support network. They may come up with a downside to a potential name or suggest an improvement you haven't thought of. Doing this type of homework is especially important if you will market your goods or services to custom-

ers who are members of several different ethnic groups. You obviously don't want to choose a name or symbol and learn later that it offends or turns off a key group of customers. For example, one organization we know couldn't figure out why it got such a cold shoulder from Mexican Americans. The answer turned out to be that the shape, size and type used on their signs were similar to a "No Trespassers—Keep Out" sign widely used in Mexico. And virtually everyone with e-mail has by now seen a widely circulated humor piece on a number of advertising translation blunders—such as Kentucky Fried Chicken's "finger lickin' good" slogan reading in China as "eat your fingers off."

• Niche businesses are often identified by their trade name, even when the focus is on the products, meaning that it is wise to pay particular attention to picking a memorable name if you will try to capture a particular, small field. The publisher of this book, Nolo Press, is a good example. Even though book buyers in other fields usually identify books they want by title or author, since Nolo books occupy a specific niche, many customers have come to recognize its name, often going into a bookstore and asking where the Nolo books are. In other words, Nolo has come to mean "self-help law" to many customers familiar with it, in contrast to the name HarperCollins—a large publisher of books on many topics—which might not evoke anything particular in most book customers' minds.

• Service businesses, or businesses that don't sell their own products, are almost always identified by their trade name. In certain fields where an owner's (or small group of owners') personal attention and savvy is important (for example, architecture or accounting), it is common to use the owner's name, as in Arthur Anderson. In other service and retail businesses, it is more common to use creative names—and not only for the business itself, but sometimes its products, too.

Example:

David and Donna operate a car wash named Storm, which develops a good deal of name recognition in the city. Besides relying on the reputation of their trade name, they come up with clever names for various service packages (such as Sunday Shower, Typhoon Tuesday and the Everyday Squall Special) in hopes that those names will catch on as well.

• Be sure your trade or business name won't restrict your ability to grow unless you are really sure your business will always be tiny. Ask yourself if your chosen name will still be appropriate as your business grows. If you open Berkeley Aquariums & Fish, will it be a problem if you want to open a second store in San Rafael? You should think twice about giving your name a geographical identifier, especially if you want Internet sales. Similarly, if you start a business selling and installing canvas awnings using the name Sturdy Canvas Awnings, your name might be a burden if you decide to also start making canvas signs. On the other hand, the name Sturdy Canvas would let you move into all sorts of canvas products, such as duffel bags, canvas signs and drop cloths.

Also, as discussed throughout this chapter, even though you plan to open, for instance, just one office to help local businesses establish security systems, it's a good idea to be sure your name is safe from trademark conflicts on a statewide or even national basis. That way if your business takes off, you won't bump into someone else who already uses the name in another area or online.

Choosing a Legal and Lucrative Business Location

For many types of businesses, location can mean the difference between feast or famine. Other enterprises will do more or less the same whether they're located in downtown San Francisco or in a deep crevasse on Mars. Not only does the importance of location vary greatly from business to business, but what makes a location desirable for one business might not work for another. Since there's no universal definition of what makes a location good for business, it's important for every business owner to figure out how location will (or will not) contribute to the success of her business, and to choose a spot accordingly.

That being said, there are a couple of basic issues to consider when choosing a business location. For one, you'll want to make sure the location makes economic sense. Even the best-run business will fail if its customers can't find it or don't want to go to an unsafe neighborhood. But it's just as true that you won't want to spend a fortune for a spot on an exclusive commercial strip unless it's really going to pay off. And, of course, the location that you choose needs to be legally approved for whatever you plan to do there. Especially if you are planning to work from home or a non-business area, you'll need to check zoning laws to see if they prohibit your type of business. This chapter will help you figure out how to find a suitable place that meets all the needs of your business and complies with your local laws.

Planning to work from home? If you plan to use your home as your office, you can skip directly to Section D, which discusses special issues for home businesses. Working from home can be a much simpler arrangement than renting a separate space, but it could put you in violation of zoning and other laws that regulate business spaces. In Section D, we'll alert you to what laws you may need to comply with and discuss other legal issues such as the home-office tax deduction.

A. Picking the Right Spot

Number one on your list should be to figure out how important location is to your business. For some businesses, the classic "location, location, location" advice definitely applies. But for others, location may be a lot less important than getting an affordable rental. And for plenty of businesses, location is practically irrelevant: wholesalers, service businesses that do all their work at the customer's location (like a roofer or a plumber), mail-order companies and Internet-based businesses are just a few examples. Especially if you can pass on your rent savings to your customers, picking a spot in an out-of-the-way area might be to your advantage. In other words, if location isn't that crucial to your business, don't blow all your start-up money on an expensive space in a thriving location.

If, on the other hand, you determine that location will be important to your business success, you'll need to figure out the best place to locate so that lots of customers can find you. It's one thing to know that you need a good location, but it can be harder to figure out what makes a location good. Ask yourself questions like these:

- Will customers come on foot?
- Will customers drive and, if so, where will they park?
- Will more customers come if you locate near other similar businesses?
- Is it the reputation of the neighborhood or even of a particular building that will help draw customers?

Often there is no one answer. As you struggle to answer these and similar questions, here are a few things you'll want to consider.

1. Planting Yourself in Rich Soil

Picking a profitable location obviously means different things to different businesses. The key is to figure out what factors will increase customer volume for your unique business, and then to concentrate on finding a location that achieves as many of them as possible. For example, if you're opening a coffee shop, you may assume your customer volume will be highest if there's lots of pedestrian traffic nearby during the hours you plan to be open. Furthermore, if you envision your coffeehouse to be a mellow place to sit and read, you'd probably prefer a university area or shopping district full of people with time to kill rather than an area buzzing with busy businesspeople. If, on the other hand you plan to open a small shop with no tables, just fast, high-volume service, a busy downtown office district might be the right spot.

Keep in mind that different types of businesses attract customers in different ways. One key distinction is foot traffic versus automobile traffic. An auto repair shop, for example, will obviously draw customers in radically different ways than the coffee shop. For the auto shop, the choicest locale is a well-traveled street, where it will be seen by many drivers who will easily be able to pull into the lot. For an urban coffee shop, on the other hand, a popular location might be in an area where there are lots of people passing on foot. But of course no rule is absolute, and even some coffee shops thrive because commuters stop for "to go" coffee and baked goods every morning.

Also think about whether it would benefit your business to be around similar businesses that are already drawing the type of customers that you want. A women's clothing store, for example, would no doubt profit from being near other clothing shops, since many women shopping for clothes tend to spend the day or at least a few hours in a particular area. The point is, the perfect location for any business is a very individual matter. Spend some time figuring out the habits of the customers you want to attract, and then choose a location that fits.

Don't sabotage your business by picking a cheap, but bad, location. This may seem obvious, but sometimes new business owners become blind to common wisdom when presented with an opportunity to rent a super-cheap space. Even if they've already determined that location will play a key role in their success, they either believe that the savings in rent will make up for slow sales or they convince themselves that they'll be the pioneers in a new area that is sure to swell into a hot business district by the middle of next week. While this does occasionally happen (god bless those brave pioneers), it's generally a poor idea to move into a dead section of town since it almost certainly won't bloom fast enough to support your business in its financially vulnerable start-up days. Unless you have a sound reason to believe that you'll get enough customers in your oddball location, don't let the lure of low rent tempt you into a bad business decision.

2. Getting the Right Physical Features

When picking your space, the biggest consideration is sometimes not where it is but what it is. Ask yourself: Are the building facilities appropriate or adaptable for my business? For example, if you're planning to open a coffee house, you might fall in love with a beautiful brick warehouse space in a funky shopping district, but if the place doesn't have at least minimal kitchen facilities, you should probably forget it. Unless you can convince your landlord to put in the needed equipment—plumbing, electrical work and the rest (which is discussed below)—it's highly unlikely that laying out the cash to do it yourself will be worth it. Sure, some improvements might be relatively cheap, such as putting up a wall or two or adding new light fixtures. But if the building lacks something that is essential to your business operation, you should take it as a sign that the place isn't right for you—even if it has loads of other great qualities. You'll have to decide for yourself which features your business absolutely can't live with or live without.

Example:

Charlotte and Sandra plan to open an alternative health store offering products such as medicinal herbs, aromatherapy products and yoga supplies. They also plan to offer services such as aromatherapy sessions and consultations with nutritionists and herbalists. Since they have high hopes for the service side of their business, Charlotte and Sandra know that their physical space needs to be comfortable and appealing to customers. After looking at a number of storefront spaces in their chosen neighborhood (near the university, of course), they find one that seems just perfect—until they notice the lack of windows. Except for the glass front door, the place has almost no natural light. Even though not having windows doesn't absolutely prevent them from doing business, Charlotte and Sandra decide that given their expected customer base (and their own feelings), they need a brighter space.

Another common need for many businesses is adequate parking. If a significant percentage of your customers will come by car and there isn't enough parking at your chosen spot, it's probably best to look elsewhere. In fact, the city might not allow you to operate there anyway if parking isn't adequate. (See Section B on zoning laws regarding parking.)

Find Out What's Required of Your Particular Business

Before you spend lots of time searching for a space, you should find out if your type of business is subject to local planning or health department requirements. For instance, if you're starting a small food manufacturing business to produce Healthy Bites energy bars, at the very least you'll need to rent a space with a certain number of vents, a fire-resistant roof and walls of proper material and adequate thickness. Contact your city or county departments of planning, health, fire or other appropriate agency to find out.

B. Complying With Zoning Laws

Legally speaking, it's far less important whether a certain spot is a good one for your business than if it's properly zoned for what you plan to do. As you may know, local zoning laws (often called ordinances or land use regulations) prohibit certain activities from being conducted in particular areas. For instance, a nightclub wouldn't be allowed to operate in a district zoned for residential use. Sure, only a fool would try to open a disco on a quiet residential street—but there are less obvious zoning no-nos that you need to observe.

Zoning ordinances typically allow certain categories of businesses to occupy each district of a city or county; mixed commercial and residential uses might be allowed in one district while another district allows heavy industry and warehouses. So if you open your small jewelry-making business in a space zoned for commercial use, you could be in for a real headache if zoning officials decide you're a light-industrial business not allowed to operate in a commercial district.

Besides regulating the types of businesses in certain areas, zoning laws also regulate specific activities. Depending on your area, you might be subject to laws regulating parking, signs, water and air quality, waste management, noise, and visual appearance of the business (especially in historic districts). And in addition to these regulations, some cities restrict the number of particular types of businesses in a certain area, such as allowing only three bookstores or two pet shops in a particular neighborhood. Finally, some zoning laws specifically regulate home businesses. Home-office regulations are discussed separately in Section D, below.

Expect Zoning Laws on Parking Spaces and Business Signs

Local zoning laws commonly require a business to provide parking. They also may regulate the size and type of business signs. Be prepared for your city or county to look into both these issues. If there's already a parking problem in your proposed area, you may have to come up with a plan for how to deal with the increased traffic your business will attract. Also be ready for zoning officials to get really nitpicky about your business sign. Many local laws limit the size of business signs (no signs over 5 feet by 3 feet, for instance), their appearance (such as whether they're illuminated, flashing, colorful or made of neon), and their placement (flat against the building, hanging over the sidewalk or mounted on a pole). There are even some regulations attempting to limit the use of foreign language on signs. Be sure to find out what your local regulations are before spending money on having signs made.

One of the key things to understand about zoning laws is that more often than not, they're enforced for the sake of the other people and companies in the neighborhood (this is particularly true of home-based businesses). While some areas are strict about their zoning laws, most of the time you won't have a zoning official knocking unannounced on your door unless neighbors have complained or you're in flagrant violation of the laws. Since enforcement is often triggered by complaints, it's a good idea to get to know your neighbors and develop good relationships with them.

1.   Making Sure That You Comply

The first thing to remember is that you should *never* sign a lease for a business space without first knowing that you'll legally be able to do business there. (One exception to this is that it's okay to sign a contingent lease, with a clause stating that the lease won't be binding if you don't get zoning approval.) Being forced to move your business is a headache enough, but not nearly as catastrophic as being held liable for payment on a lease for a space that you can't use.

For answers to zoning questions, never rely on what the previous occupants of the space did. Don't assume that you'll be allowed to do a certain activity simply because the previous tenants of your space did it. For all kinds of reasons, some businesses get away with zoning violations, even for long periods of time. Typically, however, new occupants are scrutinized more carefully than already existing businesses. It may not be fair, but it's common for a new business to be told it can't do what an old one had long been doing.

It's also possible that the previous tenants, without violating the zoning rules, were doing something that is no longer allowed in the area. For example, the previous occupants could have had a zoning variance (an exception to zoning laws) for their particular business—one that won't apply to you. And lots of times zoning laws change, but businesses that are already in a space are allowed to keep doing what they were doing, even if the activity violates the new zoning law (a system referred to as "grandfathering"). When a tenant with a grandfathered exception leaves and new occupants come in, the new business will normally have to abide by the new law.

How do you find out whether a given location is properly zoned for your business and whether you need to get other approvals (for example, based on the number of other similar businesses that operate there)? The answer varies from area to area. In some cities and counties, zoning approval is part of the tax registration process (discussed in Chapter 6). In San Diego, for instance, when you apply for your business tax certificate you must also pay a $12 Zoning Use Clearance fee to have your business approved for the location listed on your application. And the City of Oakland won't accept your new business application without prior approval of your business location by the city's zoning division. Other cities such as San Francisco don't require proof of zoning approval before issuing a tax registration certificate—but that doesn't mean you should take the zoning laws any less seriously. Whether or not you're required to deal with your local zoning department before starting your business, you'll still be subject to their monitoring and enforcement on an ongoing basis.

Audrey Wackerley,

owner of RetroFit, a vintage clothing store in San Francisco:

When we first opened we got a space in the perfect neighborhood, with lots of thrift stores, coffee shops and other walk-in type businesses on a strip with lots of foot traffic (plus, it was only a few blocks from my apartment). But we were on a cross street a few doors around the corner from Valencia Street, the main strip. We did okay, but nothing like the shops on Valencia itself. Finally we got a good deal on a storefront on Valencia Street, and we moved. Our business practically tripled! We do pay a bit more for the better space, but our boost in sales more than makes up for it.

How Vigilant Are Zoning Officials?

There's a world of difference in how strict zoning officials are from area to area. Many zoning departments aren't terribly rigid about enforcement, mostly responding to complaints from neighbors or other citizens about businesses that create a nuisance or other trouble. In a few areas, however, zoning agents relish sniffing out minor infractions and enforcing their zoning ordinances to the letter.

If you're considering going ahead with your business despite what you consider to be a minor zoning problem, you should do your best to find out how strict the zoning police are in your area. Start by asking other local business people about their experiences. If they tell you that there's little enforcement other than responding to complaints, you can breathe a little easier about a minor infraction such as including tennis-racquet stringing (technically a light-industrial activity) at your sports shop in an area zoned only for commercial use. Even so, it never pays to engage in a prohibited activity that is fundamental to your business—tennis rackets could be strung elsewhere, but a health club wouldn't want to locate its juice bar two blocks away.

But no matter how mellow your zoning department, at the very least you need to know what the rules are for your proposed location. Paying scant attention to the rules while counting on lax enforcement is just plain dumb.

If your city doesn't include zoning approval as part of its start-up requirements for new businesses, you'll need to do some detective work. Generally this involves talking with your local zoning officials. Most zoning agencies are part of city or county planning departments. Look under "Planning" or "Zoning" in the government section (blue pages) of your white-pages phone book. If your business will be located in a city, you probably only need to worry about city zoning ordinances. Businesses in rural areas should contact the county zoning/planning offices.

2. If There's a Zoning Problem

If your zoning board has a problem with any of the activities you plan to conduct at your chosen location, you'll have a few options, usually ranging from making appropriate changes to your business to giving up on that location and finding a new one. Obviously, some zoning conflicts are simply not fixable, such as opening a nightclub in a quiet cul-de-sac. But the good news is that a creative (and, when necessary, assertive) business owner can often persuade zoning officials or the zoning appeals board to work out an acceptable accommodation that will allow the business to use the desired location.

Overly restrictive zoning rules can often be circumvented legally. For borderline situations, one approach is simply to advocate an interpretation of the zoning law that's favorable to you. Sometimes this can be done proactively, by communicating with zoning officials to get their seal of approval before they make a decision.

If officials have already decided against you, it's usually possible to appeal their decision. In some cases, a zoning board may grant an exception—called a variance—to the local zoning laws. Another common type of exception is called a conditional use permit, which is granted to exempt a business from a specific zoning law, often in return for compliance with certain basic conditions.

When lobbying for an exemption from a zoning requirement, remember that you're asking for special treatment, so make your case as persuasive as possible. If your business will be valuable to the community, present evidence of that fact. Proof can include demographic data about the area, testimony from community leaders or statements from other local business people. Your goal is to show that the value of allowing your business in the area is greater than the trivial zoning conflicts that may exist. If you can compromise in some other area, offer to do so.

Example:

Carolyn wants to open a small printing shop, Nelson's Press, on a commercial strip where storefront space is cheap and plentiful. Before signing a lease, she applies for zoning approval. The local zoning board rejects her application because Carolyn's proposed location is zoned commercial, while her print shop would technically be a light-industrial business. Carolyn decides to try to get an exception, because her printing operation will be small (only one small offset printing press) and would be an asset to the neighborhood, which needs new businesses.

She submits to the zoning board detailed plans of her business, showing its small scope and including specific protocols for dealing with toxics such as ink. (At the same time she files a Certificate of Disclosure of Hazardous Substances with her city's Office of Emergency Services.) She also submits letters from other business owners in the area documenting how commerce in the area has languished for years and arguing that new businesses would help revitalize the strip. Many of the business owners also note that a local printer would be convenient for the existing area businesses, who currently have to go across town for their print jobs. A few weeks later, Carolyn gets a conditional use permit allowing her to proceed with her printing business, as long as she doesn't expand her business with additional presses and follows a number of standard rules governing the chemicals she'll use in printing.

C. Commercial Leases

Chances are that you'll rent rather than buy a space for your business. But just because you've rented plenty of apartments or flats over the years, don't assume that you know the score when it comes to leasing business space.

It's crucial to understand from the get-go that, practically and legally speaking, there are oceans of differences between commercial leases and residential leases. Commercial leases are not subject to most consumer protection laws that govern residential leases—for example, there are no caps on deposits or rules protecting a tenant's privacy. Also, since a business will often need to modify the existing space (add cubicles, raise a loading dock, rewire, etc.), the terms of commercial leases are usually subject to at least some negotiation. Of course, your bargaining power will vary a great deal from situation to situation. For example, getting a landlord to accept your demands will probably be a lot easier for a long-term lease in a largely vacant business building, than it will if you want a six-month lease in a hot commercial area.

When negotiating a commercial lease, keep in mind that the success or failure of your business may ride on certain terms of the lease. The amount of the rent is an obvious concern, as is the length of the lease. But other, less conspicuous items spelled out in the lease may be just as crucial to your business's success. For instance, if you expect your shoe-repair business to depend largely on walk-in customers, be sure that your lease establishes your right to put up a sign that's visible from the street. And if you are counting on being the only sandwich shop inside a new commercial complex, make sure your lease prevents the landlord from leasing to a competitor.

The following checklist includes many items that are often addressed in commercial leases. For more detailed information on negotiating commercial leases, see attorney Fred S. Steingold's *Legal Guide for Starting and Running a Small Business, Volume 1* (Nolo Press). Pay attention to terms regarding:

- rent, including allowable increases and method of computation
- security deposit and conditions for return
- length of lease (also called the lease term)
- whether the rent you pay covers utilities, taxes and maintenance (called a gross lease) or whether you will be charged for these items separately (called a net or, if the tenant must cover three additional costs, a triple net lease)
- whether there's an option to renew the lease
- if and how the lease may be terminated, including notice requirements
- what space is being rented, including common areas such as hallways, rest rooms and elevators
- specifications for signs, including where they may be placed
- whether there will be improvements, modifications or fixtures (often called buildouts) added to the space, who will pay for them and who will own them after the lease ends
- who will maintain the premises
- whether the lease may be assigned or sublet to another party, and
- whether disputes must be mediated or arbitrated as an alternative to court.

Many businesses must comply with the Americans with Disabilities Act. The Americans with Disabilities Act (ADA) requires all businesses that are open to the public or that employ more than 15 people to have premises that are accessible to disabled people. Make sure that you and your landlord are in agreement about who will pay for any needed modifications, such as adding a ramp or widening doorways to accommodate wheelchairs.

D. When Your Home Is Your Office

For more and more entrepreneurs, the "daily grind" means stepping into the kitchen to brew a fresh pot of coffee. Now that personal computers and networking software are both powerful and affordable, it's easy for anyone to set up a inexpensive home office that can take care of virtually all the business tasks that used to be done in high-tech commercial offices.

And besides the fact that new communications technology has largely conquered the problem of physical distance, many modern businesses don't take up much physical space. In plenty of situations, space for a bookcase, a file cabinet, a phone and your computer may be all you need. Factor in the money saved by not paying commercial rent or commuting costs, and it may be foolish *not* to at least start your business from home.

But before you get too euphoric about opening a machine shop in the den, it's important to realize a home business isn't immune from a number of the requirements that affect businesses in general. Like a company operated from a commercial office space, a business run from your home needs to comply with zoning requirements in that area. You should also be aware of several key insurance and tax rules.

Is your business right for a home office? While many types of businesses lend themselves to being run out of a residence, others don't. Make sure you've considered whether using your home as your office is a good idea. Ask yourself questions like the following:

- How will you deal with customers and suppliers?

- Will customers take you and your company seriously if you work out of your house?

- Will your business require a lot of space for performing services or storing supplies?

- Can you work productively in your home, considering distractions like kids, the couch, the refrigerator and the TV?

Businesses that require nothing but a small office and don't generate much coming and going—such as graphic design, accounting and Web development businesses—and businesses where most of the dirty work is routinely done off-site—such as construction and plumbing—are particularly well suited for home offices.

Kimberly Torgerson, *owner of Your Word's Worth, a freelance editing and writing service:*

Setting up my home office was much harder than navigating the licensing agencies to start up my business. Where to put the fax? How to get the monitor set up just right? How to organize a spaghetti tangle of cables? Someday I'd like to get a sleeker setup, with everything in a tailored niche, but for now I put money into upgrading equipment, not furniture.

1. Zoning Restrictions on Home Offices

As with leased office spaces, you need to make sure that the business activities you plan to do in your home are acceptable to your local zoning officials. (Zoning laws typically refer to home offices as "home occupations.") Since your home is most likely in an area zoned for residential use only (some loft-type apartments might be zoned for mixed use), the types of businesses allowed by the ordinance will likely be pretty limited. A few areas forbid home businesses altogether. But most cities and counties allow occupations that have little likelihood of causing noise or pollution, creating traffic or otherwise disturbing the neighbors. Writers, artists, attorneys, accountants, insurance brokers and piano teachers are common examples of businesspeople who cities allow to work from home.

Watch out for special, private land use restrictions.
If you live in a condo, a co-op, a planned subdivision or other rental property, you are likely subject to land use restrictions in addition to your local laws. Condo regulations, for instance, often contain language restricting or sometimes even prohibiting business use of the premises. Or your apartment lease might forbid business from being conducted on the property. Be sure to check the documents governing your property to see if there are any such rules.

If zoning laws do allow a list of certain types of home businesses or "traditional home businesses," they are likely to impose other restrictions, such as requiring that any employees also be residents of the home, limiting the number of customers that may come to your home, limiting the percentage of a home's floor space that's used for business or prohibiting signs outside of your home that advertise your business. In Sacramento, for example, home businesses are subject to dozens of rules, including a limit of two employees, both of whom must live at the residence, and a prohibition on operating trucks larger than one-half ton—which rules out many full-size pick-up trucks.

Besides regulating certain activities in general, cities often impose additional restrictions upon specific types of businesses. For instance, while a city might forbid any home business from having a neon sign, it might have a special rule for landscapers that no supplies may be kept at the home office. Be sure to find out if there are special rules for your type of business in your city.

Finally, some localities require you to get a special permit to conduct business from home, for which they charge a fee. Sacramento, for instance, charges $45 for a home occupation permit, and Los Angeles charges $25.

To find out how your city or county deals with home offices, call the planning department and ask them for any information they have on home occupations. Some areas have special pamphlets of information explaining home office restrictions and how to obtain any necessary permits. In other places, all that's available might be a grainy photocopied copy of the municipal code that you'll have to decipher yourself. If there's no approval or permit process for home businesses in your area, that generally means that it's up to you to comply with your area's zoning code. Keep in mind that the best way to avoid trouble is to do your best to minimize your business's impact on the neighborhood. As long as you're not in flagrant violation of the zoning laws regarding home businesses, you'll probably be fine as long as your neighbors are happy (see Tip, below).

Below, we've listed some home occupation restrictions and permit fees for a few of California's larger cities. It's a good general guide to the types of regulations home businesses face across the state. There are, of course, exceptions to these rules and they are subject to change, so be sure to check with your city for its specific laws regulating home occupations.

City	Home Office Restrictions	Required Permit for Home Offices	Fees for Home Offices
Fresno	• any employees must be residents of home • business may not use more than one room of home • business may not use space outside the main home structure (e.g. no business activities in the garage) • business vehicle may not weigh more than one ton, and must be stored in an entirely enclosed garage	None	None
Oakland	• any employees must be residents of home business • sign may not be larger than one square foot, must be nonmoving, and may be lit only indirectly without flashing lights • if business is conducted in garage, garage door must be closed • any vehicle with sign advertising business may not be visible from the edge of the property	Same zoning approval requirements as all other businesses ($10 fee for zoning clearance)	$10 zoning clearance fee (applies to all businesses, not just home occupations)
Los Angeles	• may conduct business between 8 a.m. and 8 p.m. • one client per hour allowed on premises during business hours • no signs allowed	Home Occupation Permit	$25 for annual permit
Sacramento	• only two employees allowed, both of whom must be residents of home • no customers or clients allowed on premises • only one truck weighing up to 1/2 ton allowed • no signs allowed	Home Occupation Permit	$45 for annual permit
San Diego	• may conduct business between 8 a.m. and 5 p.m. Monday through Friday • only one employee or partner allowed on premises during business hours • employee or partner must be resident of home • clients allowed on premises only one at a time, by appointment only, and only during business hours • no signs allowed	Home Occupation Permit * Exception: No permit required if no employee, partners or clients will be on premises, and if only one business vehicle will be kept at premises	$157.50 for annual permit
San Francisco	• no more than 1/4 of home's floor space may be used for business • any employees must be residents of home • no inventory may be kept on premises	None	None
San Jose	• any employees must be residents of home • only two clients allowed on premises at one time • clients allowed only between 9 a.m. and 9 p.m. • only one vehicle under 10,000 pounds may be kept at residence • business sign may not be larger than one square foot	None	None

Keep in mind that the zoning agency is probably not the only land-use regulatory agency in your area. While your activity might be okay with zoning officials, operating out of your home may not pass other departments' requirements. For example, if you're starting a catering business, your county health department will likely not let you work out of your home kitchen. You may be allowed to convert your garage or another separate structure into a professional kitchen, but of course that invites building permits as well as county health inspections and zoning permission.

Let your neighbors in on your business plans. As mentioned earlier, getting to know your neighbors can be a huge help in avoiding problems with zoning officials. For instance, if your business requires people to be coming and going from your house or packages to be delivered daily, your neighbors might jump to the nutty conclusion that you're a drug dealer and report you to the city. Even though you can show your drug of choice is vitamin C, the city might discover technical zoning violations that never would have otherwise turned up. In short, communicating with your neighbors and dealing with any of their concerns about issues such as parking and noise will greatly reduce the likelihood that the zoning police will come knocking on your door.

2. The Home-Office Tax Deduction

If your office is located in your home, you may be able to claim a portion of your home expenses— such as rent, depreciation, property taxes, utilities and insurance—as a special deduction when reporting federal taxes. (This deduction will also flow through to your state tax return.) The IRS's general rule is that if your home office qualifies (discussed below), you can deduct a pro rata share of home-office expenses—which simply means a share that's proportional to the percentage of home space that you use for your business. To qualify, your home-office space must be used exclusively and regularly as a principal place of business.

No question, the words "exclusively," "regularly" and "principal place of business" are IRS-speak, and have specific, nit-picky meanings. First, we'll explain these terms so that you'll know whether you can deduct your home-office expenses, and then we'll tell you how to figure out just how much is actually deductible. (For information on how businesses in general are taxed, refer to Chapter 8, "Getting to Know Your Taxes.")

Many business expenses are fully deductible without the home-office deduction. A common misconception is that you need to qualify for the home-office deduction before you can claim any expenses associated with your home-based business. Not true. You can deduct business expenses necessary for your business whether they're incurred in your home or anyplace else, even if you don't qualify for the home-office deduction. For instance, you can always deduct the portion of your home long-distance phone bill that you spend on business-related calls. Other deductible business expenses might include office supplies, furniture and equipment that you use in your home office, and the cost of bringing a second telephone line into your home for business use. For the rest of this chapter, when we mean expenses that can only be claimed as home-office deductions, we'll say "home-office expenses."

a. Using Your Home Office Exclusively and Regularly for Business

The IRS will allow you to deduct home-office expenses only for office space in your home that is dedicated to business use. For example, a graphic designer who sometimes sits at the kitchen table to do illustrations can't claim business deductions for using the kitchen (assuming the kitchen is also sometimes used for nonbusiness uses like cooking and eating). A spare room, however, that's set up as an office space and used only for business would probably meet the "exclusive use" test. But if the room contains a bed for the occasional overnight guest or doubles as storage space for clothing, technically, it wouldn't qualify.

The "regular use" test is generally pretty easy to pass (and the IRS rarely conducts inspections). As long as you use a home-office space for business on a continuing basis, rather than for a once-in-a-while garage sale or lemonade stand, the "regular use" test will probably be satisfied.

Example 1:

Stacey runs a hat-making business. She makes the hats in an extra room of her house where she has a sewing machine and all her supplies, as well as a computer and a file cabinet containing her sales and other financial information. Since the only use of that room is for the hat-making business, it will meet the IRS's criteria of exclusive use. And since Stacey has made and sold hats for a couple years, with consistent monthly sales, she'll have no trouble proving that she uses the space regularly for business.

Example 2:

Parisha has a full-time job at a plant nursery, but also does occasional freelance work in photography. She has a darkroom in her basement that she uses to develop photos for her assignments. Her darkroom is dedicated to her photography business, but she spends most of her time working at the plant nursery and has only done one photo shoot in the last six months. Parisha would be ill-advised to claim her darkroom expenses as a home-office deduction since she doesn't regularly use it for business.

b. Using Your Home Office as Your Principal Place of Business

Besides fulfilling the exclusive and regular use requirement, your home-office space must also be the main place where you do business—with two exceptions explained below in "Exceptions to the Principal Place of Business Rule." Basically, if you do all your work at your home office, you'll satisfy this requirement. If you have a home office, but also conduct business in other locations—for example, you make house calls to do TV repair work or you play music at nightclubs—you can only deduct your home-office expenses if your home office is your principal work space. It can sometimes be tricky to figure out which work location is "principal"—and sometimes, no single location will qualify as the principal one. The IRS weighs two factors to approach this question:

- **How important are the activities at the various locations?** This test to determine whether your home office is your principal work space focuses on whether the activities carried on at your home office are really central or key to your business. Consider, for instance, a tennis instructor who gives lessons at a local public court and maintains an office at home to keep track of clients. Since giving the actual tennis lessons to students is clearly more important to the business than the administrative side of things, this "central to the business" test would not be met (the home office could not be considered the principal business location).

  But what about a math tutor who sometimes teaches children at her home, and sometimes at the students' homes? Clearly her business activities at and away from her home are both a core part of her business, so this test alone might not give a clear answer as to whether her home office is her principal place of business.

- **How much time is spent at each location?** Another approach to figuring out which business location is principal is to compare how much time you spend in each location. Using the above examples, chances are that the tennis teacher spends far more time at the tennis court than at his home office. Since both IRS criteria for the principal place of business would show the tennis instructor's principal place of business to be the tennis court, he wouldn't be able to deduct his home-office expenses.

On the other hand, say the math tutor teaches at home 20 days a month and at students' homes five days a month. Plus, she also uses her home office to prepare her lesson plans and keep track of billing information. All told, since most of her work time is spent at home on activities that are central to her business, her home office would be considered her principal place of business, making her home-office expenses deductible.

Finally, you should also be aware that the law is about to change, making it easier for home offices to satisfy the "principal place of business" requirement. Beginning in 1999, your home office will qualify as a principal place of business if:

- you use the office to conduct administrative or management activities for your business, and

- you do not have an office or other business location outside your home where you conduct a large part of your administrative or management activities.

Exceptions to the Principal Place of Business Rule

If your home office doesn't qualify as your principal place of business under the tests described above, there are two other ways you may be able to qualify for the home-office deduction:

- you regularly meet clients or customers at home, or

- you use a separate structure on your property for your home office.

In these cases, it doesn't matter whether your home office or separate structure is your principal work space. But remember—the rule still applies that your home office must be exclusively and regularly for business.

---

c. Figuring Your Deductible Home-Office Expenses

Once you've determined that your home-office expenses are, in fact, deductible, you'll need to figure out exactly how much you can deduct. Obviously you can't deduct all of your housing costs—only the expenses that are attributable to business purposes.

The general rule is that expenses that are unrelated to the business space are not deductible at all, such as the cost of repainting your bedroom or replacing your dining room window. Expenses that affect the specific business space (called direct expenses) are fully deductible, such as installing new carpeting for your office space, replacing a broken window in the office and repairing the heating vent in your office space. Expenses that affect the whole house (called indirect expenses) are deductible, but only to the exent that they are business-related. For instance, you could deduct a percentage of the cost of a new foundation, a new water heater, real estate taxes and the gas and electric bill.

To calculate the portion of indirect costs attributable to your business, you should first figure out what percentage of your home you use for business purposes. Then you'll use that percentage to calculate how much of your regular home expenses can be deducted as home-office expenses.

You can calculate the percentage of your home being used for business in one of two ways: the square footage method or the number of rooms method. Either approach is acceptable to the IRS. The square footage method simply divides the square footage of the business space by the square footage of the whole house. For instance, if you use 250 square feet for business, and your whole house takes up 1000 square feet, then your business space uses 25% (250/1000) of your home. The number of rooms method is just as simple: if your house has five similarly sized rooms, and you use one of them for business, then the business uses 20% (1/5) of your home.

Once you have a space percentage for your business, you'll use it to calculate how much of your home expenses are deductible home-office expenses. Rent is an easy expense to prorate. For instance, if your business uses 25% of your home, and your rent is $800 per month, then $200 per month is a deductible home-office expense (25% x $800).

Home owners, however, need to calculate a depreciation deduction, which is somewhat more complicated than simply figuring a percentage of their monthly mortgage payments. First, you'll need to break down the value of your home into the value of the building itself versus the value of the land. Then calculate yearly depreciation for the building only—not the land. The depreciation rate for the building will depend on when it was purchased, so you'll have to do some research as to the tax rules in effect at that time. Finally, divide the yearly depreciation figure by the percentage of space your business takes up in your home. That figure—the depreciation deduction—can be claimed as a business expense.

Claiming a depreciation deduction may subject you to capital gains taxes. Under current tax laws, when you sell your home you're exempted from capital gains taxes on gains up to $250,000 as long as you've owned and lived in the home for at least two of five years. However, if you claim depreciation deductions for a home office, the total of those deductions will be subject to capital gains tax when you sell your house. In other words, if you sell your house at a gain of $200,000, you'll be exempt from capital gains taxes. But if over the years you'd claimed $10,000 in depreciation deductions for an office you ran from home, that $10,000 would be subject to capital gains tax. A way to avoid this is to stop using your home office for two years before selling your home.

Other expenses such as home insurance, utilities, repairs and taxes can be partially deducted, depending on how much they're used for the business. Generally speaking, you can use the percentage of space your business uses in the home to prorate these expenses. It's important to note, however, that the IRS has specific rules as to which indirect expenses may be deducted for a home office. For instance, if your business space takes up 25% of your home, you may not be able to simply deduct 25% of your water bill, since your business doesn't use 25% of your home's water—most of the water goes for home uses such as washing clothes and dishes, bathing and watering the garden. For more detailed information on tax deductions for home offices, read *Tax Savvy for Small Business*, by attorney Frederick W. Daily (Nolo Press). Also, IRS Publication 587, "Business Use of Your Home," contains many details and specific rules for deductible expenses.

3. Business for Pleasure: Hobby Businesses

For many small business owners, their business is more a labor of love than a reliable source of income. This is most often the case when an owner has other means of financial support—such as a regular job or a spouse who brings home wages or other income—allowing the microbusiness to continue even though it makes little or no money. These types of tiny businesses are usually operated from the home (renting an office would be too expensive) and are often based on activities near and dear to the owner, which has earned them the nickname "hobby businesses."

There is no one type of hobby business, but examples might include a basement jewelry studio, a jazz band for hire, or an antique-refinishing business. The owners would probably keep on making jewelry, playing jazz or restoring antiques even if they never made a penny, but are making a go of turning their hobby into a profitable business.

Often, profits fail to materialize. For most regular businesses, anything more than a year or so of losing money is a cue to close up shop. But if you love doing whatever you're doing, it might make sense for you to stick with your losing business rather than fold it up. Why? Because if you have another source of income (as many owners of hobby businesses do), the losses from your hobby business can be used to offset that income. Deducting business losses—including everyday expenses and depreciation on assets—can not only lower the amount of income upon which taxes are calculated, but also may drop you into a lower tax bracket. This is what is commonly referred to as a tax shelter: an unprofitable business whose losses offset the owner's taxable income from other sources. (For more detailed information on taxes, see Chapter 8, "Getting to Know Your Taxes.")

Of course, most entrepreneurs would much rather earn a healthy profit than lose money with their business. And the savings made possible by a tax shelter do not always justify continuing a marginal or losing business. But they definitely can make a difference in a decision of whether it's worth it to keep your unprofitable—but enjoyable!—business going.

Example:

Kay and Reza are married and file joint tax returns. Reza earns a salary as a chef in a local restaurant, and Kay is a magazine editor. Kay has a passion for plants, and decides to try making a business of selling some of the hundreds of plants she grows and propagates in her backyard greenhouse. After she's spent thousands of dollars on exotic plants and better lighting equipment, the greenhouse heater goes on the fritz and over 300 of Kay's expensive, exotic plants die. Her expenses for the year total nearly $10,000, and she has not yet sold any plants. The silver lining for Kay and Reza comes at tax time, when they deduct the $10,000 loss from their joint taxable income of $105,000. By reducing their joint taxable income to $95,000, they not only are taxed on less income, but their tax bracket is reduced from 31% to 28%—a tax savings of nearly $6,000.

On the down side, if you consistently use your business as a tax shelter, deducting your losses from your other income year after year, you'll likely catch the attention of the IRS. An issue that often arises with hobby businesses is whether the venture is really a business at all. An important thing to understand about tax shelters is that in order to deduct expenses from your taxable income, those expenses must have been incurred by a legitimate profit-motivated business—not merely a personal hobby. As you might expect, not every hobby counts as a hobby business. If you claim expenses from your hobby business as tax deductions and you're audited, you'll have to prove to the IRS that your hobby is in fact a legitimate business.

a. Proving Your Business is a Business

Before you start claiming deductions for the costs of your favorite art projects or toy car collections, make sure your venture will pass IRS scrutiny and qualify as a real business. Thankfully, the IRS's definition is fairly broad. Basically, any activity that you engage in to make a profit counts as a business. In other words, you need only prove to the IRS that you're *trying*—not necessarily succeeding—to make a profit with your venture. The IRS uses a few different criteria for deciding whether your business truly has a profit motive.

The main test for profit motive is called the "3-of-5" test. If your business makes a profit in three out of five consecutive years, it is legally presumed to have a profit motive. You may be surprised—and relieved—to know that the amount of the profit is irrelevant; even if you just barely break even and earn only $1 profit in your business year, you've officially had a profitable year.

While the IRS gives a lot of weight to the 3-of-5 test, it is not conclusive. In other words, if you flunk the 3-of-5 test, you still may be able to prove that your business is motivated by profit. You can use virtually any kind of evidence to this. Business cards, a well-maintained set of books, a separate business bank account, current business licenses and permits, and proof of advertising will all help to persuade an IRS auditor that your activity is in fact a business.

b. Watch Out for Local Rules

When planning out your hobby business, don't forget that local requirements and taxes will increase your costs of doing business, both in time and money. Lots of small business people are surprised to find out that state and local regulations for small businesses can be more of a bear than IRS rules. If you sell tangible products, you may be subject to state sales taxes. Plus, many cities impose taxes on small businesses and require them to go through some sort of registration process, and counties often have similar requirements for businesses in rural areas. Generally speaking, these rules technically apply to any money-making activity within the area—even if the hobby business doesn't intend to claim any federal or state tax deductions. (See Chapter 6 for registration requirements for small businesses.)

In practice, many tiny hobby businesses—so tiny that the word "business" even seems excessive—might be able to get away unnoticed. Even so, you should be aware that depending on your local rules, you may be penalized if you're caught doing business without having gotten the permits or licenses required by your state or local goverment. These penalties may include fines and any back taxes that apply.

4. Insurance and the Home Business

While lots of businesses might not have to worry too much about insurance in their very early days, there are a few special issues to watch out for if you plan to run a business from home. In a nutshell, don't expect your homeowner's or renter's policy to automatically cover you for business-related losses, including property theft or damage, as well as personal injury claims. Not having additional coverage can be a real catastrophe if your computer system is stolen or destroyed in an earthquake, or if a client trips and falls over your garden hose on the way up your front walk.

Potentially even worse, your regular homeowner's or renter's policy might be voided entirely—even for home-related claims—if the insurance company finds out you are running a business in the home without their knowledge. Some companies require you to tell them about any home business (and may bill you for added coverage), or else have your policy invalidated. Compared to the risks of having the whole policy yanked from under you, paying some extra premium dollars will probably be well worth it.

For more information on small business insurance, see Chapter 7.

C H A P T E R 5

Drafting an Effective Business Plan

If you think only Type A personalities compose business plans, you're wrong. Talk to a random sample of successful business owners, and you'll be amazed at how many—even the most laid-back—took the time to put their business plans into writing. If you're truly determined to succeed, you'll follow their example. Why? Because without a plan, you're leaving far too many things to chance. Just as a blueprint is used to ensure that a building will be structurally sound, a business plan will help you see whether your business will be financially able to stay afloat.

The idea of a business plan is simple: to bring together in one document the key elements of your business. These include what products or services you'll sell, what they'll cost to produce and how much sales revenue you expect during your first months and years of operation. Most important, your plan will help you see how all the disparate elements of your business relate to one another, which will allow you to make any necessary alterations in order to maximize your business's potential to turn a profit.

Business plans are often written by business owners who want to borrow money or attract investors. This is good as far as it goes—lenders or investors do want to understand as much as possible about how a business will work before deciding whether to back it financially. Unless you're prepared to show them a well thought-out plan for how you expect your business to become profitable, you won't have much chance of convincing them to finance your project.

But creating a business plan is just as good an idea if you don't need to raise start-up money. The discipline involved in developing financial projections such as a break-even analysis and a profit and loss forecast will help you decide if your business is really worth starting, or if you need to rethink some of your key assumptions. As any experienced businessperson will tell you, the business you decide not to start (often because a business plan doesn't pencil out) can be more important to your long-term success than the one you bet your economic future on.

This chapter will explain how to create a thorough business plan. If you've already written one, you may want to skip this chapter—or you might find the information here useful in double-checking your plan. Yes, of course we remember you have zero time to waste, so we will keep our focus on the essential elements and spare you the fluff.

Recommended reading on business plans. *For the full treatment, read Mike McKeever's* How to Write a Business Plan *(Nolo Press). This book describes the many different items of financial information you can include in your plan in far more detail than we have space for here, and explains how to put them together into a plan that fits your needs.*

A. Different Purposes Require Different Plans

All good business plans have two basic goals: to describe the fundamentals of your business idea, and to provide financial calculations to show that it will make good money. But, depending on how you intend to use it, a business plan can take somewhat different forms.

- If you will use your plan to borrow money or interest investors, it should be carefully written and edited to sell your vision to skeptical people. Normally this means that it should include a persuasive introduction and request for funds, in-depth market research information, an evaluation of your main competitors, your key marketing strategies, and a management plan. In addition, it should contain detailed financial information, including your best estimates of start-up costs, revenues and expenses. Finally, since your plan will be submitted to people you don't know well, the writing should be polished and the format clean and professional.

- If your plan will primarily be for your own use—that is, if you don't need to raise money—don't worry so much about making a sales pitch or slick presentation. But don't skimp when it comes to doing your numbers. The last thing you want is to experience the very real misery of starting a business that never had a chance to make a solid profit.

Plan to get the help you need. Not all business people are great writers. But excellent writing skills can be a big help in creating a compelling business plan. Consider paying a freelance writer with small business savvy to help you polish your plan. Similarly, if you are challenged by numbers, find a bookkeeper or accountant to provide needed help.

B. Describing the Business, and Yourself

The first several sections of your plan should describe the beauty of your business idea. If you will show your plan to potential lenders, investors or people you want to work with, show them that you've hit upon a product or service that customers really want. In addition, you want to show that you are exactly the right person to make your fine idea a roaring success. Your goal is to have them say, "Wow! What a great business idea! And yes, I see exactly why Carlos Burns is the ideal person to make it a big success."

To accomplish these goals, you should include the following:

- a statement of the purpose of your business
- a detailed description of how the business will work
- an analysis of your market
- an analysis of your competitors
- a description of your marketing strategy, and
- a résumé setting forth your business accomplishments.

Again, depending on how you intend to use your business plan, you may be able to skip some of these elements. For example, if you don't need to raise start-up money and are writing a plan mostly for your own use, you may decide to skip the résumé of your own business accomplishments. But think twice before you leave out too much. Any new business will need to introduce itself to loads of people—suppliers, contractors, employees and key customers, to name a few—and showing them part or all of your business plan can be a great way to do it.

1. State Your Business's Purpose

Why does the great big world—or your small town or narrow niche market—need the product or service you want to offer? The first paragraph of your plan should address this question as directly and compellingly as possible. For example, if you're planning to open a pet-grooming salon, you might start with the proposition that in today's increasingly busy world, pet owners need and want to keep their pets clean and groomed, but often don't have time to do it themselves. You might add that many pet owners have more than enough disposable income to pay for your top-of-the-line service. Similarly, if you want to start a sea kayaking guide service, you might start with the proposition that more and more people are participating in this exciting sport, but need equipment, planning, training and logistics to do it in other parts of the world.

A statement of business purpose doesn't generally need to be complicated or lengthy. In fact, some of the best state the obvious. No problem—if the need for your business will be clear to lenders or investors (for example, a sandwich shop in a fast-growing office area), one paragraph may be all you need. But if the value of your business idea isn't so readily apparent (for example, an innovative software company), you will want to say more. Show how your business will solve a real problem or fill an actual need. And, just as important, explain why customers will pay you to accomplish the task.

2. Describe Your Business

Once you've stated the need that your business will fill, describe exactly how you'll accomplish it. In this section, don't write a bunch of fluffy text about how brilliant your entrepreneurial idea is. Instead, outline in detail exactly how your business will operate. Your description should include:

- how you will go about providing your product or service
- where you will buy key supplies
- how customers will pay you
- how many employees you will have and what they will do
- what hours you will operate, and
- where you will be located (if possible, include details about how your customers will find you).

Keep in mind that even the smallest, simplest business involves a swarm of pesky details. Don't assume there's anything obvious about your business, even if it's a tiny one-person operation. For example, if you plan to start a pet-grooming business, how many different types of services will you offer—shampooing? flea bathing? nail cutting? hair trimming? teeth cleaning? Will you charge separately for each individual service, sell them in packages, or both? How will you attract customers and regularly stay in touch with the best ones? How will you accommodate animals with special needs such as allergies or with behavioral problems such as aggressiveness? How will people drop off and pick up their pets? Will your business need insurance in case an animal is injured or dies while in your care?

A little repetition is okay. The description of how your business will operate is likely to be the longest section of your plan and will probably discuss one or more topics that are also covered elsewhere. No problem. For example, a key issue like how you will establish and keep a competitive edge is appropriate to mention as part of your big-picture business description as well as in its own section.

Never hesitate to take advantage of your business description as a tool to change or refine your business idea. Almost always, when you write and rewrite this section you'll come up with ideas and questions you haven't yet thought through. If so, great—this gives you an opportunity to fill in the gaps cheaply and easily before you actually open for business. And again, even if you discover a flaw so big that you decide not to start the business after all, your business plan has done its job. While undoubtedly disappointing, it's far better for your business to fail on paper than in real life.

3. Define Your Market

Who will buy your product or service? Even the most innovative business will fail if it doesn't quickly find enough customers to make a profit. In this section, your task is to demonstrate to a potential investor or lender (and convince yourself) that there are indeed customers out there ready and willing to buy your product or service. Use whatever data you can get your hands on to demonstrate this. And don't neglect your imagination—unconventional arguments are fine as long as they are convincing. Here is a brief list of points you may wish to make:

- Similar businesses have been successful. For example, if several fitness clubs with Internet access are all the rage in L.A., you might explain why this is a good indication that your similar business would succeed in Sacramento, where the market is currently dominated by less cutting-edge gyms.

- Marketing surveys or demographic reports point to a growing need for your product or service. For instance, to buttress your contention that there will be a need for your new line of paralegal training materials, point to U.S. government reports listing paralegals as being one of the fastest-growing occupations.

- Media reports confirm the popularity of and demand for your business. For example, include newspaper clips or transcripts of television news reports on the surge of demand for antibacterial air fresheners as evidence that your germ-killing Sani-Scent™ will sell.

- Your conversations with potential customers show a need for your business. It's often a good idea to carry out a detailed survey of your most likely customers and include the result. For example, if you will run a business repairing and reconditioning acoustic guitars and similar stringed instruments, you might include results of a survey of guitarists and other musicians on what kind of repair services they need, as well as quotes from them saying that they'd use your services.

Besides claiming that there is a solid market for your business, do your best to define and describe exactly who makes it up. If you're opening a bar with live entertainment, for instance, you might identify your market as primarily childless, urban 18- to 35-year-olds who tend to have more disposable income and leisure time than others. Similarly, if you're planning an antique restoration service, you might identify your target market as professionals and others in the 40–70 age range with household incomes of $100,000 or more. The better you can show that you know exactly who your market is, the more confident investors will be that you can actually find these people and sell to them.

Include a profile of your target customer. Explain what this fictional person's needs are and why and how she uses your product or service. Do your best to flesh out a believable person, right down to the color of her socks. Creating a typical customer gives a face to an otherwise abstract market definition, and can give your market analysis more impact.

Think twice before you attempt to compete on price. No matter how efficient your business is and how little you charge, someone will always charge less. Given the purchasing power and other efficiencies of big business, few little operators can successfully compete on pricing alone. Far better to look for another edge—quality, uniqueness and customer convenience, to mention a few.

4.　Analyze Your Competition

Just because you have a great business idea doesn't mean you'll be successful; other businesses may have already cornered the market or be poised to do so. For example, lots of small-business owners who opened movie-rental businesses were wiped out when chains like Blockbuster rolled out thousands of megastores. It's often all too easy for a bigger, better-capitalized outfit to copy your best features and pull the rug out from under your business. Use this section to explain why your business really will have few direct competitors—or, if competitors will abound (as is far more likely), to show how your business will develop and keep an edge. Don't be shy about detailing competitors' strengths as well as weaknesses as part of showing why your business will better meet customers' needs.

In discussing the competition, it's important to put yourself in the shoes of a customer who is comparing your business to theirs. From the customer's perspective, what factors are most important in choosing which business to patronize? Some obvious considerations are quality of products or services, convenience (access), reliability and price. Your competitors will probably excel in some of these areas and be weaker in others. The same will probably be true of your business. The trick is for you to find a spot, or niche, among the competition, and offer a combination of elements—such as price and convenience—that no one else offers.

Example:

John O'Toole's Classic Cars

John wants to open a business to sell and service classic cars. In developing his business idea, he discovers that there are about a dozen existing companies within a 20-mile radius of his proposed location who already provide some or all of the services he envisions. Before finally committing to opening the business, he needs to identify a convincing competitive edge. One day, talking to a friend, he realizes that his edge could be the development of a better system for finding parts. If he could locate new and used classic car parts nationwide, rather than just in his region, he would have a huge advantage over other shops. John begins by developing a database of Websites that specialize in classic and reproduction car parts, organized by make and model. By using these online dealers—plus the other dealers nationwide who aren't online, but whom John will become familiar with as he attends regional trade shows and does more national business—John will be able to get parts faster than any of his competitors. Putting some extra energy into the parts aspect of his business gives John a key marketing hook to convince his knowledgeable (and often finicky) customers that his business really is a step ahead.

Businesses With Specialized Knowledge Are Hard to Copy

The business with the most knowledge usually wins. But what is business knowledge, and how can you exploit it? In the broad sense, it's anything a business knows how to do that can give it a meaningful edge over competitors. Common examples include:

- the ability to buy products for resale cheaper than competitors can

- a great location

- a unique, hard-to-duplicate product

- a terrific reputation for customer service, and

- superior customer accessibility—longer hours, better parking, etc.

Consider the example of Laura and Brad's import business. They were importing clothing from Guatemala, but with competition from hundreds of other small importers, it was hard to make a dime. Then, leaving Brad to manage the business for a few weeks, Laura spent some time working with a dozen weavers in a small Guatemalan town. They focused on creating specially woven and dyed Guatemalan fabric suitable for luxury window coverings. Realizing that the high end of the import business was an underexploited niche, Laura quickly created a product with a hard-to-copy look and a solid profit margin. In short, she transformed a not particularly savvy, barely profitable import business into a highly intelligent, highly profitable one.

5. Describe Your Marketing Strategy

By now you've shown that there are people out there who will buy your product or service from you instead of from your competitors. Great, but your job isn't done. Investors and others interested in supporting your business will want to know how you'll reach your customers in a cost-effective way. Explaining how you'll go about this is essentially outlining your marketing strategy.

Any marketing strategy worthy of the name should be based on the particular characteristics of the market you're trying to reach, with the goal being to reach as many customers as possible for the least expense. If you're trying to reach a very tiny group of people, such as left-handed ophthalmologists, or even a slightly larger audience, such as digital video editors, it makes no sense to spend the big bucks required for television advertising. On the other hand, if your market consists of all children between the ages of six and ten, TV advertising might be an efficient way to reach them.

Marketing without advertising can be successful. Especially in niche or local markets, people often make purchasing decisions on the recommendations of people they respect, not on ads. If you doubt this, think about how you chose your dentist, plumber or the company that recently fixed your roof. Chances are good that you got a recommendation from people you trusted. To be the beneficiary of positive word of mouth, you need to run an excellent business. Assuming you do, there are loads of cost-effective ways to let potential customers know about your great service. For a book full of great ideas, read *Marketing Without Advertising*, by Michael Phillips and Salli Rasberry (Nolo Press). Its subtitle, "Inspire Customers to Rave About Your Business to Create Lasting Success," explains exactly why every small business person should read it.

6. Describe Your Business Accomplishments

Above and beyond demonstrating the beauty of your business idea, you'll want to show that you're the right person to run it. Do this by creating a business accomplishments résumé. Here you have the chance to highlight all of your relevant experience and training, as well as any other personal information likely to inspire confidence in you as a businessperson.

Prospective lenders or investors will want to know the following things about you:

- **Do you understand the business?** Emphasize that you understand the basic tasks of the business inside and out. Surprisingly, lots of people start small businesses in areas where they are amateurs. (For example, a person who isn't mechanically inclined but who loves German cars may want to open a VW repair shop.) Lack of hands-on experience will likely be a red flag to investors, who know a non-expert boss can't roll up her sleeves and help out in emergencies. Do your best to show them otherwise.

- **Can you manage people?** All sorts of organizations, including small businesses, fail because their leaders—no matter how technically competent—can't work well with others. Bad people management is one of the surest ways to create a poor workplace atmosphere, one with low morale, mediocre productivity and high turnover. If you have successfully worked with, and preferably led, people, you should emphasize this experience.

- **Do you understand money?** A surprising number of people who open small businesses don't know how to make money. Even though their business idea is a good, competitive one and their employees are energetic, they manage to make such poor financial decisions that their businesses don't prosper. Knowing this, people who will consider funding your business will want to see if you or another key person in your business has money-making skills. If you do—even if your experience was in a very different business—emphasize it.

C. Making Financial Projections

Besides describing how your business will work, including how it will reach plenty of customers and fend off competitors, you'll also need to do some number-crunching to show that it will in fact turn a profit. All the rosy descriptions in the world won't make your business a success if the numbers turn up red. Projecting the finances of your business may seem intimidating or difficult, but in reality it's really not terribly complex. Basically, it consists of making educated guesses as to how much money you'll need to spend and how much you'll take in, and using these estimates to calculate whether your business will be sufficiently profitable.

Needless to say, predicting and planning the finances of your business is an important task, not just to attract investors, but to demonstrate to you and your family whether or not your business idea will fly. If your first projections show your business losing money, you'll have an opportunity while still in the planning stage to make sensible adjustments, such as raising your prices or cutting costs. If you neglect to make tight financial projections, you won't realize your plan is a money-loser until you actually start losing money. At that point, it may be too late to turn things around.

Nonetheless, many new entrepreneurs avoid crunching their numbers, often due to fear that their estimates will be wildly off-base and yield useless results. This is a poor reason to avoid forecasting your finances. If you do your best to make realistic predictions of expenses and revenues and accept that your guestimates will not be absolutely correct, you can learn a great deal about what the financial side of your business is likely to look like in its early months and even years of operation. Even a somewhat inaccurate picture of your business's likely finances will be much more helpful than having no picture at all.

For a basic understanding of your business's projected financial situation, you'll need to make the following estimates and calculations, all of which are discussed in detail in the rest of this chapter:

- **a break-even analysis.** Here you use income and expense estimates for a year or more to see whether, in theory at least, your business will be able to turn a profit. If you have trouble projecting a solid profit, you might need to consider abandoning your idea altogether.

- **a profit/loss forecast.** Here you'll refine the sales and expense estimates that you used for your break-even analysis into a formal, month-by-month projection of your business's net profit for at least the first year of operations.

- **a start-up cost estimate.** As the name suggests, this is simply the total of all the expenses you'll incur before your business opens. These costs should be included in your business plan to give a true picture of how much money you'll need to get your business off the ground.

- **a cash flow projection.** Even if your profit/loss forecast tells you that your business will have higher revenues than expenses, that doesn't mean that you'll always have enough cash available on key dates such as when rent is due or when you need to buy more inventory. A cash flow projection lays out how much cash you'll have—or how much you'll be short—month by month. This lets you know if you'll need to get a credit line or set up other arrangements to raise funds.

Get to Know Your Numbers

The calculations involved in accounting aren't terribly complex. The main reason people get confused is not that they're bad at math—it's that they don't understand what the numbers mean. It's important that you take a little time early on to learn what your key financial numbers are, and how they relate to one another. To help you keep the numbers straight, keep in mind this formula:

sales revenue

− costs of sale (variable costs)

= gross profit

− fixed costs (overhead)

= net profit (take-home profit)

− taxes

= after-tax profit

You'll have a much easier time understanding all the various financial calculations involved in accounting—including break-even, profit/loss and cash flow analysis—once you're familar and comfortable with this basic formula.

All you really need to make these financial forecasts are a calculator and some simple ledger sheets, though if you have a computer and accounting software your job will be even easier. Blank ledger sheets, which are nothing more than blank rows and columns for you to fill in with your numbers, are available at any office supply store. If you use accounting software, most of your calculations can be done automatically, with the click of a button, which can be very helpful when you're in the planning stages and trying out lots of different numbers. If you plan to use software for your bookkeeping and accounting once your business is started, you might as well also use it for preparing your financial projections. Accounting software is relatively easy to learn and will definitely save you lots of time in the long run. Quicken and Quickbooks, both by Intuit, are very popular and priced within reach of just about any budget. Magazines such as *Home Office Computing*, *MacWorld* and *PC World* are good sources of information on other programs.

Once you start shopping for accounting and bookkeeping software, you'll probably also find special business plan software. These programs, however, usually provide you with only a word processing function and some empty spreadsheets to fill in. Most accounting software allows you to do the same kinds of spreadsheets, and usually a lot more. Chances are the word processing program you already have is a lot more powerful than whatever is offered with a business plan program.

The rest of this chapter will walk you step by step through each of these financial forecasts, which, when completed, will tell you whether your business will actually make enough money to pay the bills and turn a profit. Assuming the answer is yes, you'll also see whether you need to obtain start-up money from investors or lenders and, if so, how much. Finally, once your business is up and running you can refer back to your forecasts to see how your performance is measuring up.

D. Break-Even Analysis

Your break-even point is the amount of income you'll need to cover your expenses before you make a dime of profit. Expenses include the costs of your product or service to you (also known as variable costs, since they change depending on how much product or service you provide), plus your overhead, like rent, your salary and utility bills (commonly called fixed costs).

Since break-even analysis offers a glimpse of your ultimate profitability, it's a great tool for weeding out losing business ideas. For example, if you see that you'll need to achieve a highly optimistic sales number just to cover your costs, you'll probably want to rethink your entire business plan. Maybe there will be a way you can adjust parts of your business so that a more reachable sales volume will result in a profit. If not, it might be best to ditch your less-than-brilliant business idea.

To find your break-even point, first make a best-guess estimate of your sales revenue for the products or services you plan to sell. Then predict how much profit you'll make on each sale, and what your fixed costs such as rent and insurance will be. After a few calculations, you'll see whether the profit you'll make on each individual sale (also called gross profit) adds up to enough to cover your fixed costs. Before we explain how to do the calculations, we'll quickly discuss two items that you need to understand before actually crunching your numbers: making financial estimates and categorizing your expenses.

1. Making Estimates

Your income and expense estimates should extend over enough time to catch up with seasonal fluctuations. Depending on your type of business, your revenue and expenses may vary wildly from month to month. For example, if you plan to manufacture custom snowboards, most of your sales will be in late fall and early winter months, while the opposite would be true if you made surfboards. A good way to account for this is to make estimates for each month of the year, then add them up to get a yearly figure. We recommend covering at least a one-year period, which is enough time to account for normal ups and downs, but not so long as to be overly speculative.

Don't change your numbers without a very good reason. When confronted by too high a break-even point, you may be tempted to tweak and squish your numbers into a profitable forecast, even if those numbers aren't realistic. Unless you really do have a good reason to think you can break even at a lower point, this is a temptation to guard against. For example, to have your plan pencil out in the black, you might boost your sales estimates in hopes that you'll somehow be able to pull it off. But can you really sell 500,000 Sausage Shooters™, 3,000 books on medieval dentistry or 2,000 Tori Spelling mini-tees per month? If the answer is no, there may be other aspects of your business that you can change, such as your area of distribution, method of delivery or even the product itself. As you do this, it's best to focus on your costs—the most reliable way to tilt a business from the red to the black is to reduce what you will pay out, not to make a more optimistic projection of what you'll take in.

2. Categorizing Your Expenses

Your business expenses need to be divided into two categories: fixed expenses and variable expenses. This division is not only important for your break-even analysis, it's a standard method of categorizing expenses for accounting and tax reporting. It's key that you understand the difference.

- **Fixed costs.** These include all regular expenses not directly tied to the product or service you provide. Rent, utility bills, phone bills, payments for outside help like bookkeeping services, postage and salaries (usually) are common fixed costs.

- **Variable costs.** These costs—sometimes also called product costs or costs of sale—are directly related to the products or services you provide and include inventory, packaging, supplies, materials and sometimes labor used in providing your product or service. They're called "variable" precisely because they go up or down depending on the volume of products or services you produce or sell. (In the case of services, one of the biggest variable expenses is almost always the salary of the service provider—see "Salaries and Labor Costs— Fixed or Variable?")

Salaries and Labor Costs— Fixed or Variable?

Whether you'll categorize labor expenses as fixed or variable costs often depends on the type of workers you pay and the kinds of products or services you're selling. Salaries or wages of managers and employees who are necessary to keep your business going (your bookkeeper, for example) are usually best seen as fixed costs. But salaries or wages for employees who create the products or provide the services you sell may be more appropriately treated as variable costs. For example, an ad agency that pays six freelance copywriters to service clients' accounts should treat their paychecks as variable costs.

A good test of whether a labor cost should be designated as fixed or variable is to ask yourself: If I sell one, ten or 100 more products or services this week, will my labor costs go up? If not, you're probably looking at a fixed cost. For instance, suppose you're trying to decide whether your receptionist's salary should be categorized as a variable cost or a fixed cost. If you produce and sell 100 more Tori Spelling mini-tees, will your reception costs go up? Probably not. So your receptionist's salary should be part of your overhead. But if you have to hire five temporary employees to handle the phones at Christmastime to handle the spiking demand for mini-tees, their wages should be classified as variable costs. (Hint: money paid to workers who are temps or independent contractors are usually categorized as variable costs, because it's usually tied to providing a product or service.) Of course, at some point selling more products or services at a permanently increased level will probably lead to expansion of your business and increased overhead, because you'll have to hire more support staff, managers and other necessary employees just to get along. At that point, you might revisit your allocation of fixed and variable costs.

3. Estimate Your Sales Revenue

Start your break-even analysis by making your best estimate of annual sales revenues. Your estimate will obviously depend on several different variables, such as your type of business, what you plan to charge for each product or service you'll offer and how successful you'll be at selling products and services. Though at first it may seem overwhelming to project revenues based upon so many untested variables, it is essential that you take the plunge and try out some numbers. Even though your estimates won't be anywhere near 100% accurate, they'll force you to focus and refine key elements of your business idea and may even help you spot big potholes in your plan.

One good way to estimate how much money you'll be bringing in is to compare your business with similar ones. Retail businesses, for example, often measure annual sales revenue per square foot of retail space. Thus, if you plan to open a pet supply store, you'll want to find out the annual sales revenue per square foot of other pet supply shops. While direct competitors probably won't share this information, industry trade publications almost always provide it. Attending industry trade shows where you can meet and talk to people who own similar businesses in other parts of the country is also a good way to gather valuable information.

Example:

Inga is planning to open a used bookstore in San Francisco called Inga's Book Haus. She plans to sell mostly used books, which generally have a high profit margin, but will also stock a limited selection of new books at the front of the store to attract more customers. She'll also sell some miscellaneous trinkets like postcards and magnets.

As part of trying to figure out how much sales revenue she can realistically expect for Inga's Book Haus, Inga calls up a couple friends who happen to be in the book business. One who works at a nearby used bookstore confides to Inga that the store sells approximately $450 worth of books per square foot per year. Another friend

owns a new-and-used bookstore in a Pasadena; she tells Inga that they bring in about $400 annually per square foot. Neither of these stores is exactly like the one Inga envisions; the one in San Francisco doesn't sell any new books, and the one in Pasadena does a healthy trade in textbooks, which Inga doesn't expect at her store. To round out her information, Inga also looks into some trade publications and does a bit of sleuthing at local new-and-used bookstores, examining their prices and how busy they seem to be. Ultimately she decides that an annual income of $350 per square foot is realistic. She has her eye on a few storefronts, all around 1200 square feet, so she estimates her annual revenues to be $420,000.

If yours is a service business, your estimate of sales revenue will depend on how many billable sales you'll be able to make each month. A big part of doing this is to estimate how many hours you and any employees will work and how much you'll be paid per hour. But don't overlook the fact that all of your time won't be billable—you won't be providing services every hour you're at work. For example, if you run a landscaping business, a sizable portion of your time will not be performing landscaping work but managing your accounts, maintaining your equipment and soliciting new clients. You'll need to make a realistic assessment of how much of your time is taken up by these non-billable activities to get an accurate picture of how much money will be flowing in.

4. Calculate Your Average Gross Profit

Your next task is to figure how much of your estimated sales income will be left over after paying for the costs of the products or services themselves. If your business sells a doghouse for $200, for example, part of that amount has to cover what it cost you to provide that doghouse—say $110. The costs to you of your product or service are called your variable costs, also sometimes called costs of sale. What's left over is called gross profit, sometimes called your profit margin. Calculating your gross profit on the dog house would look like this:

Sales revenue	$200
– Variable cost	$110
= Gross profit	$90

If you're selling products bought from a wholesaler, your variable costs may be as simple as what you pay for the products themselves. If you'll assemble the products, then include your costs for the parts and labor needed to put them together. For service businesses, costs of sale basically include the salaries (minus time spent on administrative tasks and managing accounts) of whoever provides the services (you or perhaps an employee). Also remember to include items like packaging or freebies in your variable costs.

One kink in figuring out your business's average gross profit is that your selling prices and variable costs—the two figures that determine gross profit—may vary a great deal from product to product (or service to service). For instance, say you buy cat collars for an average of $4, and sell them for an average price of $10. Doghouses, on the other hand, cost you an average of $110, and you sell them for an average price of $220. To account for these differences you should categorize your products or services, figure average gross profit for each category, and then figure average gross profit for your business as a whole. There are a few steps to follow, but hang in there—each one is pretty simple.

First, estimate your average selling price and average variable cost for products or services with roughly similar selling prices and variable costs. For instance, you might group all your animal collars together—for cats, dogs and ferrets—since their selling prices ($9 to $13) and variable costs ($3 to $5) aren't too different. Don't lump together products or services with considerably different selling prices or variable costs. As a general rule, the more tightly you define your categories, the more accurate your estimates will be.

Subtract the average variable cost from the average selling price for each category, and you'll have an average gross profit dollar figure.

	Animal collars	Bird-houses	Dog-houses
Average selling price	$11	$60	$220
– Average variable cost	$4	$30	$110
= Average gross profit	$7	$30	$110

The next step is to figure out a gross profit percentage for each category. A gross profit percentage tells you how much of each dollar of sales income is gross profit. To calculate each category's gross profit percentage, divide the average gross profit figure by the average selling price.

Animal collars category:

Average gross profit	$7.00
/ Average selling price	$11.00
= Gross profit percentage	63.6%

Using the above example, it follows that if you sold $1500 in cat collars, 63.6% of that—$954—would be gross profit, or the amount left over after paying costs of sale. As you can see, converting your gross profit into a percentage allows you to quickly figure out how much of your income will be left over after variable costs have been covered.

Next, estimate your annual sales revenue per category. Earlier you estimated your total annual sales revenues; now divide that figure as best you can into your estimates for each category. For example, if you estimated total annual revenues of $100,000 for your pet supply business, divide that into your categories, such as collars, birdhouses and doghouses—say $25,000 in collar sales, $40,000 in birdhouses and $35,000 in doghouses. Then, for each product category, multiply the estimated sales by the category's gross profit percentage (arrived at above) to arrive at your total gross profit dollars per category.

Finally, add together the gross profit dollar amounts for each category to arrive at a total annual gross profit. Divide the total annual gross profit figure by the total annual sales for all products. The result will be an average gross profit percentage for your business.

Let's look at how this process works with Inga's Book Haus.

Example:

As you may recall, Inga plans to sell new and used books, plus some peripheral items such as postcards and refrigerator magnets. Since the profit margins for new books, used books and trinkets are different, Inga figures a gross profit percentage for each of these categories. To accomplish this, first she estimates an average variable cost for each category. In addition to the cost of the merchandise, she includes the cost of free bags, bookmarks and wrapping paper for gifts.

For instance, used books cost her an average of $3, and she figures the bookmarks and bags that go with each sale will cost her an average of 10¢. So her total average variable cost in the used book category is $3.10. (Inga might want to establish separate categories for hardback, paperback and coffee table books, but we'll keep things simple.) She doesn't include fixed costs, like rent or salaries, here.

Next, Inga fills in an average selling price for each product category. Her average selling price for used books, for example, is $7. She then subtracts the average variable cost (arrived at above) from the average selling price to get an average gross profit figure for each product category. Subtracting her average variable cost for used books ($3.10) from her average selling price for used books ($7.00) leaves her with an average gross profit for used books of $3.90.

Used book category:

Average sales price	$7.00
– Average variable cost	$3.10
= Average gross profit	$3.90

To determine the gross profit percentage, she'll simply divide the gross profit by the selling price in each category to get a gross profit percentage for each category. Dividing her average gross profit for used books ($3.90) by her average selling price ($7.00) gives Inga a gross profit percentage of 56% for used books, a good percentage. That means that for every dollar she'll bring in from used books, .44 will be eaten up when Inga buys the book (and freebies), leaving .56 per dollar to cover fixed costs and make a net profit. Her gross profit percentage for new books is 33%, and for trinkets it's an impressive 70%.

Trinkets category:

Average gross profit	$1.40
/ Average selling price	$2.00
= Gross profit percentage	70%

Using the gross profit percentages and estimated sales revenues for each category, Inga can calculate the gross profit dollar figure for each category. For example, her estimated annual sales of used books is $300,000. By multiplying $300,000 by the category's gross profit percentage (56%), she estimates an annual gross profit of $168,000. Adding up the gross profit figures for each category, Inga figures that her total gross profit will be $215,000. Finally, by dividing this amount by her annual estimated revenues of $420,000, she easily determines her total gross profit percentage, which is 51.2%.

	New Books	Used Books	Trinkets	Total
Average costs per product	$8.00	$3.00	.50	
+ bookmarks, bags	.10	.10	.10	
= Average total cost	$8.10	$3.10	$.60	
Average selling price	$12.00	$7.00	$2.00	
− Average total cost	$8.10	$3.10	$.60	
= Gross profit	$3.90	$3.90	$1.40	
Gross profit	$3.90	$3.90	$1.40	
/ Average selling price	$12.00	$7.00	$2.00	
= Gross profit %	33%	56%	70%	
Annual sales	$100,000	$300,000	$20,000	
x Gross profit %	33%	56%	70%	
= Annual gross profit	$33,000	$168,000	$14,000	
Total annual gross profit				$215,000
/ Total annual sales				$420,000
= Average gross profit percentage				51.2%

5. Estimate Your Fixed Costs

Next, estimate monthly fixed expenses. Include items like rent, utility bills, office supplies, bad debts—basically, any costs that you can count on independent of the product or service you sell. Since many of these costs recur monthly, it's usually easiest to estimate them per month and total them for one year. It's also a good idea to throw in a little extra, say 10% or so, to cover miscellaneous expenses that you can't predict. Once you've arrived at a total, you'll know that you'll need to make at least this much gross profit (and probably a healthy chunk more) to keep your business afloat.

Example:

Here is a list of Inga's monthly fixed costs estimates.

Rent	$3,500
Wages for part-time clerks	$2,500
Utilities	$800
Telephone	$700
Office equipment	$700
Insurance	$500
Advertising	$700
Accounting	$300
Electronic payment system fees	$300
Misc.	$1,000
Total fixed expenses per month	$11,000
Annual total fixed expenses (monthly expenses x 12)	$132,000

Don't forget you have to eat. Notice that Inga has chosen not to list her salary here as an expense. She figures that her savings, help from friends and family, and some extra crumbs the business may produce should be enough to live on for the short term. Once she figures out how much profit the business will bring in regularly, she'll decide on a salary for herself and add it to her fixed costs. Not including a salary in the planning stages, however, can be dangerous, at least if you're planning to live off your business's profits from the get-go. If this is your plan, you should add to your fixed costs the minimum salary that will cover your living expenses. If you can't project your income to be higher than your costs when your basic salary for living expenses is included, you'll know you can't plan on living off the company. This may be a clue that your business is not a good bet.

Keep fixed costs as low as reasonably possible. If your business is slow to get started—and lots of businesses take months or even years to become solidly profitable—high fixed costs can quickly eat up your savings. Rather than committing yourself to high overhead, it's usually better to keep expenses low, allowing increases only when your income justifies spending more. For example, few businesses really depend on a pricey physical location. If your business won't depend on a big casual walk-in trade, don't overpay for a trendy zip code. Operating from a low-cost warehouse district, an older office building or even your garage may work just fine.

6. Calculate Your Break-Even Point

Once you have estimated your fixed costs (from Section D5) and your average gross profit percentage (from Section D4), it's easy to figure out how much revenue you'll need to break even. Simply divide your estimated annual fixed costs by your gross profit percentage. The result is your break-even point—the amount of sales revenue you'll need to bring in just to break even.

If your estimated revenue exceeds your break-even point, great—but that's not the same thing as saying you are free to put the excess money in your pocket. Much of the excess revenue will be spent on variable costs. To figure out how much is actual profit, multiply the excess revenue by the gross profit percentage for the entire business. The result is your net profit.

Example:

The break-even point for Inga's Book Haus will equal her annual fixed expenses divided by her average gross profit percentage.

Annual fixed expenses	$132,000
/ Average gross profit percentage	51.2%
= Break-even point	$257,813

Earlier, Inga estimated her annual sales revenue to be $420,000—over $160,000 more than she needs to break even. To figure out how much of Inga's excess revenue will be actual profit, she multiplies it by her gross profit percentage.

Estimated revenue	$420,000
− Break-even point	$257,813
= Excess revenues	$162,187
x Gross profit percentage	51.2%
= Net profit	$83,040

Inga is happy to see her projections show a profit. But she needs to remember that none of her estimates included her own salary, meaning all personal income must come out of the business's profits.

E. Profit/Loss Forecast

If your break-even analysis shows that, based on realistic estimates of revenue and expenses, your business will turn a profit, your next job is to use these figures to create the profit/loss forecast component of your business plan. Similar to a break-even analysis, a profit/loss forecast (sometimes called a P & L forecast) uses your estimates for sales revenue and variable costs to calculate your gross profit, then subtracts your fixed expenses from gross profit to arrive at net profit. The main difference between this financial tool and the break-even analysis just discussed has to do with timing. A break-even analysis looks at profit and loss on a yearly basis, while your P & L forecast calculates monthly net profit. If you use accounting software, it will generate a P & L statement automatically once you enter monthly sales and expense estimates.

Here's how to translate your break-even figures into a profit/loss forecast. Start by breaking down your annual sales estimate into monthly amounts. If you expect significant seasonal fluctuations in sales, account for them here.

Next, figure your gross profit for each month. The easiest way to do this is to multiply each month's sales revenue by the gross profit percentage for your business as a whole, which you calculated earlier. (If you rounded off your gross profit percentage, you'll get a slightly different annual gross profit figure here than you did in your break-even analysis.)

Then enter your fixed expenses by category per month, and add them together to get monthly totals. For each month, subtract your total fixed expenses from your gross profit and enter the result in the net profit row. If the result is a negative number, it means your expenses are more than your gross profit. Put parentheses around the result; in accounting symbols, a number in parentheses is a negative number.

Your profit/loss statement doesn't include all your income or expenses. Other income and costs such as loans and start-up expenses aren't included in your P & L statement, which reflects only money earned and spent as part of providing your product or service. For the full picture of all money that comes into and goes out from your business— including start-up costs, loans, taxes and other money that isn't earned or spent as part of your core business operation—you'll need to do a cash flow analysis. (Predicting your cash flow is covered in Section G.)

Example:

Here's Inga's one-year profit/loss forecast for her bookstore:

Inga's Book Haus Profit/Loss Forecast: Year One Total

	Jan	Feb	Mar	April	May
Sales Revenues	$30,000	$35,000	$35,000	$35,000	$35,000
Gross Profit (51.2%)	$15,360	$17,920	$17,920	$17,920	$17,920
Fixed Expenses					
Rent	$3,500	$3,500	$3,500	$3,500	$3,500
Salaries	$2,500	$2,500	$2,500	$2,500	$2,500
Utilities	$800	$800	$800	$800	$800
Telephone	$700	$700	$700	$700	$700
Office Equipment	$700	$700	$700	$700	$700
Insurance	$500	$500	$500	$500	$500
Advertising	$700	$700	$700	$700	$700
Accounting	$300	$300	$300	$300	$300
Fees for electronic payment system (EPS)	$300	$300	$300	$300	$300
Miscellaneous	$1,000	$1,000	$1,000	$1,000	$1,000
Total Fixed Expenses	$11,000	$11,000	$11,000	$11,000	$11,000
Net Profit (Loss)	$4,360	$6,920	$6,920	$6,920	$6,920

June	July	Aug	Sept	Oct	Nov	Dec	Year Total
$35,000	$35,000	$35,000	$35,000	$35,000	$35,000	$40,000	$420,000
$17,920	$17,920	$17,920	$17,920	$17,920	$17,920	$20,480	$215,040
$3,500	$3,500	$3,500	$3,500	$3,500	$3,500	$3,500	$42,000
$2,500	$2,500	$2,500	$2,500	$2,500	$2,500	$2,500	$30,000
$800	$800	$800	$800	$800	$800	$800	$9,600
$700	$700	$700	$700	$700	$700	$700	$8,400
$700	$700	$700	$700	$700	$700	$700	$8,400
$500	$500	$500	$500	$500	$500	$500	$6,000
$700	$700	$700	$700	$700	$700	$700	$8,400
$300	$300	$300	$300	$300	$300	$300	$3,600
$300	$300	$300	$300	$300	$300	$300	$3,600
$1,000	$1,000	$1,000	$1,000	$1,000	$1,000	$1,000	$12,000
$11,000	$11,000	$11,000	$11,000	$11,000	$11,000	$11,000	$132,000
$6,920	$6,920	$6,920	$6,920	$6,920	$6,920	$9,480	$83,040

F. Start-up Cost Estimate

If your break-even analysis and profit/loss forecast show your projected income will be higher than expenses, great—but you haven't yet accounted for an important category of expenses: business start-up costs. The worst part about start-up costs is that you need to pay them before your business is actually making any money. That's why you should have a firm grasp on what you really need to spend to successfully start your business and have a plan for where that money will come from. Of course, potential lenders or investors will want to see that you've accounted for these costs in your planning. But it's also important that you understand for yourself how high this initial financial hurdle will be so that you can figure out how to clear it. Obviously, you don't want to start a business with high start-up costs but low projected profits, since it will take you far too long to recover your initial investment.

Buy only what your business really needs. Too many new small-business owners load their new enterprises down with unneeded start-up costs. Unless a particular item is absolutely necessary to generate revenue, don't buy it—or, if you do, spend as little as possible on it. Sure you need a desk, but unless customers will see it (and sometimes even if they will), repainting a door and laying it across a couple of secondhand filing cabinets at a net cost of $40 makes a lot more sense than laying out $800 for a new one.

Compared to the projections we just went through, estimating your start-up costs is a breeze—just list them and add them up. Include items like business registration fees and tax deposits you need to pay up front, rent and security deposits you'll have to pay before business starts, costs of any initial inventory, office supplies, equipment and anything else you'll have to cover before your business starts bringing in money.

If you don't have enough cash to pay all start-up costs out of pocket, you'll either need to come up with the money or figure out a way to spread the costs over the first few months of business when you'll have at least some cash flowing in. For instance, maybe you could lease, rather than buy, needed equipment. The next (and final) financial projection we'll do as part of your business plan—a cash flow projection—will help you plan and manage your incoming and outgoing cash so that you can cover needed expenses when they come due.

Example:

Inga makes a list of the start-up expenses she expects to pay before she'll start selling books.

Initial inventory	$20,000

Rent deposit
    (security deposit
    and last month's rent)
	$7,000

Office supplies, stationery	$500
Fax machine	$500
Business registration fees	$200
TOTAL	$28,200

G. Cash Flow Projection

To round out the collection of financial information in your business plan, you should include a cash flow projection. While your profit/loss forecast may have shown that your business would make enough sales at a high enough price to cover your estimated expenses, a cash flow projection analyzes whether the cash from those sales, as well as from other sources such as loans or investments, will come in fast enough to pay your bills on time. Cash flow management is important once your business is up and running, especially if you plan to stock a good-sized inventory or extend credit to customers. A high sales volume won't be enough to cover your expenses if your customers are slow to pay you and your checking account is empty.

Cash flow projection is also important in your planning stages in order to show how you plan to survive the first few lean months of business—particularly after you figure in your start-up expenses. If you'll have more than enough cash to cover your expenses for the first months of business, then you're one of the lucky few. More likely you'll be pressed to figure out how to cover a cash deficit for at least the first few months, and maybe longer. One way to do this is to put off some expenses. Another is to get a loan or sell part of your business to investors. The important thing is to do your best to predict your cash needs in advance, both to give yourself ample time to come up with a plan for getting the cash, and to inspire more confidence in lenders or investors.

Your cash flow projection will use many of the same figures you developed for your profit/loss forecast. The main difference is that you'll include all cash inflows and outflows, not just sales revenues and business expenses. Also, you'll record costs in the month that you expect to incur them, rather than simply spreading annual amounts equally over 12 months. Inflows and outflows of cash that belong in your cash flow analysis include loans, loan payments and start-up costs. Once you're turning a profit, you'll also include tax payments in your cash flow analysis, but for now let's assume that you'll be free from taxes for your first year.

For each month, simply start your projection with the actual amount of cash your business will have on hand. Next, fill in your projected cash-ins for the month, which should include sales revenues, loans, transfers of personal money—basically any money that goes into your business checking account. Add these together along with the cash you have at the beginning of the month to get your total cash-ins for the month.

Next enter all your projected cash-outs for the month, such as your fixed expenses and any loan payments. Remember also to include costs of your products, materials you use in your products or services like costs of inventory. Add together all your cash-outs to obtain a total for the month. Subtract cash-outs from cash-ins and the result will be your cash left at the end of the month. That figure is also your beginning cash balance at the start of the next month; transfer it to the top of the next month's column, and do the whole process over again.

Example:

Inga projects her cash flow for her first year in business. She starts her projection one month early to account for the money she must spend before she opens her bookstore. In her cash-in section, she figures in $15,000 that she will put into the business: $10,000 of her own savings and an interest-free loan from her sister of $5,000. In her cash-out section, she includes what she'll pay for the initial set-up of the business, as well as that month's rent and a $500 allowance for unexpected expenses. Inga also includes in her cash-out section a $500 payment each month to her sister for the loan.

Notice that Inga's cash-outs look a bit different than her expenses in her profit/loss forecast, even though they add up to the same totals. The reason is that Inga's cash-out section of her cash flow projection reflects that some expenses are paid in lump sums, such as her insurance, which is paid twice a year. She also breaks up her estimates for office expenses into lump payments, as she doesn't expect to spend equal amounts each month.

Also notice that Inga's estimated paid sales for the year come to the same total as her estimated annual sales revenue. That's because for her first year at least, Inga doesn't plan to take credit cards or checks, only cash and ATM purchases. That way all her sales will be paid immediately.

Inga's Book Haus Cash Flow Projection: Year One

	Dec	Jan	Feb	Mar	Apr	May
Cash at Beginning of Month	$0	($17,200)	($16,540)	($8920)	($3400)	$4220
Cash-ins						
Sales Paid	$0	$30,000	$35,000	$35,000	$35,000	$35,000
Loans and Transfers	$15,000	$0	$0	$0	$0	$0
Total Cash-ins	$15,000	$12,800	$18,460	$26,080	$31,600	$39,220
Cash-outs						
Start-up Costs	$28,200	$0	$0	$0	$0	$0
Books & Other Products	$0	$14,640	$17,080	$17,080	$17,080	$17,080
Rent	$3,500	$3,500	$3,500	$3,500	$3,500	$3,500
Salaries	$0	$2,500	$2,500	$2,500	$2,500	$2,500
Utilities	$0	$800	$800	$800	$800	$800
Telephone	$0	$700	$700	$700	$700	$700
Office Equipment	$0	$1,400	$0	$2,100	$0	$0
Insurance	$0	$3,000	$0	$0	$0	$0
Advertising	$0	$700	$700	$700	$700	$700
Accounting	$0	$300	$300	$300	$300	$300
EPS fees	$0	$300	$300	$300	$300	$300
Loan Payments	$0	$500	$500	$500	$500	$500
Misc.	$500	$1,000	$1,000	$1,000	$1,000	$1,000
Total Cash-outs	**$32,200**	**$29,340**	**$27,380**	**$29,480**	**$27,380**	**$27,380**
CASH AT END OF MONTH	($17,200)	($16,540)	($8,920)	($3,400)	$4,220	$11,840

June	July	Aug	Sept	Oct	Nov	Dec	Year Total
$11,840	$17,360	$21,980	$29,600	$34,420	$42,040	$49,660	$165,060
$35,000	$35,000	$35,000	$35,000	$35,000	$35,000	$40,000	$420,000
$0	$0	$0	$0	$0	$0	$0	$15,000
$46,840	$52,360	$56,980	$64,600	$69,420	$77,040	$89,660	$600,060
$0	$0	$0	$0	$0	$0	$0	$28,200
$17,080	$17,080	$17,080	$17,080	$17,080	$17,080	$19,520	$204,960
$3,500	$3,500	$3,500	$3,500	$3,500	$3,500	$3,500	$45,500
$2,500	$2,500	$2,500	$2,500	$2,500	$2,500	$2,500	$30,000
$800	$800	$800	$800	$800	$800	$800	$9,600
$700	$700	$700	$700	$700	$700	$700	$8,400
$2,100	$0	$0	$2,800	$0	$0	$0	$8,400
$0	$3,000	$0	$0	$0	$0	$0	$6,000
$700	$700	$700	$700	$700	$700	$700	$8,400
$300	$300	$300	$300	$300	$300	$300	$3,600
$300	$300	$300	$300	$300	$300	$300	$3,600
$500	$500	$500	$500	$500	$500	$500	$6,000
$1,000	$1,000	$1,000	$1,000	$1,000	$1,000	$1,000	$12,500
$29,480	**$30,380**	**$27,380**	**$30,180**	**$27,380**	**$27,380**	**$29,820**	**$375,160**
$17,360	$21,980	$29,600	$34,420	$42,040	$49,660	$59,840	$224,900

Inga's happy to see that by the end of April she should have cash left in the bank after all her expenses are paid. Still, she needs to close the cash deficits that she predicts for her first three months in business. Based on her cash flow projection, an extra $17,200 up front would keep her cash flow in the black. She decides to apply for a loan of $15,000 and try to juggle expenses to cover the remaining $2,200 shortfall.

Your cash flow projection will be more complicated if you do any credit transactions. Since cash flow analysis is concerned with when your business receives or spends money, not when sales or purchases are made, you'll need to account for delayed payments if you do any sales or purchases on credit.

Mike McKeever's *How to Write a Business Plan* (Nolo Press) offers more detail on how to complete your cash flow analysis, including how to deal with credit transactions.

H. Putting It All Together

Congratulations! You've finished the descriptive and financial aspects of your business plan. While you kick back and enjoy a cold one, think about how you want to put all the information together. If you put the plan together for your own information, then you might want to simply review it, edit anything that needs fixing, print it out and put it into a binder for your reference. If you plan to present the information as part of a loan request or as a package for investors to review, you might want to do some extra polishing. As mentioned earlier, you might want to get a writer to help you develop the information into a well-written, persuasive document. The bottom line is to package the information as needed for different purposes.

6

Federal, State and Local Start-up Requirements

By now you've finished hammering out the details of how you plan to operate your business. In a perfect world, you could hang up your "open" sign and start selling your products or services at a nice profit. Sorry! In the real world of California business, things are not quite that easy. Before a business can legally begin, it needs to complete a number of pesky requirements with governmental agencies from the city to the federal level. Although none of these requirements are difficult or even terribly time-consuming, lots of entrepreneurs get stymied at this point because it's so hard to find one centralized source of information that explains what they need to do. They're left to ferret out each bureaucratic requirement one by one and hope they've found all of them by the time they start doing business.

For example, your city tax office can tell you what forms you must file there, but won't tell you how to obtain a California seller's permit in order to sell retail goods. And while the state Board of Equalization can tell you everything you need to know about the process of getting a seller's permit, they will be of no help in explaining the process of obtaining a federal employer identification number, which is required for most businesses (even those without employees). The process of finding out what you need to do and how to go about doing it can feel like putting together a jigsaw puzzle without knowing how many pieces it has or how it should look when completed.

To remedy the woeful lack of condensed information, we've pulled all the basic start-up requirements for California businesses together into one chapter for you. It will guide you through the bureaucratic maze and explain exactly what you must do to satisfy all the registration requirements that apply to your business. (There are a few extra requirements for businesses with employees, which are outlined in Chapter 11.) Sure, dealing with city and state bureaucrats can be a mind-numbing endurance of pain. But once you understand what you need to do, where you need to do it and how much it will cost, you'll see that the entire process can be easily accomplished in just one day. Yes, it will be a busy day, but once you've left the last office on your list you will have transformed your good entrepreneurial idea into a fully legal business.

New One-Stop Shopping for Information on Government Requirements

One of the few centralized sources of small business start-up information is a new online clearinghouse called CalGOLD. It's maintained by the California Environmental Protection Agency (CalEPA), but the information it offers isn't restricted to environmental permit issues. When you enter your type of business and the city and county where it's located, this interactive site will pull up a comprehensive list of registration requirements and contact information for the agencies that administer them. The Web address is http://www.calgold.ca.gov/.

The CalEPA also hosts 13 permit assistance centers around the state that help small business start-ups figure out which permits and licenses they need and where to get them. Call 800-GOV-1-STOP or go to http://www.calepa.ca.gov for a list of centers you can visit.

Jennifer Mahoney,

owner of an illustration service in Northern California:

I'm lucky enough to have a technical skill to combine with a regular drawing skill that puts me in a market niche among illustrators. Lacking any entrepreneurial "uncles," it took me a while to get a clue about the business world, like finding untapped markets, understanding agreements, getting paid, handling copyright issues, and finding out how many regulatory bodies need a portion of my modest income. It all felt like groping in the dark: where are all the rules written down? I'm doing well for myself now, supporting my family, but I wish it hadn't taken me so long to figure out.

It may take more time to start a corporation, LLC or limited partnership. Although it is theoretically possible to start a company with limited liability—a corporation, LLC or limited partnership—in one day, the process is more complex than for sole proprietorships and general partnerships. While this chapter outlines the basic start-up requirements, you will need to understand the additional formalities and requirements of these business structures. For example, if you plan to create one of these types of businesses, you'll need to comply with federal and state securities laws. As we mention in Section A, below, Nolo publishes several books that give in-depth, detailed information about starting and running these business types. If you're planning to start a corporation, LLC or limited partnership, be sure you study one of these excellent manuals. Once you have organized your corporation, LLC or limited partnership, you'll be ready to use the information in this chapter on permits, licenses and tax-filing requirements.

Here is a list of the steps we walk you through below:

Step 1:

File organizational documents with the California Secretary of State (corporations, LLCs and limited partnerships only).

Step 2:

Obtain a federal employer identification number (FEIN).

Step 3:

Register your fictitious business name with your county.

Step 4:

Obtain a local tax registration certificate (a.k.a. business license).

Step 5:

Obtain a State of California seller's permit.

Step 6:

Obtain specialized licenses or permits if necessary.

Understanding why such tangled bureaucracy governs small businesses can go a long way in helping you conquer it with a minimum of time and frustration. At the most basic level, there are three purposes to the various permit and license requirements that businesses must complete.

- **To identify you.** No matter what kind of business you run, society has an interest in seeing to it that you are accountable for your actions. That's why any business that doesn't use its owner's name as part of its business name must register a fictitious business name statement with the county. That way, if a member of the public has a problem with Racafrax Designs or Acme Sandblasting, she can easily find out who the owners are and, if necessary, sue them.

- **To protect the public.** Government agencies issue permits and licenses in an attempt to ensure that your business offers safe products or services that won't harm people or the environment. For example, if you open a food service business, the Department of Health understandably wants to make sure that your kitchen is sanitary, and must issue a permit of approval before you can start serving snacks.

- **To keep track of your finances for tax purposes.** Several of the registration requirements are based on the government's nasty habit of taxing everything that moves (and lots of things that don't). To be sure that they collect every possible tax and fee, local, state and federal governments use various registration requirements in order to keep tabs on your business.

A. Step 1: File Organizational Documents With the California Secretary of State (Corporations, LLCs and limited partnerships only).

Unlike sole proprietorships or partnerships, businesses with limited liability don't just pop into existence as soon as their owners start selling products or services. You need to take the step of explicitly creating a corporation, LLC or limited partnership by filing registration papers with the California Secretary of State. For corporations, the necessary papers are called Articles of Incorporation; for LLCs they're called Articles of Organization. Limited partnerships must file a Certificate of Limited Partnership (LP-1). Samples of all three types of organizational documents appear in Appendix C, though this book does not contain the rest of the forms or information necessary to create one of these business types. We've provided the samples for your reference only; to create these business forms you'll need to do additional reading or consult other resources (see "More Information on Creating a Corporation or an LLC," below.)

When you file your organizational documents with the Secretary of State, you will be registering your corporate, LLC or limited partnership name at the same time. The Secretary of State must approve all names before they can be registered, however; otherwise your papers will be rejected. A major factor in whether a name is approved is whether or not another California business of the same legal structure (corporation, LLC or limited partnership) has already taken that name. A California corporation may not use a name that's used by an existing corporation, an LLC may not use a name that is used by another California LLC, and so on.

If you file your organizational papers without checking on your business name, you always run the risk of having to redo the papers with a new name and refile them. To save time and headaches, before you file your papers you should submit potential names to the Secretary of State to be checked for availability. Simply mail in a name reservation form, with multiple names ranked in priority, and a check for the name reservation fee (currently $10). Going down your list of preferred names, the Secretary of State will reserve the first one that's not already taken. Then when you file your organizational documents, your business name is sure to be accepted.

You may also be able to do a name search in person at one of the California Secretary of State offices (addresses appear below). Call ahead of time to find out if that office will allow you to search in person. However you do your search, we highly recommend that once you find a name that's available, you reserve it with a reservation form as described above.

Kimberly Torgerson,

owner of Your Word's Worth, a freelance editing and writing service:

It took me much less than 24 hours to get started as a freelance editor and writer; I wandered to the Berkeley business licensing office, talked with the helpful folks there, paid some fees, and bought a used computer. My biggest challenge starting out was convincing my mother that my business was real.

More Information on Creating a Corporation or an LLC

For detailed information and forms necessary to start a corporation or an LLC, see *How to Form Your Own California Corporation* or *Form Your Own Limited Liability Company*, both by attorney Anthony Mancuso (Nolo Press). These books offer specific instructions on filling out Articles of Organization and Incorporation, as well as the other documents that must be kept in your business records. They also cover the legal and tax implications of these types of businesses, plus detailed information on how to manage them in compliance with various state and federal laws. Forms are included in the back of each book and on accompanying disks. For more information on limited partnerships, see *The Partnership Book* by attorneys Denis Clifford and Ralph Warner.

You can also get information on incorporated businesses from the California Secretary of State. Its Website offers information and downloadable forms for LLCs and corporations. You'll find the California Secretary of State online at http://www.ss.ca.gov/.

California Secretary of State Offices

Sacramento Headquarters	1500 11th St. 916-657-5448
Fresno Branch	2497 West Shaw #101 & 102 209-243-2100
Los Angeles Branch	300 S. Spring 213-897-3062
San Diego Branch	1350 Front St. #2060 619-525-4113
San Francisco Branch	235 Montgomery St., Suite 725 415-439-6959

B. Step 2: Obtain a Federal Employer Identification Number.

If you're starting a sole proprietorship or a partnership, getting a federal employer identification number (FEIN) from the Internal Revenue Service should be your first task in registering your business, mainly because you can get one without having to be registered with any other agency and before you've filled out any other forms.

Corporations and LLCs must also apply for an FEIN, but they must first file their organization documents with the Secretary of State (see Step 1, above).

1. What an FEIN Is and Who Needs One

A business's federal employer identification number (alternately called an FEIN, an EIN and an employer ID) is roughly equivalent to a Social Security number for an individual. It's a number used by the government to identify your business, which you'll use over and over again on most of your important business documents. To mention just a few places you'll use it, you'll typically need to enter it on your business's local tax registration forms, your federal tax return and applications for licenses.

Some of you are probably saying, "But I don't plan to have employees—why do I need an employer ID number?" Blame the IRS for the confusing terminology. Although it's called an "employer" ID number, FEINs are required for most businesses, even if they don't have employees. The one exception is that sole proprietors with no employees can use their own Social Security number instead of an FEIN (but we highly recommend obtaining an FEIN anyway; see Tip below). Partnerships, LLCs and corporations need FEINs whether they have employees or not.

Even sole proprietors without employees should get an FEIN. Sole proprietors should get an FEIN, even though it is not technically required. First, government agencies of all sorts expect you to have one—it's far easier to produce your FEIN than to explain why you don't have one. Second, it helps you distinguish between your personal finances and those of your business. With different ID numbers for yourself and your business, there's less chance of confusion on the part of banks, credit agencies, government offices and whoever else may ask you for your social security number.

2. Applying for an FEIN

There's no fee for an FEIN, and thanks to a mail-in and phone system getting one is super easy. Simply fill out and submit IRS Form SS-4, according to the instructions below. (This book contains two copies of Form SS-4: one in Appendix C which you can tear out and use, and one on CD-ROM, along with the IRS's instructions for completing the form.) If you submit the form by mail you'll get your FEIN in about four weeks. Better yet, you can file by phone and get your number the same day, again for no charge, and then send in Form SS-4. Although most of the information you'll have to put on the form is pretty basic, the following tips will help get the job done.

- **Line 1** asks for the legal name of the entity that is applying for the FEIN. Sounds simple enough, but depending on your business it can get a little tricky.

  Sole proprietors should enter their full individual name—first, last and middle initial. Do not enter any fictitious business name you use or plan to use.

  A partnership should use the legal name of the partnership as it appears in the partnership agreement. For example, Pakroo and Snood own a partnership that they name "Pakroo and Snood, Partners" in their agreement. This is the name they would put for Item 1. If you own a partnership but don't have a written partnership agreement (and you definitely should; see Chapter 2), insert the name you plan to use for all official business and on all government forms—either a name containing each partner's last name, or the trade name that you will present to the public (also known as your fictitious business name or your DBA name). (See Chapter 3 for the full spiel on business names.)

An LLC should enter the official company name as it appears in the Articles of Organization.

A corporation should use its legal name as it appears in the Articles of Incorporation.

• **Line 2** asks for the trade name of the business. This is the same as asking for your "doing business as" (DBA) name. You can leave this line blank if you plan to do business under the same name you entered in line 1. For example, if Pakroo and Snood plan to do business under the name Pakroo and Snood, Partners, they can leave line 2 blank. Similarly, if a sole proprietor named Peder Johnson will use just his name to identify his freelance computer consulting services, he too can leave line 2 blank.

But if Peder uses a different business name—even a business name that contains his legal name, say Johnson's Database Design—he should enter "Johnson's Database Design" on line 2. And a partnership that wants to do business under any name other than its legal name would do the same thing. For example, if "Pakroo and Snood, Partners" want to do business under the trade name "SnooRoo Enterprises," they will enter "Pakroo and Snood, Partners" on line 1 and "SnooRoo Enterprises" on line 2. As long as the legal name is not the same as the trade name, lines 1 and 2 should be filled in with different names.

While it may seem like we're splitting hairs, this is actually very important. Think about it: the FEIN form introduces you and your business to the IRS, and identifies you in an official way. Not only do you want to be sure to give the IRS the correct names,

but, more importantly you want to be consistent with the names you give in order to avoid snafus with the IRS and other government agencies. For example, if the Pakroo and Snood partnership goes back and forth between calling their business "Pakroo and Snood" and "SnooRoo Enterprises," they will almost surely experience a raft of bureaucratic headaches.

To get your FEIN the same day, use the IRS's free Tele-TIN phone-in system. Simply call the appropriate Tele-TIN number for your location (listed below) and state the information from your completed SS-4 form to the IRS representative, who will then give you your FEIN over the phone. Enter the FEIN in the upper right corner of the SS-4, sign and date the form, and mail or FAX it to the Tele-TIN service center within 24 hours of the phone call.

Tele-TIN Phone Numbers and Addresses

Counties of Alpine, Amador, Butt, Calaveras, Colusa, Contra Costa, Del Norte, El Dorado, Glenn, Humboldt, Lake, Lassen, Marin, Mendocino, Modoc, Napa, Nevada, Placer, Plumas, Sacramento, San Joaquin, Shasta, Sierra, Siskiyou, Solano, Sonoma, Sutter, Tehama, Trinity, Yolo and Yuba:

Attn: Entity Control
Mail Stop 6271-T
P.O. Box 9950
Ogden, UT 84409
801-620-7645

All other California counties:
Attn: Entity Control
Fresno, CA 93888
209-452-4010

C. Step 3: Register Your Fictitious Business Name With Your County.

Recall from Chapter 3 that any trade name that doesn't contain the names of the owners (for sole proprietorships or general partnerships) or that doesn't match the company's corporate, limited partnership or LLC name on file with the state is called a fictitious business name (FBN). Fictitious business names are sometimes also called "DBAs" for "doing business as"—as in, "Spikey Andrews, doing business as Coffee Corner" or "Alibi Corporation, doing business as Ferryville Bait and Tackle." California requires every business that uses a fictitious business name to file a fictitious business name statement with the county clerk in the county where its primary business site is located. Details of who needs to register are covered below, in Section 2.

Counties keep track of business names and who uses them for a couple of reasons. One is to prevent customer confusion, which can occur when two local businesses use the same name; in most counties, you'll be required to search the county database of registered names before filing your name to make sure it isn't already being used. Another reason is to give customers a quick way to find out who the owner of a company is without having to hire a private investigator. This allows customers to easily contact the owners with a complaint or to take legal action against them. Requiring owners to register their business names with the county makes it harder for fly-by-night businesses to operate anonymously and defraud customers.

Searching the county database usually isn't enough. Ironically, the county clerk's request that you search its database of registered fictitious business names may well do more harm than good. Why? Because lots of people who find that no one in the county has registered a certain name are misled into believing that the name is free to use. The truth of the matter is that only the tiniest of businesses can feel safe by doing merely a county-wide search of a name they want to use. If someone else is using the name in a neighboring county, or even in a different state, you may well run into legal trouble, depending on your geographical scope and the products or services you sell. And even geographical distance is becoming irrelevant as the World Wide Web is making neighbors out of businesses on opposite sides of the globe.

To avoid being accused of unfair competition or trademark infringement, it is wise to check neighboring counties' FBN databases, look into state registries of corporate and LLC names, or even do a full international trademark search. Failing to do an appropriate search puts you at risk not only of lawsuits, but of having to change your name down the line when you already have stationery, business signs and invoices printed up. Be sure to read Chapter 3 on trademark and business name issues for more information on choosing and researching a name that won't get you into legal trouble.

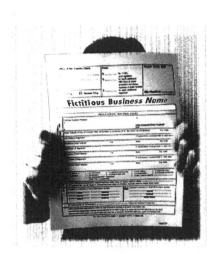

require a fictitious name statement to be filed indicating that it really is John O'Toole's business.

> **If your business name implies more than one owner is involved, a fictitious business name statement must be filed.** If Jason Todd were a sole proprietor, for example, and named his business Jason Todd and Sons, or Jason Todd & Associates, he would have to file an FBN statement, even though he included his last name in the business name.

1. The Importance of Filing an FBN Statement

Do not neglect or put off registering your fictitious business name. If you do, you will not be eligible to file a lawsuit in California. (This may even include lawsuits completely unrelated to your business!) Of even more immediate importance, without proof of registration, most banks will not open an account under your business name. Also, if you don't register your name, it won't appear in the county database, so new businesses that check the database won't find out you're using it. Even though you have other legal avenues to stop another business from using a name that you used first (see Chapter 3), the possibility of customer confusion and a name dispute with another business are definitely things you should try to avoid. If you lose a dispute over a name, at the very least you'll have to redo stationery, signs and anything else that contains the name, such as T-shirts or maybe even your logo.

2. Who Needs to Register

Here's the lowdown on how fictitious business name rules apply to different business forms:

Sole proprietorships. If a sole proprietor includes his last name in the business name—such as John O'Toole's Classic Cars—he does not need to file an FBN statement. But it is not enough to include just initials or part of a name, such as a nickname. For example, a business called J.R.'s Classic Cars would

Partnerships. If a partnership includes the last names of all the partners—for example, Lawrence Anderson and Nancy Fawcett name their business "Anderson and Fawcett Metal Designs"—no statement needs to be filed. In all other situations, filing an FBN statement is necessary. For example, if four partners, White, Black, Pink and Titmouse, did business only under the name "White, Black & Pink," an FBN statement would be required.

Corporations, LLCs and Limited Partnerships. Any business whose name is registered with the California Secretary of State—that includes corporations, LLCs and limited partnerships—does not need to file an FBN statement unless it operates under a name different from its official name as stated in its Articles of Incorporation, Articles of Organization or Certificate of Limited Partnership. For example, an LLC that registered with the Secretary of State under the name "Landmark Lanes, LLC" wouldn't have to file an FBN statement as long as it conducted business under the name "Landmark Lanes, LLC." Any other trade name, "Landmark Bowl," for instance—or even "Landmark Lanes" without the "LLC" tacked onto the end—would count as fictitious and would have to be registered with the Secretary of State. The same is true for corporations: if "Inc." is included in the name in the Articles of Incorporation, it must also be included in the company's trade name; otherwise an FBN statement must be filed.

Office of the County Clerk	**Fees**	**FILING STAMP ONLY**
Address _____ City _____ ☐ First Filing ☐ Renewal Filing	$ _____ for 1 FBN and registrant $ _____ for each additional FBN filed on same statement and doing business at same location $ _____ for each additional registrant	 **File Number:** _____

FICTITIOUS BUSINESS NAME STATEMENT

THE FOLLOWING PERSON(S) IS (ARE)

1

Fictitious Business Name(s)

1

2

3.

Articles of Incorporation Number (if applicable)
AL#

2 Street Address & City of Principal Place of Business in California (P.O. Box alone not acceptable)   Zip Code

3 Full Name of Registrant   if corporation—incorporated in what state

Residence Street Address   City   State   Zip Code

3a Full Name of Registrant   if corporation—incorporated in what state

Residence Street Address   City   State   Zip Code

3b Full Name of Registrant   if corporation—incorporated in what state

Residence Street Address   City   State   Zip Code

4 This Business is conducted by:

( ) an individual   ( ) a general partnership   ( ) joint venture   ( ) a business trust
( ) co-partners   ( ) husband and wife   ( ) a corporation   ( ) a limited partnership
( ) an unincorporated association other than a partnership   ( ) other—please specify _____

5
( ) The registrant commenced to transact business under name or names listed on (date): _____
( ) Registrant has not yet begun to transact business under the fictitious business name or names listed herein.

6 If registrant is not a corporation or a limited liability company sign below:

SIGNATURE	TYPE OR PRINT NAME
SIGNATURE	TYPE OR PRINT NAME
SIGNATURE	TYPE OR PRINT NAME

6a If registrant is a corporation or a limited liability company sign below:

COMPANY NAME

SIGNATURE & TITLE

TYPE OR PRINT NAME AND TITLE

This statement was filed with the County Clerk of _____ County on date indicated by file stamp above.

NOTICE—THIS FICTITIOUS NAME STATEMENT EXPIRES FIVE YEARS FROM DATE IT WAS FILED IN THE OFFICE OF THE COUNTY CLERK.

A NEW FICTITIOUS BUSINESS NAME STATEMENT MUST BE FILED PRIOR TO THAT DATE. The filing of this statement does not of itself authorize the use in this state of a fictitious business name in violation of the rights of another under federal, state, or common law (SEE SECTION 14400 et seq., Business and Professional Code).

This form should be **typed** *or* **printed** *legibly in* **black ink**.

3. Filing With Your County

The law governing fictitious business names (Business and Professions Code § 17900 to 17930) applies to the whole state, but is administered by each county. The result is a mammoth exercise in governmental inefficiency, with each county in California issuing different forms and charging different fees for registering an FBN. In Appendix C and on the CD-ROM, we provide a form that contains all the information required by state law for FBN statements. Logically, each county should accept this form, but, of course, some clerks insist that you use a specific form provided by their office.

Your first step should be to call your county clerk's office to find out its requirements and fees. Or, unless you live a good distance from the nearest county clerk, it may be easiest just to go to the office to complete the process in person. If you'd rather do the process by mail, call and ask if the office will accept our standard form and, if so, how many copies you must submit and what fees must be paid. If the clerk's office requires filers to use a specific county form, then use that form. The clerk will tell you how to obtain one. Many counties allow you to order the form by phone; others require you to send a written request for it along with a self-addressed stamped envelope. You'll find a list of county clerks' offices and contact in Appendix B.

a. Searching the County Database

In most counties, you'll be instructed to search the county database of registered fictitious business names before submitting your statement, in order to see if anyone else has already registered the name you want to use. Typically, you can search a county's database (often an easy-to-search computerized system) for free if you go to the office in person, or you can sometimes pay a fee for a staff person to do the search for you. If you want the clerk's office to do the search, you must usually submit the request and fee by mail.

b. Completing and Submitting an FBN Statement

If you've determined that the name you've chosen is free to use, simply fill out the FBN statement and submit it to your county clerk along with the appropriate fees. The following instructions are for the standard form (below) that we've included in Appendix C and on the CD-ROM.

Item 1: Insert the fictitious business name or names. If you enter more than one, such as "Loaded for Bear Publishing" and "Bear Bones Comics," be sure to number them to make it clear that they're separate names. You're only allowed to register business names used at one address on a single FBN statement. For instance, if the same owners use more than one fictitious business name at the same location, such as "Snak Central Cafe" and "Turtle Tavern" all under one roof, both names can be registered on one statement. Business names used at different locations—or by different owners at the same location—must be registered on separate FBN statements.

Item 2: Enter the street address of the business. P.O. Boxes aren't acceptable. If you're working from home, just enter your home address.

Item 3: Enter the legal name and residence address of the person(s), LLC or corporation that's registering the fictitious business name. Partnerships should enter this information for each general partner. For LLCs and corporations, use the name in the Articles of Organization or Incorporation that was filed with the Secretary of State and the business's principal address (again, no P.O. boxes). LLCs and corporations should also indicate which state they're organized or incorporated in (probably California), and enter their Articles of Organization or Incorporation number.

Item 4: Indicate what legal type of business entity you are operating, most likely a sole proprietorship, general partnership, LLC or corporation. For corporations and LLCs, some counties, such as Los Angeles, require a certified copy of the Articles of Organization or Incorporation to be attached. Check with your county for its requirements.

Item 5: Enter the date you started your business or check the box that indicates you haven't opened for business yet. State law requires an FBN statement to be filed within 40 days of using a fictitious business name (though this rule isn't strictly monitored).

Item 6: Enter the appropriate signatures. The following people may sign for each specific business type:

Sole proprietorship:	Sole proprietor
Partnership:	General partner
LLC:	Officer or manager
Corporation:	Officer

Whoever signs for an LLC or corporation must indicate his or her title.

You can submit the form in person or by mail. Depending on the county, the fee is generally between $10 and $40 for registering one business name and one business owner. You can also pay an additional fee, around $5 or so, to register additional business names to be used at the same business location or additional owners. In other words, the more owners a business has, the more expensive it is to file an FBN statement. See the chart in Appendix B for contact and fee information for each county in California.

Attention: San Francisco filers. *The procedure of registering an FBN in San Francisco is a bit more complicated than in other counties, because the San Francisco county clerk won't accept an FBN statement without proof that you've already registered with the city tax collector and paid the appropriate fees. Here is the best way to proceed. First, check San Francisco's FBN database for the name you want to use. At that point you'll have to take a detour and register your business with the city tax collector's office—using the business name you just checked for availability, even though you haven't registered it yet—and obtain a Temporary Verification of Registration (TVR). Then take the TVR back to the county clerk's office and finish registering your business name. When you show the clerk the TVR as proof that you've registered your business with the city, she will accept your FBN statement along with the fees.*

c. Publishing Notice of Your FBN Statement

Once you've filed your name and paid the necessary fees, you are free to do business—but there is one more catch to using a fictitious business name. Within 30 days of your filing date, you must have your FBN statement published in an approved newspaper in the county where you filed it. The county clerk often will provide a list of acceptable publications for posting your FBN statement, though by state law any newspaper of general circulation in the county will suffice (really, no one reads these notices anyway). Publishing your statement is dead simple; just take a copy of your completed statement to your publication of choice, which will have a standard format to present the required information.

Obscure publications often charge the lowest fees. As long as a newspaper is on the approved list or otherwise doesn't violate your county's rules (for instance, in Alameda County you can't publish your FBN statement in a free newspaper), there's nothing wrong with picking the cheapest one.

The published notice must run once a week for four consecutive weeks. Within 30 days after the last publication, an affidavit (sometimes called Proof of Publication) must be filed with the county clerk to show that publication has been completed. Many newspapers that provide publication services will automatically send in the affidavit for you after your ad has completed its run. Make sure to find out whether the publication you use will do this or not (and it's not a bad idea to double check after the four weeks whether they've actually done it). If not, you'll have to get the affidavit from the publication after the four weeks is up and submit it to the county clerk yourself within the 30-day deadline. If the affidavit isn't filed in time, you may have to start the process all over again.

Save your ad receipt. For practical reasons, you may need to prove that you completed your fictitious business name filing requirements, specifically publication, before your ad has actually run for four weeks. Banks, for instance, want to see that you have met fictitious name rules before they allow you to open an account in that name. Fortunately, a receipt from the newspaper that's publishing your statement, showing that you have paid for publication, along with a copy of the FBN statement, certified by the county clerk, is generally sufficient to prove that you've met all the registration requirements even though the ad hasn't yet run for four weeks. So be sure to get a certified copy of your FBN statement back from the county clerk when you submit it, as well as a receipt from the newspaper when you pay for publication of the statement.

4. After You've Filed

Legally, your FBN statement must be renewed every five years. You (or someone at your business) should keep track of your expiration date—five years after the date of initial filing. The county clerk will *not* notify you when your expiration approaches. Also, you must renew your FBN statement if there is any change in the facts in the statement (except for changes of residence of an owner). You'll have to promptly file a new FBN statement when facts change or your FBN statement will expire in 40 days. If you no longer want your FBN registered, your FBN statement will expire as soon as you file a statement of abandonment, which usually costs around $10 to $40.

Changes to Your Business Which Require a New FBN Statement

- Business name change
- Business address change
- Change of business ownership (unless a withdrawing partner files a statement of withdrawal)
- Change of business type (for example, you change your partnership to an LLC).

D. Step 4: Obtain a Local Tax Registration Certificate (a.k.a. Business License).

As you're now learning, there's a whole host of licenses, permits and registrations you may need in order to start your business—and then there's what's commonly called your "business license." Many people use the term "business license" to refer to a tax registration certificate that every business needs in order to do business. This can be misleading. True licenses, which are discussed in Section F, below, must be obtained by certain businesses if they engage in regulated activities, such as selling alcohol or cutting people's hair. Getting such a license often involves taking a test or otherwise proving you're qualified to do a certain activity.

Getting a so-called business license, on the other hand, is nothing more than the simple act of registering with your local tax collector. Most cities in California require businesses to register with that city's tax collector, regardless of business structure, size, name or type of business. This includes home businesses. Businesses located in rural, unincorporated areas must usually register with the county clerk. (While we often refer to city tax collectors and city requirements for businesses in this chapter, just keep in mind that if you're operating outside of a city, the same types of requirements generally apply, but are often administered by county government instead.)

Depending on where you register, the locality may use different names for the process: tax registration, business tax application, or tax certification, to name a few. We use the terms "tax registration" and "tax registration certificate" in this book—and we recommend that you don't use the term "business license" when you really mean "tax registration certificate" (or whatever term is used in your locality for tax registration).

Some businesses need additional licenses and permits. It's important to understand that your tax registration certificate (a.k.a. business license) is not the same as a specialized license your business might need—such as a permit from the local health department for handling food, or from the Federal Communications Commission for broadcasting a radio station, or from a regional air management district for emitting particles into the air. Section F, below, discusses these specialized licenses and permits. Whether or not you need one of these licenses or permits, you'll still need to get a tax registration certificate.

Why do you need to register with your local tax collector? Because just like the federal and state governments, your local government wants a cut of your business income. And the tax registration requirement is basically your local government's way of keeping track of your business so that it will be able to collect any taxes it owes. Cities and counties have been known to tax businesses with even more flair and creativity than the feds or the state does. Localities tax businesses based on criteria such as net profit, gross income, number of employees, total payroll, number of vehicles, number of machines and sometimes even seating capacity. In addition, most cities categorize businesses and use different tax structures for each category. Oakland's 1997 tax rates, for instance, taxed media firms at $1.20 per $1,000 of gross receipts, recreation/entertainment businesses at $4.50 per $1,000 of gross receipts, and limousine companies at $75 per vehicle.

For the privilege of registering to pay local taxes, you'll have to pay a fee, which varies a lot from city to city. Usually the annual fee depends partly on how much tax your business is expected to owe the following year, based on city (or county) tax rates. Often, at least part of the registration fee is a non-refundable administrative fee. To register in Oakland, for instance, you'll need to pay a non-refundable fee of $30, plus your estimated tax based on your business category and your estimated income for the next year. The estimated tax portion will be credited towards your tax bill for the next year. The chart below gives you an idea of the variety of ways that cities register new businesses.

Local ordinances on business tax registration change often. Please use the following chart only as a general illustration of the range of tax registration requirements in some California cities. Each city's rules are much more particular than what appears below, and are subject to sudden and significant change. You definitely need to contact the tax registration agency in your area for the specific procedures and fees that will apply to your business.

	Name of Permit	Fee Structure	Additional Information
Fresno	Business Tax Certificate	$10 application processing fee plus minimum tax (e.g. $8.50 for general business services)	Minimum tax credited to tax bill at year-end.
Los Angeles	Tax Registration Certificate	Minimum tax (e.g. $106.43 for general business services)	Minimum tax credited to bill at year-end.
Oakland	Business Tax Certificate	$30 registration fee plus estimated tax	Estimated tax credited to tax bill at year-end
San Diego	Business Tax Certificate	$34 fee for businesses with 12 or less employees; $125 plus $5 per employee for businesses with 13 or more employees	Fees not credited toward tax bill at year-end
San Francisco	Business Tax Registration Certificate	Registration fee ($25 to $500) based on estimated tax due	Registration fees not credited to tax bill at year-end.
San Jose	Business Tax Certificate	Prepaid tax (e.g., general service businesses pay base rate of $154.50, plus $18.54 for each employee in excess of 8)	Prepaid tax is credited to tax bill at year-end.

For your city's requirements, call your city tax collector, whose office will probably be listed under "Tax Collector" in the city government section of your white pages. The tax collector's office will be able to provide you with the forms necessary to register in your city, as well as a breakdown of business categories and tax tables. If you're doing business outside city limits, call your county clerk, who'll usually be listed under "County Clerk" in the county government section of the phone book.

E. Step 5: Obtain a State of California Seller's Permit.

Sellers of merchandise must get a seller's permit from the California Board of Equalization (BOE), which is in charge of collecting taxes from businesses that do retail sales. The permit allows your business to collect sales taxes from customers to cover the sales tax that you'll owe to the BOE (if any). You'll pay any taxes you owe at year-end, or quarterly if your sales volume is high enough. The BOE uses a threshold of approximately $17,000 in sales revenues per month—or about $1,200 in taxes due per month—to trigger a quarterly reporting requirement. Businesses with incomes or expected taxes below those levels will generally be able to report yearly. We discuss collecting, reporting and paying state sales taxes more fully in Chapter 8. In this section we just explain how to get a seller's permit, so you can get on with your business.

1. Who Needs a Seller's Permit?

Any business—whether it's a sole proprietorship, corporation or any other type—must have a seller's permit if it sells any tangible goods to the public. Tangible goods are things you can touch, like furniture or food. Businesses that sell only services and no tangible goods are exempt from the seller's permit requirement.

It's important to understand that if you plan to sell tangible goods, you'll need a seller's permit *whether or not those sales will be taxable.* While a seller's permit is required if you sell tangible goods, taxes are due on those sales only if the tangible goods are sold to an in-state final user. In other words, you'll need a seller's permit even to conduct nontaxable sales of tangible goods—such as to a wholesaler or to an out-of-state customer. This means you'll need to get a sales permit before you begin to sell tangible goods; when the sales are made you'll distinguish the taxable ones from the nontaxable ones. When it comes time to report and pay sales taxes to the state, you'll be taxed only on the taxable sales. (We cover reporting and paying sales taxes in more depth in Chapter 8.)

Unfortunately, it's sometimes tricky to figure out whether a permit is required (or whether a sale is taxable), often because of a blurry line between service sales (no permit required) and product sales (permit required). A graphic design business, for example, performs services such as typesetting and graphic production but usually also provides its customers a hard copy of the job. Is the business merely performing a service or is it selling a product (the hard copy) like a retailer? The BOE says that transferring graphic art to a customer either on paper or on disk amounts to selling a product, so a seller's permit is required and a tax will be due. If you think this doesn't quite make sense, welcome to the world of the BOE, where there are lots of oddball rules and where common sense doesn't apply.

Pending legislation may exempt graphic artists from needing a seller's permit. A long-running controversy between the BOE and California's graphic artists has resulted in a bill that could change California's sales tax law as it applies to graphic artists. Senate Bill 331 was drafted in an attempt to exempt graphic artist from having to pay sales taxes on licensing artwork, and from needing a seller's permit to conduct this type of business. Amendments threaten to gut the bill however. To find out the latest status of S.B. 331, visit the Northern Chapter of the Graphic Artists Guilds Website at http://www.gag.org/sanfran/salestax.html. You can also get legislative information from the California State Senate's Website at http://www.sen.ca.gov/.

Keep track of your service and product sales separately. Many businesses both perform services and sell products. A metalsmith, for instance, both repairs jewelry and sells his raw materials, such as precious metals and gemstones. If a business sells both labor and goods, it definitely needs a seller's permit. Plus, to assure proper tax reporting, that business will need to keep its labor sales separate from sales of goods. (Chapter 10 explains simple bookkeeping and how to account for taxable sales separately from tax-exempt sales.)

If you're still in doubt as to whether your business needs a seller's permit, try reading the BOE's pamphlets (see "Commonly Requested BOE Publications"). Chances are you'll still have questions. The only way to get a definitive answer as to whether your specific business needs a seller's permit may be to ask an agent of the BOE. You can call the BOE at 1-800-400-7115 and ask for an agent. When describing your business to an agent, give as much detail as you can about what you'll be doing—but be careful not to attract an audit! It's a good idea not to identify yourself or arouse too much interest in your business.

Commonly Requested BOE Publications

Besides the application forms for seller's permits, the BOE offers hundreds of free publications, including specific regulations and tax tips for particular businesses.

Some of the more popular BOE pamphlets are

Pamphlet 22, Tax Tips for the Dining & Beverage Industry

Pamphlet 24, Tax Tips for Liquor Stores

Pamphlet 25, Tax Tips for Auto Repair Garages and Service Stations

Pamphlet 32, Tax Tips for Purchasers from Mexico

Pamphlet 35, Tax Tips for Interior Designers and Decorators

Pamphlet 37, Tax Tips for the Graphic Arts Industry

Pamphlet 76, Audits and Appeals

Pamphlet 80B, Electronic Funds Transfer Program

Commonly requested regulations include

Regulation 1501, Service Enterprises Generally

Regulation 1502, Computers, Programs and Data Processing

Regulation 1574, Vending Machine Operators

Regulation 1602, Food Products

Regulation 1668, Resale Certificates

Many of these publications are available in Chinese, Spanish, Korean and Vietnamese.

There are a number of different ways to get BOE publications.

- You can use one of the BOE's order forms to order information by mail. Order forms are included in Appendix C; you can also download them from the BOE's Website at http://www.boe.ca.gov boelist.htm.

- If you already know which publication you want, you can call the BOE at 1-800-400-7115 and order it 24 hours a day by leaving a message. Or call during business hours so that you can talk with an agent about which publication you need.

- All publications are also available in person at any of the BOE's field offices, which are listed in Appendix A.

- Finally, a limited selection of the BOE's publications can be downloaded directly from the Web by going to http://www.boe.ca.gov/boelist.htm.

2. Obtaining a Seller's Permit

To obtain a seller's permit, a sole proprietor or partnership must submit form BT-400-MIP to the Board of Equalization. LLCs and corporations must use form BT-400-MCO, which is only slightly different. A sample of BT-400-MIP appears below. This book contains both BT-400 forms for you to fill out and use (tear-out forms are in Appendix C; digital copies are on the CD-ROM). The BOE's instructions are included with the forms.

You'll need a seller's permit for each location where you sell goods, but you don't need to apply separately for each one. If you'll sell goods from more than one location, just include the addresses of all locations with your application, and the BOE will issue as many permits as you need from the single application.

Most of the items on the BT-400 form are self-explanatory, but we'll go through a few details for both kinds of forms.

Note: You will need to include a photocopy of each owner's driver's license and Social Security card with your application. Generally this applies to everyone who signs the application, including sole proprietors, general partners, LLC members and corporate officers.

▪ **BT-400-MIP (for sole proprietorships and partnerships)**

Section I, Item 1: Indicate whether your business is a sole proprietorship (sole owner), a husband/wife co-ownership or a partnership. If you and your spouse are co-owners, either as a partnership or a husband/wife sole proprietorship, the BOE wants you to check the husband/wife co-ownership box. But if one spouse is a sole proprietor and the other an official employee, then check the sole proprietorship box. (See Chapter 2, Section A on different business structures and how a husband and wife can jointly own a business formed as a sole proprietorship.)

Example:

Chris and his wife Amy are starting a small business selling chile peppers which they grow on their ranch in the Central Valley. Since they will both actively work in the business, they will be partners for tax purposes. When filling out their application for a seller's permit, they check the "Husband/Wife Co-ownership" box.

Example:

Tim is starting a business selling imports from Brazil and other South American countries. His wife Abby will do some work for the business, but won't share in management decisions. If Tim decides to hire Abby as an employee and pay employment taxes, he should check the "Sole Proprietorship" box on his seller's permit application. But if he doesn't want to pay employment taxes, he could take advantage of the IRS's rule that allows Abby to work for the business without being classified as an employee. In that case they would be a husband/wife sole proprietorship, and Tim would check the "Husband/Wife Co-ownership" box on the seller's permit application.

Note for partnerships: The BOE's instructions included with the BT-400-MIP form state that partnerships should include a partnership agreement with the application. If your business is a partnership and you have a written agreement (which we highly recommend, see Chapter 2), then include it. If you have not yet drafted your partnership agreement, you may still be okay, since most BOE offices don't enforce this rule. If you're concerned about this requirement, check with your local office to find out whether it requires you to submit a partnership agreement. (See Appendix A for a list of BOE offices and contact information.) If the answer is yes, but you haven't created one yet, you might take this opportunity to do something that you really need to do anyway. See Chapter 2 for information on drafting partnership agreements.

BOE - 400 - MIP (S2F) REV. 12(5-98)

**APPLICATION FOR SELLER'S PERMIT AND REGISTRATION
AS A RETAILER (INDIVIDUALS/PARTNERS)**

STATE of CALIFORNIA
BOARD OF EQUALIZATION

SECTION I: OWNERSHIP INFORMATION

	FOR BOARD USE ONLY

1. PLEASE CHECK TYPE OF OWNERSHIP *(use additional sheet to include information about additional co-owners or partners)*

TAX	OFFICE	NUMBER
S		

☐ Sole Owner   ☐ Husband/Wife Co-ownership

☐ Partnership (If partnership enter Federal
Employer Indentification Number (FEIN) numbers)

Photocopy of
Driver's License and
Social Security Card
is required
See instruction number 6

BUSINESS CODE	AREA CODE
PREPARER	VERIFICATION: ☐ SSN ☐ DL ☐ Other

	OWNER OR PARTNER	CO-OWNER OR PARTNER
2. FULL NAME *(first, middle, last)*		
3. RESIDENCE ADDRESS *(enter full address including zip code)*		
4. RESIDENCE TELEPHONE NO.	( )	( )
5. SOCIAL SECURITY NO.		
6. DRIVER'S LICENSE NO. & DATE OF BIRTH		
7. PRESENT/PAST EMPLOYER *(enter full address including zip code & telephone no.)*		
8. NAME, ADDRESS & TELEPHONE NO. OF TWO PERSONAL REFERENCES	1. 2.	1. 2.
9. SPOUSE'S NAME		
10. SPOUSE'S SOCIAL SECURITY NO.		
11. SPOUSE'S DRIVER'S LICENSE NO. & DATE OF BIRTH		
12. SIGNATURE		

SECTION II: BUSINESS INFORMATION

1. BUSINESS NAME	BUSINESS TELEPHONE ( )

2. BUSINESS ADDRESS *(do not list P.O. Box or mailing service)*	CITY	STATE	ZIP CODE

3. MAILING ADDRESS *(if different from No. 2 above)*	CITY	STATE	ZIP CODE

4. DATE YOU WILL BEGIN SALES *(month, day & year)*	5. DAYS & HOURS OF OPERATION	SUNDAY	MONDAY	TUESDAY	WEDNESDAY	THURSDAY	FRIDAY	SATURDAY

6. TYPE OF BUSINESS *(check one)*

☐ Retail ☐ Wholesale ☐ Mfg. ☐ Repair ☐ Service ☐ Construction Contractor

CHECK ONE   ☐ Full Time ☐ Part Time ☐ Mail Order

7. TYPE OF ITEMS SOLD

8. ARE YOU

☐ Starting a new business? ☐ Adding/dropping partner? ☐ Other? _____

☐ Buying a business? *(indicate name & account number in area at right)*

FORMER OWNER'S NAME

ACCOUNT NUMBER

9. PURCHASE PRICE $	10. VALUE OF FIXTURES & EQUIPMENT	11. NUMBER OF SELLING LOCATIONS *(if 2 or more attach list of all locations)*

12. IF AN ESCROW COMPANY IS REQUESTING A TAX CLEARANCE ON YOUR BEHALF, PLEASE LIST THEIR NAME, ADDRESS, TELEPHONE NUMBER AND THE ESCROW NUMBER

13. IF ALCOHOLIC BEVERAGES ARE SOLD, PLEASE LIST YOUR ALCOHOLIC BEVERAGE CONTROL LICENSE NO. AND TYPE

BOE-400-MIP (S2B) REV. 12 (5-98)

14. NAME, ADDRESS & TELEPHONE NUMBER OF ACCOUNTANT/BOOKKEEPER

15. NAME, ADDRESS & TELEPHONE NUMBER OF BUSINESS LANDLORD

16. NAME & LOCATION OF BANK OR OTHER FINANCIAL INSTITUTION *(Note whether business or personal)*	CHECKING AND SAVINGS ACCOUNT NUMBER
17. NAME & ADDRESS OF MAJOR SUPPLIERS	PRODUCTS PURCHASED

18. OTHER ACCOUNT NUMBERS ISSUED TO YOU BY THE BOARD

SECTION III: INCOME AND EXPENSES

1. PROJECTED MONTHLY BUSINESS EXPENSES	2. PROJECTED MONTHLY SALES	3. INFORMATION CONCERNING EMPLOYMENT DEVELOPMENT DEPARTMENT (EDD)
RENT $ _____	TOTAL GROSS SALES $ _____	a. Are you registered with EDD? ☐ Yes ☐ No
PAYROLL $ _____	NON-TAXABLE $ _____	b. If no, will your payroll exceed $100 per quarter? ☐ Yes ☐ No If yes, you must make application with EDD. Number of employees See pamphlet DE 44, "California Employer's Guide."
MISC. $ _____	TAXABLE $ _____	c. I have already received pamphlet DE 44, "California Employer's Guide." ☐ Yes ☐ No
TOTAL $ _____	TAX $ _____	

SECTION IV: CERTIFICATION

The statements contained herein are hereby certified to be correct to the best knowledge and belief of the undersigned who is duly authorized to sign this application. (If spouse co-ownership both signatures must appear below.)

SIGNATURE	TITLE	SIGNATURE	TITLE
NAME *(typed or printed)*		NAME *(typed or printed)*	DATE

FOR BOARD USE ONLY
Furnished to Taxpayer

REPORTING BASIS			REGULATIONS
SECURITY REVIEW	☐ BOE-8	☐ DE-44	
	☒ BOE-324A	☐ OTHER	
☐ BT-598 $ _____	☐ BT-400Y	_____	
☐ BT-1009	☐ BOE-467	_____	PAMPHLETS
BY	☐ BOE-519	_____	
	☐ BT-1241-D	_____	
APPROVED BY	☐ REG. 1668	_____	
REMOTE INPUT DATE	☐ REG. 1698	_____	RETURNS
BY	☐ REG. 1700	_____	
☐ Permit Issued Date _____			

Section III, Item 1: Estimate your monthly expenses such as rent, payroll and supplies. Salaries of sole proprietors and general partners may not be counted as a business expense.

Item 2: Estimate your monthly revenue, dividing it into taxable and nontaxable income. Generally, taxable income includes tangible items (products) sold to the final user. Nontaxable income includes sales of services and sales of tangible items to resellers. (See Chapter 8, Section G for a detailed discussion of sales taxes.) Multiply your taxable income by the sales tax rate for your county. A list of county sales tax rates is included in Chapter 8.

Item 3: If you have employees, you must register with the Employment Development Department (EDD). (See Chapter 11 on registering with the EDD and other requirements for hiring employees.) Sole proprietors and partners are owners—not employees. Your spouse, if involved in the business, may be treated as an employee or a partner, or may be nonclassified. See Chapter 2 on husband/wife businesses and the status of your spouse as a partner or employee. Then check the applicable box.

Section I and Section IV: Be sure that all owners sign both of these sections.

- **BT-400-MCO (for corporations and LLCs)**

Section I: Be sure that all corporate officers or at least two LLC members fill in the requested information and sign at line 11. For corporate officers, check the "President," "Vice-president," "Secretary" or "Treasurer" box. If one person holds more than one title, just repeat the name in the column under that title without filling in the rest of the information, and check the appropriate title box. For LLC members, check the "Member" box.

Section III, Item 1: Estimate your monthly expenses such as rent, payroll and supplies.

Item 2: Estimate your monthly revenue, dividing it into taxable and nontaxable income. Generally, taxable income includes tangible items sold to the final user, and nontaxable income includes items sold

to resellers or sales of services. (See Chapter 8, Section G for a detailed discussion of sales taxes.) Multiply your taxable income by the sales tax for your county. A list of county sales tax rates is included in Chapter 8.

Item 3: Virtually every corporation will have at least one employee, which means it must register with the Employment Development Department (EDD). (See Chapter 11 on registering with the EDD and other requirements for hiring employees.) If your LLC has any employees (as opposed to members), it must register with this department.

Section IV: Only one corporate officer or LLC member should sign.

Submit your application for a seller's permit 30 days or less prior to your first sale. After you apply, it generally takes two to three weeks until you get your permit. If you want one right away, some BOE field offices will grant you one on the same day if you apply in person. (Field office addresses and phone numbers are listed in Appendix A.)

For sole proprietorships and partnerships there is no fee for the permit, though if you have a blemished history with a previous seller's permit—for instance, if you were late with your tax payments to the BOE—you may be required to post a deposit. Corporations and LLCs that sell retail goods must often post a security deposit, which generally amounts to half a year's estimated sales tax. If the business is diligent about paying its taxes, the BOE should refund the deposit after three years.

Businesses with higher revenues must report more often and pay larger deposits. No one wants to tie up a big deposit with the State of California or pay taxes more often than is necessary. To avoid this, your best bet is to make a low estimate as to expected revenues. Since no one knows how much you'll really sell (including you), it is usually possible to get the BOE to accept a modest number. This is especially likely to be true if you emphasize that your business will primarily provide services.

F. Step 6: Obtain Specialized Licenses or Permits

Depending on the nature of your business, you might be finished with your list of bureaucratic tasks. But before you run off to rev up your cash register, cool your jets—you may be surprised to find out that even your simple little business is subject to an extra regulation or two. Some business activities aren't allowed until you obtain a license or permit to do them, and some business locations require special approval from the local planning department for what you plan to do there. These extra requirements are especially likely to apply to your business if it has any potential for harming the environment or hurting the public, but they also apply in lots of seemingly risk-free situations.

Figuring out what additional permits or licenses you might need can be confusing, because there are literally hundreds of independent agencies from the local to the federal level that regulate various businesses. Obviously you don't want to waste your time calling each and every one of them to find out whether your business is subject to its rules. This

section will put you on the right track by first outlining the basics on what types of activities are regulated and by whom. This should help you recognize when your business is likely to face a special regulation. Then we'll direct you to a few resources that help to make sense of the crazy patchwork of local, state and federal regulations on small businesses.

Local regulations have a different focus than state or federal ones. Very generally speaking, local regulations tend to focus on the location of your business and whether it poses a nuisance or a threat to public safety. State and federal regulations typically focus more on the job you're doing and whether or not you're competent at it.

1. Zoning and Local Permits

Local business regulations usually have to do with the physical location of the business and the safety of the premises and equipment. City zoning laws, for instance, regulate which activities are allowed in particular locations. If a certain location is zoned exclusively for residential use, if there's not enough parking to support your business, or if there are too many similar businesses nearby, your business might not be approved by the zoning board. Even if your business activities are acceptable for the time being, you might not be allowed to put up the sign you want or put in additional seating once your business takes off.

If your business doesn't comply with zoning laws, you'll either need to get a Conditional Use Permit or be granted an exception to the law (sometimes called a variance). Your city or county planning department is generally in charge of zoning laws. Contact them to find out whether your business complies with local rules, and, if not, how to request a Conditional Use Permit or a zoning variance. (Chapter 4 discusses zoning laws and picking a business location.)

Assuming your business has met zoning requirements, it still might need to be approved by other city agencies, such as the fire or police departments, the building inspector or the department of public health. To ensure compliance with local laws, such as health and fire codes, noise laws and environmental regulations, you may need one or more permits from these agencies. When you register with your local tax collector, you'll often receive information on these agencies and which types of businesses need to contact them. Your county clerk might also be able to direct you to information about which regulatory agencies to contact in your particular area.

San Francisco's Permit Agencies

To give you an idea of the types of local regulations that apply to businesses, here's a partial list of agencies in San Francisco and the types of businesses that are regulated by them.

Health Department: preparers, servers, manufacturers and marketers of food; laundries

Police Department: billiard parlors; dance halls; massage parlors; street peddlers; taxicabs; valet parking services

Fire Department: garages; storage facilities; service stations; theaters; handlers of hazardous chemicals or gases

Public Works Department: apartments; hotels

---

2. State and Federal Regulations

The State of California regulates how you conduct your business—such as making sure that your cosmetologists are competent, or that your carpenters do safe work—through licensing. (There are a few federal agencies that issue licenses and permits, such as the Bureau of Alcohol, Tobacco and Firearms, the Food and Drug Administration and the U.S. Customs Office). Businesses are more likely to need a state permit if they are highly specialized or if they affect the public welfare. If there's a risk that poor handling of the business might harm the public, chances are that a state license is required. Common examples of state-licensed businesses are bars, auto shops, health care services and waste management companies.

Don't assume that your business is so simple or straightforward that you don't need a special license. You'd be amazed at how many activities the state regulates: to name a few, locksmiths must be licensed by the Bureau of Security and Investigative Services; people who train guide dogs must be licensed by the State Board of Guide Dogs; and furniture makers must be licensed by the Bureau of Home Furnishings (no, we're not making this up).

Audrey Wackerley,

owner of RetroFit, a vintage clothing store in San Francisco

Getting the right permits turned into a total hassle for our clothing store. After we'd been in business for a year and a half, a cop walked in our store and said we needed a "second-hand" permit. We had never even heard of one! It's not like we hadn't really made an effort to get all the permits we needed—before we opened we spent hours in all these different buildings downtown, waiting in endless lines (it's a lot like going to the DMV), asking a million questions to find out what permits we needed to open our store. We had a seller's permit, a sign permit...we thought we had everything we needed. But all of a sudden this cop said he'd shut us down if we didn't get the second-hand permit within five days. Five days! The permit cost $700, which was a real stretch for us right then. But what could we do? We had to scramble to get the money together and buy that stupid permit. The cop also let us know that we needed a separate jewelry permit in order to sell jewelry, but getting the second-hand permit was enough of an ordeal. We just decided to stop selling jewelry.

3. License and Permit Information Resources

Fortunately, there are a few state agencies that act as clearinghouses for information on permits and issuing agencies. If you aren't sure what regulations might apply to your business, contact one or all of them to help you figure out what you need to do to keep your business in full compliance with all license and permit regulations.

- **CalGOLD and the California EPA's Permit Assistance Centers.** The state Environmental Protection Agency (CalEPA) has just completed an impressive interactive Website that offers information on all the government requirements—not just environment-related ones—a start-up business needs to complete. The site, located at http://www.calgold.ca.gov, asks you to enter your business type and location (city and county), and after a few seconds returns a list of all the licenses and permits you'll need from the local to the federal level, as well as contact information for the agencies that adminster them. You won't find any detailed information about these requirements (as in this book), but it still is very helpful to see them all at a glance. On the down side, this Website is like any other automated information source, in that it can only handle very standard information requests. For example, if you're not sure how to categorize your business, this site won't be of much help.

  For a real person, you can contact a CalEPA Permit Assistance Center for a representative who will either help you over the phone or direct you to one of the 13 Permit Assistance Centers in the state. Again, the assistance available at these centers is for all business requirements, not only those related to environmental concerns. The CalEPA Permit Assistance Centers have one main phone number that will route your call to the office nearest you. Call 800-GOV-1-STOP.

- **California's Office of Small Business.** This office (which is part of the California Trade and Commerce Agency) will refer you to one of the local Small Business Development Centers (SBDCs) that it oversees. Each SBDC can provide information about license and permit requirements of all governmental levels for your type of business. The Office of Small Business (which is also the lead SBDC) can be reached at 916-322-5790, or for online information, go to http://commerce.ca.gov/business/small/licensing.html.

- **California's Office of Permit Assistance (COPA).** This agency specializes in information about environmental regulatory agencies. Although COPA is officially meant only to assist with the state permitting process, it may be able to direct you to local or federal agencies dealing with toxics or other environmental hazards. Most often, the regulations COPA specializes in are triggered by new construction projects or other types of land development. COPA also publishes the very useful California Permit Handbook. You can reach COPA at 916-322-4245. Its Web address is http://commerce.ca.gov/business/permits_assist.

Insuring Your Business

Except for some specific types of insurance, such as liability insurance for a vehicle or unemployment insurance if you have employees, there's no legal requirement that you obtain property or liability insurance for your business. But just because you don't have to do it doesn't mean it's not a good idea. Even if you incorporate your business and shield your personal assets from business liabilities (see Chapter 2 for information on incorporating), that won't protect you from losing your business if disaster strikes. Careful as we may be, fate does sometimes deal us a blow, and you'll undoubtedly be thankful you've taken the steps to protect yourself if and when it does.

There is something of an art to insuring your business: you want to get the maximum protection from insurance without blowing your whole bankroll on policies for every conceivable risk. Once you start to look, you'll find every imaginable type of insurance policy out there, though your business will likely need only a few of them at most. The two most common and generally useful types of policies are property insurance and liability insurance. We'll explain the basics of these two types, and introduce you to the many other kinds of policies you can purchase to cover specific risks involved in your business. We'll also shine some light on the process of shopping for and buying the policies you need.

Employers are subject to special insurance rules. As discussed in Chapter 11, if you are an employer you will need to carry workers' compensation insurance, California Unemployment Insurance and State Disability Insurance. These insurance programs are specifically for employers and are largely regulated by the state. Refer to that chapter for the special rules governing employers' and employees' contributions to these insurance programs.

A. Property Insurance

As the name implies, property insurance simply covers you for damage or loss to your business property. There is, of course, a good deal of variation—on what property and what risks are covered, and to what extent—from policy to policy. Be sure you're absolutely clear on these issues when choosing a policy. As far as what property is covered, you'll want to make sure that the premises themselves, as well as the business property that's kept there are covered, including:

- fixtures to the property such as lighting systems or carpeting
- equipment and machinery
- furniture
- computers and accessories (monitors, CD-ROM drives, modems)
- inventory and supplies, and
- personal property that's kept at the business site.

If you rent your business space, your lease may require that you obtain a specific amount or type of property coverage. Be sure to check your lease for any insurance requirements before you purchase a policy.

If the policy you're considering excludes one or more items that you want covered, find out whether it can be included and at what cost. You may have to purchase what's commonly called a rider to add special coverage to the policy. There also may be other ways to bring the property you want covered under the scope of policy. For example, if you want the policy to cover your personal stereo, which you keep at your office, but the policy only covers business property, one option is to transfer title of the stereo to the business.

Besides establishing what property is covered under a property insurance policy, you'll need to understand which types of losses will be covered. Read a policy carefully to determine what causes of damage are insurable. The causes of damage that are commonly covered include fire, explosions, storms, smoke, riots, vandalism and sprinkler leaks. Often an insurance company will offer various packages, such as low-cost "basic coverage" that covers a certain number of risks and "broader coverage" that covers more risks for a higher premium. If a package covers almost all the risks, you're worried about but excludes one or two, such as flood damage, you can often have that coverage added to the policy for an extra premium.

If you have a home-based business, you may need to adjust your homeowner's policy. As discussed in Chapter 4, it's important for owners of home-based businesses to figure out whether their homeowner's policy forbids business use of the home or excludes coverage of business-related claims. You need to make sure that your homeowner's policy won't be limited or voided entirely by running a business out of your home. It's better to come clean with your insurance company about your home business and maybe spend some extra premium dollars than to find out after a catastrophe that your homeowner's coverage has been voided by your business activities. (See Chapter 4, Section D for more on home businesses.)

Finally, be sure you clearly understand the dollar limits on your policy, any deductibles or co-payments you'll have to make, and whether the policy covers the current value of property or its replacement cost.

B. Liability Insurance

Liability coverage insures you against the notorious slip-and-fall situation: someone injures himself on your premises and sues you for the ranch. A general liability policy (versus a product liability or vehicle liability policy, discussed below) will cover damages your business is ordered to pay to an individual (customer, supplier, business associate, whoever) who was injured on your property. Say, for instance, someone puts their foot through a floorboard weakened by dry rot, or trips on an electric cord, or is hit by a shelving unit that falls over. In this age of fast and furious personal injury lawsuits, one accident like this could result in a verdict against your business for thousands, tens of thousands or even millions of dollars, even if you were only marginally at fault. For this reason, liability insurance is advised for any business that has even minimal contact with the public.

A related, though technically different, type of insurance is product liability insurance, which protects you from lawsuits by customers claiming to be hurt by a product you provided. Remember the woman who sued McDonald's for millions after she was burned by their hot coffee? That's the type of thing product liability insurance is designed to protect against. If your business provides a product to the public that has a risk of harming anyone, you might consider this type of insurance—even if your risk seems as absurd as the scalding-coffee scenario. It can be expensive, but a lot less so than a multimillion dollar award to a victorious plaintiff.

Finally, be sure to obtain liability insurance (at the least) for any vehicles used for business, including employees' personal cars that are used for business purposes. This coverage will not be provided by a general liability policy (if you have one), and is required by California law.

C. The Wide World of Specialized Insurance Policies

Property and liability insurance are the two most important types of coverage for small businesses, but there are loads of other kinds of policies as well, many of which are designed for particular businesses. The following list includes some of the more common ones. Keep in mind that a broad property or liability policy might already cover one or more risks listed here. For instance, a reasonably broad property insurance policy should insure you against burglary. Check with your insurance agent or broker about whether your specific business might need one or more of these special types of coverage.

- Business interruption insurance

- Malpractice insurance

- Theft insurance, including burglary, robbery and employee theft

- Credit insurance for accounts receivable

- Intellectual property insurance

- Disability insurance for owners of the business (not the same as state-mandated disability insurance for employees, discussed in Chapter 11).

Valerie Hoecke,

owner of Fire Engine Red, a Web development firm:

I strongly recommend finding a reputable insurance broker in your area who can help you seek out affordable insurance (liability, property, even health) for your company. These people work off commissions from insurance companies, so you need to be sure you have an agent that is looking out for your needs at least as much as his or her own. A good agent that you trust can do a lot of legwork for you and can help you make informed decisions.

D. Investigating and Purchasing a Policy

The key to making an intelligent and cost-effective insurance purchase is to do your homework. Realize up front that understanding the fine-print details is absolutely essential in order to compare policies and purchase the best one for you. For example, when pricing out different insurance companies it's useless to compare two policies unless they cover the same types of property, the same risks, and up to the same dollar amounts. All these details need to be fully fleshed out and understood before you can make an informed decision.

Insurance brokers who gather information from different insurance companies can be of great help in deciphering policies and figuring out your best deal. Preferably, use a broker who's familiar with your type of business. Make sure she understands all the nooks and crannies of your specific business activities and the risks that are, or may be, involved.

You'll probably encounter insurance companies that offer package deals, which can often be cheaper than buying each individual policy separately. As long as all your needs are met, these package deals can be a good way to go. As always, be sure you understand the extent of each area of coverage rather than relying on any promises that the package covers "all your business needs."

Getting to Know Your Taxes

I t's no fun for any profitable business to share a big chunk of its hard-won earnings with the government. But like it or not, as soon as your business is in the black everyone, from your city and county to your state and, of course, the IRS, will demand a piece of the action. Although it's not necessary to become a tax expert before going into business, it is important for you to know what taxes you'll be subject to and how to go about paying them. Understanding the taxes you'll face will help you in at least three ways:

- You'll be better able to plan your finances, which may even involve deciding whether you'll have enough cash to stay in business.

- You'll be able to avoid tax-reporting and deposit errors, which can result in hefty—sometimes even business-threatening—penalties.

- You'll be able to make good business decisions that will also reduce your tax burden.

Even if your business won't make a fast profit, you may owe taxes. Lots of new businesspeople believe that if there is no profit, there is no tax. Sorry, but local taxes on gross receipts and taxes on sales of retail goods (sales taxes) are but two examples of taxes that need to be paid regardless of whether a business is turning a profit. So even if your business may not be profitable for a year or two, you need to prepare yourself for paying some taxes.

This chapter will give you simple, straightforward information on the taxes that owners of sole proprietorships, partnerships and LLCs will face. It will also provide basic instructions for filing and paying them correctly and on time. After covering the basics, we offer three sections that discuss the specific tax rules that vary according to business type. There's a separate section for sole proprietorships, partnerships and LLCs. Simply read the section that's appropriate for your business form. Then, in the next three sections, we cover paying estimated taxes, local taxes and taxes on

retail sales of goods, all of which apply more or less evenly to all business types. If your business has employees, refer to Chapter 11, "Your Healthy, Growing Business," for information on the special taxes faced by employers.

The details of corporate taxation are beyond the scope of this book. This chapter offers only some broad outlines of corporate taxation. The full maze of corporate tax rules is far too complicated for us to cover in detail. If you're thinking about incorporating, keep in mind that doing so will subject you to more complicated (and occasionally seriously unpleasant) tax rules. We present an overview of the potential tax advantages and disadvantages of this business form in Chapter 2, Section C. If you need detailed information beyond that, take a look at *Tax Savvy for Small Business*, by attorney Frederick Daily, or *How to Form Your Own California Corporation*, by attorney Tony Mancuso, both by Nolo Press.

You may need professional help to deal with your taxes. Tax rules and filing procedures can be quite complex, even for a relatively simple business. This chapter is meant to give you the big picture. Especially if your business is large, is incorporated or has a number of employees, you will likely need to do additional reading and possibly hire an experienced accountant or even a tax lawyer. Chapter 12 discusses other resources and publications for small business people, as well as how to work with experts.

A. Tax Basics

One of the first things you should understand is that there's little rhyme or reason to the world of taxes. Don't drive yourself nuts by trying to figure out the logic of a system that has virtually none. The bottom line is that in the U.S.—and especially in California—everything that breathes or moves (and lots of things that do neither) are taxed. And this includes virtually every aspect of a business that can be quantified. For example, depending on the type of business and its location, a business might be taxed on its gross income, net profit, gross retail sales, how many employees it has, how much employees are paid, how much property the business owns or leases, the seating capacity of the business, how many vehicles the business owns—the list goes on and on.

To complicate matters further, the many different taxes are administered by different government agencies, each with its own rules, forms and filing procedures. It's little wonder that the mere mention of taxes often induces nausea and sometimes even panic in otherwise well-adjusted businesspeople.

Talking About Income—Key Terms Defined

A lot of different jargon is used to describe the money that comes into and flows out of your business. These financial terms are discussed in more detail elsewhere in the book where we discuss financial projections and accounting (Chapters 5 and 10). But since these concepts are also important in understanding your taxes, here are some brief definitions.

- **Gross vs. net.** It's crucial to understand this distinction. "Gross" means total income, before deducting anything such as expenses. "Net" means what you have left over after subtracting costs and expenses. Thus "gross income" (sometimes called "gross receipts" or "gross sales") refers to the total money brought in by your business before any expenses such as rent or the cost of the product have been paid.

- **Fixed vs. variable expenses.** Fixed expenses are the ones that will be more or less the same regardless of how much business you're doing. They include rent, utility bills, insurance premiums and loan payments. Variable expenses are the costs of the products or services themselves and anything that goes along with your product, like packaging or shipping.

- **Current vs. capital expenses.** Current expenses include ordinary, day-to-day business expenses such as office supplies or salaries. For tax purposes, you can deduct them from your business income in the year that you pay them. Capital expenses, on the other hand, include payments for business assets (also called capital, fixed or depreciable assets) that have a useful life of at least one year. Capital expenses generally can't be deducted in the year they occur, but need to be deducted over a number of years—a process known as depreciation, capitalization or amortization.

- **Gross profit** refers to how much money you make on each sale above the cost of the item itself (its variable cost). The term "profit margin" or "gross margin" is also sometimes used to mean the same thing. The key thing to remember about gross profit is that fixed expenses such as rent or utility bills still haven't been taken from it.

- **Net profit** is what's left over after subtracting fixed expenses from gross profit. Put another way, net profit means the amount of money you have left over after subtracting all expenses—fixed and variable—from your gross income. Sometimes the term "net income" is used to mean the same thing as "net profit."

1. The Agencies Behind the Taxes

The first step in understanding small business taxes is to recognize who levies which taxes. Here's a quick breakdown.

- **Federal Taxes:** The United States Internal Revenue Service, the top dog of tax agencies, collects the following taxes from small businesses and their owners: taxes on personal or corporate income; self-employment taxes (which go to the Social Security and Medicare systems); and payroll taxes. (See Chapter 11 for information on payroll taxes.)

- **California Taxes:** The State of California collects the following taxes: taxes on personal or corporate income; franchise taxes on corporations; LLC taxes on LLCs; limited partnership taxes on limited partnerships; and sales taxes on sales of retail goods. (See Chapter 11 for information on payroll taxes.) California also collects special taxes (called excise taxes) on certain types of business activities such as distributing alcohol, cigarettes or gasoline.

- **County and City Taxes:** Your city or county, or both, will impose taxes on your business based upon several factors. Most cities assign businesses to categories (for example, retail businesses, wholesalers, services, to name a few) and then tax each category based on certain criteria such as gross receipts, gross payroll or number of employees. Counties in California assess and collect property taxes on real and personal property owned by businesses within the county. Cities and counties also impose a tax on retail sales of goods, though this tax is calculated and collected by the state along with the state sales tax.

A tax by any other name…is a fee. In addition to the taxes listed above, your business may have to pay additional fees for things like licenses and tax registration. For instance, many California cities and counties require all businesses in the area to register with the local tax collector and pay a registration fee. And if your business requires a special license such as a permit to handle food or a cosmetology license, you'll usually have to pay for it. While these fees arguably could be called taxes, we don't deal with them as such in this chapter. The various registration, permit and license requirements—including fees—for California small businesses are dealt with in Chapter 6, "Federal, State and Local Start-Up Requirements."

Forms and Schedules and Returns, Oh My!

We talk a lot in this chapter about tax forms, tax schedules and tax returns. Basically, these are simply different names for the papers you fill out with your financial information and submit to your federal, state or local tax agency. Technically, a tax form is the principal document that a taxpayer (either an individual or a corporation) completes with all the basic information about the taxpayer's income. For instance, a person who earns wages from a job simply fills out Form 1040. But if a taxpayer has income other than from a regular job, she must also file an additional sheet, called a schedule, to report that income. For instance, a business owner must submit Schedule C with the financial info from her business. Or if she earns royalties from a book she's written, she needs to report the royalty income on Schedule E. A tax return is a general term for the whole package you send off to the IRS: your form and any schedules.

2. Understanding Deductions

Maximizing profits while keeping taxes as low as possible is the name of the game in any business. The main way to do this is by claiming deductions, which means subtracting certain expenses from your taxable income. But of course you can't deduct just any old expense you want. To stay out of trouble with the IRS, California's Franchise Tax Board and your local tax collector, you need to understand which deductions are allowed and which ones are not.

Allowable deductions are outlined in great length (to put it mildly) in the Internal Revenue Code. You'll need to follow these rules when submitting your federal tax return to the IRS reporting your business income and deductions. When you file your state income tax return, you'll fill out a special form (Schedule CA) that uses the information from your federal return and makes adjustments to reflect California's different rules on deductibility of expenses. As far as local taxes go, they're often based on gross income (also called gross receipts), so no deductions are allowed. In short, the main rules for deductibility of business expenses that you need to worry about are the federal ones.

The Internal Revenue Code says that any ordinary and necessary expenses for your business can be subtracted from your business income for federal tax purposes (IRC § 162). For lots of expenses, it's a no-brainer whether they qualify. The cost of your products, rent for office space, equipment and machinery, office supplies, your business computer system, business insurance and office utility bills are just a few examples of costs that easily count as deductible expenses. As long as an expenditure is in fact made for business—not personal—purposes, the general rule is that you can deduct it from your business's gross income. But in addition to determining whether an expense is deductible, you need to understand a number of special rules that govern how particular expenses may be deducted.

One major distinction is between current expenses and capital expenses. Current expenses can best be described as your everyday costs of doing business, such as rent, supplies, utility bills and the like. These expenses are fully deductible in the year they occur. Capital expenses, on the other hand, are not fully deductible in the year you incur them. When you purchase an item with a useful life of at least one year—called a business asset—that expense qualifies as a capital expense. Business assets include items such as vehicles, furniture, heavy equipment (like a fork lift or printing press) and real estate. Rather than fully deducting a capital expense in the year it was made, you must spread out the deduction over a number of years. This process is variously called depreciation, amortization, or capitalization. Different types of assets have different depreciation rules, such as the number of years over which it must be depreciated. Depreciation rules are explained in IRS Publication 534, "Depreciation," as well as other IRS publications that cover specific types of assets.

		Federal Tax Requirements	State Tax Requirements	Local Tax Requirements
Sole Proprietorships	Business	• Employment taxes if there are employees	• Sales tax on sales of retail goods (Form BT-401) • Excise taxes on special activities	• Business Tax depends on local rules • Property tax assessed and collected by county
	Owner	• Income tax (Form 1040 with Schedule C) • Self-employment tax (Form 1040 with Schedule SE) • Estimated tax payments (Form 540-ES)	• Income tax (Form 540 with Schedule CA) • Estimated tax payments (Form 540-ES)	
Partnerships	Business	• Informational return (Form 1065, plus Schedule K-1 for each partner) • Employment taxes if there are employees	• Informational return (Form 565, plus Schedule K-1 (565) for each partner) • Sales tax on sales of retail goods (Form BT-401) • Excise taxes on special activities	• Business tax depends on local rules • Property tax assessed and collected by county
	Owners	• Income tax (Form 1040 with Schedule E) • Self-employment tax (Form 1040 with Schedule SE) • Estimated tax payments (Form 1040-ES)	• Income tax (Form 540 with Schedule CA) • Estimated tax payments (Form 540-ES)	
LLCs (partnership tax status)	Business	• Informational return (Form 1065, plus Schedule K-1 for each member) • Employment taxes if there are employees	• LLC tax (Form 3522) • LLC annual fee (Form 568) • Informational returns for each member's share of income (Schedule K-1 for each member submitted with Form 568) • Sales taxes on sales of retail goods (Form BT-401) • Excise taxes on special activities	• Business tax depends on local rules • Property tax assessed and collected by county
	Owners	• Income tax (Form 1040 with Schedule E) • Self-employment tax (Form 1040 with Schedule SE) • Estimated tax payments (Form 1040-ES)	• Income tax (Schedule CA with Form 540) • Estimated tax payments (Form 540-ES)	

		Federal Tax Requirements	State Tax Requirements	Local Tax Requirements
S Corporations	Business	• Informational return (Form 1120-S, plus Schedule K-1 for each shareholder) • Employment taxes if there are employees	• Franchise tax (Form 100-S) • Commencement tax (paid to Secretary of State when when Articles of Incorporation are filed) • Sales taxes on sales of retail goods (Form BT-401) • Excise taxes on special activities	• Business tax depends on local rules • Property tax assessed and collected by county
	Owners	• Income tax (Form 1040 with Schedule E) • Estimated tax payments (Form 1040 ES)	• Income tax (Form 540 with Schedule CA) • Estimated tax payments (Form 540-ES)	
C Corporations	Business	• Income tax (Form 1120) • Quarterly deposits of estimated tax (Form 8109) • Employment taxes if there are employees	• Franchise tax (Form 100) • Commencement tax (paid to Secretary of State when Articles of Incorporation are filed) • Estimated tax payments (Form 100-ES) • Sales taxes on sales of retail goods (Form BT-401) • Excise taxes on special activities	• Business tax depends on local rules • Property tax assessed and collected by county
	Owners	• Income tax (Forms vary depending on whether income is wages or dividends)	• Income tax (Forms vary depending on whether income is wages or dividends)	

For your reference as you read this chapter, here's a chart of all the basic tax-reporting and paying requirements for all types of businesses, including corporations. We've divided the taxes into those that are levied on the business itself (such as sales taxes) and those imposed on the business owner (such as income taxes) to give you a better idea of just which entity is actually being taxed. Of course, sole proprietors and partners are personally liable for the debts of their business—including any and all taxes.

There's a big exception to the rule that all capital expenses must be depreciated. The IRS allows businesses to treat a certain amount of capital expenditures as current expenses, and fully deduct them in the year they were made. This major exception is known as a 179 deduction, because it's established in the Internal Revenue Code section 179. In 1998, businesses can write off up to $18,500 in expenses that would normally qualify as capital expenditures. The limit goes up to $19,000 in 1999, and up to $20,000 in the year 2000. Whether and how much you should take advantage of a 179 deduction depends on your circumstances. Good general advice is to take a 179 deduction only when your taxable income is high enough that you'll get a decent tax benefit right away. Businesses with low incomes might want to depreciate assets instead, so that they'll have deductions available in future years when income might be higher. For more detailed information on the pros and cons of 179 deductions, see *Tax Savvy for Small Business,* by tax attorney Frederick W. Daily (Nolo Press).

Another important rule is that start-up expenses must be depreciated—you can't deduct their full cost in the year you make them. For lots of businesses, this rule isn't too much of a big deal because their profits in the first year of operation are so small that a big tax deduction wouldn't result in a lot of savings anyway.

Finally, the IRS has special rules for certain expenses such as travel, entertainment and vehicle expenses. These costs are deductible, but only according to special IRS rules.

The introduction to tax deductions we've given you in this section is only the tiniest scratch on the surface of a huge and complex body of information. The book *Tax Savvy for Small Business,* by tax attorney Frederick W. Daily (Nolo Press), does an excellent job of leading you through the maze. Especially as your business grows and its finances become more complicated, you may well want to hire an attorney or tax advisor to help you use the tax rules to your best advantage. (See Chapter 12 on hiring and working with attorneys and other professionals.)

Where to Get Tax Forms and Schedules

We don't include many federal or state tax forms in this book because they change from year to year, and are readily available from other sources. Besides the flood of tax forms that are available at post offices and libraries as April 15 comes near, you can always obtain the most current forms, schedules and publications by ordering them over the phone or downloading them off the Web.

- Order federal tax forms and other publications from the IRS by calling 800-829-3676. Or download them from the Web at http://www.irs.ustreas.gov/prod/forms_pubs/index.html.

- California Franchise Tax Board (FTB) forms can be ordered by phone at 800-338-0505, or downloaded from the Web at http://www.ftb.ca.gov/forms.

- Order forms from the California Board of Equalization (BOE) by calling 800-400-7115, or download them from the Web at http://www.boe.ca.gov/boelist.htm.

- Local tax forms and instructions are generally sent to businesses automatically once they've registered with their city or county.

B. Income Taxes for Sole Proprietors

As mentioned throughout this book, a sole proprietorship is one and the same as its owner (the sole proprietor) for most legal and tax purposes. It follows that federal and state income taxes must be paid directly by the sole proprietor on any profit she earns from her business.

1.   Federal Income Taxes

You're probably already familiar with the process of filing IRS Form 1040, based on income you earned at a job. Good—this means much of the process of filing federal income taxes as a sole proprietor will already be familiar to you. That's because income from your business will be treated as personal income, which you report on Form 1040 much as you report wages or returns on investments. But there are two additional steps: you'll use a separate sheet (called Schedule C) to report your business profit, and you'll also have to pay self-employment taxes based on your income (and file Schedule SE).

a.   Income Tax

Sole proprietors report business profits or losses on Schedule C (Profit or Loss From Business), which is submitted once a year with your 1040 return, usually by April 15. (See Sidebar in Section E3 for information on using a business year other than the calendar year for tax-reporting purposes.) If a sole proprietor owns more than one business, a separate Schedule C is used for each. An example of 1998 Schedule C and Form 1040 appears below. (See "Where to Get Tax Forms and Schedules" on page 8/8 for information on obtaining the most current forms.)

You're not required to file Schedule C if your sole proprietorship doesn't make at least $400 profit in the business year, though it's a good idea to file one anyway. One reason is that if your business loses money in any year, filing Schedule C allows that loss to be deducted from any other income you make for that year to reduce your total taxable income. Or you can carry over the loss into a future profitable year to offset those profits and thereby reduce your taxes. Another reason to report losses or profits under $400 on Schedule C is that doing so triggers the beginning of the time window during which the IRS can audit you (otherwise, the IRS can audit you virtually forever).

Simplified Tax Form for Super-Small Businesses

Teeny businesses may be able to use a simplified form to report their income, Schedule C-EZ. To use this simplified form, which provides the same Schedule C benefits as discussed in the text, the following criteria must be met:

- you have less than $25,000 in gross income
- you claim less than $2,500 in business expenses
- you have no inventory
- you have no employees
- you use the cash method of accounting
- you don't claim depreciation expenses to write off assets, and
- you don't report a net business loss.

Though it's easier to fill out than Schedule C, you won't save enough time or trouble to warrant trying to squeeze a too-large business into Schedule C-EZ. Don't, for example, neglect to claim over $2,500 in business expenses or to claim depreciation expenses just so you qualify to use the form. The marginal convenience of the simplified form just isn't worth it.

Besides using Schedule C, there's an important procedural difference between reporting and paying taxes on income from a job and income from a sole proprietorship: regular employees are subject to tax withholding by their employer, but sole proprietors must usually estimate their tax for the year and pay it in quarterly installments. The IRS is a stickler when it comes to making these quarterly payments and won't hesitate to fine you for doing it incorrectly or late, or especially for not doing it at all. Even if you pay your taxes in full by April 15 (or whenever your business year ends), failure to make quarterly payments means you'll be charged a steep penalty (9% annually). Be sure to read Section E, below, on who needs to make estimated quarterly tax payments and how to do it.

b. Self-Employment Taxes

Sole proprietors must also make separate payments for Social Security and Medicare, called self-employment taxes. Again, people who work as employees contribute to these programs through deductions from their paychecks that are matched by their employers. But sole proprietors and other self-employed individuals who make more than $400 profit per year must do so through federal self-employment taxes. For 1998, these include:

- Social Security tax of 12.4% on profits up to $65,400, and

- Medicare tax of 2.9% on all profits.

In other words, profits of $65,400 and less will be taxed at 15.3% (both Social Security and Medicare), and profits above that will be taxed at 2.9% (Medicare only). Fortunately, there is a small silver lining to this dark tax cloud; half of the total self-employment tax you'll pay can be deducted from your taxable income at year-end. And if your sole proprietorship makes less than $400 profit in the business year, no self-employment taxes need to be filed or paid.

Reporting and Paying Are Not the Same

As we discuss the often complex rules of taxes, keep in mind that a requirement that you must report income is not the same as an obligation to pay. Sometimes, a tax agency like the IRS or the California Franchise Tax Board requires you to submit a tax return even if you don't owe any taxes. Generally, a "filing" or "reporting" requirement means simply that you need to provide income and expense information, which may or may not add up to an actual tax obligation.

Self-employment taxes are reported on Schedule SE, which, like Schedule C (Profit or Loss from a Business), is submitted yearly with your 1040 income tax return. A sample of Schedule SE appears on page 8/14. (See "Where to Get Tax Forms and Schedules" on page 8/8 for information on obtaining the latest forms.) Once you determine the self-employment taxes you owe on Schedule SE, the result is entered on your 1040 form in the "Other Taxes" section, which is added to your personal income tax obligation. Remember, however, that many sole proprietors must estimate their total taxes for the year and pay them in quarterly installments. Read Section E, below, for details on estimated tax payments, which must be paid by most businesses owners.

2. California Income Taxes

California income tax is filed and paid in much the same way as federal income tax. Any profit generated by a sole proprietorship is treated as personal income of the sole proprietor and reported on Schedule CA, which is submitted with Form 540, California Resident Income Tax Return. Most 1998 California tax forms aren't available until January 1999. (See "Where to Get Tax Forms and Schedules" on page 8/8 to find out how to get current California tax forms.) Unlike the federal rule, you must file Schedule CA even if your business loses money. Obviously, you won't owe any taxes unless you've made a profit, but you must file the form in any case.

Like federal taxes, California income taxes for many businesses must be paid in quarterly installments. Estimating your taxes and making quarterly payments is covered in Section E, below.

C. Income Taxes for Partnerships

When it comes to federal and state income taxes for partnerships, the main thing to remember is that a partnership itself does not pay taxes, but it does need to submit returns to the IRS and the California Franchise Tax Board to report its income. As is true for a sole proprietorship, taxes are paid only by the partners (business owners), not the business itself. This section will explain what partnerships need to do to comply with the rules of the IRS and California's FTB.

SCHEDULE C (Form 1040)

Department of the Treasury
Internal Revenue Service   (99)

Profit or Loss From Business
(Sole Proprietorship)

▶ Partnerships, joint ventures, etc., must file Form 1065 or Form 1065-B.

▶ Attach to Form 1040 or Form 1041.   ▶ See Instructions for Schedule C (Form 1040).

OMB No. 1545-0074

98

Attachment Sequence No. 09

Name of proprietor

Social security number (SSN)

A Principal business or profession, including product or service (see page C-1)

B Enter NEW code from pages C-8 & 9 ▶

C Business name. If no separate business name, leave blank.

D Employer ID number (EIN), if any

E Business address (including suite or room no.) ▶
City, town or post office, state, and ZIP code

F Accounting method: (1) ☐ Cash (2) ☐ Accrual (3) ☐ Other (specify) ▶

G Did you "materially participate" in the operation of this business during 1998? If "No," see page C-2 for limit on losses   ☐ Yes ☐ No

H If you started or acquired this business during 1998, check here ▶ ☐

Part I Income

1 Gross receipts or sales. Caution: If this income was reported to you on Form W-2 and the "Statutory employee" box on that form was checked, see page C-3 and check here ▶ ☐ ... 1

2 Returns and allowances ... 2

3 Subtract line 2 from line 1 ... 3

4 Cost of goods sold (from line 42 on page 2) ... 4

5 Gross profit. Subtract line 4 from line 3 ... 5

6 Other income, including Federal and state gasoline or fuel tax credit or refund (see page C-3) ... 6

7 Gross income. Add lines 5 and 6 ▶ 7

Part II Expenses. Enter expenses for business use of your home only on line 30.

8 Advertising ... 8
9 Bad debts from sales or services (see page C-3) ... 9
10 Car and truck expenses (see page C-3) ... 10
11 Commissions and fees ... 11
12 Depletion ... 12
13 Depreciation and section 179 expense deduction (not included in Part III) (see page C-4) ... 13
14 Employee benefit programs (other than on line 19) ... 14
15 Insurance (other than health) ... 15
16 Interest:
a Mortgage (paid to banks, etc.) ... 16a
b Other ... 16b
17 Legal and professional services ... 17
18 Office expense ... 18

19 Pension and profit-sharing plans ... 19
20 Rent or lease (see page C-5):
a Vehicles, machinery, and equipment ... 20a
b Other business property ... 20b
21 Repairs and maintenance ... 21
22 Supplies (not included in Part III) ... 22
23 Taxes and licenses ... 23
24 Travel, meals, and entertainment:
a Travel ... 24a
b Meals and entertainment ...
c Enter 50% of line 24b subject to limitations (see page C-6) ...
d Subtract line 24c from line 24b ... 24d
25 Utilities ... 25
26 Wages (less employment credits) ... 26
27 Other expenses (from line 48 on page 2) ... 27

28 Total expenses before expenses for business use of home. Add lines 8 through 27 in columns ▶ 28

29 Tentative profit (loss). Subtract line 28 from line 7 ... 29
30 Expenses for business use of your home. Attach Form 8829 ... 30
31 Net profit or (loss). Subtract line 30 from line 29.
c If a profit, enter on Form 1040, line 12, and ALSO on Schedule SE, line 2 (statutory employees, see page C-6). Estates and trusts, enter on Form 1041, line 3.
c If a loss, you MUST go on to line 32. ... 31
32 If you have a loss, check the box that describes your investment in this activity (see page C-6).
c If you checked 32a, enter the loss on Form 1040, line 12, and ALSO on Schedule SE, line 2 (statutory employees, see page C-6). Estates and trusts, enter on Form 1041, line 3.
c If you checked 32b, you MUST attach Form 6198.
32a ☐ All investment is at risk.
32b ☐ Some investment is not at risk.

For Paperwork Reduction Act Notice, see Form 1040 instructions.   Cat. No. 11334P   Schedule C (Form 1040) 1998

Schedule C (Form 1040) 1998   Page 2

Part III Cost of Goods Sold (see page C-7)

33 Method(s) used to value closing inventory: a ☐ Cost b ☐ Lower of cost or market c ☐ Other (attach explanation)

34 Was there any change in determining quantities, costs, or valuations between opening and closing inventory? If "Yes," attach explanation ... ☐ Yes ☐ No

35 Inventory at beginning of year. If different from last year's closing inventory, attach explanation ... 35
36 Purchases less cost of items withdrawn for personal use ... 36
37 Cost of labor. Do not include any amounts paid to yourself ... 37
38 Materials and supplies ... 38
39 Other costs ... 39
40 Add lines 35 through 39 ... 40
41 Inventory at end of year ... 41
42 Cost of goods sold. Subtract line 41 from line 40. Enter the result here and on page 1, line 4 ... 42

Part IV Information on Your Vehicle. Complete this part ONLY if you are claiming car or truck expenses on line 10 and are not required to file Form 4562 for this business. See the instructions for line 13 on page C-4 to find out if you must file.

43 When did you place your vehicle in service for business purposes? (month, day, year) ▶ ... / ... / ...

44 Of the total number of miles you drove your vehicle during 1998, enter the number of miles you used your vehicle for:
a Business ... b Commuting ... c Other ...

45 Do you (or your spouse) have another vehicle available for personal use? ... ☐ Yes ☐ No
46 Was your vehicle available for use during off-duty hours? ... ☐ Yes ☐ No
47a Do you have evidence to support your deduction? ... ☐ Yes ☐ No
b If "Yes," is the evidence written? ... ☐ Yes ☐ No

Part V Other Expenses. List below business expenses not included on lines 8–26 or line 30.

48 Total other expenses. Enter here and on page 1, line 27 ... 48

Form **1040**
Department of the Treasury—Internal Revenue Service
U.S. Individual Income Tax Return **1998** (99) IRS Use Only—Do not write or staple in this space.

For the year Jan. 1–Dec. 31, 1998, or other tax year beginning , 1998, ending , 19   OMB No. 1545-0074

Label
(See instructions on page 18.)
Use the IRS label. Otherwise, please print or type.

Your first name and initial | Last name | Your social security number
If a joint return, spouse's first name and initial | Last name | Spouse's social security number
Home address (number and street). If you have a P.O. box, see page 18. | Apt. no.
City, town or post office, state, and ZIP code. If you have a foreign address, see page 18.

▲ **IMPORTANT!** ▲
You must enter your SSN(s) above.

Presidential Election Campaign (See page 18.)
Do you want $3 to go to this fund? ... Yes No
If a joint return, does your spouse want $3 to go to this fund?

Note: Checking "Yes" will not change your tax or reduce your refund.

Filing Status
Check only one box.
1 □ Single
2 □ Married filing joint return (even if only one had income)
3 □ Married filing separate return. Enter spouse's social security no. above and full name here. ▶
4 □ Head of household (with qualifying person). (See page 18.) If the qualifying person is a child but not your dependent, enter this child's name here. ▶
5 □ Qualifying widow(er) with dependent child (year spouse died ▶ 19). (See page 18.)

Exemptions
6a □ Yourself. If your parent (or someone else) can claim you as a dependent on his or her tax return, do not check box 6a.
b □ Spouse
c Dependents:
(1) First name Last name | (2) Dependent's social security number | (3) Dependent's relationship to you | (4) ✓ if qualifying child for child tax credit (see page 19)

No. of boxes checked on 6a and 6b
No. of your children on 6c who:
● lived with you
● did not live with you due to divorce or separation (see page 19)
Dependents on 6c not entered above
Add numbers entered on lines above

If more than six dependents, see page 19.
d Total number of exemptions claimed

Income
Attach Copy B of your Forms W-2, W-2G, and 1099-R here.
If you did not get a W-2, see page 20.
Enclose, but do not staple, any payment. Also, please use Form 1040-V.

7 Wages, salaries, tips, etc. Attach Form(s) W-2 ... 7
8a Taxable interest. Attach Schedule B if required ... 8a
b Tax-exempt interest. DO NOT include on line 8a ... 8b
9 Ordinary dividends. Attach Schedule B if required ... 9
10 Taxable refunds, credits, or offsets of state and local income taxes (see page 21) ... 10
11 Alimony received ... 11
12 Business income or (loss). Attach Schedule C or C-EZ ... 12
13 Capital gain or (loss). Attach Schedule D ... 13
14 Other gains or (losses). Attach Form 4797 ... 14
15a Total IRA distributions 15a | b Taxable amount (see page 22) 15b
16a Total pensions and annuities 16a | b Taxable amount (see page 22) 16b
17 Rental real estate, royalties, partnerships, S corporations, trusts, etc. Attach Schedule E ... 17
18 Farm income or (loss). Attach Schedule F ... 18
19 Unemployment compensation ... 19
20a Social security benefits 20a | b Taxable amount (see page 24) 20b
21 Other income. List type and amount—see page 24 ... 21
22 Add the amounts in the far right column for lines 7 through 21. This is your **total income** ▶ 22

Adjusted Gross Income
If line 33 is under $30,095 (under $10,030 if a child did not live with you), see EIC inst. on page 36.

23 IRA deduction (see page 25) 23
24 Student loan interest deduction (see page 27) 24
25 Medical savings account deduction. Attach Form 8853 25
26 Moving expenses. Attach Form 3903 26
27 One-half of self-employment tax. Attach Schedule SE 27
28 Self-employed health insurance deduction (see page 28) 28
29 Keogh and self-employed SEP and SIMPLE plans 29
30 Penalty on early withdrawal of savings 30
31a Alimony paid b Recipient's SSN ▶ 31a
32 Add lines 23 through 31a ... 32
33 Subtract line 32 from line 22. This is your **adjusted gross income** ▶ 33

For Disclosure, Privacy Act, and Paperwork Reduction Act Notice, see page 51.   Cat. No. 11320B   Form **1040** (1998)

Form 1040 (1998)   Page 2

Tax and Credits

34 Amount from line 33 (adjusted gross income) ... 34
35a Check if: □ You were 65 or older, □ Blind; □ Spouse was 65 or older, □ Blind.
Add the number of boxes checked above and enter the total here ... ▶ 35a
b If you are married filing separately and your spouse itemizes deductions or you were a dual-status alien, see page 29 and check here ... ▶ 35b □

Standard Deduction for Most People
Single: $4,250
Head of household: $6,250
Married filing jointly or Qualifying widow(er): $7,100
Married filing separately: $3,550

36 Enter the larger of your itemized deductions from Schedule A, line 28, OR standard deduction shown on the left. But see page 30 to find your standard deduction if you checked any box on line 35a or 35b or if someone can claim you as a dependent ... 36
37 Subtract line 36 from line 34 ... 37
38 If line 34 is $93,400 or less, multiply $2,700 by the total number of exemptions claimed on line 6d. If line 34 is over $93,400, see the worksheet on page 30 for the amount to enter ... 38
39 **Taxable income.** Subtract line 38 from line 37. If line 38 is more than line 37, enter -0- ... 39
40 **Tax.** See page 30. Check if any tax is from a □ Form(s) 8814 b □ Form 4972 ▶ 40
41 Credit for child and dependent care expenses. Attach Form 2441 41
42 Credit for the elderly or the disabled. Attach Schedule R. 42
43 Child tax credit (see page 31) 43
44 Education credits. Attach Form 8863 44
45 Adoption credit. Attach Form 8839 45
46 Foreign tax credit. Attach Form 1116 if required 46
47 Other. Check if from a □ Form 3800 b □ Form 8396 c □ Form 8801 d □ Form (specify) 47
48 Add lines 41 through 47. These are your **total credits** ... 48
49 Subtract line 48 from line 40. If line 48 is more than line 40, enter -0- ... 49

Other Taxes
50 Self-employment tax. Attach Schedule SE ... 50
51 Alternative minimum tax. Attach Form 6251 ... 51
52 Social security and Medicare tax on tip income not reported to employer. Attach Form 4137 52
53 Tax on IRAs, other retirement plans, and MSAs. Attach Form 5329 if required 53
54 Advance earned income credit payments from Form(s) W-2 54
55 Household employment taxes. Attach Schedule H 55
56 Add lines 49 through 55. This is your **total tax.** ▶ 56

Payments
Attach Forms W-2 and W-2G on the front. Also attach Form 1099-R if tax was withheld.

57 Federal income tax withheld from Forms W-2 and 1099 57
58 1998 estimated tax payments and amount applied from 1997 return. 58
59a Earned income credit. Attach Schedule EIC if you have a qualifying child b Nontaxable earned income: amount ▶ and type ▶ 59a
60 Additional child tax credit. Attach Form 8812 60
61 Amount paid with Form 4868 (request for extension) 61
62 Excess social security and RRTA tax withheld (see page 43) 62
63 Other payments. Check if from a □ Form 2439 b □ Form 4136 63
64 Add lines 57, 58, 59a, and 60 through 63. These are your **total payments** ▶ 64

Refund
Have it directly deposited! See page 44 and fill in 66b, 66c, and 66d.

65 If line 64 is more than line 56, subtract line 56 from line 64. This is the amount you **OVERPAID** 65
66a Amount of line 65 you want **REFUNDED TO YOU.** ▶ 66a
▶ b Routing number c Type: □ Checking □ Savings
▶ d Account number
67 Amount of line 65 you want **APPLIED TO YOUR 1999 ESTIMATED TAX** ▶ 67

Amount You Owe
68 If line 56 is more than line 64, subtract line 64 from line 56. This is the **AMOUNT YOU OWE.** For details on how to pay, see page 44 ... 68
69 Estimated tax penalty. Also include on line 68 69

Sign Here
Joint return? See page 18.
Keep a copy for your records.
Under penalties of perjury, I declare that I have examined this return and accompanying schedules and statements, and to the best of my knowledge and belief, they are true, correct, and complete. Declaration of preparer (other than taxpayer) is based on all information of which preparer has any knowledge.
Your signature | Date | Your occupation
Spouse's signature. If a joint return, BOTH must sign. | Date | Spouse's occupation
Daytime telephone number (optional)

Paid Preparer's Use Only
Preparer's signature | Date | Check if self-employed □ | Preparer's social security no.
Firm's name (or yours if self-employed) and address | EIN | ZIP code

Form **1040** (1998)

1.   Federal Income Taxes

As discussed elsewhere in this book, partnerships are called "pass-through tax entities," which means that profits pass right through the business to the owners, who report them on their personal income tax returns. (Although few do, partnerships can also elect to be taxed as a separate entity like corporations, by submitting Form 8832 and electing corporate tax status.) The partnership itself is not taxed, though it must report its income and losses each year. Besides income taxes, partners must also file and pay self-employment taxes.

a.   Income Tax

Even though the partnership itself does not pay taxes on profits, it must report profits and losses using an informational return, Form 1065, U.S. Partnership Return of Income. No tax is due with this return, which is generally due by April 15. (See Sidebar in Section E3 for information on defining a business year other than the calendar year.)

Along with Form 1065, the partnership must also submit a Schedule K-1, Partner's Share of Income, Credit and Deductions, for each partner, reporting each partner's share of profits or losses. (The K-1 form is also used to inform the IRS of your chosen profit division. Often, partners own equal shares of the business, which normally means they will choose to share profits and pay taxes equally—such as four partners each getting 1/4 of a business's profits and paying 1/4 of its taxes. But if they so choose, partners can divide profits and losses in another way. See Chapter 2 for more on partnerships.) A copy of the completed K-1 must also be given to each partner on or before the date that the partnership return is due to the IRS. (Page 8/8 includes information on obtaining current forms.)

As we mentioned above, profits earned by a partnership are taxed as personal income of the individual partners. Each partner reports business income or losses on their personal federal income tax return (Form 1040) using Schedule E (Supplemental Income and Loss). Schedule E, which has enough space to report income from up to five

different partnerships, repeats the information reported about that partner's income on Schedule K-1 (which each partner should have received from the partnership). Since the partnership already filed Schedule K-1, partners do not need to. An example of Schedule E appears on page 8/16.

Partners who earn income from a profitable partnership often must estimate their taxes in advance and pay the total in quarterly installments. Section E, below, covers estimated tax payments, an important aspect of taxes for all small businesses.

b.   Self-Employment Taxes

Partners and other self-employed individuals who earn more than $400 profit in the business year must contribute to Social Security and Medicare through federal self-employment taxes. In 1998, self-employment taxes include:

- Social Security tax of 12.4% on profits up to $65,400, and

- Medicare tax of 2.9% on all profits.

Profits of $65,400 and less will be taxed at 15.3% (both Social Security and Medicare), and profits above that will be taxed at 2.9% (Medicare only). Fortunately, there is a small silver lining to this dark tax cloud; half of the total self-employment tax you'll pay can be deducted from your taxable income at year-end. And if your partnership makes less than $400 profit in the business year, no self-employment taxes need be filed or paid. (See Sidebar in Section B1, above, if you're confused about the difference between filing taxes and paying them.)

Self-employment taxes are reported on Schedule SE which, like Schedule E (Supplemental Income and Loss), is submitted yearly with a partner's 1040 return. (See page 8/14 for a sample of Schedule SE.) Once you determine your self-employment tax with Schedule SE, the result is entered on your 1040 form in the "Other Taxes" section, which is added to your personal income tax obligation. But don't forget about paying taxes in advance—most profitable businesses must do so, or face the IRS's penalties. Ouch. (See Section E, below.)

SCHEDULE SE
(Form 1040)
Department of the Treasury
Internal Revenue Service

Self-Employment Tax

► See Instructions for Schedule SE (Form 1040).
► Attach to Form 1040.

OMB No. 1545-0074

98

Attachment Sequence No. 17

Name of person with self-employment income (as shown on Form 1040)

Social security number of person with self-employment income ►

Who Must File Schedule SE

You must file Schedule SE if:

c You had net earnings from self-employment from other than church employee income (line 4 of Short Schedule SE or line 4c of Long Schedule SE) of $400 or more, OR

c You had church employee income of $108.28 or more. Income from services you performed as a minister or a member of a religious order is not church employee income. See page SE-1.

Note: Even if you had a loss or a small amount of income from self-employment, it may be to your benefit to file Schedule SE and use either "optional method" in Part II of Long Schedule SE. See page SE-3.

Exception. If your only self-employment income was from earnings as a minister, member of a religious order, or Christian Science practitioner and you filed Form 4361 and received IRS approval not to be taxed on those earnings, do not file Schedule SE. Instead, write "Exempt-Form 4361" on Form 1040, line 50.

May I Use Short Schedule SE or MUST I Use Long Schedule SE?

DID YOU RECEIVE WAGES OR TIPS IN 1998?

Was the total of your wages and tips subject to social security or railroad retirement tax plus your net earnings from self-employment more than $68,400?

Are you a minister, member of a religious order or Christian Science practitioner who received IRS approval not to be taxed on earnings from these sources, but you owe self-employment tax on other earnings?

Did you receive tips subject to social security or Medicare tax that you did not report to your employer?

Are you using one of the optional methods to figure your net earnings (see page SE-3)?

Did you receive church employee income reported on Form W-2 of $108.28 or more?

YOU MAY USE SHORT SCHEDULE SE BELOW

YOU MUST USE LONG SCHEDULE SE ON THE BACK

Section A—Short Schedule SE. Caution: Read above to see if you can use Short Schedule SE.

1 Net farm profit or (loss) from Schedule F, line 36, and farm partnerships, Schedule K-1 (Form 1065), line 15a ... **1**

2 Net profit or (loss) from Schedule C, line 31; Schedule C-EZ, line 3; Schedule K-1 (Form 1065), line 15a (other than farming); and Schedule K-1 (Form 1065-B), box 9. Ministers and members of religious orders, see page SE-1 for amounts to report on this line. See page SE-2 for other income to report ... **2**

3 Combine lines 1 and 2 ... **3**

4 Net earnings from self-employment. Multiply line 3 by 92.35% (.9235). If less than $400, do not file this schedule; you do not owe self-employment tax ... **4**

5 Self-employment tax. If the amount on line 4 is:

c $68,400 or less, multiply line 4 by 15.3% (.153). Enter the result here and on Form 1040, line 50.

c More than $68,400, multiply line 4 by 2.9% (.029). Then, add $8,481.60 to the result. Enter the total here and on Form 1040, line 50 ... **5**

6 Deduction for one-half of self-employment tax. Multiply line 5 by 50% (.5). Enter the result here and on Form 1040, line 27 ... **6**

For Paperwork Reduction Act Notice, see Form 1040 instructions.   Cat. No. 11358Z   Schedule SE (Form 1040) 1998

Schedule SE (Form 1040) 1998   Page 2

Name of person with self-employment income (as shown on Form 1040)

Social security number of person with self-employment income ►

Attachment Sequence No. 17

Section B—Long Schedule SE

Part I   Self-Employment Tax

Note: If your only income subject to self-employment tax is church employee income, skip lines 1 through 4b. Enter -0- on line 4c and go to line 5a. Income from services you performed as a minister or a member of a religious order is not church employee income. See page SE-1.

A If you are a minister, member of a religious order, or Christian Science practitioner and you filed Form 4361, but you had $400 or more of other net earnings from self-employment, check here and continue with Part I ... ► ☐

1 Net farm profit or (loss) from Schedule F, line 36, and farm partnerships, Schedule K-1 (Form 1065), line 15a. Note: Skip this line if you use the farm optional method. See page SE-4 ... **1**

2 Net profit or (loss) from Schedule C, line 31; Schedule C-EZ, line 3; Schedule K-1 (Form 1065), line 15a (other than farming); and Schedule K-1 (Form 1065-B), box 9. Ministers and members of religious orders, see page SE-1 for amounts to report on this line. See page SE-2 for other income to report. Note: Skip this line if you use the nonfarm optional method. See page SE-4. ... **2**

3 Combine lines 1 and 2 ... **3**

4a If line 3 is more than zero, multiply line 3 by 92.35% (.9235). Otherwise, enter amount from line 3 ... **4a**

b If you elected one or both of the optional methods, enter the total of lines 15 and 17 here ... **4b**

c Combine lines 4a and 4b. If less than $400, do not file this schedule; you do not owe self-employment tax. Exception. If less than $400 and you had church employee income, enter -0- and continue ► ... **4c**

5a Enter your church employee income from Form W-2. Caution: See page SE-1 for definition of church employee income ... **5a**

b Multiply line 5a by 92.35% (.9235). If less than $100, enter -0- ... **5b**

6 Net earnings from self-employment. Add lines 4c and 5b ... **6**

7 Maximum amount of combined wages and self-employment earnings subject to social security tax or the 6.2% portion of the 7.65% railroad retirement (tier 1) tax for 1998 ... **7** 68,400 00

8a Total social security wages and tips (total of boxes 3 and 7 on Form(s) W-2) and railroad retirement (tier 1) compensation ... **8a**

b Unreported tips subject to social security tax (from Form 4137, line 9) ... **8b**

c Add lines 8a and 8b ... **8c**

9 Subtract line 8c from line 7. If zero or less, enter -0- here and on line 10 and go to line 11 ... ► **9**

10 Multiply the smaller of line 6 or line 9 by 12.4% (.124) ... **10**

11 Multiply line 6 by 2.9% (.029) ... **11**

12 Self-employment tax. Add lines 10 and 11. Enter here and on Form 1040, line 50 ... **12**

13 Deduction for one-half of self-employment tax. Multiply line 12 by 50% (.5). Enter the result here and on Form 1040, line 27 ... **13**

Part II   Optional Methods To Figure Net Earnings   (See page SE-3.)

Farm Optional Method. You may use this method only if:

c Your gross farm income [1] was not more than $2,400, or

c Your gross farm income [1] was more than $2,400 and your net farm profits [2] were less than $1,733.

14 Maximum income for optional methods ... **14** 1,600 00

15 Enter the smaller of: two-thirds (⅔) of gross farm income [1] (not less than zero) or $1,600. Also, include this amount on line 4b above ... **15**

Nonfarm Optional Method. You may use this method only if:

c Your net nonfarm profits [3] were less than $1,733 and also less than 72.189% of your gross nonfarm income [4] and

c You had net earnings from self-employment of at least $400 in 2 of the prior 3 years.

Caution: You may use this method no more than five times.

16 Subtract line 15 from line 14 ... **16**

17 Enter the smaller of: two-thirds (⅔) of gross nonfarm income [4] (not less than zero) or the amount on line 16. Also, include this amount on line 4b above ... **17**

[1] From Sch. F, line 11, and Sch. K-1 (Form 1065), line 15b.   [2] From Sch. C, line 31; Sch. C-EZ, line 3; Sch. K-1 (Form 1065), line 15a; and Sch. K-1 (Form 1065-B), box 9.
[3] From Sch. F, line 36, and Sch. K-1 (Form 1065), line 15a.   [4] From Sch. C, line 7; Sch. C-EZ, line 1; Sch. K-1 (Form 1065), line 15c; and Sch. K-1 (Form 1065-B), box 9.

Schedule SE (Form 1040) 1998

2. California Income Taxes

Like the federal government, the state of California requires partnerships to file an informational return reporting business income and losses. Fortunately, California Form 565—which is filed with the state Franchise Tax Board (FTB)—is almost identical to the federal Form 1065. Also like the federal system, a partnership must submit to the FTB a Schedule K-1—in California aptly called a Schedule K-1 (565)—for each partner indicating the partner's share of the business profit or loss, and give each partner a copy. The California version of Schedule K-1 (565) is similar to the federal version, but accounts for differences between California and federal tax laws. No tax is due with the partnership return or schedules.

Any partnership profit is taxed as personal income of the partners, who report their share on Schedule CA, which should reflect the information from California Schedule K-1 (565). Schedule CA is submitted with Form 540, California Resident Income Tax Return. Partners do *not* submit the state Schedule K-1 (565) with their state return. Unlike the federal rule for partners, a partner must file Schedule CA with the FTB even if the partnership loses money and no taxes are due.

Finally, like federal taxes, California income taxes must be paid in quarterly installments. Estimating your taxes and making quarterly payments are covered in Section E, below.

D. Income Taxes for LLCs

The limited liability company (LLC), which is explained in greater detail in Chapter 2, Section D, is a relatively new business form. LLCs combine several key attributes that distinguish the traditional partnership and corporation, allowing LLC owners (usually called members) to enjoy the limited personal liability of a corporation, yet avoid the complicated and often expensive corporate tax system by choosing to be taxed as individuals (like a sole proprietor or partners). Although LLC members can also choose to be taxed like a corporation, this choice is somewhat unusual (but see Chapter 2, Section D, for why some LLCs may decide to be taxed like a corporation); this section will assume your LLC will stick with pass-through tax status.

1. Federal Income Taxes

Like owners of partnerships, most LLC owners will report business profits on their personal income tax returns. Although this means the LLC itself is not taxed, it must still report its income and losses each year. Besides regular income taxes, members must pay self-employment taxes, which are also based on business income.

a. Income Tax

Even though the LLC itself does not pay taxes on profits, like a partnership it must file an informational return with the IRS. Since the IRS hasn't yet come up with tax forms specifically for LLCs, LLC profits and losses are reported on Form 1065, U.S. Partnership Return of Income. No tax is due with this return, which is generally due by April 15. (See Sidebar in Section E3 for information on defining a business year other than the calendar year.)

Along with Form 1065, an LLC must also submit a Schedule K-1 (again, the same form used by partnerships) to the IRS for each member reporting each member's share of profits or losses. (The K-1 form is also used to inform the IRS of your chosen profit division. Often, members own equal shares of the business, which normally means they will choose to share profits and pay taxes equally—such as four members each getting 1/4 of a business's profits and paying 1/4 of its taxes. But if they so choose, LLC members can divide profits and losses in another way. (See Chapter 2, Section D for more on LLCs and ownership shares). A copy of the completed K-1 must also be given to each member on or before the date that the LLC return is due to the IRS.

SCHEDULE E (Form 1040)

Department of the Treasury
Internal Revenue Service (99)

OMB No. 1545-0074

98

Attachment Sequence No. **13**

Supplemental Income and Loss

(From rental real estate, royalties, partnerships,
S corporations, estates, trusts, REMICs, etc.)

▶ Attach to Form 1040 or Form 1041.   ▶ See Instructions for Schedule E (Form 1040).

Name(s) shown on return

Your social security number

Part I Income or Loss From Rental Real Estate and Royalties   Note: Report income and expenses from your business of renting personal property on Schedule C or C-EZ (see page E-1). Report farm rental income or loss from Form 4835 on page 2, line 39.

1 Show the kind and location of each rental real estate property:

A

B

C

2 For each rental real estate property listed on line 1, did you or your family use it during the tax year for personal purposes for more than the greater of:
  - 14 days, or
  - 10% of the total days rented at fair rental value?
  (See page E-1.)

	Yes	No
A		
B		
C		

Income:

Properties

		A	B	C	Totals (Add columns A, B, and C.)
3	Rents received				3
4	Royalties received				4

Expenses:

5	Advertising				
6	Auto and travel (see page E-2)				
7	Cleaning and maintenance				
8	Commissions				
9	Insurance				
10	Legal and other professional fees				
11	Management fees				
12	Mortgage interest paid to banks, etc. (see page E-2)				12
13	Other interest				
14	Repairs				
15	Supplies				
16	Taxes				
17	Utilities				
18	Other (list) ▶				
19	Add lines 5 through 18				19
20	Depreciation expense or depletion (see page E-3)				20
21	Total expenses. Add lines 19 and 20				
22	Income or (loss) from rental real estate or royalty properties. Subtract line 21 from line 3 (rents) or line 4 (royalties). If the result is a (loss), see page E-3 to find out if you must file Form 6198				
23	Deductible rental real estate loss. Caution: Your rental real estate loss on line 22 may be limited. See page E-3 to find out if you must file Form 8582. Real estate professionals must complete line 42 on page 2			( )	
24	Income. Add positive amounts shown on line 22. Do not include any losses				24
25	Losses. Add royalty losses from line 22 and rental real estate losses from line 23. Enter total losses here				25 ( )
26	Total rental real estate and royalty income or (loss). Combine lines 24 and 25. Enter the result here. If Parts II, III, IV, and line 39 on page 2 do not apply to you, also enter this amount on Form 1040, line 17. Otherwise, include this amount in the total on line 40 on page 2				26

For Paperwork Reduction Act Notice, see Form 1040 instructions.   Cat. No. 11344L   Schedule E (Form 1040) 1998

Schedule E (Form 1040) 1998   Attachment Sequence No. 13   Page 2

Name(s) shown on return. Do not enter name and social security number if shown on other side.   Your social security number

Note: If you report amounts from farming or fishing on Schedule E, you must enter your gross income from those activities on line 41 below. Real estate professionals must complete line 42 below.

Part II Income or Loss From Partnerships and S Corporations   Note: If you report a loss from an at-risk activity, you MUST check either column (e) or (f) on line 27 to describe your investment in the activity. See page E-5. If you check column (f), you must attach Form 6198.

27

	(a) Name	(b) Enter P for partnership, S for S corporation	(c) Check if foreign partnership	(d) Employer identification number	(e) All is	(f) Some is not at risk
A						
B						
C						
D						
E						

Passive Income and Loss | | | Nonpassive Income and Loss | | |

	(g) Passive loss allowed (attach Form 8582 if required)	(h) Passive income from Schedule K-1	(i) Nonpassive loss from Schedule K-1	(j) Section 179 expense deduction from Form 4562	(k) Nonpassive income from Schedule K-1
A					
B					
C					
D					
E					
28a Totals					
b Totals					

29	Add columns (h) and (k) of line 28a		29	
30	Add columns (g), (i), and (j) of line 28b		30 ( )
31	Total partnership and S corporation income or (loss). Combine lines 29 and 30. Enter the result here and include in the total on line 40 below		31	

Part III Income or Loss From Estates and Trusts

32

	(a) Name
A	
B	

Passive Income and Loss | | Nonpassive Income and Loss | |

	(b) Employer identification number	(c) Passive deduction or loss allowed (attach Form 8582 if required)	(d) Passive income from Schedule K-1	(e) Deduction or loss from Schedule K-1	(f) Other income from Schedule K-1
A					
B					
33a Totals					
b Totals					

34	Add columns (d) and (f) of line 33a		34	
35	Add columns (c) and (e) of line 33b		35 ( )
36	Total estate and trust income or (loss). Combine lines 34 and 35. Enter the result here and include in the total on line 40 below		36	

Part IV Income or Loss From Real Estate Mortgage Investment Conduits (REMICs)—Residual Holder

37

	(a) Name	(b) Employer identification number	(c) Excess inclusion from Schedules Q, line 2c (see page E-6)	(d) Taxable income (net loss) from Schedules Q, line 1b	(e) Income from Schedules Q, line 3b

| 38 | Combine columns (d) and (e) only. Enter the result here and include in the total on line 40 below | | 38 | |

Part V Summary

39	Net farm rental income or (loss) from Form 4835. Also, complete line 41 below		39	
40	TOTAL income or (loss). Combine lines 26, 31, 36, 38, and 39. Enter the result here and on Form 1040, line 17 ▶		40	
41	Reconciliation of Farming and Fishing Income. Enter your gross farming and fishing income reported on Form 4835, line 7; Schedule K-1 (Form 1065), line 15b; Schedule K-1 (Form 1120S), line 23; and Schedule K-1 (Form 1041), line 14 (see page E-6)	41		
42	Reconciliation for Real Estate Professionals. If you were a real estate professional (see page E-4), enter the net income or (loss) you reported anywhere on Form 1040 from all rental real estate activities in which you materially participated under the passive activity loss rules	42		

Profits earned by an LLC are taxed as personal income of the individual members. The information from Schedule K-1 is used by members to report business income or losses on their personal federal income tax returns (Form 1040) using Schedule E (Supplemental Income and Loss). Since the LLC already filed Schedule K-1, members do not need to. Schedule E has enough space to report income from up to five different businesses. (See page 8/16 for an example of Schedule E; page 8/8 provides information on getting current forms.)

Like sole proprietors and partners, LLC members will have to estimate their taxes for the year and pay them in advance in quarterly installments. Read Section E, below, on estimated tax payments.

b. Self-Employment Taxes

The current rule is that LLC members who are actively involved in the business must pay self-employment taxes, which include payments to the Social Security and Medicare systems. If an LLC member is non-active and merely an investor in the company, she is exempt from the self-employment tax obligation. Self-employment taxes include:

- Social Security tax of 12.4% on profits up to $65,400, and

- Medicare tax of 2.9% on all profits.

   This translates into a 15.3% tax on profits up to $65,400 (both Social Security and Medicare), and a 2.9% tax on profits above that amount (Medicare only).

The rules on self-employment taxes for LLCs are far from settled. Due to the somewhat contradictory nature of LLCs—partnership-like in some respects, corporation-esque in others—it's not clear to what extent LLC owners are subject to self-employment tax. If the issue affects you, it may be wise to do some research or consult a business attorney to find out the latest word on how these taxes apply to LLC members. Chapter 12 gives information on legal resources beyond this book.

Fortunately, if self-employment taxes are due, half of the total self-employment taxes you pay can be deducted from your taxable income at year-end. And if your LLC made less than $400 profit in the business year or lost money, you're totally exempt from having to file or pay self-employment taxes. (See Sidebar in Section B1, above, on the distinction between filing taxes and paying them.)

Self-employment taxes are reported on Schedule SE, which, like Schedule E (Supplemental Income and Loss), is submitted yearly with an LLC member's 1040 return. (A sample of Schedule SE appears on page 8/14.) Once you determine the self-employment taxes you owe on Schedule SE, the result is entered on your 1040 form in the "Other Taxes" section, which is added to your personal income tax obligation. If the LLC member is required to pay advance quarterly tax installments, however, any self-employment taxes will be included in those payments. See Section E, below, for information on estimating taxes and paying them in advance. This is a requirement all businesses need to understand.

2. California Taxes: Special LLC Tax and Fee

While the federal government treats LLCs that have chosen pass-through tax status almost exactly like partnerships, the State of California's tax treatment is annoyingly schizophrenic. Like an owner of a partnership, an LLC member is subject to California income taxes on her share of business profits. However, California also imposes special taxes on LLCs themselves, despite treating them as pass-through tax entities in most other respects.

See page 8/8 for information on getting the latest forms.

a. LLC Tax and Fee

LLCs need to make two payments to the Franchise Tax Board (FTB): one prepayment of what California calls an LLC tax, and one payment of what the state calls an LLC fee. To make matters more confusing, the LLC tax is really more like a fee, and the LLC fee seems much more like a tax. Here's how this screwy system works.

The "LLC tax" is an $800 annual payment (it may help you to think of it as a prepaid minimum tax) that the FTB collects, in its words, "for the privilege of doing business in California." It applies to all LLCs even if they're losing money. For newly formed LLCs, the tax is due within 3 months and 15 days of forming the LLC. For ongoing LLCs, this tax is due each year within 3 months and 15 days from the *beginning* of the business year. On the plus side, the $800 can be credited toward the other tax the LLC may owe at year-end. The LLC tax is paid with Form 3522, Limited Liability Tax Voucher. A sample of Form 3522 appears on page 8/20.

The other tax that California imposes on LLCs is the "LLC fee." The LLC fee is due 3 months and 15 days after the *end* of the business year (usually a calendar year, making the deadline the familiar April 15). It's reported and paid with Form 568, Limited Liability Company Return of Income. The LLC fee varies according to the LLC's total income, which is

calculated on Schedule Q which is attached to Form 568. The tax applies as follows:

Total Income	LLC Fee
0 to $250,000	$0
$250,000 to $499,000	$500
$500,000 to $999,999	$1,500
$1,000,000 to $4,999,999	$3,000
$5,000,000 and over	$4,500

All LLCs doing business in California (and classified as partnerships) must file Form 568 regardless of how much or little income the LLC has made. On that return, you'll subtract the $800 tax that you prepaid for the year, but since you'll also need to prepay for the next year, you'll always be $800 behind (until you dissolve your LLC).

Since the LLC tax is due 3 1/2 months after the start of the business year, and the LLC fee is due a 3 1/2 months after the end of the year, once your LLC is up and running you'll have to simultaneously pay two taxes (assuming you bring in a gross income of more than $250,000 per year). For instance, assuming that you use a calendar year, your $800 LLC tax for the year of 2000 and your LLC fee for 1999 will both be due April 15, 2000.

Example:

Chad plans to open his restaurant, Kitty B's Catfish Shack, as a limited liability company. He files his Articles of Organization on May 31, 1999, which means his $800 minimum tax for the year is due September 15, 1999. When Chad reports taxes for the Catfish Shack the following April in the year 2000, he can count the $800 he prepaid toward any LLC taxes the restaurant owes. However, he'll have to pay another $800 minimum tax by April 15, 1999, as prepayment for that year of business.

Note that there is no requirement to make advance estimated payments for the LLC tax and the LLC fee.

Instructions for Form FTB 3522
Limited Liability Company Tax Voucher

General Information

A Purpose

Form FTB 3522 is used to pay the annual limited liability company (LLC) tax of $800 for taxable year 1998. LLCs should use this form if they:

- Are doing business in California, or
- Have articles of organization accepted by the California Secretary of State (SOS), or
- Have a certificate of registration issued by the SOS.

B Who Must Pay the Annual LLC Tax?

Every LLC that is doing business in California or that has articles of organization accepted or a certificate of registration issued by the SOS is subject to the annual LLC tax of $800. The tax must be paid for each taxable year until a certificate of cancellation of registration or of articles of organization is filed with the SOS.

C How to Complete the Form

Please complete all information requested on this form. To assure timely and proper application of the payment to your account, please remember to enter the file number assigned upon registration of the LLC with the SOS and the federal employer identification number (FEIN).

D Where to Mail the Annual LLC Tax and Voucher

Mail the annual LLC tax and voucher to:

FRANCHISE TAX BOARD
PO BOX 942857
SACRAMENTO CA 94257-0631

E When to Pay the Annual LLC Tax

The annual LLC tax is due and payable on or before the 15th day of the 4th month after the beginning of the LLC's taxable year. **Note:** The taxable year of an LLC that was not previously in existence begins when the LLC is organized, registered or begins doing business in California.

If the 15th day of the 4th month of an existing foreign LLC's taxable year has passed before the foreign LLC commences business in California or registers with the SOS, the LLC annual tax should be paid immediately after commencing business or registering with the SOS.

Example:

LLC1, newly-formed calendar year taxpayer, organizes as an LLC in Delaware on June 1, 1998. LLC1 registers with the SOS on August 12, 1998, and begins doing business in California on August 13, 1998. Because LLC1's initial tax year began on June 1, 1990, the annual LLC tax is due September 15, 1998 (the 15th day of the 4th month of the short period taxable year). LLC1's short period (6/1/1998-12/31/1998) tax return is due April 15, 1999, and its annual tax payment with form FTB 3522 is also due April 15, 1999.

F Penalties and Interest

If the LLC fails to pay its total tax by the 15th day of the 4th month after the beginning of the taxable year (fiscal year filers) or April 15, 1998 (calendar year filers), a late payment penalty plus interest will be added to the tax due. The penalty and interest will be computed from the due date of the tax payment to the date paid.

For information on the calculation of the penalty, see the instructions for Form 568, General Information H, Penalties and Interest.

G Late Payment of Prior Year Annual LLC Tax

If a prior year LLC tax of $800 was not paid on or before the 15th day of the 4th month after the beginning of the taxable year, the tax should be remitted as soon as possible, using the appropriate year form FTB 3522, Limited Liability Company Tax Voucher. **Do not** use any other form for payment of the tax. This will assure proper application of the payment to the LLC account.

- - - - - - - - - - - - - - - - DETACH HERE - - - - - - - - - - - - - - - - -

TAXABLE YEAR **1998**	**Limited Liability Company Tax Voucher**	CALIFORNIA FORM **3522**

For calendar year 1998, or fiscal year beginning ⬚⬚⬚ 1 9 9 8 , and ending ⬚⬚⬚⬚ 1 9 .

Limited Liability Company name

Federal employer identification number (FEIN)

DBA/Attention

Secretary of State file number

Delivery Address

City, town or post office

State   ZIP code

Make your check or money order payable to "Franchise Tax Board." Write your FEIN and "Form FTB 3522 1998" on it. Mail this voucher and your check or money order to: FRANCHISE TAX BOARD
PO BOX 942857
SACRAMENTO CA 94257-0631
For Privacy Act Notice, see form FTB 1131.

Due 15th day of 4th month of taxable year.

Amount of payment

$ 800.00

FTB 3522   1997

b. Regular State Income Taxes for Members

Aside from these special rules for the LLC tax and fee, filing state income taxes for LLCs is very similar to the procedure at the federal level. An LLC must file Form 568, Limited Liability Company Return of Income, accompanied by Schedule K-1 (565) for each LLC member reporting that member's share of profit or losses. The LLC also needs to supply each member with a copy of the Schedule K-1 (565) submitted to the FTB.

All profits or losses that pass through the LLC to its owners must be reported on their personal California income tax returns, Form 540, using Schedule CA. Schedule CA should reflect the profit or losses reported on the state K-1 (565) return that was provided to each member by the LLC. Unlike the federal rule, an LLC member must file Schedule CA with his Form 540 even if the LLC loses money. The member won't owe any taxes unless the LLC made a profit, but the form must be filed in any case.

Like federal taxes, California income taxes for members must generally be paid in quarterly installments. Estimating your taxes and making quarterly payments is covered in Section E below.

E. Estimating and Paying Your Taxes in Advance

An important federal and state tax rule for anyone who earns income from a business is that income taxes must generally be paid in quarterly installments over the course of the business year. (Some businesspeople who expect a very low level of taxation are exempt from these estimated payment requirements. See Section I, below.) At year-end, if you've paid more than what you owe, you'll get a refund. If, on the other hand, you didn't pay enough in your quarterly installments, you will owe more.

While it might not seem so at first, this system isn't all that different from the way taxes on employment wages are handled. From each paycheck, the state and federal governments require an employer to withhold income tax from each employee's wages based on her expected salary or hourly pay. At year-end the employee calculates and reports her taxes based on how much money she actually earned during the year. Depending on the dollar amount of her tax obligation, she'll either owe more money or be due a refund. The IRS requires wages to be withheld or tax payments to be estimated and paid in advance for a simple, practical reason: it knows that a sudden multi-thousand dollar bill on April 15 can be difficult for anyone. Spreading out payments by wage withholding or estimated payments is the IRS's way of making your life a little easier—and to make sure it gets its money.

Unfortunately, it's much easier for an employer to figure out an employee's estimated tax burden knowing his yearly salary or hourly wage than it is for a small business owner to estimate taxes based on future income from a new and unproven business. If you're wondering, "How can I estimate taxes on business income that hasn't come in yet?" you're not alone. Projecting future income in order to estimate your tax obligation can be a dicey task, especially for brand-new business owners whose income hasn't yet evened out into any predictable rhythm. To make matters worse, you'll be socked with a penalty if your estimates are off and you don't pay enough each quarter.

But here's the good news: you don't need to start making estimated tax payments until you earn enough income to subject you to a threshold quarterly payment requirement. Usually this gives you enough time to get a pretty good feel for how much and how quickly money—and, by extension, taxable profits—are coming into your business. And even if you do underpay estimated taxes and face a penalty of a few hundred dollars, you can at least take heart that you owe a little extra only because your business has become profitable sooner than you anticipated.

1. Federal Estimated Taxes: Who Must Pay?

You must pay federal estimated taxes if:

a) you expect to owe at least $1,000 in federal taxes (including income and self-employment taxes) after subtracting wage withholding, if any, and

b) if you have a job where the company takes out taxes, you expect wage withholding to be less than the smaller of

- 100% of your total tax owed for the prior year, or
- 90% of your total tax for that year.

This formula sounds complicated, but it's not. It requires you to make estimated payments only if you expect to owe at least $1,000 to the IRS at year-end, above and beyond any taxes withheld from wages. Obviously, if you don't have a day job and all your income comes from your business, you won't be subject to wage withholding, and will be more likely to have to pay estimated taxes (assuming your business is turning even a modest profit).

In a nutshell, if you expect to take home over $3,000 to $4,000 per year in salary, bonus or profits, and you don't make wages or a salary elsewhere, you'll probably have to make estimated payments of federal tax.

Example 1:

On December 31, 1998, as part of a New Year's resolution Jason quits his job as computer salesman and opens a river-rafting outfit called the Rapids Transit Company. For the first few months of 1999, every dollar he takes in pays for equipment, insurance and marketing. At the rate he's going, he doesn't know if he'll make a profit at all that year, so he doesn't worry about estimated taxes. However, starting in June with the heavy tourist season, he starts clearing about $800 per month, after all deductions. He thinks he may have at least 4 more months like that before winter slows business down. If so, his annual profit will be about $4,000 ($800 x 5 months).

Depending on his tax status, he'll probably owe between $1,000 and $1,300 in taxes at the end of the year. He realizes he'd better start making estimated quarterly payments or risk a penalty.

Example 2:

Nels works as a manager of an auto parts store, which pays him a salary and deducts federal and state taxes from each paycheck. He starts a sole proprietorship called Falcon's Auto Tow. In the first few months of his auto-towing business, Nels operates at a loss. Since his only taxable income during those months is his paychecks, from which taxes are being withheld, he doesn't have to worry about estimated payments. In the fifth month he starts to turn a profit, at which point Nels starts to pay attention to whether he must pay estimated taxes. If he thinks his wage withholding will account for at least 90% of his total tax bill at the end of the year, he doesn't need to file and pay estimated taxes. In other words, if he thinks that taxes on his small business income will account for less than 10% of his total tax bill, he'll just file his taxes at year-end like most people whose income is all subject to wage withholding.

Nels' salary from the auto parts store is $28,000. He expects that his wage withholding should be enough so that he won't owe any taxes at year-end. Based on how much is withheld each paycheck, he sees that the yearly withholding will come to approximately $6,000. Based on these numbers, Nels sees that if he makes more than $2,000 profit from the business, his business income tax for the year will be approximately $667, and his $6000 wage withholding would be just about 90% of the total tax bill ($6,667). Nels, however, expects to make about $4,000 from his business over the course of the year. He'll end up owing the IRS about $7,333 ($6,000 from auto shop salary plus $1,333 from business profit) that year—which means that his wage withholding will be only about 82% of his total tax bill. (In keeping an eye on the taxes he's racking up, Nels keeps in mind that in addition to regular income taxes on his business profits, he'll owe self-employment tax on them at the rate of 15.3%.) Nels will need to start submitting Form 1040-ES to the IRS and paying quarterly estimated payments.

If you're not sure, help is available. IRS form 1040-ES contains a worksheet to use to calculate your estimated tax. You can obtain the form by calling 800-829-3676, or at http://www.irs.ustreas.gov/prod/forms_pubs/index.html. Or, even better, if you have a computerized accounting program, it can help you with the calculations.

Income made during:	Tax installment due:
Jan. 1 through Mar. 31	April 15
Apr. 1 through May 31	June 15
June 1 through Aug. 31	September 15
Sept. 1 through Dec. 31	January 15 of the next year

2. California Estimated Taxes: Who Must Pay?

The state rule has the same idea as the federal one, but the formula and the numbers are a bit different. Estimated state taxes must be paid if:

a) you expect to owe at least $100 in state taxes after any wage withholding has been accounted for, and

b) if you earn wages subject to withholding, you expect the wage withholding to be less than 80% of the total estimated tax for the current year, and

c) any wage withholding for the previous year was less than 80% of the tax owed that year, and

d) any income subject to withholding will be less than 80% of your estimated adjusted gross income for the current year.

3. When to Make Estimated Tax Payments

You become subject to the state and federal estimated tax payment requirements when you expect to earn enough profit during a business year to trigger the payment requirement. If you do, you need to do your best to estimate your income for the year and pay a quarterly installment based on the taxes due. Each quarterly payment must be filed a half-month after the end of the quarter. For estimated tax purposes for both federal and state taxes, the quarterly periods are as follows:

If your business uses a fiscal rather than a calendar year, your payments will be due the 15th day of the 4th, 6th, and 9th months of your fiscal year and the 1st month of the following fiscal year.

Defining Your Business Year

Except for C corporations, a business must use the calendar year as its business year unless it gets permission from the IRS to choose a different starting and ending point. A bit of tax jargon is important here. Any one-year period that a business uses for tax purposes, other than the calendar year (ending on December 31), is called a fiscal year, a tax year or an accounting period. The IRS allows sole proprietorships, partnerships, LLCs and S corporations to use a fiscal year only if there is a valid business reason for it, such as significant seasonal fluctuations in business. Fiscal years must begin on the first day of a month and end on the last day of the month one year later. A business that wants to use a fiscal year must submit Form 8716, "Election to Have a Tax Year Other Than a Required Tax Year" to the IRS and have it approved. This form is included in Appendix C and on the CD-ROM.

4. Calculating and Paying Your Estimated Tax

There are three ways to properly estimate your taxes. You can

- base it on how much tax you owed last year

- estimate your current year's income and deductions, and calculate the taxes you'd owe for those figures, or

- calculate your tax liability after each quarter (called the annualized income installment method), prorating your deductions and personal exemptions (you must also file Form 2210 if you use this method).

With the exception of the first method, you'll need help making these calculations. Instructions and worksheets that can help you calculate your estimated tax payments are included with the federal Form 1040-ES and the California Form 540-ES (the forms you'll send to the IRS and to the California FTB). These forms also include vouchers to submit with each periodic payment. Both the Appendix and the CD-ROM that accompanies this book contain 1998's version of these forms, along with the instructions and worksheets. See page 8/8 for information on getting the latest forms.

For more information on federal estimated tax payments, refer to IRS Publication 505, "Tax Withholding and Estimated Tax." For more state estimated tax information, call the Franchise Tax Board at 800-852-5711.

Don't Overlook Your Self-Employment Taxes

Self-employment taxes (see Section A1b, B1b or C1b, above), like income taxes, are subject to the estimated tax payment requirement. Be sure to include them when figuring your estimated tax burden for the year.

F. City and County Taxes

Unlike the federal or state governments, most cities and counties in California impose taxes directly on your business, even if your business is a pass-through entity such as a sole proprietorship. Of course, sole proprietors and partners are personally liable for these financial obligations, but the difference is that your business itself—not merely the profits that flow through to you and any other owners—incurs taxes by local governments. Often, these taxes are more substantial than federal or state taxes because many of them are based on business income with fewer deductions taken out, sometimes none at all. Some areas, for instance, impose a gross receipts tax, which calculates the tax based simply on how much total income your business has, without regard for your expenses.

Local taxes vary a lot from one area to the next, but basically your business will face some sort of a "business tax" from your city or county, as well as property taxes imposed by your county.

1. Business Taxes

This vague term simply refers to the money your local government imposes on all businesses within the city or county limits. Businesses in rural areas will probably only deal with their county tax authority. Whether the tax is imposed by a city or a county tax authority, the information about business taxes discussed in this section generally applies.

Unlike the IRS or the California FTB, which simply collect taxes once they're incurred, most local tax collectors require you to go through a registration process before starting business. (Information on how this generally works is provided in Chapter 6, Section D). Once you've registered, you'll obtain what's commonly called a tax registration certificate (or sometimes called a "business license"). Registration gives notice to your local tax authority that your business exists and allows them to charge taxes upon it, based on whatever method your locality has adopted for your type of business.

The schemes used to tax your business in various California cities and counties are usually based on certain attributes of your business. Most localities divide businesses into a number of different categories or types, such as retail sales, wholesale sales, hotels/apartments, and service businesses. Each category uses a certain criterion to calculate taxes on, also called a tax base. The most common tax base, for example, is "gross receipts" (total income, before expenses). Each category also has a certain tax rate for each tax base.

For example, in San Francisco, for retail sales businesses (category 08) the tax rate is $1.50 per $1000 of gross receipts (tax base). Contractors (category 02) in San Francisco also have gross receipts as their tax base, but the tax rate is $3.00 per $1000. Other criteria used as tax bases include total payroll, number of employees or number of company vehicles. In Oakland, for example, limousine companies pay a tax rate of $75 per vehicle. And San Jose charges all businesses a basic rate of $154.50 and adds $18.54 for each employee. Other tax bases exist as well. In Sacramento, for instance, certain professionals such as accountants, attorneys and podiatrists are taxed based on the number of years they have been licensed in the state of California.

In many cities and counties, you actually start paying your local taxes when you purchase your business license or registration certificate. Often, a locality will base its registration fee on your expected tax for the year. In some localities, your registration fee is like a prepaid tax that can be applied toward your total year-end tax. In other places, the registration cost is purely an administrative fee and cannot be applied to your tax bill. And in still other areas, part of the registration cost is a prepaid tax that can be credited towards your tax bill, and part is an administrative fee. Since rules vary widely from city to city and county to county, you'll need to check with the appropriate local agency. When looking up the appropriate tax agency, look in the government section of your white pages under City Government (or County Government if you live in an unincorporated area) for names such as "Tax Collector," "Business Licenses and Permits" or "Business Tax Division."

Since local taxation of businesses is usually closely tied to start-up registration requirements, most businesses will automatically receive tax-filing information either when they register or soon thereafter by mail. (For more information on start-up registration requirements, see Chapter 6.)

2. Property Taxes

Under state law, each county is responsible for assessing and collecting tax on certain kinds of property within the county. For businesses, this includes real estate and business equipment (sometimes called "business personal property"). An important exception is that business inventory (or items that will go into making a product or providing a service) is *not* subject to property tax.

Real estate is appraised by the county assessor only when it changes ownership or when construction is completed. Business personal property, on the other hand, is assessed every year. Some businesses must send the assessor a property statement each year, with information on the cost of all supplies, equipment and fixtures at each business location.

The tax rate is 1% on the assessed value of the property, plus any additional tax that may have been approved by voters in your county. The average tax across the state as of March 1998 is 1.06%. For specific information on your county's property tax system, call your county assessor's office, which is often part of the county clerk's office.

G. Sales Taxes

Sales tax rules are closely related to seller's permit requirements. Recall from Chapter 6, Section E, that all businesses that sell tangible goods must apply for a seller's permit. All businesses that have a seller's permit must file a sales tax return, even if the business ultimately made no taxable sales. Refer to Chapter 6, Section E, to figure out whether your business needs a seller's permit. Then use this section to help you determine whether you'll owe sales tax.

In California, retail sales of tangible items are subject to state, county and local district taxes. We often just refer to them as state sales taxes, since they're filed and paid to the California Board of Equalization (BOE) with just one return. It's up to the BOE to distribute the taxes to the counties and districts across the state.

1. Who Actually Owes Sales Taxes?

When you sell a taxable item to a customer, you, the seller, incur a tax on the sale, which you'll owe when your sales-tax return is due. To avoid paying the tax out of your own pocket, you can pass it along to your customers by adding it to the amount you charge for the item. Since virtually all retail businesses do just that, most consumers falsely believe that they are responsible for paying sales taxes. Not so—if business owners fail to collect sales tax from their customers, they will still owe the tax.

2. Taxable vs. Non-Taxable Sales

For a sale to be taxable, it must:

• involve the sale of a tangible item, not a service, and

• be made to the final user of the item.

a. Tangible Item

The first condition for a sale to be taxable is that it must involve a tangible item rather than a service—and you'll need to figure out whether you'll be selling tangible items before you open your business. As we mentioned above, businesses that sell tangible goods must obtain a seller's permit from the state before sales begin, even if the sales aren't taxable (such as wholesale sales, discussed below). Selling tangible goods without a seller's permit is technically a misdemeanor crime, but typically the BOE will give you the opportunity to comply (get a permit) before it files any criminal charges. But if you made any sales that were taxable before you got your seller's permit, the BOE will not only require you to get a permit, but to pay all back taxes that are due.

Sales Tax Exemptions

Part of the reason that the rules on sales taxes can be so convoluted is that the "rules" are clouded by swarms of exceptions and exemptions. Here are some of the most common exemptions from sales tax:

• some groceries (but not restaurant food)

• sales to out-of-state consumers

• sales to the U.S. government, and

• some sales related to entertainment industry.

Graphic Artists Beware!

Licensing reproduction rights to graphic artwork is currently considered by the BOE to be a taxable sale, despite the general rule that only sales of tangible goods are taxable. A number of California artists have been stung quite harshly by the BOE's interpretation, which has generated much support for reform of the current law.

At the heart of the issue is whether sales taxes should apply when graphic artists create artwork such as logos or book illustrations and sell the rights to use that artwork to their clients. (Selling rights is also known as licensing.) Artists argue that these transactions shouldn't be subject to sales taxes because they're not sales of physical goods; rather, what's being sold are intangible reproduction rights. Sales of original artwork, artists agree, should be subject to sales tax. But according to the BOE, even royalties from licensing reproduction rights are taxable when the graphic artist gives the client a tangible copy of the work on a piece of paper or on computer disk. Since the hard copy or disk is tangible, says the BOE, the sale is taxable—even when the disk or hard copy is given only temporarily for the client to make a copy. The BOE exempts these transactions from sales tax only when the artwork is delivered via intangible e-mail.

As this book goes to press, legislation is pending that could change California's sales tax law as it applies to graphic artists. Senate Bill 331 was originally drafted in an attempt to exempt graphic artists from having to pay sales taxes on licensing artwork, and from needing a seller's permit to conduct this type of business. The bill has gone through significant amendments, however, so its future is uncertain. To find out the latest status of S.B. 331, visit the Northern Chapter of the Graphic Artists Guild's Website at http://www.gag.org/sanfran/salestax.html. You can also get legislative information from the California State Senate's Website at http://www.sen.ca.gov/.

b.   Final User

The second condition for a sale to be taxable is that it is made to the final user. The fact that a sale is made directly to an end user (a consumer), rather than a reseller, is what differentiates retail sales (taxable) from wholesale sales (nontaxable). This means that if you operate as a wholesaler and sell tangible goods to a reseller who will in turn sell them to a consumer, you are exempt from sales tax. The idea behind this rule is to make sure that items are taxed only once. Rather than taxing the sale of a lamp, for instance, each time it is sold—from its manufacturer, to wholesaler, to the final customer—it is taxed only when it is sold to the final consumer. (Some transactions that are exempt from sales tax, however, may be subject to a nearly identical tax, a use tax. See Section 4, below.)

How can you tell whether a customer is a final user or not? Customers that intend to resell your product should present you with a resale certificate, which states that the property is being purchased for resale. The certificate must contain certain information, including:

- the purchaser's name and address
- the number of the purchaser's seller's permit
- a description of the property to be purchased
- a statement that the property is being used for resale, in terms such as "will be resold" or "for resale" (language such as "nontaxable" or "exempt" is not enough),
- the date of the sale, and
- the signature of the purchaser or her authorized agent.

If you are not presented with such a certificate, you should assume the customer is the final user and treat the sale as taxable. If you sell to the same customer repeatedly, you need only to collect one resale certificate, which should be kept on file at your office. From then on, whenever you sell items to that company, there is no need to collect another resale certificate. Likewise, if you buy regularly from the same supplier, you need only to present one resale certificate.

3. Using a Resale Certificate

Just as your customers can escape paying sales taxes to you by presenting a resale certificate, you can use one to purchase goods and supplies for legitimate resale free of sales tax. Appendix C and the CD-ROM that comes with it contain blank resale certificates approved by the BOE. Simply give a completed resale certificate, with your valid seller's permit number and the information above, to any company you're buying things from in order to be exempt from sales tax. There is no need to file a copy of the form with the state.

Keep in mind, however, that you are not allowed to use a resale certificate when you plan to use an item in your own business (and not resell it or use it in manufacturing). For example, if you purchase a computer to keep track of your sales, you shouldn't give the person who sells it to you a resale certificate, you should pay the sales tax on that purchase. Also, if your business performs services, you still have to pay sales taxes on your supplies. For example, a hairdresser must pay sales tax on the shampoo he uses to wash people's hair. When purchasing a combination of goods, only some of which you intend to resell, you must clearly indicate which items are for resale and pay sales taxes on the rest.

4. Use Taxes

To a certain degree, the rules regarding sales taxes are a myth. That's because of a little-understood tax called the use tax. While it's true that many sales of tangible goods are exempt from sales tax, many of these transactions will actually be subject to a use tax. In keeping with its name, a use tax is due when you *use* a tangible good in the state of California on which you didn't pay sales tax. The use tax rate is the same as the sales tax rate in that county.

Use taxes commonly apply to purchases of tangible goods from out of state that are used in California. For instance, if you order 20 computers, 20 chairs and 20 desks for your office from an out-of-state mail order catalog, you probably didn't pay sales taxes on those items, because most states don't allow businesses to collect sales tax from out-of-state purchasers. But under California's use tax law, it can collect use taxes from you, the buyer, thus making up for the revenue it would have gotten if you had bought the equipment within the state. In that way, California collects taxes from the purchaser that it can't collect from the out-of-state seller.

Other transactions subject to use tax include purchases of items you originally intended to resell (and bought tax-free because you used your resale certificate), but used for another purpose. Items that you buy to incorporate into a new product that you sell (and use your resale certificate when buying to avoid paying sales tax), as well as items you lease, are also subject to the use tax. Inventory that you store for future resale is *not* subject to use tax.

You report the use taxes you owe at the same time you report sales taxes, on Form BT-401, "California State, Local and District Sales and Use Tax Return," by adding up the use tax you owe and putting it on Line 2 of the return. (But if you paid another state's sales or use tax for some purchases, do not include the tax you paid in your total on line 2. Put the tax you paid on line 20 instead—you may get a credit for this amount.) If you are in doubt about how the sales and use tax law applies to your specific activity or transaction, you should call the State Board of Equalization office at 800-400-7115.

5. Keeping Track of Your Sales

When you obtain a seller's permit, you obligate yourself to file a sales (and use) tax return, and that means you'll need to keep careful records of both your sales and purchases. The BOE requires that you keep:

- books or computer files recording your sales and purchases
- bills, receipts, invoices, contracts or other documents supporting your books of account (called "documents of original entry"), and
- all schedules and working papers used in preparing your tax returns.

In addition, if you conduct business in more than one county, you'll need to keep separate records of sales made in each county.

Your records should show all sales your business made, even sales that aren't taxable.

6. Calculating, Paying and Filing Sales Taxes

The standard statewide sales tax rate is 7.25%, which is the total of a 6% state tax, a .25% county tax, and a 1% local tax. However, if you conducted business in an area that has imposed an additional tax (there are a number of them, listed in sidebar called "Special Tax Districts"), your sales in those areas will be subject to the higher rate. In mid-1998, the maximum sales tax rate in California is 8.5%.

Special Tax Districts

(Counties unless otherwise noted)

Alameda	8.25%
Contra Costa	8.25%
Del Norte	7.75%
Fresno	7.75%
Imperial	7.75%
City of Calexico	8.25%
City of Clearlake	7.75%
Inyo	7.75%
Los Angeles	8.25%
Madera	7.75%
Monterey	7.25%
Orange	7.75%
Riverside	7.75%
Sacramento	7.75%
San Benito	8.25%
San Bernardino	7.75%
San Diego	7.75%
San Francisco	8.5%
San Joaquin	7.75%
San Mateo	8.25%
Santa Barbara	7.75%
Santa Clara	7.75%
Santa Cruz	8.25%
Sonoma	7.5%
Stanislaus	7.375%
Tulare	7.75%

Fortunately, you can report and pay all of your sales taxes with one form, BT-401, California State, Local and District Sales and Use Tax Return. (Many small businesses can fill out a shortened version of that form, BT-401EZ. See Sidebar.) All types of businesses, including sole proprietorships, partnerships, LLCs and corporations (for-profit as well as non-profit) use the same form and are subject to the same sales tax rules.

Any business that has been issued a seller's permit will automatically receive Form BT-401 in the mail, along with an account number, due date and filing instructions. Depending on your sales volume, you'll need to submit your sales tax return yearly, quarterly or monthly.

If you have a seller's permit, you must file a sales tax return. If you applied for and received a seller's permit because you anticipated selling goods but never made a sale, you'll need to submit Form BT-401 anyway. Likewise, if you didn't make any *taxable* sales, you won't owe any taxes, but you still need to submit the form. If you don't, you risk losing your sellers' permit.

Simplified Sales Tax Return

Some businesses can fill out a simplified sales tax return, Form BT-401EZ. Your business can use the simplified form if you:

- sell in only one county
- do not sell fixed-price contracts or leases
- do not sell fuel, cars, boats or aircraft, or sell to aircraft common carriers
- do not claim sales tax exemptions for discounts, returned items or bad debts, and
- do not claim a credit for sales tax paid to another state.

C H A P T E R 9

Drafting Contracts and Agreements

As a business owner, you may often have to enter into agreements (legal contracts) with other businesses and people: suppliers, customers, creditors and the landlord, for example. While a few of these transactions will be so simple and short-term that it's enough to complete them with a handshake, most will be sufficiently complicated, long-term, or financially important that a written contract is essential. Thankfully—and contrary to what many people believe—a contract is often a fairly simple legal creature that sets forth mutual promises to do whatever specific acts are listed in the contract. (A promises to pay B $1,000 if B delivers 50,000 twist-ties to A's warehouse on or before March 1, 1999.) A written contract will usually include the main terms of the agreement: the price of goods, important dates, and the time and place of delivery. For most contractual agreements, standard forms are readily available. Except in the relatively few instances where lots of money or cutting legal issues are involved, lawyers won't normally be needed.

Simple as some types of contracts may be, the important thing to remember about them is that they are legally enforceable. If you fail to keep your end of the bargain, you can be sued and forced to pay monetary damages to the other party or, in some circumstances, to do the things you promised in the contract.

This chapter will explain the basics behind binding, legal contracts, such as what makes a contract enforceable and which contracts are legally required to be in writing. We'll also go over some common contract clauses and explain in plain English what they really mean and whether they contain hidden pitfalls.

Kimberly Torgerson,
owner of Your Word's Worth, a freelance editing and writing service:

Several years ago, I took on a short-term project managing the last-minute editing for a medical software program. The timeline was extremely tight, and I needed to locate and manage about 10 additional freelance editors, who got paid directly from the company who hired me. Because I had not worked with the company before, or many of the editors I had located, I drafted an agreement that spelled out delivery, completion and payment terms for everyone involved. To draft this agreement, I looked at my previous professional service agreements and a Nolo book, and ran it by a friend who is a lawyer. A seat-of-the-pants approach, but it worked.

A. Contract Basics

Although lots of contracts are filled with mind-bending legal gibberish, there's no reason why this has to be true. For most contracts, legalese is not essential or even helpful. On the contrary, the agreements you'll want to put into a written contract are best expressed in simple, everyday English.

Don't be afraid to redraft contract language. When reading a contract that has been presented to you, your first task is to be sure you understand all of its terms. It is just plain foolish to sign a contract if you're unclear on the meaning of any of its language. If a clause is poorly written, hard to understand or doesn't accomplish your key goals, rewrite it in clearer language. By refusing to sign at the X unless your goals are clearly met, you'll be less likely to find yourself in a breach-of-contract lawsuit later on. (A breach of contract occurs when one party fails to live up to the terms or promises of the contract.) For more on changing contract language, see Section D, below, on reading and revising a contract.

1. Elements of a Valid Contract

A contract will be valid if the following elements are present:

- all parties are in agreement (after an offer has been made by one party and accepted by the other)

- something of value has been exchanged, such as cash, services or goods (or a promise to exchange such an item), for something else of value, and

- in a few situations, to be a valid contract the agreement must be put into writing. (Of course, because oral contracts can be difficult or impossible to prove, it is wise to write out most agreements.)

Now let's look at each of these elements in more detail.

a. Agreement Between Parties, a.k.a. Offer and Acceptance

Although it may seem like stating the obvious, an essential element of a valid contract is that all parties really do agree on all major issues. In real life there are plenty of situations that blur the line between a full agreement and a preliminary discussion about the possibility of making an agreement. To help clarify these borderline cases, the law has developed some rules defining when an agreement legally exists.

The most basic rule of contract law is that a legal contract exists when one party makes an offer and the other party accepts it. For most types of contracts, this can be done either orally or in writing. (For a few, discussed in Section A2, below, the offer and acceptance must be made in writing.)

Let's say, for instance, you're shopping around for a print shop to produce brochures for your business. One printer says (or faxes) that he'll print 5,000 two-color flyers for $200. This constitutes his offer. If you tell him to go ahead with the job, you've accepted his offer. In the eyes of the law, when you tell the printer to go ahead, you create a contract, which means you're liable for your side of the bargain (in this case, payment of $200). But if you tell the printer you're not sure and want to continue shopping around (or don't even respond, for that matter), you clearly haven't accepted his offer and no agreement has been reached. Or if you say his offer sounds great, except that you want the printer to use three colors instead of two, no contract has been made, since you have not accepted all of the important terms of the offer—you've changed one term of the offer. (Depending on your wording, you may have made a counteroffer, which is discussed below.)

Sure enough, in real, day-to-day business the seemingly simple steps of offer and acceptance can become quite convoluted. For instance, sometimes when you make an offer it isn't quickly and un-equivocally accepted; the other party may want to think about it for a while or try to get a better deal for himself. And before he accepts your offer, you might change your mind and want to withdraw or amend your offer. Delaying acceptance of an offer and revoking an offer, as well as making a counteroffer, are common situations in business transactions that often lead to confusion and conflict. To minimize the potential for dispute, here are some general rules you should understand and follow.

■ **How long an offer stays open.** Unless an offer includes a stated expiration date, it remains open for a "reasonable" time. What's reasonable, of course, is open to interpretation and will vary depending on the type of business and the particular situation. To leave no room for doubt as to when the other party must make a decision, the best way to make an offer is to include an expiration date. And if you want to accept someone else's offer, the best approach is to do it as soon as possible, while there's no doubt that the offer is still open. Keep in mind that until you accept, the person or company who made the offer—called the offeror—may revoke it. Revocation is discussed below.

Include an expiration date clause in all bids. In many types of businesses, from replacing roofs to redesigning Websites, it is common to bid (in other words, to make an offer to create a contract) on lots more jobs than you really need or want. But sometimes this strategy can backfire. With lots of offers floating around, there is always the possibility that too many will be accepted, raising the embarrassing specter of your not being able to cope with all the work. One easy way to minimize this problem is to print right on your offer form that all offers are good for only ten days (or some other relatively short period) unless extended in writing.

■ **Counteroffers.** Often when an offer is made, the response will not be to accept the terms of the offer right off, but to start bargaining. Of course, haggling over price is the most common type of negotiating that occurs in business situations. When one party responds to an offer by proposing something different, this proposal is called a "counteroffer." When a counteroffer is made, the legal responsibility to accept, decline or make another counteroffer shifts to the original offeror. For instance, if your printer (here, the original offeror) offers to print 5,000 brochures for $300 and you respond by saying you'll pay $250 for the job, you have not accepted his offer

(no contract has been formed), but instead have made a counteroffer. If your printer then agrees to do the job exactly as you have specified for $250, he's accepted your counteroffer and a legal agreement has been reached.

Inconsequential differences between offer and acceptance don't nix a contract. While it is true that a contract is only formed if the accepting party agrees to all substantial terms of an offer, this doesn't mean you can rely on inconsequential differences to void a contract later. For example, if you offer to buy 100 chicken sandwiches on one-inch-thick sourdough bread, there is no contract if the other party replies he will provide 100 emu filets on rye bread. But if he agrees to provide the chicken sandwiches on one-inch-thick sourdough bread, a valid contract exists, and you can't later refuse to pay if the bread turns out to be a hair thicker or thinner than one inch.

■ **Revoking an offer.** Whoever makes an offer can revoke it as long as it hasn't yet been accepted. This means if you make an offer and the other party says she needs some time to think it through or makes a counteroffer with changed terms, you can revoke your original offer. Once she accepts, however, you'll have a binding agreement. Revocation must happen before acceptance.

An exception to this rule occurs if the parties agree that the offer will remain open for a stated period of time. This type of agreement is called an option, and it usually doesn't come for free. Say someone offers to sell you a forklift for $10,000, and you want to think the offer over free of the worry that the seller will withdraw the offer or sell to someone else. You and the seller could agree that the offer will stay open for a certain period of time, say thirty days. Often, however, the offeror will ask you to pay for this 30-day option—which is understandable, since during the 30-day option period he can't sell to anyone else. Payment or no payment, when an option agreement exists, the offeror cannot revoke the offer until the time period ends.

Generally speaking, an advertisement to the public does not count as an offer in the legal sense. In other words, if you advertised your catering services in your local weekly newspaper, and included a price quote of $300 for your standard menu serving 20 people, you would not be legally bound to live up to that service if someone called you and said, "I accept!" If, for instance, you were too busy with other catering jobs and unable to do the job for the eager caller, you could decline. Since your ad wasn't, legally speaking, an offer, the caller couldn't claim that he "accepted" it to create a binding contract.

That being said, you do need to watch what you say in your advertisements. California law requires retailers to stock enough of an advertised item to meet reasonably expected demand. Otherwise, your ad needs to state that stock is limited.

Of course, false or misleading advertising is always a bad idea. Federal laws regulating trade and state consumer protection laws prohibit deceptive advertising, even if no one was in fact misled. And check your ad's facts—false advertising is illegal, even if you believed the ad to be truthful.

b. Exchange of Things of Value

In addition to both parties agreeing to the terms, a contract isn't valid unless both parties exchange something of value—in anticipation of the completion of the contract. The "thing of value" being exchanged—which every law student who ever lived has been taught to call "consideration"—is most often a promise to do something in the future, such as a promise to perform a certain job or a promise to pay a fee for that job. For instance, let's return to the example of the print job. Once you and the printer agree on terms, there is an exchange of things of value (consideration): the printer has promised to print the 5,000 brochures and you have promised to pay $250 for them.

The main importance of requiring things of value to be exchanged is to differentiate a contract from generous statements and one-sided promises that are not enforceable by law. If a friend offers you a gift, for instance, such as offering to stop by and help you move a pile of rocks, without asking anything in return, that arrangement wouldn't count as a contract because you didn't give or promise him anything of value. If the other party never followed through with his gift, you would not be able to enforce his promise. However, if in exchange for helping you move rocks on Saturday, you promise your friend you'll help him weed his vegetable garden on Sunday, a contract exists.

Although the exchange of value requirement necessary to form a valid contract is met in most business transactions by an exchange of promises ("I'll promise to pay money if you promise to paint my building next month"), actually doing the work can also satisfy the rule. If, for instance, you leave your printer a voice-mail message that you'll pay an extra $100 if your brochures are cut and stapled when you pick them up, the printer can create a binding contract by actually doing the cutting and stapling. And once he does so, you can't weasel out of the deal by claiming you changed your mind.

2. Oral vs. Written Contracts

Before answering the question "Does a contract have to be in writing to be legally enforceable?" here's some advice: Put your contracts in writing. For compelling practical reasons, all contracts of more than a trivial nature should be written out and signed by both parties. Here is why:

• Writing down terms tends to make both parties review them more carefully, eliminating fatal flaws that oral contracts often have from the start.

- An oral agreement—no matter how honestly made—is hard to remember accurately.

- Oral agreements are subject to willful misinterpretation by a not-so-innocent party who wants to get out of the deal.

- Oral contracts are often difficult, and commonly impossible, to prove and, therefore, to enforce in court.

That's our good advice; now here's the legal rule: By statute §1624 of the Civil Code, the state of California (and, with minor differences, every other state) requires that certain contracts be in writing. These include the following:

- An agreement that by its terms can't be completed in a year or less. For example, a contract for a bakery to provide fresh bread to a restaurant for two years must be in writing. On the other hand, if the contract might take longer than a year to complete but could be completed within a year, it doesn't need to be in writing. For example, a contract for a gardener to landscape five big properties within the next 15 months would not need to be written, because it is quite possible that the landscape would finish the work within one year. Similarly, a contract for a bakery to bake bread for a restaurant with no time period stated would not need to be in writing.

- A lease whose term is longer than one year, or an agreement authorizing an agent to execute such a lease on your behalf.

- Any sale of real estate or of an interest in real estate, or an agreement authorizing an agent to purchase or sell real estate or interest in real estate on your behalf.

- An agreement that by its terms will not be completed during the lifetime of one of the parties.

- A promise to pay someone else's debt, such as a business partner's promising to pay your car payments, or an agreement that the person who prints your brochure will also pay the cost of photographic work done at another shop.

- An agreement by the purchaser of real estate to pay the seller's debt, if it's backed (secured) by a mortgage or trust deed.

- An agreement for a professional creditor, such as a bank, to lend money or extend credit of more than $100,000, if the loan is not primarily for personal, family or household purposes.

In addition to California's Civil Code, the state has a special body of law on commercial issues called the Uniform Commercial Code (UCC). Under California's UCC § 2201, a sale of goods for $500 or more requires at least a brief written note or memo indicating the agreement on the sale of the goods. The note can be much less detailed than a normal contract; it needs only to show an agreement between the parties and the quantity of goods being sold. Other terms that are typically covered in contracts, such as the price of goods or the time and place of delivery, don't need to be included to satisfy the UCC rule. This written memo usually needs to be signed, although if one party doesn't object to the memo within 10 days of receiving it then her signature isn't required.

Jennifer F. Mahoney,
owner of an illustration service in Northern California:

My creativity is exercised just as much by drawing up a good agreement with a client as it is by the way I create art for that client.

There are special legal requirements for contracts in some businesses. California state law imposes additional requirements for contracts involving particular businesses or certain kinds of transactions. For instance, contracts for weight-loss services and dating services must be in writing. Plus, the law requires some contracts to include special language. For example, California dating service contracts must include the following language in at least 10-point boldface type:

"You, the buyer, may cancel this agreement, without any penalty or obligation, at any time prior to midnight of the original contract seller's third business day following the date of this contract, excluding Sundays and holidays. To cancel this agreement, mail or deliver a signed and dated notice, or send a telegram which states that you, the buyer, are canceling this agreement, or words of similar effect." (California Civil Code § 1694.2.)

Unfortunately, there's no centralized place where a business owner can learn if any special contract laws apply to his type of business. One way to is to read over California's statutes for mentions of your type of business. Contracts are discussed in the Civil Code, beginning at Section 1549, and in various sections of the Uniform Commercial Code.

If doing legal research is too time-consuming or overwhelming for you, a good alternative is to use the limited help of a lawyer who's generally familiar with small business issues and, if possible, already works with businesses in your field (other plant nurseries, Website designers or restaurants, for example). Many lawyers are now more flexible in offering just as much or as little help as clients need, and offer coaching services to those who want to handle their simple legal affairs themselves. Using a legal coach is especially useful for small business people who often need simple legal questions answered, rather than full-blown attorney services. Chapter 12 discusses working with lawyers and finding one that's willing to coach you through simple legal matters.

As an illustration of how the process of writing a contract can produce a better result, consider the following example.

Example:

Kay opens a plant shop called The Green Scene, and is in the process of installing all the necessary equipment in her storefront space. Because she needs specialized grow-lights for her extensive line of tropical plants, she checks with several contractors familiar with installing lighting systems. One company, Got a Light, says they will install a system for $3,000, which would include the lights themselves and installation. Their quote is the lowest among the companies Kay has checked, so she tells them she'll accept their offer but only with a written contract.

When they send her a contract detailing the job, she notices that nothing in the contract addresses rewiring her shop. She calls Got a Light and talks with Dan, who tells her that, indeed, she needs to have an electrician add several new circuits and provide six specialized outlets before Got a Light can install the lighting system. Based on this discovery, Kay and Dan discuss exactly what needs to be done before Got a Light's work begins and include this new agreement in an additional contract clause. Dan recommends an electrician, whom Kay hires to do the rewiring. She also manages to negotiate a lower price with Got a Light, based on the fact that the rewiring will be done according to Got a Light's specifications, making their installation much easier.

B. Using Standard Contracts

By now you should understand that your contracts should be written, but you may still be clueless about how to write the ones you'll need. Luckily for you and most other businesspeople, virtually every type of business transaction is covered by a readily available standard contract. Anyone who has ever picked up a fill-in-the-blank lease or promissory note from an office supply store, torn one out of a self-help law book or downloaded one from a Website is familiar with how this works.

For especially common transactions—service contracts, rental agreements, independent contractor agreements, contracts for sales of goods and licensing agreements are just a few examples—you should easily be able to find a blank-form contract that you can fill in and, if necessary, modify before signing. Blank rental agreements, for example, are widely available at office supply stores, through landlords' associations, at most public libraries, in Nolo's LeaseWriter software and from many other sources.

If you can't easily find a blank-form contract that meets your needs, try these sources:

- Trade associations are excellent resources for fill-in-the-blank contracts.

- Your competitors might be less than willing to share their contracts with you, but similar businesses in far-away locations (which you won't be competing with) might be willing to show you theirs.

- The Web has oceans of information for small businesses, including sample contracts. Try searching for terms particular to your type of business to find specific contracts you need.

- Nolo Press books offer many different blank-form agreements. For general business contracts, a great resource is the *Legal Guide for Starting and Running a Small Business, Volume 2: Legal Forms,* by attorney Fred S. Steingold.

Once you've found a contract that generally fits your needs, you can amend it for your particular situation. It's entirely appropriate and often necessary to change clauses of a fill-in-the-blank contract to suit your needs. Of course, it's crucial that you understand what you're doing. Don't just strike a clause because you don't understand what it means, or add a clause without fully knowing the consequences of including it. To help you educate yourself about typical contract language, the next section explains which clauses commonly appear in contracts and what they mean.

C. How to Draft a Contract

If you can't find a form agreement or if you find one that needs a load of revisions, you may need to draft a clause or two—or possibly even the whole contract—from scratch. Don't be intimidated. Either way, your goal is simple: to state clearly what each party is agreeing to do and the specifics of how they'll do it (usually called the terms of the contract). Put another way, your written contract should be the most accurate reflection possible of the understanding you have with the other party.

Good Ideas to Keep Your Contracts Crystal Clear

- Avoid the use of "he," "she," "they" or other pronouns in your contracts to prevent confusion over whom you're talking about. Use either the actual names of the parties or their roles, such as Landlord and Tenant. It might seem repetitive or clumsy to write this way, but your goal is to be clear—not to write beautiful prose.

- Stay away from legalistic words like wherefore, herewith or hereinafter. Far from making your contract sound more impressive, this type of language is simply unnecessary and outdated. Stick to modern, clear English.

- Make at least a couple drafts of your contract. After the first draft, let it rest a day or so and then reread it. Does it leave any questions in your mind? If it does, you need to fill in the gaps with more information.

This section explains the important things to include in most contracts and alerts you to the situations that might require more specialized provisions. The information we provide will help you in editing or drafting amendments to a standard contract, or in drafting a contract from scratch if necessary. We'll present examples of how to state certain terms—although, as mentioned above, clear English is really all that's usually necessary.

Don't paralyze your contract with too many specifics. Although a good contract covers all the important aspects of a deal, there is no need to be too anal when it comes to specifying every minute detail. For instance, if you hire a cleaning service to scrub your floors, you probably don't need to specify what type of brushes they'll use. Better to put your energy into picking the right person or company to do the job and to leave some of the specifics of the actual work up to them. How do you know when enough detail is enough? You'll simply have to judge for yourself which nit-picky details are so important that they should be covered in your contract and which ones you can safely ignore. For example, if you need fresh salmon for a party at 6 p.m., the time of delivery and quality of the fish are extremely important points, but the exact weight of each fish or the method of delivery may be a lot less so.

1. What to Include in a Basic Contract

So you've reached an agreement with another party and are ready to put your agreement into writing. Before you start editing a form contract or writing one on your own, step back a moment to consider the goals of all contracts:

- to clearly outline what each party is agreeing to do (including payment arrangements),
- to anticipate areas of confusion or points of potential conflict, and
- to provide for recourse (remedy) in case the agreement is not followed through to completion.

Also remember that the more you have at stake, the more carefully you'll have to approach the task of putting together your contract. For example, if you're entering into a contract to buy a truckload of bicycle tires for $1,000, you won't need your agreement to be outlined nearly as meticulously as you would in a contract for the construction of a building. For high-stakes, complex agreements, don't leave any of your bases uncovered. In fact, if the stakes are high enough, you might want to hire an attorney or other expert to help with some or all of the contract-writing process (see Sidebar, below) or at least to check your draft and make suggestions.

For complex agreements, you may need an attorney. More complex contracts—especially those in areas unfamiliar to you—are often best handled with the help of a lawyer. Certainly if a transaction is so huge or elaborate it makes your head spin, you shouldn't go it alone. First, decide how much help you need. Rather than having an attorney draft your contract from start to finish, you could simply have her look over a contract that you or the other party has written. Ideally, you should hire a lawyer with some experience with small business, preferably your type of business. Even better would be an attorney with whom you have a long-term working relationship so that she knows the ins and outs of your business. See Chapter 12 on getting legal assistance.

Except where noted, no special wording is required in a contract. Section D, below, offers some tips on how to make your clauses as clear as they can be. Let's look at the information most contracts include and how that info is presented.

- **Title.** Generally a contract will have a simple, to-the-point title like "Contract for Printing Services" or "Agreement for Sale of Ball Bearings."

- **The names and addresses of all the parties.** It should be clear what role each party has in the contract, such as seller or buyer; landlord or tenant; client or service person. The addresses of the parties generally appear at the end of a contract in the section with the signatures.

Example:

Christopher Johnson ("Client") desires to enter into a contract with Virgil's Printing ("Printer") for printing services for Client's newspaper.

- **A brief description of the background of the agreement (called "recitals").** While not always included, this type of information is often necessary to frame the contents of the agreement. Typically this section includes a brief description of what kinds of businesses the parties run and the nature of the transaction being entered into in the contract.

Example:

Client prints and distributes a free, weekly, 24-page newspaper called El Norte *with a circulation of 40,000. Printer operates a full-service print shop with three print-*

ing presses. The subject of this contract is an agreement that Printer shall print Client's newspaper each week in exchange for payment.

- **A full description of what each party is promising to do as part of the agreement.** This section is sometimes called the "specifications," or just "specs." If a product is being sold, describe the product and then state when it will be delivered. If a service is being performed, describe the job and then state when it will be completed, including any intermediate deadlines that must be met before the final completion date. Indicate whether strict compliance with deadlines is necessary by throwing in the phrase "Time is of the essence." If specifications are complicated (for example, intricate performance details for a software contract), they should normally be set out in attachments, which may include scale drawings, formulas or other detailed information about the transaction.

Example:

Client promises to deliver materials ("boards") for printing to Printer's shop no later than 10:00 a.m. each Wednesday morning. Printer promises to print, fold and bundle 40,000 copies of Client's newspaper and have them ready for Client to pick up from Printer's shop by 8:00 p.m. that same Wednesday. Time is of the essence regarding this contract. If, however, Client fails to deliver boards to Printer by 10:00 a.m. Wednesday morning, Printer may take extra time to complete the job. The amount of extra time will depend on how late Client is in delivering the boards and on Printer's schedule of other jobs, but in no case shall be longer than 24 hours after delivery of the boards.

- **The contract term.** This sentence establishes how long the contract will be in effect.

Example:

This contract will remain in effect for a period of one year, or until it is terminated by one of the parties under Paragraph 4, whichever is first.

Example :

This contract will remain in effect for a period of one year, or until it is terminated by one of the parties under Paragraph 4, whichever is first.

- **The price of the product or service.** This section states how much one party will pay for the other party's goods or services. If the price may vary (say, based on the time or quality of performance) or if it will be established later, a description of how it will be calculated should be included.

Example :

Client will pay Printer $1,000 for every 10,000 24-page newspapers printed, up to 50,000 newspapers. The price will be renegotiated if Client orders more than 50,000 newspapers, or if the number of pages per newspaper changes.

- **Payment arrangements.** This section should explain when payment is due, whether it will be paid all at once or in installments, whether interest will be charged if payments are late, plus any other special requirements, such as whether payment must be by certified or cashier's check (otherwise a garden-variety check will normally suffice). Again, if strict compliance with payment deadlines is necessary, use the phrase "Time is of the essence."

Example :

Client will pay Printer the full amount of each week's printing cost within 3 days of picking up the completed newspapers.

- **A statement of any warranties made by either party regarding the product or service being provided.** If a guarantee is provided by either party, the contract should state what will happen if the guarantee isn't satisfied—for instance, if certain standards aren't met, the party who got the raw end of the deal will be given a refund or may give the other party another chance to do the job right.

Example :

Printer warrants that the completed newspapers shall be free from printing defects or errors attributable to the printer. In case such errors do occur, Printer and Client may negotiate a discount not to exceed actual damages suffered by Client.

- **A statement whether either party may transfer the contract to an outside party.** Transferring contract rights is also called assigning. If you have chosen a company because of particular characteristics, such as good personal service or artistic detail, you may not want that company to be able to hand off the job to someone else, who may not do as good a job.

Example :

Neither Printer nor Client may assign this contract or any part of it to another party.

- **A description of any conditions under which either party may terminate the agreement.** For some types of contracts (for example, contracts to provide an ongoing service), a termination clause often states that either party must give a written termination notice in order to end the contract, often 30 or 60 days in advance. But you may not want either party to be able to terminate the contract just any old time they feel like it. In this case, you can specify a limited number of certain events that might allow a party to end a contract early. For instance, say you own a rock shop that sells lots of agate, so you contract with a miner to sell you a half-ton of agate each month for a year. To protect yourself, you could include a clause in your contract stating that if you resell less than a quarter-ton of agate in any calendar month, you may terminate the agreement.

Example :

Upon written notice of at least 30 days to the other party, either Printer or Client may terminate this agreement.

- **An outline of how you will deal with a breach-of-contract situation.** Though signing a contract may not head off a subsequent dispute, it may be able to channel the dispute in ways that will lead to it being resolved as quickly and cheaply as possible. There are a number of different approaches you can take.

You can pre-set the amount of damages to be paid (called liquidated damages) by a breaching party in order to avoid the often lengthy and contentious process of calculating damages after a contract has been breached. In order for a liquidated damages clause to be valid, the dollar amount of damages that you set must be a reasonable estimate of what actual damages would be, not merely a pre-set penalty.

Another option is for both parties to agree to try mediation and, if that fails, arbitration to settle a dispute as an alternative to court.

Or, if for some reason one or both of you prefers going to court, you can arrange for the prevailing party in a dispute to pay the other party's legal fees, or you can establish that each party is responsible for their own legal fees regardless of who prevails.

Example:

If any dispute arises under the terms of this agreement, the parties agree to select a mutually agreeable, neutral third party to help them mediate it. The costs of mediation will be shared equally. If the dispute is not resolved after 30 days in mediation, the parties agree to choose a mutually agreeable artibrator who will arbitrate the dispute. The costs of arbitration will be assigned to the parties by the arbitrator. The results of any arbitration will be binding and final.

- **For contracts with out-of-state entities, a statement of which state's laws apply to the transaction.** Although contract law in all states is very similar, using California law will generally be the simplest for you, since you'll have more California resources at your disposal, including law libraries and people knowledgeable in California law.

Example:

This contract shall be governed by and interpreted in accordance with the laws of California.

- **Signatures and Dates.** Your signature section should always include room for the date the contract was signed, as well as the addresses of the parties.

2. Putting Your Contract Together

Besides making sure your contract includes all the necessary information, you'll need to present it in an easy-to-follow, professional format. Generally, contract clauses are organized in a series of numbered paragraphs for easy reference to specific terms.

If your agreement includes any hard-to-articulate details, such as the specifications of a software product, the drawing of a company logo, or architectural blueprints, you can include them as attachments to the main contract. If you do include an attachment, be sure to label it and refer to it in the main contract. To officially make it a part of the contract, state somewhere in the main contract that you "include the Attachment in the contract," or that you "incorporate the Attachment into the contract."

Example 1:

Company agrees to pay artist $100 for use of logo. Logo is attached to this contract as Attachment A and is hereby included in this contract.

Example 2:

Contractor agrees to complete remodeling within one year. The final plans are attached to this contract as Exhibit B and are hereby incorporated into this contract.

Jennifer F. Mahoney,

owner of an illustration service in Northern California:

It's helpful to learn about the accounts payable process for each client and to understand who releases checks. It's often an entirely different person or department from the one who calls you to offer work. You don't necessarily want to strain your relationship with the person who calls offering you work just because a different department of their business doesn't pay on time. Pave the way for timely payments as much as possible by getting to know the correct procedure, and when it's time to press for payment, you'll know the right person to call.

D. Reading and Revising a Contract

If you don't like certain terms of a contract that's presented to you, you can propose changes to the contract. By doing this, you are technically making a counteroffer. Contracts are commonly negotiated back and forth (offer and counteroffer) this way until all the terms are accepted by both parties. (Remember, if the parties aren't in agreement, there's no contract—oral or otherwise. See Section A, above, on offers and counteroffers.)

Changes to a contract—whether to a form contract or one drafted from scratch—can be made in a number of ways. One is by simply crossing out language and filling in new language directly on the contract itself. Each party should initial any such changes to show that each approves of them, and should then sign the contract as a whole.

In today's world, however, it's more than likely that you'll have an electronic copy of the contract either on your computer, your lawyer's, or the other party's. If so, it makes much more sense to make the necessary changes on the computer and then print out a clean copy for both parties to sign. In some industries, on the other hand, it's common to use a separate document when making a counteroffer that states the desired changes and refers back to the original offer. In that case, both the original offer and the counteroffer form the contract.

A contract can also be amended at a later date with a separate document called an addendum. The addendum should state that its terms prevail over the terms of the original contract, especially if the terms are in direct conflict, as would be the case if the price or completion time for a job is changed. Both parties should sign the addendum.

CHAPTER 10

Bookkeeping, Accounting and Financial Management

Perhaps the hardest part of accounting is getting over the psychological hang-up that most people seem to have about it. Many of us are loath to balance our checkbooks on any regular basis, much less keep detailed accounts of how our money comes and goes. The good news is that you don't need to be a financial wizard to start a small business; you just need a comfortable working knowledge of the basics.

If you read Chapter 5, "Drafting an Effective Business Plan," some of this material may be a review. In that chapter, we explained how to generate financial projections using sales and expense estimates to see if your business was likely to turn a profit. The financial tools used in business planning—particularly profit/loss analysis and cash flow projection—are the same tools used in accounting, just used slightly differently. In this chapter, we'll focus on how to use these and other tools to keep track of the actual financial data (as opposed to projections) of your business.

This chapter will give you an idea of what records your business should keep and will describe simple ways to keep them. We'll also explain how to use the information in your financial records to calculate how much profit your business is making and to ensure that enough cash is regularly flowing through your business to pay your important bills on time.

Fortunately for today's entrepreneurs, inexpensive, powerful and easy-to-use software, such as Quickbooks or Quicken, is available that will help simplify the accounting process. Once your income and expenses are entered into the system, you're only a few mouse clicks away from sophisticated financial reports that would have taken many hours and considerable skill to generate just a decade ago. In fact, these programs are so affordable (around $100) and user-friendly it makes little sense not to use one of them.

Don't expect your accounting software to do your accounting for you. Don't simply rely on a software program to spit out numbers for you that you don't fully understand. The accounting concepts and processes described in this chapter are the same whether done manually or by computer—and you should take the time to learn them. Either way, you'll still need to save your receipts and enter them into periodic summaries. And either way, you'll use the numbers in those summaries to tell you key information about the financial health of your business. While accounting software makes it much easier to manipulate the numbers you've entered and to generate informative financial reports, you still need an understanding of what all the numbers mean in order to make them work for your business.

It often pays to get help with bookkeeping and accounting tasks. The basic information provided in this chapter will be valuable for all business owners who are unfamiliar with accounting basics. Depending on the size and type of your business, you may eventually want to do additional reading or hire experienced help. Our approach here is to provide enough information to get a new businessperson sensibly started. But even so, the owner of a small, relatively simple business can almost always benefit from an hour or two with an experienced small-business accountant who can often offer creative strategies for keeping records, selecting and configuring your computerized accounting system, and managing your money.

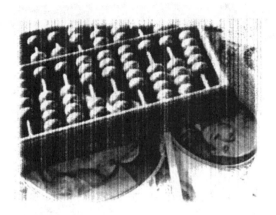

Organization is everything. One thing that all good bookkeeping systems have in common is organization. A well-organized system with accessible, reasonably neat files will not only be a godsend in the event of an audit, but it will help you keep track of your business as well.

The actual process of accounting is easy to understand when broken down into three steps.

1) Keep receipts or other acceptable records of every payment to and every expenditure from your business.

2) Summarize your income and expenditure records on some periodic basis (generally daily, weekly or monthly).

3) Use your summaries to create financial reports that will tell you specific information about your business, such as how much monthly profit you're making or how much your business is worth at a specific point in time.

And, of course, whether you do your accounting by hand on ledger sheets or use accounting software, these principles are exactly the same.

A. Accounting Basics

Accounting has two basic goals:

• to keep track of your income and expenses, thereby improving your chances of making a profit, and

• to collect the necessary financial information about your business to file your various tax returns and local tax registration papers.

Sounds pretty simple, doesn't it? And it can be, especially if you remind yourself of these two goals whenever you feel overwhelmed by the details of keeping your financial records. Hopefully you will also be reassured to know that there is no requirement that your records be kept in any particular way. (There is a requirement, however, that some businesses use a certain method of crediting their accounts. See Section B, below, on accrual accounting.) In other words, there's no official "right" way to organize your books—as long as your records accurately reflect your business's income and expenses, the IRS will find them acceptable.

Accounting Glossary

A big part of understanding the financial side of your business consists of nothing more than learning the language of accounting. Once you're familiar with basic terms, you'll be well prepared to make sense of basic written reports and better able to communicate with others about important financial information. And you'll also be well positioned to cope with a common business problem: many people use key financial terms imprecisely or even incorrectly, thus needlessly confusing themselves and others.

- **Accounting** is a general term that refers to the overall process of tracking your business's income and expenses, and then using these numbers in various calculations and formulas to answer specific questions about the financial and tax status of the business.

- **Bookkeeping** refers to the task of recording the amount, date and source of all business revenues and expenses. Bookkeeping is essentially the starting point of the accounting process. Only with accurate bookkeeping numbers can meaningful accounting be done.

- An **invoice** is a written record of a transaction, often submitted to a customer or client when requesting payment. Invoices are sometimes called **bills** or **statements**, though the latter term has its own technical meaning (see below).

- A **statement** is a formal written summary of an account. Unlike an invoice, a statement is not generally used as a formal request for payment, but is more of a reminder to a customer or client that payment is due.

- A **ledger** is a physical collection of related financial information, such as revenues, expenditures, accounts receivable and accounts payable. Led-

gers used to be kept in books preprinted with lined ledger paper (which explains why a business's financial info is often referred to as the "books"), but are now commonly computer files that can be printed out.

- An **account** is a collection of financial information grouped according to customer or purpose. For example, if you have a regular customer, the collection of information regarding that customer's purchases, payments and debts would be called his "account." A written record of an account is called a **statement.**

- A **receipt** is a written record of a transaction. A buyer receives a receipt to show that he paid for an item. The seller keeps a copy of the receipt to show she received payment for the item. Receipts are sometimes called **sales slips**.

- **Accounts payable** are amounts that your business owes. For example, unpaid utility bills and purchases your business made on credit would be included in your accounts payable.

- **Accounts receivable** are amounts owed to your business that you expect to receive. Accounts receivable includes sales your business made on credit.

Are you to beginning believe that you don't need to be afraid of accounting? Good, because it's something you absolutely need to embrace as part of running any business. Failing to keep track of income and expenses is one of the surest ways to run any business off a cliff. Here are a few more ways that a simple set of books will help your business.

- **You'll be able to price your goods and services more competitively.** Only by staying on top of your business's income and expenses will you know how much money you'll need to bring in each week, month or year to make a profit. And, of course, this knowledge is essential to allow you to price your goods and services appropriately. For instance, if you don't know your break-even point, you will only be able to guess at how much to charge your customers for products or services, with the likely result that you'll charge too low (and make an inadequate profit) or too high (and alienate customers).

- **You'll be able to pace your growth more effectively.** A good set of books will give you the information you need to decide when and how to expand your business. If your numbers tell you that sales and profits have been growing consistently for several months, that may be a signal that it's time to hire additional employees or enter into a new market—or both. Without meaningful financial numbers, making any decisions about growth can be a gamble. For example, just because your business has a lot of money in its checking account doesn't necessarily mean you're making good money (you might have received several big payments from past sales, while current sales are actually slowing down).

- **Your taxes can be minimized.** Knowing your company's finances well, inside and out, will help you save money when tax time comes around. For example, if the end of the year is nearing and your up-to-date records clearly show the year to be profitable, you can purchase needed supplies or equipment before the end of the year and write off these expenses, thus reducing your

taxable income. Also, keeping careful track of your expenses will prevent you from simply forgetting to claim them as deductions at year-end. Businesses that are sloppy about bookkeeping often miss opportunities for saving tax dollars. Don't be one of them.

- **You'll avoid tax penalties.** Besides being positioned to legally save tax dollars, responsible bookkeeping will help you avoid errors in your tax returns that can subject you to fines and other penalties. No question, if your business is audited, the IRS can be really nasty if it finds your books in bad shape—in extreme situations it may even refuse to recognize perfectly legitimate expenses. In short, neglecting your responsibility to maintain basic, accurate records is highly likely to result in the kind of trouble with the IRS that you might not even wish on your worst enemy.

B. Cash vs. Accrual Accounting

Before we discuss several simple systems for keeping your records, you need to understand the basics of the two principal methods of keeping track of a business's income and expenses: cash method and accrual method (sometimes called cash basis and accrual basis). In a nutshell, these methods differ only in the timing of when transactions—both sales and purchases—are credited or debited to your accounts. If you use the cash method, income is counted when cash (or a check) is actually received and expenses are counted when actually paid. But under the more common accrual method, transactions are counted when they happen—regardless of when the money is actually received or paid.

So with the accrual method, income is counted when the sale occurs, and expenses are counted when you receive goods or services—you don't have to wait until you see the money, or until you actually pay money out of your checking account. With some transactions, it's not so easy to know when the sale or purchase has occurred. The key date here is the job completion date. Not until you finish a service or deliver all the goods a contract calls for can do you put the income down in your books. If a job is mostly completed but will take another 30 days to add the finishing touches, technically it doesn't go on your books until the 30 days pass.

Say you purchase a new laser printer on credit in May and pay $2,000 for it in July, two months later. Using cash-method accounting you would record a $2,000 payment for the month of July, the month when the money is actually paid. But under the accrual method, the $2,000 payment would be recorded in May, when you take the laser printer and become obligated to pay for it. Similarly, if your computer installation business finishes a job on November 30, 1998, and doesn't get paid until January 10, 1999, you'd record the payment in January 1999 if you use the cash method. Under the accrual method the income would be recorded in your books in November of 1998.

The most significant way your business is affected by the accounting method you choose involves the tax year in which income and particular expense items will be counted. (See Sidebar on tax years and accounting periods.) For instance, if you incur expenses in the 1998 tax year but don't pay them until the 1999 tax year, you won't be able to claim them in 1998 if you use the cash method. But as you should now understand, you would be able to claim them if you use the accrual method, since the very essence of that system is to record transactions when they occur, not when money actually changes hands.

Example 1:

Zara runs a small flower shop called ZuZu's Petals. On December 22, 1999, Zara buys a set of new lighting equipment for her shop for which she will be billed $400. She installs the lighting equipment that day, but according to the terms of the purchase doesn't pay for it for 30 days. Under her accrual system of accounting, she counts the $400 expense during the December 1999 accounting period, even though she didn't actually write the check until January of the next year. This means that Zara can deduct the $400 from her taxable income of 1999.

Example 2:

Scott and Lisa operate A Stitch in Hide, a leather repair shop. They're hired to repair an antique leather couch, and they finish their job on December 15, 1999. They bill the customer for $750, which they receive on January 20, 2000. Since they use the accrual method of accounting, Scott and Lisa count the $750 income in December 1999, because that's when they earned the money by finishing the job. This income must be reported in their 1999 tax return even though they don't receive the money that year.

The cash and accrual methods can produce the same results. As you can readily see, the results produced by the cash and accrual accounting methods will only be different if you do some transactions on credit. If all your transactions are paid in cash as soon as completed, including your sales and your purchases, then your ledgers will look the same, regardless of what method you use.

Most businesses that have sales of less than $5 million per year are free to choose which accounting method to adopt. But if your business stocks an inventory of items that you will sell to the public, the IRS requires that the accrual accounting method be used. Inventory includes any merchandise you sell as well as supplies that will physically become part of an item intended for sale.

Whichever method you use, it's important to realize that either one only gives you a partial picture of the financial status of your business. While the accrual method shows the ebb and flow of business income and debts more accurately, it may leave you in the dark as to what cash reserves are available—which could result in a serious cash flow problem. For instance, your income ledger may show thousands of dollars in sales, while in reality your bank account is empty because your customers haven't paid you yet.

And though the cash method will give you a truer idea of how much actual cash your business has, it may offer a misleading picture of longer-term profitability. Under the cash method, for instance, your books may show one month to be spectacularly profitable, when actually sales have been slow and, by coincidence, a lot of credit customers paid their bills in that month. To have a firm and true understanding of your business's finances, you need more than just a collection of monthly totals; you need to understand what your numbers mean and how to use them to answer specific financial questions.

C. Step One: Keeping Your Receipts

Comprehensive summaries of your business's income and expenses are the heart of the accounting process. But they can't legally be created in a vacuum. Each of your business's sales and purchases must be backed by some type of record containing the amount, the date and other relevant information about that sale. This is true whether your accounting is done by computer or on hand-posted ledgers.

From a legal point of view, your method of keeping receipts can range from slips kept in a cigar box to a sophisticated cash register hooked into a computer system. Practically, you'll want to choose a system that fits your business needs. For example, a small service business that handles only relatively few jobs may get by with a bare-bones approach. But the more sales and expenditures your business makes, the better your receipt filing system needs to be. This section discusses common ways of keeping your receipts. The bottom line is to choose or adapt one to suit your needs.

1. Receipts of Income

Every time your business brings in money, you need a record of that income. Most of your revenue will come from sales of your products or services. How you keep track of sales will vary a great deal depending on what type of business you run and how many sales you make. Businesses like grocery stores that make hundreds or even thousands of sales a day will likely need a cash register to produce a record of each sale. Other businesses with slower sales, such as a hair salon or an auto shop, could get by simply writing out a receipt for each sale from a receipt book. The main thing is to establish a system that works with your particular type of business.

Whether you use a cash register tape or hand-written receipts, make sure that you and your employees know the system and use it consistently. Hand-written receipts should include the date and a brief description of the goods or services sold. If some of your sales are made on credit, your receipts should indicate whether the customer paid, and if not, when payment is due. If your income records aren't accurate, neither will be the ledgers or financial statements you make from them.

Receipts are more important for you than your customers. Sales receipts (records) are more important for your own accounting purposes than they are for your customers (who, unless they are a business, will likely throw them out). While it's good business practice to give receipts to customers who purchase goods or services, it's a legal requirement that you keep a copy for yourself. Therefore, if you write out your own receipts, you'll need to make two copies—one for you, and one for the customer. Cash registers and most receipt books make each record in duplicate.

One huge distinction your income records need to reflect is whether a sale is taxable or not for state sales-tax purposes. To compute and file your California sales taxes, you'll need to keep taxable sales separate from nontaxable sales. (See "Taxable Sales vs. Taxable Income," below.) If you use a cash register, this distinction can be made by the push of a button at the time of each sale. At the end of the day, the register (assuming it's a relatively modern one) will give you totals for taxable sales and nontaxable sales. If you write out a receipt of each sale by hand, be sure to show any sales tax separately, not just as part of a total, and if the sale is nontaxable make that clear by writing "no tax," "nontaxable" or the like.

Taxable Sales vs. Taxable Income

As discussed above (and in more detail in Chapter 8), many sales of goods are subject to California sales tax, which retailers must pay to the state. But other large categories of sales are exempt from sales tax, such as sales of services, sales to California non-residents or sales to resellers. So some sales income is taxable and some is not. But it is crucial to understand that whether a sale is taxable or not for sales tax purposes is a different issue from whether income is taxable or not for income-tax purposes. Generally, taxable income—that is, money you take in which is subject to income taxes at the end of the year—includes any money earned by your business, minus certain deductions, and will be taxed on your year-end income-tax return. This includes all income your business brings in, whether or not it is subject to sales tax. Be sure you keep these two different issues straight.

You should also document any income your business receives from sources other than sales, and keep these receipts separate from your sales receipts. If you get a loan or contribute your own personal money to the business, record this fact with some sort of a receipt or a promissory note. The key here is to be sure your written records adequately describe the source of income so you can tell whether to count it as taxable income or not. Most sales income, for example, will be taxed at the end of the year, while income that you personally contribute to the business will not be subject to tax.

Assuming you follow our advice to keep your receipts of taxable sales separate from receipts of nontaxable sales and income, posting them to your accounting system (discussed below) should be easy. If you plan to post daily, a simple method involves keeping your receipts for the day in two envelopes or two sections of an accordion folder (one for taxable sales, one for nontaxable) and adding them up at the end of the day. If you use a cash register, the process is simplified because you can simply run totals at the end of the day for taxable sales and nontaxable sales. Depending on your machine, you may also be able to print out totals for other periods of time, such as one week or a specified number of days.

2. Expenditure Receipts

Ever hear the business wisdom that the key to small-business success is to keep your costs down? While this isn't the only thing a successful business owner needs to do, watching those pennies is always a good idea. The first step in keeping costs down is keeping accurate track of what they are. Just as you keep a record of each individual sale, you need to keep a record of each time you spend money for your business. Business expenditures include paychecks to employees, money spent on supplies, and payments on loans, as well as all other costs associated with your business. Legally and practically, each and every one of these expenses must be recorded.

First of all, be sure to get a written receipt for every transaction in which you spend money for the business. Not only is keeping and tallying these receipts an easy way to keep track of your expenses, but receipts also come in handy if there's a problem with any of the goods or services you purchased or a dispute over whether you paid a particular bill.

Many business people like to use their checkbook registers to keep track of expenses. This is fine, but there are two thorns to watch out for. Since many of your expenditures will be paid for by check, for these transactions you may have two records of the same transaction: the notation in your checkbook and the receipt from the seller. *Make sure you don't count that transaction twice!* And don't forget to record cash purchases—they won't show up in your checkbook register. There are several easy ways to avoid counting some expenses twice and forgetting others. One is to use your receipts as the sole record of expenditures, and not to count the amounts in your checkbook. Since most businesspeople don't want to sort through a pile of odd-sized bits of paper, another way is to rely solely on your checkbook for expenditure records, instead of on receipts. Fine, as long as you make sure you include the receipts of cash transactions.

Don't let multiple receipts screw up your bookkeeping. *Sometimes you'll receive a number of sales slips for just one purchase: a credit card slip, a register receipt and an itemized statement, for example. If you throw all three receipts into your files to be posted later, you run the risk of counting all three separately. You might think that you'll remember the transaction, or that it will be obvious to you as you're posting your ledger that the three receipts correspond to a single transaction, but when dealing with dozens of receipts at the end of a long day of work it's all too easy for mistakes to creep into your paperwork. To avoid counting transactions more than once, either discard multiple copies of receipts immediately after the transaction or staple them all together.*

Each record of an expenditure should include the date, the amount, the method of payment, who was paid and—most important—a description of what type of expense it was, such as rent, supplies or utilities. The description is important because later, when you post (enter) your expenses to your ledgers, you'll need to assign them into categories such as rent, advertising, supplies, utilities and taxes. (We discuss expense categories below.) These categories are important for tax purposes because different types of expenses have different rules for deductibility. So to make your bookkeeping job easier, make sure your expense receipts contain enough information for you to be able to assign the expense to the appropriate category when you post it in your ledger. Also, it's best to keep your expense receipts separated by category during the month before you post them. In other words, keep all of your utilities receipts in one box or envelope, your supplies receipts in another, and so on.

D. Step Two: Setting Up and Posting Ledgers

A completed ledger is really nothing more than a summary of revenues, expenditures, and whatever else you're keeping track of (entered from your receipts according to category and date). Later, you'll use these summaries to answer specific financial questions about your business—such as whether you're making a profit, and if so, how much.

You'll start with a blank ledger page (a sheet with lines) or, more often these days, a computer file of empty rows and columns. On some regular basis—like every day, once a week or at least once a month—you should transfer the amounts from your receipts for sales and purchases into your ledger. Called "posting," how often you do this depends on how many sales and expenditures your business makes and how detailed you want your books to be.

Generally speaking, the more sales you do, the more often you should post to your ledger. A retail store, for instance, that does hundreds of sales amounting to thousands or tens of thousands of dollars every day should probably post daily. With that volume of sales, it's important to see what's happening every day and not to fall behind with the paperwork. To do this, the busy retailer should use a cash register which totals and posts the day's sales to a computerized bookkeeping system at the push of a button. A slower business, however, or one with just a few large transactions per month, such as a small Website design shop, dog-sitting service or swimming-pool repair company, would probably be fine if it posted weekly or even monthly.

To get started on a hand-entry system, get ledger pads from any office supply store. Alternatively, you can purchase an accounting software program that will generate its own ledgers as you enter your information. All but the tiniest new business are well advised to use an accounting software package to help keep their books (and micro-businesses can get by with personal finance software such as Quicken). That's because once you've entered your daily, weekly or monthly numbers, accounting software makes preparing monthly and yearly financial reports incredibly easy.

Learn bookkeeping by hand to prevent computer-induced ignorance. Even though a computerized accounting system allows you to generate sophisticated financial reports with a few mouse clicks, you should still take the time to understand how the numbers fit together and what they mean. A good way to do this is to learn how financial reports are done by hand, even if you plan to use a computer to generate them. The more you know about your numbers and the relationships between various figures, the more power you'll have to make positive and profitable business decisions.

Every business should have both an income ledger and an expenditure ledger to post its transactions. We'll walk you through each of these ledgers below, and offer samples of each type. We'll also introduce you to some other types of ledgers that you may want to use, depending on your business.

1. Income Ledger

Despite its name, an income ledger should include only money earned in the course of business—your sales income, not income from every source. For example, income such as a loan or transfer of personal money into the business should not be included with sales income on this ledger.

Check out the following example.

Income for May 1999							
1	**2**	**3**	**4**		**5**		**6**
Date	**Sales Period**	**Taxable Sales**	**Sales Tax**		**Nontaxable Sales**		**Total Sales**
				Sales to Retailers	Nontaxable Labor Sales	Other	
I		$452.58	$38.47	$96.50	$75.00	$45.00	$707.55
2	closed						
3							
4	(May 3-4)	$765.50	$65.07	$143.50	$125.00	$65.75	$1,164.82
5...		$407.88	$34.67	$76.25	$60.00	$45.00	$623.80
...31		$502.45	$42.71	$105.00	$90.00	$53.50	$793.66
Totals		**$9,456.82**	**$803.83**	**$1,845.50**	**$1,365.50**	**$854.00**	**$14,325.65**

Most income ledgers—whether on paper or part of your accounting software—are set up like the above sample, covering a one-month period and allowing space for daily entries. Your income should be divided into taxable sales, sales tax and nontaxable sales.

You must group your nontaxable sales by type. *The California Board of Equalization requires that you keep records of your nontaxable sales in separate categories, such as food sales, sales to retailers and sales to the U.S. government. The categories you must use may vary depending on what kind of business you run. Contact the BOE for information on the specific categories your particular business must use. The BOE has a number of published regulations on recordkeeping and tax tip pamphlets that explain the bookkeeping requirements for various businesses. See Appendix A for a list of available publications.*

When you're ready to post your sales income, however often you decide to do it, go through your receipts for that period and enter the totals into the appropriate columns. Mark each receipt or cash-register tape "posted" (stamping is often easiest) once you've recorded it in your ledger. If you post daily, you'll have entries on each line except for days your business is closed, in which case you should enter "closed" in the Sales Period column. If you don't post daily, indicate in the Sales Period column which days are included for the totals you're entering (for example, "June 3 to June 6").

At the end of each month, total the entries in each column. Voila! You now have an income ledger for one month of business. As you can see, even without the help of a computer creating one is easy.

After an income ledger has been completed each month for a year, it's easy to add the monthly totals to arrive at your yearly sales income, broken down into taxable and nontaxable sales and sales tax amounts. Simply use a separate ledger sheet or computer file to post your monthly totals into a year-end income ledger. It will look very similar to your monthly income ledgers. Here's a sample:

Income for 1999					
1	**2**	**3**	**4**		**5**
Month	**Taxable Sales**	**Sales Tax**	**Nontaxable Sales**		**Monthly Totals**
			Sales to Retailer	Nontaxable Labor	Other
January	$7,873.46	$669.24	$1,595.75	$1,310.75	$749.50	$12,198.70
February	$8,567.45	$728.23	$1,787.25	$1,280.75	$683.00	$13,046.68
March	$8,349.05	$709.67	$1,640.50	$1,150.50	$745.50	$12,595.22
April...	$8,995.65	$764.63	$1,788.00	$1,335.75	$823.70	$13,707.73
...December	$10,483.88	$891.13	$1,825.25	$1,458.50	$880.50	$15,539.26
Total for Year	$100,468.48	$9,108.72	$20,364.50	$14,076.25	$9,539.90	$153,557.85

2. Expenditure Ledger

The process of creating an expenditure ledger is quite similar to the income ledger process, but there are some key differences. Most importantly, the categories you must divide your expenses into are different. These categories are especially important because different types of expenses have different rules for deductibility for tax purposes. Some expenditures can be deducted right away in full, others may be deducted only over multiple tax years (referred to as depreciation), while other costs may not be deductible at all. The sample expenditure ledger below shows the most commonly used expense categories. But if your business has different regular expenses (for example, a carpenter might have a category for wood and another for nails, while a

Web designer might have a category for printing costs, and one for computer disks), you will want to add or change one or more categories to suit your needs.

The IRS has oceans of rules on deductible expenses. For more information on different types of business expenses and their deductibility, read *Tax Savvy for Small Business*, by tax attorney Frederick Daily (Nolo Press). Reading the rules issued by the IRS isn't a bad idea, either. IRS Publication 334, "Tax Guide for Small Businesses" is a good place to start.

Expenditures for February 1999

1 Date	2 Payment Method/ Check #	3 Transaction/ Payee	4 Supplies	5 Rent	6 Utilities	7 Misc.	8 Monthly Totals
2-1	ck. 1204	rent/landlord		$1,000.00			
2-5	Visa	stationery/ Office Depot	$ 78.00				
2-13	cash	business lunch/ Monte Vista café				$ 32.00	
2-22	ck. 1206	electric bill/PG&E			$ 65.00		
Feb. Totals			**$78.00**	**$1,000.00**	**$ 65.00**	**$ 32.00**	**$1,175.00**

Just as with your income receipts, you must periodically transfer (post) the information from your expenditure receipts to your expense ledger. Ideally you should do this reasonably promptly after you incur the expense. In the Payment Method/Check # column, enter "cash" if you paid in cash; the name of the credit card if you paid with plastic; or the check number if you paid by check. (Remember, if you use cash basis accounting, you will only record expenditures when they are paid—not when you incur them—so instead of recording credit card purchases, you'd only record when you pay your bill.) In the Transaction/Payee column, enter a brief description of the purchase and whom you paid. Then enter the amount of the purchase in the appropriate category column.

Unlike your income ledgers, a new expenditure ledger isn't started each month—you'll have one running expense ledger. At the end of the month, simply add up the expenses for that month in each category, and enter each category's total in the next empty row. Then add up all the totals for each category and enter the result in the Monthly Totals column. Draw a double line under the monthly totals, and then continue entering expenses for the next month on the same sheet. Use a new sheet when you run out of room.

At year-end, you'll summarize your monthly expenditure totals on a separate ledger in much the same way that you summarized your monthly income totals. Remember that if you use the accrual accounting method, you'll need to include expenses for the year even if you haven't paid for them yet. Do this by including the totals of any unpaid bills in the Accounts Payable row, categorized like your other expenses, and added to your yearly total.

Year-end Expenditure Summary					
1	2	3	4	5	6
Month	Rent	Supplies	Utilities	Misc.	Totals
January	$1,100	$120	$254	$154	$1,628
February	$1,100	$75	$236	$209	$1,620
March	$1,100	$56	$244	$130	$1,530
April...	$1,100	$90	$197	$104	$1,491
...December	$1,100	$62	$230	$185	$1,577
Accounts Payable	$75	$210	$62	$347	$694
Year Totals	$13,275	$1,082	$2,164	$1,845	$18,366

3. Designing a Ledger System for Your Business

The two ledgers just described help you keep track of your most basic business functions—earning and spending money. Depending on how you conduct your business, you may also need to use one or more additional ledgers. If you sell products or services on credit, you'll want to keep track of these sales (the amount you are owed) using an accounts receivable ledger. Similarly, if you make purchases on credit, you can keep track of what you owe with an accounts payable ledger. And if your business has assets such as machinery, computers or vehicles, you'll need to keep track of their depreciation with an equipment ledger. (Depreciation is explained in Chapter 8.) You'll find prototypes of various types of ledgers at office supply stores, or as a component of any accounting software product.

E. Step Three: Creating Basic Financial Reports

Financial reports are important because they bring together several key pieces of financial information about your business in one place. Think of it this way—while your income ledger may tell you that your business brought in a lot of money during the year, you have no way of knowing whether you turned a profit without measuring your income against your expenses. And even comparing your monthly totals of income and expenses won't tell you whether your credit customers are paying fast enough to keep adequate cash flowing through your business to pay your bills on time. That's why you need financial reports: to combine data from your ledgers and sculpt it into a shape that shows you the big picture of your business.

The financial reports we talk about in this section are nothing to freak out about—they're really just the income and expense numbers from your ledgers, tweaked a bit in order to help you answer questions about how your business is doing. For instance, the mysterious-sounding "profit and loss statement" consists of nothing more than your company income and expense numbers coupled with one another so that you know how much profit (or loss) you're making over a specified period of time. As long as you've been consistent and thorough in keeping your ledgers, you'll be able to easily and quickly generate this and other reports (which will make you as popular with your bank as having a six-pack of beer on prom night).

1. Profit and Loss Statement

If the typical owner of a small business start-up got a nickel for every time she asked herself, "Will my business make a profit?" she'd probably be rich enough to retire before the doors were even open. A profit and loss statement (also called a P & L, or an income statement) is designed to answer this very question. (In Chapter 5, "Drafting an Effective Business Plan," we discussed creating a profit and loss statement with projected numbers. Here we explain how to do it after you've opened your doors and have actual numbers to work with.) A P & L is made by totaling your revenues and then subtracting your expenses from that total, for specific periods of time, usually per month. If you use accounting software, it will generate a P & L automatically with the data you enter from your sales and expense records. For each month you'll be able to see whether your revenues are higher or lower than your expenses and by how much. At year-end you can total the monthly results to obtain your annual profit or loss.

To create a profit and loss statement, you'll need to subtract your "fixed costs" and your "variable costs" from your sales revenue, but first you'll need to understand the difference between the two. Variable costs (also called costs of sale, or product costs, or labor costs) are the expenses that are directly tied to the product or service that you're selling. Fixed costs (also called overhead) are the costs associated with running your business in general, not with individual products or services themselves. For example, say your business produces and sells greeting cards. Your variable costs would include the cost of the paper and printing of the cards, and the labor cost for the workers that make, package and distribute the cards. As the name implies, these costs will vary depending on the amount and type of product (in this case the individual card) you make and sell or service that you perform. For example, if you produce more or less of a particular card, if you use color or black and white, or if you emboss or use a heavier grade of card stock, your variable expenses will be affected.

Labor costs are sometimes considered variable, sometimes fixed. *If you ask a group of accountants whether the labor costs associated with a making a product are fixed or variable, you're likely to get conflicting answers. Some argue that as long as the workers will get paid regardless of whether they're working on that product, their salaries should be considered fixed, like rent or utilities. Others say that to have accurate financial records you need to reflect the cost of the labor that goes into a product. You or your accountant can decide how you want to categorize labor costs for making a product. Labor costs for providing services, on the other hand, are almost always treated as variable costs.*

But other costs—your fixed costs—will not go up or down depending on the products you make or the services you perform. These costs, such as your rent, your office utility bills and the insurance you purchase for your company vehicles (as well as your own salary, probably) will be more or less the same, regardless of the types or amount of greeting cards you make. This is exactly why age-old business wisdom says to keep your overhead costs as low as reasonably possible. In times of slow sales, you want to be saddled with as few fixed costs as possible.

Now that you know the distinction between variable and fixed costs, you need to understand how they're each subtracted from your revenue on a typical profit and loss statement (hang in there—we're almost done).

- A profit and loss statement starts with your total sales revenues (remember, you collected that on your income ledger), and then subtracts your variable costs (collected in one or more columns of your expenditure ledger). The result is called your gross profit—how much money you've earned from sales of your products or services above their cost to you.

- Next you subtract your fixed costs from your gross profit. Any money you're left with is your real profit—also called net income, net profit, or pre-tax profit. Other than the various taxes you'll need to pay on this income, this is your money.

The formula used in a profit and loss statement is basically as follows:

sales revenue

– variable costs (a.k.a. costs of sale)

――――――――――――――――――

= gross profit (a.k.a. gross margin)

– fixed costs

――――――

= net profit

Here's a typical P & L:

1999 Profit/Loss Forecast							
	January	**February**	**March**	**April**	**May...**	**...December**	**Year Total**
Sales Revenues	$ 1,900	$1,950	$2,000	$1,850	$2,000	$2,100	$23,550
Variable Costs	$ 300	$310	$350	$300	$325	$350	$3,840
Gross Profit	$ 1,600	$1,640	$1,650	$1,550	$1,675	$1,750	$19,180
Fixed Expenses							
Rent	$ 700	$700	$700	$700	$700	$700	$8,400
Supplies	$ 150	$100	$75	$90	$125	$100	$1,220
Utilities	$ 200	$200	$200	$200	$200	$200	$2,400
Advertising	$ 150	$150	$150	$150	$150	$150	$1,800
Misc.	$ 75	$80	$65	$70	$75	$85	$830
Total Fixed Expenses	$ 1,275	$1,230	$1,190	$1,210	$1,250	$1,235	$14,650
Net Income (Loss)	**$ 325**	**$410**	**$460**	**$340**	**$425**	**$515**	**$4530**

The P & L will not only tell you whether you're making or losing money, but is also an absolutely crucial tool to help you identify which aspects of your business need tinkering with in order to boost profits. Often, a profitability problem can be found in your expenses. Being able to see the totals of each of your various expense categories over the course of several months all on one sheet can help you pinpoint areas where you're spending too much money (and hopefully help give you the courage to do something about it). And, of course, accurately tracking income totals month by month will help you quickly spot a downturn and see if you need to take action to boost sales.

2. Cash Flow Projection

We discussed cash flow projections in Chapter 5, "Drafting an Effective Business Plan," as a way to find out if your business would be able to pay its bills once it got started. A cash flow projection is also a crucial tool to use in your ongoing business. It's essential that your business have enough cash available at any given time to pay for its costs of operation. Having lots of customers and thriving sales isn't enough, especially if you sell on credit. If your customers pay you in 90 days, but you must pay your expenses in 30 days, or even immediately, you may face a situation where, even though your financial statement says you are making a profit, you can't pay your rent, utilities, delivery services or other key bills. Unless you make some changes, you may even have to close up shop.

Understanding how this can happen—and how to take steps to avoid it—is where a cash flow projection comes in. A cash flow projection focuses on the actual cash payments made to and by your business. We call these payments cash-ins and cash-outs (or inflows and outflows) to differentiate them from sales and expenses, which may not be paid right away. Estimating your cash-ins and cash-outs for upcoming months can help you predict when you might run short, allowing you to take action early by tightening up on your credit terms, raising more capital by getting a loan, or putting more effort into collecting accounts receivable. Without a prediction of when a cash shortage might happen, by the time it does it may be too late to do anything about it other than lock your doors.

Especially when you're in the early stages of a business and don't have much of a business history, predicting your cash-ins and cash-outs isn't easy. You'll need to make estimates of how much income will come in and what expenses must be covered—a task that may seem only slightly easier than reading tea leaves. The key is to do your best—with an emphasis on "do." Accept the fact that your estimates won't be close to 100% accurate, but make them anyway. As the months tick by and the flow of cash into and out from your business settles into daily, weekly and monthly patterns, you'll be able to use numbers from previous periods to help you create a realistic picture of the future.

Your cash flow projection will use most of the same numbers as your profit and loss statement, along with a few new ones. The big difference is that your cash flow projection will include all your sources of income—not just sales income—and only income that's paid in cash (not credit). In other words, while your profit and loss statement is concerned with how much money your business is earning through sales of its product or service, your cash flow analysis is designed to show you how much cash you will have on hand from all sources, including paid sales, loans, investments, transfers from your personal accounts, lottery winnings, whatever. That's because when it comes to paying bills, the bottom line is whether you have money, period.

Here's a brief outline of how to use income and expense information to create a cash flow projection. If you use accounting software, the process will be automatic once you've entered income and expense numbers. Though automated, the calculations are basically the same. The basic formula is

$$
\begin{aligned}
&\text{cash in bank at beginning of month} \\
+\ &\text{cash receipts for the month} \\
-\ &\text{cash disbursements for the month} \\
\hline
=\ &\text{cash in bank at end of month}
\end{aligned}
$$

Generally, you'll start a cash flow projection with a couple months' worth of actual information (or one month's, if you've just opened). Then you'll use those figures to project income and expense amounts for the following months.

For each month, start with the amount of money you have in the bank. (This will generally be the same amount that's left over from the previous month.) Add to that amount any cash that you expect to come in during the month in all relevant categories, such as sales income, loans, interest earned and any personal money you put into the business—your total cash-ins for the month. Next, figure out how much money you expect to spend during the month, your cash-outs. (Cash-outs are often easier to predict than cash-ins because you have more control over them and many costs recur each month.) Subtract your cash-outs from cash-ins and you're through!

Hopefully you'll have cash left over. If not, don't panic. First, pat yourself on the back for doing a cash flow analysis and figuring out ahead of time that you won't be able to cover all your expenses. Then come up with a plan—either put off any expenses that can wait, get more money (perhaps through collecting accounts receivable or getting a short-term loan), or sell, sell, sell.

Here's an example of a cash flow projection you can do on a simple spreadsheet.

Cash Flow Projection, completed April, 1999

	Jan	Feb	March	April	May	June	July	Aug	Sep	Oct	Nov	Dec	Year 19___
Cash at Beginning of Month	$200	$125	$60	$70	$35	$10	($30)	$15	$0	$0	($55)	$30	$460
Cash-ins													
Sales Paid	$1,500	$1,475	$1,550	$1,475	$1,550	$1,500	$1,610	$1,625	$1,550	$1,525	$1,675	$1,690	$18,725
Loans and Transfers	$0	$0	$0	$0	$0	$0	$0	$0	$0	$0	$0	$0	$0
Cash-outs													
Variable Costs	$300	$310	$350	$300	$325	$315	$345	$350	$325	$330	$340	$355	$3,945
Rent	$700	$700	$700	$700	$700	$700	$700	$700	$700	$700	$700	$700	$8,400
Supplies	$150	$100	$75	$90	$125	$90	$110	$85	$100	$110	$95	$90	$1,220
Utilities	$200	$200	$200	$200	$200	$200	$200	$200	$200	$200	$200	$200	$2,400
Loan Payments	$150	$150	$150	$150	$150	$150	$150	$150	$150	$150	$150	$150	$1,800
Misc.	$75	$80	$65	$70	$75	$85	$60	$155	$75	$90	$105	$85	$1,020
Total Cash-outs	$1,575	$1,540	$1,540	$1,510	$1,575	$1,540	$1,565	$1,640	$1,550	$1,580	$1,590	$1,580	$18,785
Cash at End of Month	$125	$60	$70	$35	$10	($30)	$15	$0	$0	($55)	$30	$140	$400

As you can see, arranging income and expense information into a cash flow projection reveals a lot about the financial workings of a business. For example, our sample cash flow forecast shows that cash is tight each and every month (look at the "Cash at End of Month" row), so the business owner might consider ways to cut costs or to tighten credit terms. Of more pressing importance are the projected cash shortages starting in June. Knowing a few months in advance that a shortage is likely will help the business owner figure out what to do while there's still time to take action. She could contribute some personal money to the business (note that the cash flow didn't include any loans or personal transfers to the business), or she could try to cut some nonessential expenses, at least until later in the year when there will be a bit (but only a small bit) more cash available.

Compare your projection to reality. Each month, replace your projections with actual results from your accounting system. It's a great way to see how good a job of projecting you're doing.

Who Needs to Do a Cash Flow Analysis?

David Rothenberg, a CPA who also happens to be Chief Financial Officer at Nolo Press, gives the following advice: "If your business is wildly profitable, you have little or no debt, you are not planning on expanding your business anytime soon and you don't grant your customers a long time to pay, you probably don't need to do a cash flow analysis—you already know you'll have plenty of cash to meet your needs. But if this doesn't sound like your business, then you probably will benefit from keeping a close eye on your cash flow. Remember, the cash flow statement isn't for the IRS and it isn't for the bank; it's for you! That's right, YOU! You're the one who won't sleep at night if your bank account is empty. So what are you waiting for? Get out there and start projecting!"

Your Healthy, Growing Business

f all your careful planning, hard work and good karma pays off, you may soon find yourself needing one or more people to help you handle your thriving business. While part of you will surely be happy that your business is taking off, another, more practical side of you may worry about what's involved in hiring help. This chapter offers a broad overview of the many legal requirements that apply to businesses that have one or more employees. If you're thinking about hiring an employee but aren't sure, the information we give here should help you understand what you're getting into—and help you figure out if there's a better way to go.

Besides the practical and financial concerns involved in hiring one or more people to work for your business, you need to be aware of several legal rules that apply to businesses with workers who are not the business owners. First of all, you'll need to understand the difference between the two types of hired help: employees and independent contractors. This distinction is a crucial one, because different rules will apply to your business depending on what kind of workers you hire. If the government considers your workers to be employees, you'll be subject to a number of state and federal laws and taxes that, generally speaking, must be strictly observed and paid. If, on the other hand, your workers can be characterized as independent contractors, you'll be spared many—but not all—of these requirements.

Consult additional resources for information on being an employer. Nolo's *The Employer's Legal Handbook* by attorney Fred S. Steingold, is an indispensable resource for employers that covers the legal rules on hiring, firing, taxes, workplace safety and much more. For information on hiring independent contractors, be sure to read *Hiring Independent Contractors: The Employer's Legal Guide*, by Stephen Fishman (Nolo Press).

A. Employees vs. Independent Contractors

Whenever someone who isn't an owner works for your business, that person is either an employee or an independent contractor. (There is an exception to this rule for persons whose spouse owns the business they work for. See Chapter 2, Section A on husband/wife sole proprietorships.) In a nutshell, an employee is someone who works for you, on your site, with your tools and equipment and according to your rules and procedures. Independent contractors, on the other hand, are in business for themselves; they work on their own time and with their own tools, and perform services for a number of different clients.

We'll cover this distinction more fully below and introduce the legal rules that go with each type of worker, but for now ingrain it in your mind that it's a distinction not to be taken lightly. The main reason it's a big deal is that businesspeople who hire employees owe a number of employment taxes, such as payroll tax and unemployment tax, while those who hire only independent contractors do not owe these taxes. If you treat an employee as an independent contractor and fail to pay employment taxes, you risk subjecting yourself a huge back-tax bill, plus interest and other state and federal penalties. More than a few businesses have been torpedoed and sunk into bankruptcy after making this mistake.

With that warning in mind, here's the lowdown on classifying your workers.

1. The Agencies That Matter

Since paying taxes is the main fallout of classifying workers as employees, it shouldn't surprise you to learn that the IRS takes a great interest in whether your workers are classified properly. At the federal level, the IRS will take swift and severe action if it finds out that you're treating a worker as an independent contractor, when he really meets the criteria of an employee. At the state level, the California Employment Development Department (EDD) is the agency that collects employment taxes and will also punish a business that avoids paying taxes by misclassifying workers.

2. The Criteria

Strangely enough, neither the IRS nor the California EDD has issued any hard or fast rules as to when workers should be treated as employees and when they can be considered independent contractors. The IRS does, however, have internal guidelines for its auditors that are generally accepted in the business world as the rules to use when deciding what legal status to give to your workers. The California EDD also has a brochure you can obtain that gives some guidance on the issue, though for the most part the California EDD uses the same standards as the IRS. (See Appendix A for contact information for the California EDD.)

A worker should normally be considered an employee, not an independent contractor, when he:

- works only for you and not for any other business
- works on your premises
- uses your tools and equipment
- follows work hours set by you
- follows your instructions on how to complete a job
- receives reimbursement for expenses incurred in doing a job
- supervises any of your other workers, and
- receives any employee benefits, such as holiday pay, vacation time or health insurance.

On the flip side, a worker should probably be considered an independent contractor if he:

- works for a number of different businesses or clients
- has his own office, studio, garage or other permanent place to work
- uses his own equipment and tools
- sets his own hours
- uses his own judgment as to how best to complete a job
- doesn't get reimbursed for expenses incurred in doing a job, and
- advertises his services to the public.

Of course, lots of times a worker you hire might display some characteristics of both categories, which makes it harder to say for sure how that worker should be classified.

Example 1:

Bob does a lot of freelance proofreading for a publisher of books on alternative health, Wholeness Press. He often works for Wholeness Press (about 10 projects per year), but he also does four or five jobs per year for other publishers. He always works at home, receives minimal instructions as to how to do his work, and does his proof-reading whenever he feels like it. Bob can probably be categorized as an independent contractor.

Example 2:

Susan programs almost exclusively for one software developer, Fizz Games, but she also does approximately one outside project per year. She sometimes works from home, but often uses a computer at Fizz Games' office. She works closely with the software development team at Fizz Games, following instructions from some of the developers while training some of the newer workers in programming techniques. The government is likely to see Susan as a true employee. It would be risky to try to treat her as an independent contractor.

In borderline situations, it's of course safer to treat a worker as an employee than risk the penalties that may result if the IRS or the EDD decides you've misclassified an employee as an independent contractor. Keep in mind that the IRS and the EDD tend to disfavor independent contractor status—they'd much rather see borderline workers treated as employees, so that they can collect taxes on them.

If you can't decide how one of your workers should be classified, there are a few ways you can proceed. One is to consult a lawyer or an accountant who understands business tax laws. Another option is to go straight to the horse's mouth and ask the IRS or the EDD to tell you how they would classify a certain worker. You can file Form SS-8, "Determination of Employee Work Status," with the IRS to request a formal ruling on a worker's status.

You can get this form from an IRS office or from their Website (contact information is in Appendix A). Don't be surprised if the IRS says they're an employee! For an EDD determination, file Form DE 1870, "Determination of Employment Taxes and Personal Income Tax Withholding," which is also available online or from a California EDD office (see Appendix A for contact information). Like the IRS, it's common for the EDD to classify workers as employees rather than independent contractors. You'll have to decide for yourself whether it makes sense to leave the determination up to these agencies, or whether you feel confident enough to classify your workers on your own.

B. Special Hurdles for Employers

As soon as you hire your first employee, you unleash a swarm of legal requirements that apply specifically to employers. Not only will you have to pay a number of employment taxes, but you'll need to register with certain government agencies, pay for certain types of insurance, and comply with various laws, such as those requiring you to keep a smoke-free workplace and to post certain notices in your business premises.

Hiring independent contractors also triggers some requirements. For instance, if you pay any independent contractor over $600 in a year, you need to report those payments on Form 1099, which gets sent to the worker and to the IRS. For in-depth information about hiring independent contractors, see *Hiring Independent Contractors: The Employer's Legal Guide*, by Stephen Fishman (Nolo Press).

While the many laws that apply to employers are beyond the scope of this book, here's an overview of the major requirements that apply to businesses with employees. If your needs can't be met by hiring an independent contractor and you must hire an employee, you'll need to consult additional resources to make sure you comply with the many state and federal laws governing employers.

In general, owners of businesses with one or more employees are required to do the following:

- Report all new hires to the EDD within 20 days of the employee's first day of work, as part of the New-Employee Registration Program.

- Obtain workers' compensation insurance and follow rules on notifying employees of their rights to workers' compensation benefits. You may purchase this insurance from the state Workers' Compensation Insurance Fund or from a private insurer.

- Comply with state and federal job safety laws, administered by the federal Occupations Safety and Health Administration (OSHA) and California's Department of Industrial Relations, Division of Occupational Safety and Health (DOSH). This includes filing an illness and injury prevention plan, reporting work-related injuries and illnesses that result in lost work-time and keeping a log of all work-related injuries and illnesses.

- Withhold federal income taxes and the two taxes known as FICA taxes—Social Security and Medicare taxes—from employees' paychecks and periodically report and deposit them with the IRS.

- Report wages and withholding to each employee and to the IRS with Form W-2.

- Pay the employer's portion of Social Security and Medicare tax for each employee, based on the employee's wages. The employer's portion is the same amount as the employee's share: 7.65% of the employee's wages up to $65,400, and 1.45% of wages in excess of that amount.

- Withhold state income taxes from employees' paychecks and periodically deposit them with the Franchise Tax Board.

- Withhold from their paychecks employees' contributions to the State Disability Insurance (SDI) program and periodically deposit them with the state. The SDI rate for 1998 is .5% of an employee's wages, with a wage cap of $31,767 per year. This translates into a maximum SDI contribution of $158.84 per year per employee.

- Register and pay for California Unemployment Insurance (UI) tax. The UI tax rate for new employers is 3.4% of each employee's first $7,000 in wages. This rate lasts for three years, then will change depending on how many benefits any former employees have claimed. The more unemployment benefits they've taken, the higher your tax will be. The range in 1998 is between .9% and 5.4% of the first $7,000 of wages per employee. Unlike disability insurance, the employer is solely responsible for paying unemployment insurance tax and may not deduct it from employee's paychecks.

- Pay Federal Unemployment Tax (FUTA). This tax may not be deducted from employees' paychecks; it's the sole responsibility of the employer.

Thinking twice about becoming an employer? There's no way around it: adding employees to your business will greatly complicate your life. (And we haven't even discussed providing optional benefits, such as health insurance and 401(k) plans.) If there's a way to meet your needs with independent contractors rather than employees, it may be a much more practical road to take. At the very least, you shouldn't jump into hiring employees without having a clear reason to do so.

Getting Professional Help

Most business owners, especially sole proprietors and partners in general partnerships, won't need to rely on professional help for the vast majority of their day-to-day business affairs. As the chapters in this book have shown, the legal tasks involved in starting a business, as well as many of those involved in its ongoing operation, involve nothing more than complying with simple bureaucratic requirements, filling out standard forms and paying fees.

But life's not always so simple, of course, and from time to time you may find yourself feeling like you're in over your head. Maybe you're struggling to decide whether it's a good time, financially speaking, to expand your business. Or perhaps there's a dispute brewing between you and a business partner. These situations are just a couple examples of the types of situations where an expert can come in handy.

Even when things are running smoothly, virtually every business should at least occasionally consult an accountant or other tax expert for help in preparing tax returns. A tax professional can also be extremely helpful in figuring out how to manage your business's finances in order to minimize your taxes. Making contact with a lawyer and a tax person early in your business life is often a sensible step. As your business grows, you'll be able to consult these pros for help with ongoing questions.

Once you decide you want to hire a professional, your next question very likely will be, "How do I find someone I can trust?" This chapter will offer strategies that will help you find and hire a professional such as a lawyer or an accountant who's competent and above board. We'll also talk about an increasingly popular type of service called "legal coaching," which is starting to replace traditional lawyering in many cases.

The basics of do-it-yourself legal research aren't that complex. Learning how to use the legal resources at the law library and online will empower you to take care of a wide range of simple, everyday matters rather than paying someone else to do them. If you are interested in doing legal research, an excellent resource is Nolo's *Legal Research: How to Find and Understand the Law*, by attorneys Stephen Elias and Susan Levinkind.

A. Working With Lawyers

Despite the fact that the attorney section of the yellow pages is often the biggest section of the phone book, a good lawyer can be hard to find. This section discusses the process of finding a lawyer who meets your needs and how to make sure you're getting the most for your hard-earned money.

1. What to Look for in a Lawyer

There are a number of different qualities that are important for your lawyer to have. For one, you want to make sure to find an attorney who has some experience with small business issues, preferably for your type of small business. Plus, you want someone who's intelligent and competent—two qualities that don't necessarily go hand-in-hand with having a law degree. And, of course, you want a lawyer whom you can trust.

In today's world of ever-increasing specialization, lawyers often focus their areas of practice rather narrowly. For example, an expert negotiator may not be an effective courtroom lawyer, and vice versa. Make sure that your lawyer can handle the particular type of problem you're facing, both in terms of its subject matter and the type of work involved.

In addition to finding a lawyer with the skills and experience relevant to your situation, it's important that you and the lawyer get along on a personal level. If an otherwise perfect lawyer—smart, experienced and trustworthy—is condescending or rude, you might as well keep looking for someone with better personal skills. This general rule is especially true for small business owners who will ideally develop a long-term relationship with a lawyer. The better an attorney knows you and your business, the more she will be able to provide the best advice and assistance for your specific situation.

2. How to Find a Lawyer

Unfortunately, the easiest and quickest ways to find a lawyer are usually the least effective. Sure, you'll find hundreds of lawyers' names in the yellow pages, but how will you choose among them? You'll have the same problem if you look in legal newspapers for attorney ads. Flashy, aggressive advertising is definitely not a good indicator of quality legal services. Also, watch out for commercial referral services that collect fees from lawyers to be included in the referral database. To filter out the lawyers who are wrong for you, you'll need to do more research.

The best way to find a good lawyer is to get a personal referral, preferably from someone who runs a small business. Even better is a referral from an owner of a business that's similar to yours. Book publishers, for instance, face different types of legal issues than do auto repair shops, and would be best served by a lawyer familiar with legal areas such as copyright and the First Amendment. Ask other business people for lawyer recommendations.

If personal referrals don't work for you, try investigating which lawyers work in your industry. Keep your eyes and ears open for names of attorneys who have worked on cases in your field. For example, a trade magazine might have an article about a current lawsuit involving a business similar to yours and mention the names of the attorneys working on it. Contact organizations and visit

Websites that focus on your type of business. They can often direct you to lawyers who have worked in the industry. Once you get some names, try calling these lawyers and asking if they're available. If not, there's a good chance they know someone else who might be able to help you.

When you call a prospective lawyer, speak with the lawyer personally, not just the receptionist. You can probably get a good idea of how the attorney operates by paying close attention to the way your call is handled. Is the lawyer available right away, and if not, is your call promptly returned? Is the lawyer willing to spend at least a few minutes talking to you to determine if she really is the best person for the job? Do you get a good personal feeling from your conversation? The way you're treated during your initial call can be a good indicator of how the lawyer treats clients in general.

3. Using a Lawyer as a Coach

In a traditional attorney/client relationship, a client hires an attorney to take care of a legal problem and then hands over any responsibility for—and control of—the matter to the lawyer. While some clients like it this way, many would rather be more involved in their cases, both to maintain some control and to save money on legal fees. But until recently, limited legal help from a lawyer wasn't much of an option. Most lawyers wouldn't take cases unless they could handle them fully on their own.

But a new model of legal services is finally emerging. In this approach, sometimes called "legal coaching" or "unbundled legal services," a lawyer provides only the services that a client wants, and nothing more. For example, if a client wanted legal help in drafting a contract, she could perhaps have a short consulting session with a lawyer to get answers to general questions, go home and draft the contract herself, and then fax it to the lawyer, who will review it and suggest changes. Or if a client wanted to represent himself in small claims court, he could use the lawyer to help him draft motions and prepare for hearings, but otherwise pursue the case on his own.

For a small business owner, using a lawyer as a coach can be especially useful. More often than not, the legal issues that arise in the course of business are relatively simple, and—with a bit of good legal advice—are within the capabilities of most people to handle. Many times, a business owner needs nothing more than some guidance through the bureaucratic maze that small businesses need to navigate. For instance, a business person facing a zoning conflict may be perfectly served by a five-minute explanation from a legal coach on the process of appealing a planning commission's decision. Rather than hiring an attorney for upwards of $1000 to deal with the problem, using a coach might cost $50 and enable the business owner to proceed on her own.

Getting limited legal help from a lawyer has become an increasingly popular approach to legal problems in recent years, though it still can take some effort to find a lawyer who is willing to be just a coach. To find a legal coach, use the same strategies discussed above (personal referrals, for example) but take the extra step of asking the lawyer directly whether he or she is willing to help you in your efforts to solve your own legal problems. If you don't find one right away, be persistent. In today's increasingly competitive legal marketplace, it's becoming easier to find lawyers willing to be flexible in the services they offer.

4. Dealing With Bills and Payments

One area of expertise in which most lawyers are well practiced is billing for their services. Before you hire any lawyer, be sure you fully understand how your fees will be calculated. All too often, clients are unpleasantly surprised by their bills because they didn't pay enough attention to the billing terms when they hired the lawyer. For instance, make sure you understand who's responsible for items like court fees, copy fees, transcription costs and phone bills. These costs aren't trivial, and can quickly send your otherwise affordable bill into the keep-you-awake-at-night range.

Lawyers generally use one of the following methods of calculating fees for their services.

- **Hourly fees.** This arrangement works just like it sounds: you pay the attorney's hourly rate for the number of hours she works on your case. Simple as this system is, there are some details to consider. One is to find out what hourly increments the lawyer uses for billing. For instance, if an attorney bills in half-hour increments, then you'll be charged a full half-hour even if you talk for just five minutes. That can easily total $100 or more for a five-minute phone call—a rate that would make even AT&T blush. You'd be better off if your lawyer uses 10- or 15-minute periods, though not all attorneys break down their time into such small increments.

Another issue to ask about is whether all time spent on the case—even if the attorney isn't doing the work—is billed at the attorney's regular rate. For example, it's reasonable to expect a discounted rate for time spent by the attorney's administrative staff on making copies or organizing paperwork. Make sure that the hourly fee for the attorney applies only to the work of the actual attorney.

Hourly fees for attorneys range from $100 or so to over $400 per hour. High rates may reflect a lawyer's extensive experience—or they might simply reflect a need to pay for a swank office. Don't pay the highest rates unless you feel the lawyer's expertise—not his Armani suit—is worth it.

- **Flat fees.** For some types of cases, attorneys will charge a flat fee for a specific task, such as negotiating a contract or filing articles of incorporation for you. As long as the job goes as expected, you'll pay only the price you and the lawyer agreed to, regardless of how many hours she spent on the job. If the lawyer hits a snag, however, or if the case becomes convoluted for some reason, it's possible for the price to go up. Be sure you and the lawyer are on the same page regarding the situations that may result in a higher fee. Also, find out if any charges such as court costs or copy fees are charged in addition to the flat fee.

- **Contingency fees.** In a contingency fee arrangement, you pay an attorney's fee only if the lawyer wins money for you through a court judgment or a negotiated settlement. In that case, the fee you'd pay would be a percentage of the monetary award, usually one-third to one-half. In contingency fee arrangements, you need to be especially careful of costs such as travel expenses, transcription fees and phone bills. Even if you don't owe attorneys' fees because your lawyer didn't recover any money, you will often be responsible for the lawyer's out-of-pocket expenses while he was working on your case.

Small business matters don't typically require contingency fee arrangements. This payment method is usually used in personal injury cases and others in which a plaintiff sues someone in hopes of a large money award.

- **Retainers.** Sometimes you can hire a lawyer to be more or less "on-call" by paying her a regular fee (usually monthly) called a retainer. This type of arrangement is useful when you have regular, ongoing legal needs such as contract review or negotiation. Based upon your expected needs, you and the lawyer settle on a mutually acceptable monthly fee. Then, you simply have the lawyer take care of any routine legal matters that arise. If you run into a sudden, complex legal dispute, it would likely require additional payments. Obviously, for this type of arrangement to work it's important that you and the lawyer have a clear understanding of the routine services that you expect. Unless your legal needs are regular and predictable, a retainer arrangement is probably not your best option.

By California state law, your fee agreement must be in writing if your lawyer estimates the total cost of legal services to be more than $1,000, or if you have a contingency fee arrangement. Don't let an attorney slide on this requirement. Even if it's not legally required, it's always a good idea to get your fee agreement in writing. A written agreement will help prevent disputes over billing, and is the best way to avoid getting gouged.

B. Working With Accountants and Other Professionals

Many, perhaps most, of the issues that small business people face can be solved by professionals other than lawyers. In particular, tax professionals are often indispensable in helping you deal with tax laws, which have a huge impact on your business both financially and legally. In fact, tax advice is so essential to a successful small business that we recommend that every small business owner consult with a tax expert at least occasionally, say once a year.

Obviously, you want to manage your business and the money flowing through it so as to minimize your tax bill. But you also need to be extremely careful not to violate any tax laws—which are insanely complex—and to avoid making simple mistakes that can result in costly penalties. While complicated tax troubles may indeed call for a tax attorney, many other more common questions can usually be answered by an accountant.

1. Different Professionals for Different Needs

For routine maintenance of your books, you probably don't need the experience—or expense—of an accountant (certified or otherwise). An experienced bookkeeper will be able to implement an effective system of tracking your income and expenses and stay on top of your important bills, including the various taxes your business will owe. Depending on the complexity of your business, you may even decide to do your own bookkeeping—a job that's undoubtedly easier these days with the availability of accounting software. As your business grows, however, the investment in an experienced bookkeeper will likely become worthwhile.

If you find yourself seeking specific tax advice, running a large business or encountering a tricky financial problem, you may need to go up a step on the professional ladder and hire an accountant who's intimate with tax laws. The top dogs of accountants are called certified public accountants (CPAs), who are licensed and regulated by the state. California also licenses uncertified accountants called public accountants. Since the licensing requirements for CPAs are more stringent, they are considered to be the most experienced and knowledgeable type of accountants, and accordingly will be the most expensive.

In addition to bookkeepers and accountants, there are other professionals out there who specialize in tax preparation. The main thing to keep in mind is that some are licensed and some are not. An enrolled agent (EA) is a tax professional licensed by the IRS who can answer tax questions and help you prepare your returns. Others who simply use the title "tax preparer" or "tax-return preparer" may not be licensed at all. If a tax professional doesn't have a license as an enrolled agent or as a public or certified public accountant, it may mean that the "professional" has no official qualifications at all.

The bottom line is to use a professional who is best suited for your needs at hand. Obviously, you shouldn't pay a CPA to do simple bookkeeping, nor should you use a bookkeeper for preparing complex tax returns. You'll need to decide for yourself what kind of professional is appropriate for your needs.

2. Finding Good Professional Help

Finding a tax professional is a lot like finding a lawyer: your goal is to find someone both competent and trustworthy. The strategies we discussed above for finding a lawyer are equally useful in finding other professionals. Getting a personal referral is the best way to find someone you can trust. Referrals from businesspeople in your field are particularly valuable. Since virtually every business has consulted a tax pro at one point or another, it shouldn't be too hard to get a decent list of names.

As with attorneys, choose your tax professional carefully, with an eye to developing a long-term relationship. Don't be shy to ask lots of questions. Find out about the person's experience with small businesses similar to yours, and about his or her knowledge of bookkeeping methods, the tax code, the IRS or anything else that's relevant to the work you want the professional to do for you.

Also be sure you understand the professional's fee structure up front, before you have her do any work. Most charge hourly fees, which vary a great deal depending on what kind of qualifications the professional has. Like your attorney fee agreement, your fee agreement with a tax professional should be in writing—written fee agreements minimize the possibility of disputes over the bill.

Government Agencies and Small Business Resources

A note on the organization of this Appendix: If a resource can be located on the Web, its Website address, along with information about what's available online, will be included in that resource's information. For instance, in the Government Agencies category, the listing for the California Secretary of State includes that office's Web address and a brief description of what you'll find at that site. There's also a separate category for interactive Websites—those that offer more than merely another way to contact a particular office. For instance, the searchable federal trademark database gets its own listing in the Website category, even though it's also listed in the Government Agencies category under the U.S. Patent and Trademark Office.

A. Government Agencies

Government agencies are a lot like Russian dolls: one office often contains another office, which often contains yet another office, and so on in a long, confusing chain of government sub-branches. Getting the right phone number and the right government clerk can be incredibly frustrating. Be patient, and be persistent. Don't be afraid to ask questions, and do your best to explain what or who you need as clearly as you can; the clerk on the other end of the line is often your best source of accurate contact information.

Find the **Internal Revenue Service (IRS)** before it finds you. Besides collecting income taxes, the IRS is also in charge of issuing federal employer identification numbers (FEINs, sometimes called EINs) to new businesses. For general questions on taxes, forms or FEINs, call 800-829-1040. Or, if it's a local call for you, use the IRS's special number for California, which is 510-839-1040. You can also visit the IRS on the Web at http://www.irs.ustreas.gov. If you have a computer, a printer and Internet access, getting forms and instructions online is super-convenient, and much more pleasant than spending an eternity on hold.

The **Small Business Administration (SBA)** specializes in assisting small businesses with financing, often by guaranteeing loans. If your small business is having trouble securing a loan through a bank, the SBA may guarantee all or part of the loan, which will make the bank much more likely to approve the loan. There are many different SBA loan programs that you can learn about at a local SBA office; contact info for District Offices appears below. Or visit the SBA online at http://www.sba.gov.

San Francisco SBA District Office

455 Market St., 6th Floor
San Francisco, CA 94105-2445
415-744-6820
Fax: 415-744-6812

Sacramento SBA District Office

660 J St., Suite 215
Sacramento, CA 95814-2413
916-498-6410
Fax: 916-498-6422

San Diego SBA District Office

550 West C Street, Suite 550
San Diego, CA 92101-3500
619-557-7250
Fax: 619-557-5894

Santa Ana SBA District Office

200 W. Santa Ana Blvd., #700
Santa Ana, CA 92701
714-550-7420
Fax: 714-550-0191

Fresno SBA District Office

2719 N. Air Fresno Dr., Suite 200
Fresno, CA 93727-1547
209-487-5791
Fax: 209-487-5292

Glendale SBA District Office

330 N. Brand Blvd.
Glendale, CA 91203-2304
818-552-3210
Fax: 818-552-3260

The **U.S. Patent and Trademark Office (PTO)** offers federal trademark information and forms. You can call the general information line at 800-PTO-9199 or 703-308-HELP. Better yet is to visit the trademark area of the PTO's Website, at http://www.uspto.gov/web/menu/tm.html. Besides the extensive information on trademark law and procedure available online, you can search the PTO's trademark database for free, and fill out and submit your trademark application electronically.

For information on disability or unemployment insurance, employment taxes, and other rules for employers, contact the **California Employment Development Department (EDD)** in Sacramento. The main EDD phone number is 916-653-0707. The Sacramento office will be able to put you in touch with your local EDD office. Or visit the EDD's Website, which offers both contact info for the EDD offices in your area and substantive information on the laws that apply to employers. The Web address is http://www.edd.cahwnet.gov.

For sales tax and seller's permit information and forms, contact the **California Board of Equalization (BOE)** at 800-400-7115 (for a live person, press 1, then 0). Or visit the BOE's Website at http://www.boe.ca.gov. Many forms and informational pamphlets are available for download. You'll also find useful, general information about property taxes, which are assessed and collected by counties but regulated by the BOE. You can download the free publication, "California Property Tax: An Overview,"

which contains lots of valuable information, including calendars of important tax deadlines and contact info for each county assessor.

The **California Secretary of State** handles a number of different business-related issues, including corporate and LLC filings and trademark and service mark registration. The phone number for general information is 916-653-6814 (for a live person, press 1, then 6, then 0). Or visit the Secretary of State online at http://www.ss.ca.gov, where you'll find a wide range of information and downloadable forms. For specific questions, contact one of the Secretary of State's special units or one of its branch offices.

Corporations Unit

916-657-5448

Limited Liability Company (LLC) Unit

916-653-3795

Trademarks & Service Marks Unit

916-653-4984

Fresno Branch Office

209-243-2100

Los Angeles Branch Office

213-897-3062

San Diego Branch Office

619-525-4113

San Francisco Branch Office

415-439-6959

The **California Franchise Tax Board (FTB)** is California's version of the IRS. This is the agency that collects state income taxes from individuals, corporations and LLCs. For general information, call 800-852-5711 (for a live person, press 1, then 4). Most California tax forms and instructions are also available online. The FTB's Web address is http://www.ftb.ca.gov.

The **California Office of Small Business,** which is part of the California Trade and Commerce Agency, provides general help to small businesses in California, with an emphasis on solving problems business owners may have with government agencies. This is a good office to call when you need help of just about any kind, because the staff people are really quite helpful and will do their best to steer you in the right direction. The Office of Small Business is also the head of a network of **Small Business Development Centers (SBDCs),** which are similarly designed to help small businesses with the problems that typically plague them. Contact the Office of Small Business at 800-303-6600 or 916-324-1295. Or visit it online at http://commerce.ca.gov/business/small.

The **California Office of Permit Assistance (COPA)** is also under the California Trade and Commerce Agency umbrella. COPA assists businesses through the permit process for activities that might impact the environment or natural resources. It acts as a clearinghouse of information and facilitates meetings between businesses and the appropriate agencies—local, state or federal—that regulate specific activities, such as disposal of hazardous waste or development of coastal areas. Contact COPA at 800-353-2672 or 916-322-4245. (Note: If a staff person is not available to answer your call, be sure to leave a message, which the office promises to return.)

B. Associations

As every new entrepreneur quickly learns, city and state laws and regulations have a significant impact on small businesses each and every day—from zoning issues to sales tax laws. The California Small Business Association is a non-profit grassroots organization dedicated to advocating the interests of small businesses to government officials. In addition to political activism, this group offers member benefits such as discounted health insurance and Internet access. Contact CSBA at 800-350-CSBA or 310-642-0838; Fax: 310-642-0849; e-mail: csba@pacbell.net. Or visit its Website at http://www.csba.com.

The **California Chamber of Commerce** tracks business-related legislation in California and lobbies for business interests. The Chamber also publishes a number of business guides. To find your local chamber, contact the central office at 916-444-6670; Fax: 916-444-6685. Or visit its Website at http://www.calchamber.com.

The **Graphic Artists Guild (GAG)** is an excellent resource for anyone in the business of visual art. In advocating for the rights and interests of working artists, GAG has been a leader in the effort to reform California sales tax laws as well as laws regulating home businesses. The Guild is also a good source of information about copyright and contract issues for professional artists. You can contact the Northern California chapter of GAG at 415-995-4905, or online at http://www.gag.org/sanfran.

C. Books and Publications

The **California Permit Handbook** is published by the California Office of Permit Assistance (COPA). It's a useful guide to California's environmental regulatory process and, what's more, it's free. COPA is currently revising the book, so you'll have to wait until January 1999 for a hard copy. Call 800-353-2672 to order one. (Note: If there's not a staff person to answer your call, be sure to leave a message, which the office promises will be returned.) Until then, you can read the book online, or download a copy from the Web. Go to http://commerce.ca.gov/business/permits.

The **California License Handbook** is published by the California Office of Small Business (OSB). It's an excellent resource that will familiarize you with all the state agencies, departments and offices and their divisions and branches that administer the swarms of licenses, permits and other business regulations in California. You can read it online for free, at http://commerce.ca.gov/business/small/management/pub/license/index.html. Or you can obtain a hard copy by sending a request for the book, along with your name, address and check or money order for $20 (which includes tax and postage), payable to the California Trade and Commerce Agency, to:

California Trade and Commerce Agency

California Office of Small Business
Attn: Koki Tanaka
801 K Street, Suite 1700
Sacramento, CA 95814

Nolo's **Legal Guide for Starting & Running a Small Business, Volume 1,** by attorney Fred S. Steingold, covers the many legal issues that new and ongoing businesses typically face. From raising start-up money to adopting smart customer policies, this book explains the details that business owners need to know. **Volume 2** of this title offers the legal forms that small business owners most often need, including an independent contractor agreement, a promissory note, a nondisclosure agreement and an equipment-rental contract.

The Partnership Book, by attorneys Denis Clifford and Ralph Warner (Nolo Press), is an indispensable guide for anyone who is—or is thinking about becoming—a partner in a business. This book is especially good at explaining partnership agreements and provides the various clauses and instructions necessary to put together your own customized agreement.

Tax Savvy for Small Business, by tax attorney Frederick Daily (Nolo Press), is a must-have for any business owner. It explains in excruciating detail—but in easy-to-read language—the ins and outs of managing your business's tax obligations and finances. From how to write off various expenses to taking advantage of fringe benefits to appealing a bad IRS judgment, this book will help you minimize your tax bill, legally.

Small Time Operator, by Bernard Kamoroff (Bell Springs Publishing), is an accessible, useful guide geared towards the special needs of small business owners. This book, written by a CPA, is especially helpful in explaining basic bookkeeping systems and small business taxes.

Running a One-Person Business, by Claude Whitmyer, Salli Rasberry and Michael Phillips (Ten Speed Press), offers helpful information for the self-employed.

Working From Home: Everything You Need to Know About Living and Working Under the Same Roof, by Paul and Sarah Edwards (Jeremy P. Tarcher/Putnam Publishing Group), offers extensive information on how to manage home businesses.

How to Write a Business Plan, by Mike McKeever (Nolo Press), gives you all the information and tools you need to put together a powerful business plan and loan application. It walks you through all the components that a businessperson might want to include in a business plan, and offers a method for putting together a quick, one-day plan to meet your short-term needs.

The Employer's Legal Handbook, by attorney Fred S. Steingold (Nolo Press), offers comprehensive guidance to the legal rights and responsibilities involved in becoming an employer. It includes detailed information on the laws governing hiring and firing employees, personnel policies, workplace discrimination, worker's compensation and more.

Knowing the legal ins and outs of putting service agreements in writing is especially important for independent workers such as freelancers and other small operators. **Consultant and Independent Contractor Agreements,** by attorney

Stephen Fishman (Nolo Press), explains how to create a solid, legal agreement when selling services.

For a thorough explanation of trademark law and the process of searching and registering trademarks, read **Trademark: Legal Care for Your Business and Product Name,** by attorneys Kate McGrath and Stephen Elias (Nolo Press). This book includes tear-out forms for registering a federal trademark.

Marketing Without Advertising, by Michael Phillips and Salli Rasberry (Nolo Press), offers practical and creative strategies for promoting your product or service without spending a fortune.

Attorney Anthony Mancuso has written a number of guides to incorporating a business, including **How to Form Your Own California Corporation, The Corporate Minutes Book,** and **How to Form a California Professional Corporation,** all published by Nolo Press. These titles explain in detail the legal and practical implications of incorporating, and walk you through the incorporation process step-by-step.

Form Your Own Limited Liability Company, by attorney Anthony Mancuso (Nolo Press), gives you all the information you need to set up a valid LLC in all 50 states.

How to Create a Buy-Sell Agreement and Control the Destiny of Your Small Business, by attorneys Anthony Mancuso and Bethany K. Laurence (Nolo Press), explains how to put together an agreement that deals with additions and departures of business owners. Without a buy-sell agreement, an ownership transition can quickly send a business into a tailspin. Understanding how to avoid this common occurrence with a simple agreement greatly improves your chances of surviving such a transition.

D. Websites

CalGOLD is a Website sponsored by the California Environmental Protection Agency, but the help it offers isn't limited to environmental matters. After prompting you to enter a bit of information about the business you're starting, this interactive site directs you to the government agencies whose registration requirements may apply to you. CalGOLD is located at http://www.calgold.ca.gov.

The **Small Business Wizard,** sponsored by the California Office of Small Business, is designed as a sort of clearinghouse of online information for small business owners. While it's light on practical, specific answers about what agencies to contact when starting a business, it does offer many links and other contact information that you may find useful. There's a good deal of information on financing, plus you'll find some interesting information about California's economy, including statistics and demographics. The URL is http://commerce.ca.gov/business/small/bizwiz/bizwizhm.html.

The California Department of Finance sponsors the **California Demographic Research Unit's** Website, which offers a range of state demographic data. At this site you can obtain a number of different reports and research papers on California's population, such as the annual percentage growth in each California city and county, for free. For small business owners, this information can be really useful—not to mention fascinating. The Web address is http://www.dof.ca.gov/html/Demograp/druhpar.htm.

Download the latest **California tax forms** from http://www.ftb.ca.gov.

Download a **seller's permit application** and other **BOE publications** from http://www.boe.ca.gov.

Download the latest **federal tax forms** from http://www.irs.ustreas.gov/plain/forms_pubs/index.html.

You can now search the **online database of federal trademarks** at the U.S. Patent and Trademark Office's Website. Go to http://www.uspto.gov/web/menu/tm.html.

InterNIC keeps track of domain names and will reserve a name for you if it hasn't already been taken. Go to http://www.internic.net.

Web search engines are tools that scan the entire Web for whatever words or phrases you choose. Here are the most popular sites from which to start your Web search. Each site has instructions that tell you how to conduct your search.

Yahoo!	http://www.yahoo.com
Hotbot	http://www.hotbot.com
AltaVista	http://www.altavista.com
Infoseek	http://www.infoseek.com
Excite	http://www.excite.com
Metacrawler	http://www.metacrawler.com
Search.com	http://www.search.com

California County Clerks

County	Fictitious Business Name Statement Filing Fees	Fees for Name Search Conducted by Staff (not including copy or certification fees)
Alameda County Clerk 1225 Fallon Street, Room G-1 Oakland, CA 94612 510-272-6363	$29 for 1 business name and 1 owner $7 each additional business name or owner	$25 per search
Alpine County Clerk P.O. Box 158 Markleeville, CA 96120 530-694-2281	$10 for 1 business name and 1 owner $2 each additional business name or owner	$5 per search
Amador County Recorder 500 Argonaut Lane Jackson, CA 95642 209-223-6468	$10 for 1 business name and 1 owner $2 each additional business name or owner	fees not established
Butte County Clerk 25 County Center Drive Oroville, CA 95965 530-538-7690	$25 for 1 business name and 1 owner $5 each additional business name or owner	fees not established
Calaveras County Clerk 891 Mountain Ranch Road San Andreas, CA 95249 209-754-6376	$10 for 1 business name and 1 owner $2 each additional business name or owner	fees not established

County	Fictitious Business Name Statement Filing Fees	Fees for Name Search Conducted by Staff (not including copy or certification fees)
Colusa County Clerk-Recorder 546 Jay Street Colusa, CA 95932 530-458-0500	$10 for 1 business name and 1 owner $2 each additional business name or owner	$5 per search
Contra Costa County Clerk 822 Main Street P.O. Box 350 Martinez, CA 94553 510-646-2365	$15 for 1 business name and 1 owner $5 each additional business name or owner	$5 per search
Del Norte County Clerk-Recorder 457 F Street Crescent City, CA 95531 707-464-7216	$15 for 1 business name and 1 owner $2 each additional business name or owner	$15 per search
El Dorado County Clerk 360 Fair Lane Placerville, CA 95667 530-621-5490	$30 for 1 business name and 1 owner (or 2 owners if husband/wife) $5 each additional business name or owner	$15 per search
Fresno County Clerk 2221 Kern Street Fresno, CA 93721 209-488-3428	$35 for 1 business name and 1 owner $7 each additional business name or owner	$5 per search
Glenn County Clerk-Recorder 526 Sycamore Street Willows, CA 95988 530-934-6412	$15 for 1 business name and 1 owner $5 each additional business name or owner	fees not established
Humboldt County Clerk 825 5th Street, Room 108 Eureka, CA 95501 707-445-7593	$25 for 1 business name and 1 owner $5 each additional business name or owner	$5 per search
Imperial County Clerk 940 W. Main Street, Suite 202 El Centro, CA 92243 760-339-4427	$1 for form $20 for 1 business name and 1 owner $20 each additional business name $5 each additional owner	$2.50 per search

County	Fictitious Business Name Statement Filing Fees	Fees for Name Search Conducted by Staff (not including copy or certification fees)
Inyo County Clerk P.O. Drawer F Independence, CA 93526 760-878-0223	$10 for 1 business name and 2 owners $2 each additional business name or owner	fees not established
Kern County Clerk 1115 Truxtun Ave. Bakersfield, CA 93301 805-868-3588	$30 for 1 business name and 1 owner (or 2 owners if husband/wife) $6 each additional business name or owner	fees not established
Kings County Clerk-Recorder Government Center 1400 West Lacey Blvd. Hanford, CA 93230 209-582-3211 ext. 2472	$10 for 1 business name and 1 owner $2 each additional business name or owner	fees not established
Lake County Clerk-Auditor 255 North Forbes Street Lakeport, CA 95453 707-263-2311	$25 for 1 business name and 2 owners $5 each additional business name or owner	fees not established
Lassen County Clerk Courthouse, Suite 5 220 South Lassen Street Susanville, CA 96130 530-251-8217	$15 for 1 business name and 2 owners $5 each additional business name or owner	fees not established
Los Angeles Business Filing and Registration 12400 E. Imperial Hwy. Norwalk, CA 90650 562-462-2177 www.co.la.us/regrec/main.htm	$10 for 1 business name and 2 owners $2 each additional business name or owner	$5 per search
Madera County Clerk 209 West Yosemite Ave. Madera, CA 93637 209-675-7721	$10 for 1 business name and 1 owner $2 each additional business name or owner	$5 per search
Marin County Clerk-Recorder P.O. Box E San Rafael, CA 94913 415-499-6415	$27 for 1 business name and 1 owner $7 each additional business name or owner	$5 per search

County	Fictitious Business Name Statement Filing Fees	Fees for Name Search Conducted by Staff (not including copy or certification fees)
Mariposa County Clerk P.O. Box 247 Mariposa, CA 95338 209-966-2007	$10 for I business name and I owner $2 each additional busines name or owner	fees not established
Mendocino County Clerk 501 Low Gap Road, Room 1020 Ukiah, CA 95482 707-463-4370	$25 for I business name and I owner (or 2 owners if husband/wife) $2 each additional business name or owner	$5 per search
Merced County Clerk 2222 M Street, Room 14 Merced, CA 95340 209-385-7541	$13 for I business name and I owner $3 each additional business name or owner	$5.50 per search
Modoc County Clerk P.O. Box 130 Alturas, CA 96101 530-233-6200	$10 for I business name and I owner $2 each additional business name or owner	fees not established
Mono County Clerk P.O. Box 237 Bridgeport, CA 93517 760-932-5241	$12.50 for I business name and I owner $2 each additional business name or owner	fees not established
Monterey County Clerk's Office P.O. Box 29 Salinas, CA 93902 408-755-5450	$20 for I business name and I owner $5 each additional business name or owner	$5 per search
Napa County Clerk-Recorder P.O. Box 298 Napa, CA 94559 707-253-4105	$30 for I business name and I owner $6 each additional business name or owner	$9 per search
Nevada County Recorder 950 Maidu Ave. Nevada City, CA 95959 530-265-1298	$28 for I business name and I owner $5 each additional business name $2 each additional owner	fees not established
Orange County Clerk-Recorder's Office P.O. Box 238 Santa Ana, CA 92702-0238	$31 for I business name and 2 owners $7 each additional business name or owner	$6 per search

County	Fictitious Business Name Statement Filing Fees	Fees for Name Search Conducted by Staff (not including copy or certification fees)
Placer Recorder's Office P.O. Box 5228 Auburn, CA 95604 530-886-5610	$27 for 1 business name and 1 owner $5.50 each additional business name or owner	fees not established
Plumas County Clerk 520 W. Main Street, Room 104 Quincy, CA 95971 530-283-6256	$20 for 1 business name and 1 owner $5 each additional business name or owner	fees not established
Riverside County Clerk and Recorder's Office P.O. Box 751 Riverside, CA 92502 909-486-7000	$31 for 1 business name and 1 owner $7 each additional business name or owner	$5 per search
Sacramento Department of Finance Business License Section 700 H Street, Room 1710 Sacramento, CA 95814 916-874-6644	$20 for 1 business name and 1 owner $5 each additional business name or owner	fees not established
San Benito County Clerk 440 5th Street, Room 206 Hollister, CA 95023 408-636-4029	$25 for 1 business name and 1 owner $5 each additional business name or owner	$5 per search
San Bernardino Fictitious Businesses 222 W. Hospitality Lane San Bernardino, CA 92415 909-386-8970	$29 for 1 business name and 1 owner $7 each additional business name or owner	$5 per search
San Diego Recorder-County Clerk 1600 Pacific Highway, Room 260 P.O. Box 1750 San Diego, CA 92112 619-237-0502	$13 for 1 business name and 1 owner $2 each additional business name or owner	$5 per search
San Francisco County Clerk 25 Van Ness Ave., Suite 110 San Francisco, CA 94102 415-252-3282	$35 for 1 business name and 1 owner $9 each additional business name or owner	$5 per search
San Joaquin County Recorder P.O. Box 1968 Stockton, CA 95201 209-468-3939	$10 for 1 business name and 1 owner $2 each additional business name or owner	fees not established

County	Fictitious Business Name Statement Filing Fees	Fees for Name Search Conducted by Staff (not including copy or certification fees)
San Luis Obispo County Clerk-Recorder 1144 Monterey Street, Suite A San Luis Obispo, CA 93408 805-781-5088	$15 for 1 business name and 2 owners $2 each additional business name or owner	$5 per search
San Mateo Special Services 6th Floor 401 Marshall Street Redwood City, CA 94063 650-363-4212	$28 for 1 business name and 1 owner $5 each additional business name or owner	$5 per search
Santa Barbara County Clerk P.O. Box 159 Santa Barbara, CA 93102 805-568-2250	$27 for 1 business name and 1 owner $5 each additional business name or owner	$5 per search
Santa Clara County Clerk 191 N. 1st Street San Jose, CA 95113 408-299-2969	$37 for 1 business name and 2 owners $7 each additional business name or owner	$6 per search
Santa Cruz County Clerk 701 Ocean Street, Room 230 Santa Cruz, CA 95060 408-454-2470	$20 for 1 business name and 1 owner $5 each additional business name or owner	$1.75 per search
Shasta County Clerk P.O. Box 990880 Redding, CA 96099-0880 530-225-5730	$28 for 1 business name and 1 owner $5 each additional business name or owner	$5 per search
Sierra County Clerk-Recorder Courthouse, Room 11 P.O. Drawer D Downieville, CA 95936	$10 for 1 business name and 1 owner $2 each additional business name or owner	fees not established
Siskiyou County Clerk P.O. Box 338 Yreka, CA 96097 530-842-8086	$10 for 1 business name and 1 owner $10 each additional business name $2 each additional owner	fees not established

County	Fictitious Business Name Statement Filing Fees	Fees for Name Search Conducted by Staff (not including copy or certification fees)
Solano Tax Collector-County Clerk 600 Texas Street Fairfield, CA 94533 707-421-7485	$20 for 1 business name and 1 owner $2 each additional business name or owner	fees not established
Sonoma County Clerk 2300 County Center Drive, Suite B177 Santa Rosa, CA 95403 707-527-3800	$26 for 1 business name and 1 owner $7 each additional business name or owner	$1.75 per search
Stanislaus County Clerk 1021 I Street, Suite 101 Modesto, CA 95354 209-525-5250	$27 for 1 business name and 2 owners $7 each additional business name or owner	fees not established
Sutter County Recorder P.O. Box 1555 Yuba City, CA 95992 530-822-7120	$30 for 1 business name and 1 owner $5 each additional business name or owner	$5 per search
Tehama County Clerk-Recorder P.O. Box 250 Red Bluff, CA 96080 530-527-3350	$15 for 1 business name and 1 owner $5 each additional business name or owner	fees not established
Trinity Recorder P.O. Box 1258 Weaverville, CA 96093 530-623-1215	$12 for 1 business name and 1 owner $2 each additional business name or owner	$5 per search
Tulare County Clerk-Recorder 221 S. Mooney Blvd., Room 105 Visalia, CA 93291-4593 209-733-6518	$30 for 1 business name and 1 owner $5 each additional business name or owner	$10 per search
Tuolumne County, Elections Department 2 S. Green Street Sonora, CA 95370 209-533-5570	$24 for 1 business name and 1 owner $4 each additional business name or owner	$5 per search

County	Fictitious Business Name Statement Filing Fees	Fees for Name Search Conducted by Staff (not including copy or certification fees)
Ventura County Clerk Hall of Administration L 1210 800 S. Victoria Ave. Ventura, CA 93009 805-654-2263	$26 for 1 business name and 1 owner $5 each additional business name or owner	$5 per search
Yolo County Clerk-Recorder P.O. Box 1130 Woodland, CA 95776 530-666-8130	$27 for 1 business name and 1 owner $5 each additional business name or owner	$5 per search
Yuba County Clerk-Recorder 935 14th Street Marysville, CA 95901 530-741-6341	$10 for 1 business name and 1 owner $2 each additional business name or owner	fees not established

Start-up Forms

Partnership Agreement

1. Partners

_____

_____ (Partners) make the following Partnership Agreement.

2. Creation of Partnership

As of _____, 19__, the Partners agree to enter into a Partnership for the purpose of operating a business known as:

_____ (Partnership Business).

The name of the Partnership (if different from name of Partnership Business) shall be:

_____ (Partnership Name).

3. Nature of Partnership Business

The Partnership Business will consist of the following business activities:

_____

4. Contributions to the Partnership

The Partners will make the following contributions to the Partnership.

Partner Name	Cash Contribution	Property Contribution (describe property; give cash value)	Total Value of Contribution
	$		$
		Total value:	
	$		$
		Total value:	
	$		$
		Total value:	
	$		$
		Total value:	

5. Profit and Loss Allocation

The Partners will share business profits and losses as follows:

☐ in the same proportions as their contributions to the business.

☐ as follows:

_____

_____

6. Management of Partnership Business

The Partners will have the following management powers and responsibilities:

☐ The Partners will have equal management powers and responsibilities.

☐ The Partners will share management powers and responsibilities as follows:

_____

_____ .

7. Addition of a Partner

A new partner may be added to the Partnership under the following conditions:

☐ unanimous vote of all Partners.

☐ majority vote of Partners.

☐ other conditions: _____ .

8. Departure of a Partner

If any Partner leaves the Partnership for any reason, including voluntary withdrawal, expulsion or death, the Partnership shall ☐ survive ☐ dissolve.

If Partnership survives, the remaining Partner(s) shall pay the departing Partner, or the deceased Partner's estate, the fair market value of the departing Partner's share of the business as of the date of his or her departure. The Partnership's accountant shall determine the fair market value of the departing Partner's share of the business according to the following method:

_____ .

9. Dispute Resolution

If a dispute arises under this Agreement, the Partners agree to first try to resolve the dispute with the help of a mutually agreed-upon mediator. Any costs and fees other than attorney fees shall be shared equally by the Partners. If it proves impossible to arrive at a mutually satisfactory solution, the Partners agree to submit the dispute to binding arbitration in the same city or region, conducted on a confidential basis pursuant to the Commercial Arbitration Rules of the American Arbitration Association.

10. Amendment of Agreement

This agreement may not be amended without the written consent of all Partners.

11. Partner Signatures

Name: _____   Name: _____

_____   _____
Signature   *Signature*

Date: _____   Date: _____

Address: _____   Address: _____

_____   _____

Social Security # _____   Social Security # _____

Name: _____   Name: _____

_____   _____
Signature   *Signature*

Date: _____   Date: _____

Address: _____   Address: _____

_____   _____

Social Security # _____   Social Security # _____

ORGANIZATION OF DOMESTIC CLOSE CORPORATIONS

Business corporations authorized to issue stock, excluding such special organizations as cooperatives, credit unions, etc., are organized under the General Corporation Law, and particularly Title 1, Division 1, Chapter 2, California Corporations Code.

Sections 200-202, California Corporations Code, outline the minimum content requirements of Articles of Incorporation for stock corporations. Section 158 of the Corporations Code specifically deals with statutory close corporations. The attached sample has been drafted to meet **minimum** statutory requirements. The sample may be used as a guide in preparing documents to be filed with the Secretary of State to incorporate. It is, however, suggested that you seek private counsel for advice regarding the proposed corporation's specific business needs which may require the inclusion of special permissive provisions or the formation of the corporation as a general stock corporation rather than formation as a close corporation.

THE FEE FOR FILING ARTICLES OF INCORPORATION ON BEHALF OF A STOCK CORPORATION IS $100.00. Additionally, the $600.00/$800.00 minimum franchise tax must be submitted with the Articles of Incorporation to enable filing. The minimum tax is $600.00 or $800.00. The Secretary of State's Office will accept either amount for filing. The applicant is responsible for determining the proper amount to submit to this office. For assistance in making this determination, the applicant may refer to California Revenue and Taxation Code Sections 23153 and 23221. The tax payment must be sent to the Secretary of State along with Articles of Incorporation, and may be included with the filing fee in a single remittance made payable to the California Secretary of State.

The Secretary of State will certify two copies of the filed Articles of Incorporation without charge, **provided that the copies are submitted to the Secretary of State with the original to be filed.** Any additional copies, submitted with the original, will be certified upon request and the prepayment of $8.00 per copy.

An additional $15.00 **special handling fee** is applicable for expedited processing of documents delivered in person, over-the-counter, to the Sacramento office or to any of the branch offices which are located in Fresno, Los Angeles and San Diego. The $15.00 special handling fee must be remitted by separate check as it will be **RETAINED WHETHER THE DOCUMENTS ARE FILED OR REJECTED.** The special handling fee does not apply to documents submitted by mail.

NOTE: CASH IS NOT ACCEPTED IN THE FRESNO BRANCH OFFICE, THE LOS ANGELES BRANCH OFFICE OR THE SAN DIEGO BRANCH OFFICE.

When forming a new corporation you may also wish to contact one or more of the following agencies for additional information:

- The Franchise Tax Board - for information regarding **franchise tax requirements**.

- The Board of Equalization - for information regarding **sales tax** or **use tax** liability.

- The Commissioner of Corporations - for information regarding **issuance** and **sale** of **securities** in California; Franchise Investment Law; Personal Property Brokers Law; Escrow Law requirements.

- The Department of Consumer Affairs - for information regarding **licensing** requirements.

- The Employment Development Department - for information regarding **disability unemployment insurance tax**.

- The Director of Industrial Relations, Division of Workers' Compensation - for information regarding **worker's compensation** requirements.

- The city and/or county clerk and/or recorder where the principal place of business is located - for information regarding **business licenses, fictitious business names** (if doing business under a name other than the corporate name), and for specific requirements regarding **zoning, building permits**, etc. based on the business activities of the corporation.

- Internal Revenue Services (IRS) - for information regarding **federal employee identification numbers.**

The Secretary of State <u>does not</u> license corporations or business entities. For licensing requirements, please contact the city and/or county where the principal place of business is located and/or the state agency with jurisdiction over the business, e.g. Contractors' State License Board.

Samples are also available for the incorporation of California **general stock** and **professional** corporations and for the various classifications of California **nonprofit** corporations.

Documents may be mailed or hand delivered for over-the-counter processing to the Sacramento office at:

Business Filings
1500 11th Street
Sacramento, CA 95814
Attention: Document Filing Support Unit
(916) 657-5448

OR

may be hand delivered for over-the-counter processing to any of the branch offices which are located in:

- Fresno   (209) 243-2100
  2497 West Shaw, Suite 101
  Fresno, CA 93711

- Los Angeles   (213) 897-3062
  300 South Spring Street, Room 12513
  Los Angeles, CA 90013-1233

- San Diego   (619) 525-4113
  1350 Front Street, Suite 2060
  San Diego, CA 92101-3690

NOTE: When filing Articles of Incorporation in a branch office it is necessary to submit duplicate original documents, plus any copies to be certified and returned. These offices do not process mailed in documents.

CLOSE CORPORATIONS

The statutory concept of a "close" corporation is often confused with two other concepts having some elements in common. The three differing concepts are as follows:

a) Statutory close corporation, as defined in Section 158, California Corporations Code.

b) Issuance of shares under a notice filing procedure with the Commissioner of Corporations pursuant to Section 25102(f) or 25102(h), California Corporations Code.

c) "S" corporation election pursuant to Section 1372, Internal Revenue Code.

Adding to the confusion, the terms "close" corporation, "closed" corporation or "closely held" corporation are often used in a nontechnical sense simply to describe a corporation having a relatively small number of shareholders.

Each of the three concepts: statutory close corporation, notice filing procedure, and "S" election, is independent of the other two. It is not a condition to the use of the notice filing procedure or to the making of an "S" corporation election that the Articles of Incorporation state that the corporation is a close corporation or limit the number of shareholders of record. Experienced corporate counsel advises that the appropriate use of the statutory close corporation, even among corporations having 35 or fewer shareholders, is infrequent.

The three differences in the mandatory provisions of Articles of Incorporation forming a statutory close corporation and the Articles of Incorporation forming a general stock corporation are the name style requirement, the inclusion of wording denoting close corporation status and the reference to the number of persons entitled to hold issued shares.

INSTRUCTIONS:

To incorporate utilizing the attached sample it will be necessary for you to complete the form with the required information. The information **must** be typed with letters in dark contrast to the paper. Documents submitted which would produce poor microfilm will be returned unfiled. Articles of Incorporation may be drafted to include all required provisions and any statutorily permissive provisions, including initial directors. The Secretary of State does not have samples containing permissive provisions.

Article I - is to be completed with the name of the corporation exactly as the name is to appear on the records of the Secretary of State. The name of a close corporation must include the word "corporation", "incorporated" or "limited" or an abbreviation of one of the three.

Article II - cannot be modified. The statement has been taken directly from the California Corporations Code as is required by law.

Article III - is to be completed with the name and California street address, or the physical location, of the agent for service of process (a post office box is not acceptable). The designated agent, individual or corporation, **must** agree to accept process on behalf of the corporation prior to designation. A proposed corporation cannot designate itself as agent for service of process. When designating another corporation as agent, the agent corporation **must** have on file, with the Secretary of State, a statement pursuant to Section 1505, California Corporations Code. When a corporate agent is used, the address of the designated corporation must be omitted from the articles.

Article IV - is to be completed with the total number of shares that the corporation is authorized to issue.

NOTE: Before shares of stock are sold or issued the co rporation must comply with the Corporate Securities Law administered by the Commissioner of Corporations. For information regarding permits to issue shares please contact that agency.

Article V - is to be retained as stated with the number of persons completed. Please note that the number of persons designated cannot exceed 35.

The Articles of Incorporation must be originally signed by an incorporator unless directors are named in the articles. If directors are named in the articles, each person named must sign and acknowledge the document. The name(s) of the person(s) signing must be typed directly below the signature(s).

The original and at least two copies of the completed documents are then mailed or hand delivered to the Secretary of State, together with the applicable fee. (If documents are to be filed in the Los Angeles, San Diego or Fresno branch office, a duplicate original is also required.)

To expedite processing, Articles of Incorporation submitted by mail should be accompanied by a self-addressed envelope and a letter referencing the proposed corporate name as well as your own name, telephone number and return address.

ARTICLES OF INCORPORATION

I

The name of this corporation is _____ *(NAME OF CORPORATION)* _____.

II

The purpose of the corporation is to engage in any lawful act or activity for which a corporation may be organized under the **GENERAL CORPORATION LAW** of California other than the banking business, the trust company business or the practice of a profession permitted to be incorporated by the California Corporations Code.

III

The name and address in the State of California of this corporation's initial agent for service of process is:

Name _____

STREET Address _____ *(DO NOT USE POST OFFICE BOX)* _____

City _____ State **CALIFORNIA** Zip _____

IV

This corporation is authorized to issue only one class of shares of stock; and the total number of shares which this corporation is authorized to issue is _____.

V

This corporation is a **CLOSE CORPORATION**. All of the corporation's issued shares of stock, of all classes, shall be held of record by not more than _____ persons.

_____ *(Signature of Incorporator)* _____
(Typed Name of Incorporator), Incorporator

State of California
Bill Jones
Secretary of State

LLC-1

LIMITED LIABILITY COMPANY
ARTICLES OF ORGANIZATION

IMPORTANT - Read the instructions before completing the form.
This document is presented for filing pursuant to Section 17050 of the California Corporations Code.

1. Limited liability company name:
   (End the name with LLC, L.L.C., Limited Liability Company or Ltd. Liability Co.)

2. Latest date (month/day/year) on which the limited liability company is to dissolve.

3. The purpose of the limited liability company is to engage in any lawful act or activity for which a limited liability company may be organized under the Beverly-Killea Limited Liability Company Act.

4. Enter the name of initial agent for service of process and check the appropriate provision below:

   _____, which is

   [   ] an individual residing in California.

   [   ] a corporation which has filed a certificate pursuant to Section 1505 of the California Corporations Code. Skip Item 5 and proceed to Item 6.

5. If the initial agent for service of process is an individual, enter a business or residential street address in California:

   Street address:

   City: State: California   Zip Code:

6. The limited liability company will be managed by: **(check one)**

   [   ] one manager   [   ] more than one manager   [   ] limited liability company members

7. If other matters are to be included in the Articles of Organization attach one or more separate pages.
   Number of pages attached, if any: [   ]

   Describe type of business of the Limited Liability Company.

Declaration: It is hereby declared that I am the person who executed this instrument, which execution is my act and deed.

_____
Signature of organizer

_____
Type or print name of organizer

Date: _____, 19 _____

For Secretary of State Use

File No. _____

SEC/STATE (REV. 2/98)   FORM LLC-1 -- FILING FEE. $70
Approved By Secretary Of State

INSTRUCTIONS FOR COMPLETING THE ARTICLES OF ORGANIZATION (LLC-1)

**All references are to the California Corporations Code unless otherwise indicated.
Type or legibly print in black ink.**

DO NOT ALTER THIS FORM

Item 1. Enter the name of the limited liability company which must end with the words "LLC", "L.L.C." or "Limited Liability Company". The words "Limited" and "Company" may be abbreviated to "Ltd." and "Co." Section 17051(a)(1). The name of the limited liability company may not contain the words "bank", "insurance company", "insurer", "trust", "trustee", "incorporated", "inc.", "corporation", or "corp." Section 17052(d).

Professional limited liability companies are prohibited from forming or registering in California.

Item 2. Enter the latest date (month/day/year) on which the limited liability company is to dissolve. Section 17051(a)(2).

Item 3. The articles of organization must contain the following statement of purpose which is preprinted on the form and may not be altered: "The purpose of the limited liability company is to engage in any lawful act or activity for which a limited liability company may be organized under the Beverly-Killea Limited Liability Company Act". Section 17051(a)(3). If the provisions limiting or restricting the business of the limited liability company are desired refer to Item 7 for instructions on attaching additional pages.

Item 4. Enter the name and address of the initial agent for service of process. Check the appropriate provision indicating whether the initial agent is an individual residing in California or a corporation which has filed a certificate pursuant to Section 1505 of the California Corporations Code. Section 17051(a)(5).

Item 5. Enter a business or residential street address in California, box numbers and "in care of" (c/o) are not acceptable.

Item 6. Check the appropriate provision indicating whether the limited liability company is to be managed by one manager, more than one manager, or the limited liability company members. Section 17051(a)(6).

Item 7. The articles of organization may contain additional provisions including, but not limited to, provisions limiting or restricting the business in which the limited liability company may engage, powers that the limited liability company may exercise, admission of members, events that will cause a dissolution, or limitations on the authority of managers or members to bind the limited liability company. Such matters must be submitted on single-sided, standard white paper. Number and identify each page as an attachment to the articles of organization. Enter the number of pages attached to the form, if any, in Item 7. Section 17051(c).

Briefly describe the general type of business that constitutes the principal business activity of the limited liability company. Note restrictions in the rendering of professional services by Limited Liability Companies. Professional services are defined in California Corporations Code 13401(a) as: "any type of professional services that may be lawfully rendered only pursuant to a license, certification, or registration authorized by the Business and Professions Code or the Chiropractic Act."

Declaration: The articles of organization must be executed with an original signature. Facsimiles and photocopies of the articles of organization are not acceptable for the purpose of filing with the Secretary of State. The person executing the articles of organization need not be a member or manager of the limited liability company. Section 17051(a).

- The fee for filing the articles of organization with the Secretary of State is seventy dollars ($70). Section 17701(b).

- Return the acknowledgment of filing to:

  Name: _____
  Firm/Company: _____
  Address: _____
  City: _____
  State: _____ Zip Code: _____

- Send the executed document and filing fee to:

  Office of the Secretary of State
  Limited Liability Company Unit
  P.O. Box 944228
  Sacramento, CA 94244-2280

State of California
Secretary of State
Bill Jones

CERTIFICATE OF LIMITED PARTNERSHIP

A $70.00 filing fee must accompany this form.
IMPORTANT-- Read instructions before completing this form

This Space For Filing Use Only

1. NAME OF THE LIMITED PARTNERSHIP (END THE NAME WITH THE WORDS "LIMITED PARTNERSHIP" OR THE ABBREVIATION "L.P.")

2. STREET ADDRESS OF PRINCIPAL EXECUTIVE OFFICE | CITY AND STATE | ZIP CODE

3. STREET ADDRESS OF CALIFORNIA OFFICE WHERE RECORDS ARE KEPT | CITY | ZIP CODE
   CA

4. COMPLETE IF LIMITED PARTNERSHIP WAS FORMED PRIOR TO JULY 1, 1984 AND IS IN EXISTENCE ON THE DATE THIS CERTIFICATE IS EXECUTED.

   THE ORIGINAL LIMITED PARTNERSHIP CERTIFICATE WAS RECORDED ON _____ 19 _____ WITH THE RECORDER

   OF _____ COUNTY. FILE OR RECORDATION NUMBER _____

5. NAME THE AGENT FOR SERVICE OF PROCESS AND CHECK THE APPROPRIATE PROVISION BELOW:

   _____ WHICH IS

   [ ] AN INDIVIDUAL RESIDING IN CALIFORNIA. PROCEED TO ITEM 6.
   [ ] A CORPORATION WHICH HAS FILED A CERTIFICATE PURSUANT TO SECTION 1505. PROCEED TO ITEM 7.

6. IF AN INDIVIDUAL, CALIFORNIA STREET ADDRESS OF THE AGENT FOR SERVICE OF PROCESS:

   STREET ADDRESS:

   CITY: | STATE: **CA** | ZIP CODE:

7. NAMES AND ADDRESSES OF ALL GENERAL PARTNERS: (ATTACH ADDITIONAL PAGES, IF NECESSARY)

   A. NAME:

   ADDRESS:

   CITY: | STATE: | ZIP CODE:

   B. NAME:

   ADDRESS:

   CITY: | STATE: | ZIP CODE:

8. INDICATE THE <u>NUMBER</u> OF GENERAL PARTNERS' SIGNATURES REQUIRED FOR FILING CERTIFICATES OF AMENDMENT, RESTATEMENT, MERGER, DISSOLUTION, CONTINUATION AND CANCELLATION.

9. OTHER MATTERS TO BE INCLUDED IN THIS CERTIFICATE MAY BE SET FORTH ON SEPARATE ATTACHED PAGES AND ARE MADE A PART OF THIS CERTIFICATE BY CHECKING THIS BOX. OTHER MATTERS MAY INCLUDE THE PURPOSE OF BUSINESS OF THE LIMITED PARTNERSHIP E.G. GAMBLING ENTERPRISE.

10. TOTAL NUMBER OF PAGES ATTACHED, IF ANY:

11. I CERTIFY THAT THE STATEMENTS CONTAINED IN THIS DOCUMENT ARE TRUE AND CORRECT TO MY OWN KNOWLEDGE. I DECLARE THAT I AM THE PERSON WHO IS EXECUTING THIS INSTRUMENT, WHICH EXECUTION IS MY ACT AND DEED.

SIGNATURE | POSITION OR TITLE | PRINT NAME | DATE

SIGNATURE | POSITION OR TITLE | PRINT NAME | DATE

SEC/STATE (REV. 7/98) | FORM LP-1 – FILING FEE: $70.00
Approved by Secretary of State

INSTRUCTIONS FOR COMPLETING CERTIFICATE OF LIMITED PARTNERSHIP (FORM LP-1)

DO NOT ALTER THIS FORM
Type or legibly print in black ink.

- Attach the fee for filing the Certificate of Limited Partnership (LP-1) with the Secretary of State. The fee is seventy dollars ($70).

- Make check(s) payable to the Secretary of State.

- Send the executed document to:

  California Secretary of State
  Limited Partnership Unit
  P.O. Box 944225
  Sacramento, CA 94244-2250

- Fill in the items as follows:

Item 1. Enter the name of the limited partnership as it appears in the partnership agreement. The name shall contain the words "limited partnership" or the abbreviation "L.P." at the end. The name of the limited partnership may not contain the words "bank," "insurance," "trust," "trustee," "incorporated," "inc.," "corporation," or "corp.". (Section 15612)

Item 2. Enter the complete street address, including the zip code, of the principal executive office. DO NOT show a P.O. Box or abbreviate the name of the city.

Item 3. Enter the complete street address, including the zip code, of the California address where the records are kept. DO NOT show a P.O. Box or abbreviate the name of the city. (Section 15614)

Item 4. This item is to be completed only by those limited partnerships formed prior to July 1, 1984. (Section 15712(b)(2))

Item 5. Enter the name of the agent for service of process in this state. The agent for service of process must be an individual residing in California or a corporation which has filed a certificate pursuant to Section 1505. Check the appropriate provision.

Item 6. If an individual is designated as the agent for service of process, enter a business or residential street address in California. DO NOT enter a P.O. Box, "in care of" (c/o), or abbreviate the name of the city. DO NOT enter an address if a corporation is designated as the agent for service of process.

Item 7. Enter the names and addresses, including the zip code, of all general partners. DO NOT abbreviate names of the cities. Attach additional pages, if necessary.

If a general partner is a trust, both the names of the trust (including the date of the trust,) if applicable and the trustee must be listed. Example: Mary Todd, trustee of the Lincoln Family Trust U/T/A 5-1-94.

Item 8. Indicate the number of general partners' signatures required for filing certificates of amendment, restatement, merger, dissolution, continuation, and cancellation.

Item 9. The Certificate of Limited Partnership (LP-1) may include other matters that the person filing the Certificate of Limited Partnership determines to include. Other matters may include the purpose of business of the limited partnership e.g. gambling enterprise. If other matters are to be included check the box in this item and attach one or more pages setting forth the other matters.

Item 10. Indicate the total number of additional pages attached. All attachments should be 8½" x 11", one-sided and legible.

Item 11. The Certificate of Limited Partnership (LP-1) shall be executed and acknowledged with the original signatures of all general partners, unless it is filed pursuant to the provisions of Sections 15625 or 15633. Facsimiles and photocopies of signatures are not acceptable for the purpose of filing with the Secretary of State.

If the Certificate is filed by any person other than the general partner(s), the signature must be followed by the words "signature pursuant to Section _____," identifying the appropriate code section.

If the Certificate is signed by an attorney-in-fact the signature must be followed by the words "Attorney-in-fact for (name of the partner)."

If an association is designated as a general partner, the person who signs for the association must state the **exact** name of the association, his/her name, and his or her position or title.

If a trust is designated as a general partner, the certificate must be signed by a trustee as follows: _____, trustee for _____ trust (including the date of the trust, if applicable). Example: Mary Todd, trustee of th Lincoln Family Trust (U/T/A 5-1-94).

- Statutory provisions can be found in Section 15621 of the California Corporations Code, unless otherwise indicated.

- For further information contact the Limited Partnership Unit at (916) 653-3365.

Form **SS-4**
(Rev. February 1998)
Department of the Treasury
Internal Revenue Service

Application for Employer Identification Number

(For use by employers, corporations, partnerships, trusts, estates, churches, government agencies, certain individuals, and others. See instructions.)

► Keep a copy for your records.

EIN

OMB No. 1545-0003

Please type or print clearly.

1 Name of applicant (legal name) (see instructions)	

2 Trade name of business (if different from name on line 1)	**3** Executor, trustee, "care of" name

4a Mailing address (street address) (room, apt., or suite no.)	**5a** Business address (if different from address on lines 4a and 4b)
4b City, state, and ZIP code	**5b** City, state, and ZIP code

6 County and state where principal business is located

7 Name of principal officer, general partner, grantor, owner, or trustor—SSN or ITIN may be required (see instructions) ► _____

8a Type of entity (Check only one box.) (see instructions)

Caution: *If applicant is a limited liability company, see the instructions for line 8a.*

- ☐ Sole proprietor (SSN) _____
- ☐ Partnership   ☐ Personal service corp.
- ☐ REMIC   ☐ National Guard
- ☐ State/local government   ☐ Farmers' cooperative
- ☐ Church or church-controlled organization
- ☐ Other nonprofit organization (specify) ►_____
- ☐ Other (specify) ►

- ☐ Estate (SSN of decedent) _____
- ☐ Plan administrator (SSN) _____
- ☐ Other corporation (specify) ►_____
- ☐ Trust
- ☐ Federal government/military
- (enter GEN if applicable) _____

8b If a corporation, name the state or foreign country (if applicable) where incorporated

State	Foreign country

9 Reason for applying (Check only one box.) (see instructions)

- ☐ Started new business (specify type) ►_____
- ☐ Hired employees (Check the box and see line 12.)
- ☐ Created a pension plan (specify type) ►
- ☐ Banking purpose (specify purpose) ►_____
- ☐ Changed type of organization (specify new type) ►_____
- ☐ Purchased going business
- ☐ Created a trust (specify type) ►_____
- ☐ Other (specify) ►

10 Date business started or acquired (month, day, year) (see instructions)

11 Closing month of accounting year (see instructions)

12 First date wages or annuities were paid or will be paid (month, day, year). **Note:** *If applicant is a withholding agent, enter date income will first be paid to nonresident alien. (month, day, year)* . . . . ►

13 Highest number of employees expected in the next 12 months. **Note:** *If the applicant does not expect to have any employees during the period, enter -0-. (see instructions)* . . . ►

Nonagricultural	Agricultural	Household

14 Principal activity (see instructions) ►

15 Is the principal business activity manufacturing? . . . . ☐ Yes ☐ No
If "Yes," principal product and raw material used

16 To whom are most of the products or services sold? Please check one box.   ☐ Business (wholesale)
☐ Public (retail)   ☐ Other (specify) ►   ☐ N/A

17a Has the applicant ever applied for an employer identification number for this or any other business? . . . . ☐ Yes ☐ No
Note: *If "Yes," please complete lines 17b and 17c.*

17b If you checked "Yes" on line 17a, give applicant's legal name and trade name shown on prior application, if different from line 1 or 2 above.
Legal name ►   Trade name ►

17c Approximate date when and city and state where the application was filed. Enter previous employer identification number if known.

Approximate date when filed (mo., day, year)	City and state where filed	Previous EIN

Under penalties of perjury, I declare that I have examined this application, and to the best of my knowledge and belief, it is true, correct, and complete.

Business telephone number (include area code)

Fax telephone number (include area code)

Name and title (Please type or print clearly.) ►

Signature '

Date ►

Note: *Do not write below this line. For official use only.*

Please leave blank '	Geo.	Ind.	Class	Size	Reason for applying

For Paperwork Reduction Act Notice, see page 4.

Cert no. 16055N

Form **SS-4** (Rev. 2-98)

General Instructions

Section references are to the Internal Revenue Code unless otherwise noted.

Purpose of Form

Use Form SS-4 to apply for an employer identification number (EIN). An EIN is a nine-digit number (for example, 12-3456789) assigned to sole proprietors, corporations, partnerships, estates, trusts, and other entities for tax filing and reporting purposes. The information you provide on this form will establish your business tax account.

Caution: *An EIN is for use in connection with your business activities only. Do NOT use your EIN in place of your social security number (SSN).*

Who Must File

You must file this form if you have not been assigned an EIN before and:

● You pay wages to one or more employees including household employees.

● You are required to have an EIN to use on any return, statement, or other document, even if you are not an employer.

● You are a withholding agent required to withhold taxes on income, other than wages, paid to a nonresident alien (individual, corporation, partnership, etc.). A withholding agent may be an agent, broker, fiduciary, manager, tenant, or spouse, and is required to file **Form 1042,** Annual Withholding Tax Return for U.S. Source Income of Foreign Persons.

● You file **Schedule C,** Profit or Loss From Business, **Schedule C-EZ,** Net Profit From Business, or **Schedule F,** Profit or Loss From Farming, of **Form 1040,** U.S. Individual Income Tax Return, **and** have a Keogh plan or are required to file excise, employment, or alcohol, tobacco, or firearms returns.

The following must use EINs even if they do not have any employees:

● State and local agencies who serve as tax reporting agents for public assistance recipients, under Rev. Proc. 80-4, 1980-1 C.B. 581, should obtain a separate EIN for this reporting. See **Household employer** on page 3.

● Trusts, except the following:

   1. Certain grantor-owned trusts. (See the **Instructions for Form 1041.**)

   2. Individual Retirement Arrangement (IRA) trusts, unless the trust has to file **Form 990-T,** Exempt Organization Business Income Tax Return. (See the **Instructions for Form 990-T.**)

● Estates

● Partnerships

● REMICs (real estate mortgage investment conduits) (See the **Instructions for Form 1066,** U.S. Real Estate Mortgage Investment Conduit Income Tax Return.)

● Corporations

● Nonprofit organizations (churches, clubs, etc.)

● Farmers' cooperatives

● Plan administrators (A plan administrator is the person or group of persons specified as the administrator by the instrument under which the plan is operated.)

When To Apply for a New EIN

New Business. If you become the new owner of an existing business, **do not** use the EIN of the former owner. IF YOU ALREADY HAVE AN EIN, USE THAT NUMBER. If you do not have an EIN, apply for one on this form. If you become the "owner" of a corporation by acquiring its stock, use the corporation's EIN.

Changes in Organization or Ownership. If you already have an EIN, you may need to get a new one if either the organization or ownership of your business changes. If you incorporate a sole proprietorship or form a partnership, you must get a new EIN. However, **do not** apply for a new EIN if:

● You change only the name of your business,

● You elected on **Form 8832,** Entity Classification Election, to change the way the entity is taxed, or

● A partnership terminates because at least 50% of the total interests in partnership capital and profits were sold or exchanged within a 12-month period. (See Regulations section 301.6109-1(d)(2)(iii).) The EIN for the terminated partnership should continue to be used. This rule applies to terminations occurring after May 8, 1997. If the termination took place after May 8, 1996, and before May 9, 1997, a new EIN must be obtained for the new partnership unless the partnership and its partners are consistent in using the old EIN.

Note: *If you are electing to be an "S corporation," be sure you file **Form 2553,** Election by a Small Business Corporation.*

File Only One Form SS-4. File only one Form SS-4, regardless of the number of businesses operated or trade names under which a business operates. However, each corporation in an affiliated group must file a separate application.

EIN Applied for, But Not Received. If you do not have an EIN by the time a return is due, write "Applied for" and the date you applied in the space shown for the number. **Do not** show your social security number (SSN) as an EIN on returns.

If you do not have an EIN by the time a tax deposit is due, send your payment to the Internal Revenue Service Center for your filing area. (See **Where To Apply** below.) Make your check or money order payable to Internal Revenue Service and show your name (as shown on Form SS-4), address, type of tax, period covered, and date you applied for an EIN. Send an explanation with the deposit.

For more information about EINs, see **Pub. 583,** Starting a Business and Keeping Records, and **Pub. 1635,** Understanding your EIN.

How To Apply

You can apply for an EIN either by mail or by telephone. You can get an EIN immediately by calling the Tele-TIN number for the service center for your state, or you can send the completed Form SS-4 directly to the service center to receive your EIN by mail.

Application by Tele-TIN. Under the Tele-TIN program, you can receive your EIN by telephone and use it immediately to file a return or make a payment. To receive an EIN by telephone, complete Form SS-4, then call the Tele-TIN number listed for your state under **Where To Apply.** The person making the call must be authorized to sign the form. (See **Signature** on page 4.)

An IRS representative will use the information from the Form SS-4 to establish your account and assign you an EIN. Write the number you are given on the upper right corner of the form and sign and date it.

*Mail or fax (facsimile) the signed SS-4 **within 24 hours** to the Tele-TIN Unit at the service center address for your state.* The IRS representative will give you the fax number. The fax numbers are also listed in Pub. 1635.

Taxpayer representatives can receive their client's EIN by telephone if they first send a fax of a completed **Form 2848,** Power of Attorney and Declaration of Representative, or **Form 8821,** Tax Information Authorization, to the Tele-TIN unit. The Form 2848 or Form 8821 will be used solely to release the EIN to the representative authorized on the form.

Application by Mail. Complete Form SS-4 at least 4 to 5 weeks before you will need an EIN. Sign and date the application and mail it to the service center address for your state. You will receive your EIN in the mail in approximately 4 weeks.

Where To Apply

The Tele-TIN numbers listed below will involve a long-distance charge to callers outside of the local calling area and can be used only to apply for an EIN. THE NUMBERS MAY CHANGE WITHOUT NOTICE. Call 1-800-829-1040 to verify a number or to ask about the status of an application by mail.

If your principal business, office or agency, or legal residence in the case of an individual, is located in: ▼	Call the Tele-TIN number shown or file with the Internal Revenue Service Center at: ▼
Florida, Georgia, South Carolina	Attn: Entity Control Atlanta, GA 39901 770-455-2360
New Jersey, New York City and counties of Nassau, Rockland, Suffolk, and Westchester	Attn: Entity Control Holtsville, NY 00501 516-447-4955
New York (all other counties), Connecticut, Maine, Massachusetts, New Hampshire, Rhode Island, Vermont	Attn: Entity Control Andover, MA 05501 978-474-9717
Illinois, Iowa, Minnesota, Missouri, Wisconsin	Attn: Entity Control Stop 6800 2306 E. Bannister Rd. Kansas City, MO 64999 816-926-5999
Delaware, District of Columbia, Maryland, Pennsylvania, Virginia	Attn: Entity Control Philadelphia, PA 19255 215-516-6999
Indiana, Kentucky, Michigan, Ohio, West Virginia	Attn: Entity Control Cincinnati, OH 45999 606-292-5467

Kansas, New Mexico, Oklahoma, Texas	Attn: Entity Control Austin, TX 73301 512-460-7843
Alaska, Arizona, California (counties of Alpine, Amador, Butte, Calaveras, Colusa, Contra Costa, Del Norte, El Dorado, Glenn, Humboldt, Lake, Lassen, Marin, Mendocino, Modoc, Napa, Nevada, Placer, Plumas, Sacramento, San Joaquin, Shasta, Sierra, Siskiyou, Solano, Sonoma, Sutter, Tehama, Trinity, Yolo, and Yuba), Colorado, Idaho, Montana, Nebraska, Nevada, North Dakota, Oregon, South Dakota, Utah, Washington, Wyoming	Attn: Entity Control Mail Stop 6271 P.O. Box 9941 Ogden, UT 84201 801-620-7645
California (all other counties), Hawaii	Attn: Entity Control Fresno, CA 93888 209-452-4010
Alabama, Arkansas, Louisiana, Mississippi, North Carolina, Tennessee	Attn: Entity Control Memphis, TN 37501 901-546-3920
If you have no legal residence, principal place of business, or principal office or agency in any state	Attn: Entity Control Philadelphia, PA 19255 215-516-6999

Specific Instructions

The instructions that follow are for those items that are not self-explanatory. Enter N/A (nonapplicable) on the lines that do not apply.

Line 1. Enter the legal name of the entity applying for the EIN exactly as it appears on the social security card, charter, or other applicable legal document.

Individuals. Enter your first name, middle initial, and last name. If you are a sole proprietor, enter your individual name, not your business name. Enter your business name on line 2. Do not use abbreviations or nicknames on line 1.

Trusts. Enter the name of the trust.

Estate of a decedent. Enter the name of the estate.

Partnerships. Enter the legal name of the partnership as it appears in the partnership agreement. **Do not** list the names of the partners on line 1. See the specific instructions for line 7.

Corporations. Enter the corporate name as it appears in the corporation charter or other legal document creating it.

Plan administrators. Enter the name of the plan administrator. A plan administrator who already has an EIN should use that number.

Line 2. Enter the trade name of the business if different from the legal name. The trade name is the "doing business as" name.

Note: *Use the full legal name on line 1 on all tax returns filed for the entity. However, if you enter a trade name on line 2 and choose to use the trade name instead of the legal name, enter the trade name on all returns you file. To prevent processing delays and errors, always use either the legal name only or the trade name only on all tax returns.*

Line 3. Trusts enter the name of the trustee. Estates enter the name of the executor, administrator, or other fiduciary. If the entity applying has a designated person to receive tax information, enter that person's name as the "care of" person. Print or type the first name, middle initial, and last name.

Line 7. Enter the first name, middle initial, last name, and SSN of a principal officer if the business is a corporation; of a general partner if a partnership; of the owner of a single member entity that is disregarded as an entity separate from its owner; or of a grantor, owner, or trustor if a trust. If the person in question is an alien individual with a previously assigned individual taxpayer identification number (ITIN), enter the ITIN in the space provided, instead of an SSN. You are not required to enter an SSN or ITIN if the reason you are applying for an EIN is to make an entity classification election (see Regulations section 301.7701-1 through 301.7701-3), and you are a nonresident alien with no effectively connected income from sources within the United States.

Line 8a. Check the box that best describes the type of entity applying for the EIN. If you are an alien individual with an ITIN previously assigned to you, enter the ITIN in place of a requested SSN.

Caution: *This is not an election for a tax classification of an entity. See "Limited liability company" below.*

If not specifically mentioned, check the "Other" box, enter the type of entity and the type of return that will be filed (for example, common trust fund, Form 1065). Do not enter N/A. If you are an alien individual applying for an EIN, see the **Line 7** instructions above.

Sole proprietor. Check this box if you file Schedule C, C-EZ, or F (Form 1040) and have a Keogh plan, or are required to file excise, employment, or alcohol, tobacco, or firearms returns, or are a payer of gambling winnings. Enter your SSN (or ITIN) in the space provided. If you are a nonresident alien with no effectively connected income from sources within the United States, you do not need to enter an SSN or ITIN.

REMIC. Check this box if the entity has elected to be treated as a real estate mortgage investment conduit (REMIC). See the **Instructions for Form 1066** for more information.

Other nonprofit organization. Check this box if the nonprofit organization is other than a church or church-controlled organization and specify the type of nonprofit organization (for example, an educational organization).

If the organization also seeks tax-exempt status, you must file either **Package 1023,** Application for Recognition of Exemption, or **Package 1024,** Application for Recognition of Exemption Under Section 501(a). Get **Pub. 557,** Tax Exempt Status for Your Organization, for more information.

Group exemption number (GEN). If the organization is covered by a group exemption letter, enter the four-digit GEN. (Do not confuse the GEN with the nine-digit EIN.) If you do not know the GEN, contact the parent organization. Get Pub. 557 for more information about group exemption numbers.

Withholding agent. If you are a withholding agent required to file Form 1042, check the "Other" box and enter "Withholding agent."

Personal service corporation. Check this box if the entity is a personal service corporation. An entity is a personal service corporation for a tax year only if:

● The principal activity of the entity during the testing period (prior tax year) for the tax year is the performance of personal services substantially by employee-owners, and

● The employee-owners own at least 10% of the fair market value of the outstanding stock in the entity on the last day of the testing period.

Personal services include performance of services in such fields as health, law, accounting, or consulting. For more information about personal service corporations, see the **Instructions for Form 1120,** U.S. Corporation Income Tax Return, and **Pub. 542,** Corporations.

Limited liability company (LLC). See the definition of limited liability company in the **Instructions for Form 1065.** An LLC with two or more members can be a partnership or an association taxable as a corporation. An LLC with a single owner can be an association taxable as a corporation or an entity disregarded as an entity separate from its owner. See Form 8832 for more details.

● If the entity is classified as a partnership for Federal income tax purposes, check the "partnership" box.

● If the entity is classified as a corporation for Federal income tax purposes, mark the "Other corporation" box and write "limited liability co." in the space provided.

● If the entity is disregarded as an entity separate from its owner, check the "Other" box and write in "disregarded entity" in the space provided.

Plan administrator. If the plan administrator is an individual, enter the plan administrator's SSN in the space provided.

Other corporation. This box is for any corporation other than a personal service corporation. If you check this box, enter the type of corporation (such as insurance company) in the space provided.

Household employer. If you are an individual, check the "Other" box and enter "Household employer" and your SSN. If you are a state or local agency serving as a tax reporting agent for public assistance recipients who become household employers, check the "Other" box and enter "Household employer agent." If you are a trust that qualifies as a household employer, you do not need a separate EIN for reporting tax information relating to household employees; use the EIN of the trust.

QSSS. For a qualified subchapter S subsidiary (QSSS) check the "Other" box and specify "QSSS."

Line 9. Check only **one** box. Do not enter N/A.

Started new business. Check this box if you are starting a new business that requires an EIN. If you check this box, enter the type of business being started. **Do not** apply if you already have an EIN and are only adding another place of business.

Hired employees. Check this box if the existing business is requesting an EIN because it has hired or is hiring employees and is therefore required to file employment tax returns. **Do not** apply if you already have an EIN and are only hiring employees. For information on the applicable employment taxes for family members, see **Circular E,** Employer's Tax Guide (Publication 15).

Created a pension plan. Check this box if you have created a pension plan and need this number for reporting purposes. Also, enter the type of plan created.

Note: *Check this box if you are applying for a trust EIN when a new pension plan is established.*

Banking purpose. Check this box if you are requesting an EIN for banking purposes only, and enter the banking purpose (for example, a bowling league for depositing dues or an investment club for dividend and interest reporting).

Changed type of organization. Check this box if the business is changing its type of organization, for example, if the business was a sole proprietorship and has been incorporated or has become a partnership. If you check this box, specify in the space provided the type of change made, for example, "from sole proprietorship to partnership."

Purchased going business. Check this box if you purchased an existing business. **Do not** use the former owner's EIN. **Do not** apply for a new EIN if you already have one. Use your own EIN.

Created a trust. Check this box if you created a trust, and enter the type of trust created. For example, indicate if the trust is a nonexempt charitable trust or a split-interest trust.

Note: *Do not check this box if you are applying for a trust EIN when a new pension plan is established. Check "Created a pension plan."*

Exception. Do **not** file this form for certain grantor-type trusts. The trustee does not need an EIN for the trust if the trustee furnishes the name and TIN of the grantor/owner and the address of the trust to all payors. See the Instructions for Form 1041 for more information.

Other (specify). Check this box if you are requesting an EIN for any reason other than those for which there are checkboxes, and enter the reason.

Line 10. If you are starting a new business, enter the starting date of the business. If the business you acquired is already operating, enter the date you acquired the business. Trusts should enter the date the trust was legally created. Estates should enter the date of death of the decedent whose name appears on line 1 or the date when the estate was legally funded.

Line 11. Enter the last month of your accounting year or tax year. An accounting or tax year is usually 12 consecutive months, either a calendar year or a fiscal year (including a period of 52 or 53 weeks). A calendar year is 12 consecutive months ending on December 31. A fiscal year is either 12 consecutive months ending on the last day of any month other than December or a 52-53 week year. For more information on accounting periods, see **Pub. 538,** Accounting Periods and Methods.

Individuals. Your tax year generally will be a calendar year.

Partnerships. Partnerships generally must adopt one of the following tax years:
● The tax year of the majority of its partners,
● The tax year common to all of its principal partners,
● The tax year that results in the least aggregate deferral of income, or
● In certain cases, some other tax year.
See the **Instructions for Form 1065,** U.S. Partnership Return of Income, for more information.

REMIC. REMICs must have a calendar year as their tax year.

Personal service corporations. A personal service corporation generally must adopt a calendar year unless:
● It can establish a business purpose for having a different tax year, or
● It elects under section 444 to have a tax year other than a calendar year.

Trusts. Generally, a trust must adopt a calendar year except for the following:
● Tax-exempt trusts,
● Charitable trusts, and
● Grantor-owned trusts.

Line 12. If the business has or will have employees, enter the date on which the business began or will begin to pay wages. If the business does not plan to have employees, enter N/A.

Withholding agent. Enter the date you began or will begin to pay income to a nonresident alien. This also applies to individuals who are required to file Form 1042 to report alimony paid to a nonresident alien.

Line 13. For a definition of agricultural labor (farmwork), see **Circular A,** Agricultural Employer's Tax Guide (Publication 51).

Line 14. Generally, enter the exact type of business being operated (for example, advertising agency, farm, food or beverage establishment, labor union, real estate agency, steam laundry, rental of coin-operated vending machine, or investment club). Also state if the business will involve the sale or distribution of alcoholic beverages.

Governmental. Enter the type of organization (state, county, school district, municipality, etc.).

Nonprofit organization (other than governmental). Enter whether organized for religious, educational, or humane purposes, and the principal activity (for example, religious organization—hospital, charitable).

Mining and quarrying. Specify the process and the principal product (for example, mining bituminous coal, contract drilling for oil, or quarrying dimension stone).

Contract construction. Specify whether general contracting or special trade contracting. Also, show the type of work normally performed (for example, general contractor for residential buildings or electrical subcontractor).

Food or beverage establishments. Specify the type of establishment and state whether you employ workers who receive tips (for example, lounge—yes).

Trade. Specify the type of sales and the principal line of goods sold (for example, wholesale dairy products, manufacturer's representative for mining machinery, or retail hardware).

Manufacturing. Specify the type of establishment operated (for example, sawmill or vegetable cannery).

Signature. The application must be signed by (a) the individual, if the applicant is an individual, (b) the president, vice president, or other principal officer, if the applicant is a corporation, (c) a responsible and duly authorized member or officer having knowledge of its affairs, if the applicant is a partnership or other unincorporated organization, or (d) the fiduciary, if the applicant is a trust or an estate.

How To Get Forms and Publications

Phone. You can order forms, instructions, and publications by phone. Just call 1-800-TAX-FORM (1-800-829-3676). You should receive your order or notification of its status within 7 to 15 workdays.

Personal computer. With your personal computer and modem, you can get the forms and information you need using:

● IRS's Internet Web Site at **www.irs.ustreas.gov**
● Telnet at **iris.irs.ustreas.gov**
● File Transfer Protocol at **ftp.irs.ustreas.gov**

You can also dial direct (by modem) to the Internal Revenue Information Services (IRIS) at 703-321-8020. IRIS is an on-line information service on FedWorld.

For small businesses, return preparers, or others who may frequently need tax forms or publications, a CD-ROM containing over 2,000 tax products (including many prior year forms) can be purchased from the Government Printing Office.

CD-ROM. To order the CD-ROM call the Superintendent of Documents at 202-512-1800 or connect to **www.access.gpo.gov/su_docs**

Privacy Act and Paperwork Reduction Act Notice. We ask for the information on this form to carry out the Internal Revenue laws of the United States. We need it to comply with section 6109 and the regulations thereunder which generally require the inclusion of an employer identification number (EIN) on certain returns, statements, or other documents filed with the Internal Revenue Service. Information on this form may be used to determine which Federal tax returns you are required to file and to provide you with related forms and publications. We disclose this form to the Social Security Administration for their use in determining compliance with applicable laws. We will be unable to issue an EIN to you unless you provide all of the requested information which applies to your entity.

You are not required to provide the information requested on a form that is subject to the Paperwork Reduction Act unless the form displays a valid OMB control number. Books or records relating to a form or its instructions must be retained as long as their contents may become material in the administration of any Internal Revenue law. Generally, tax returns and return information are confidential, as required by section 6103.

The time needed to complete and file this form will vary depending on individual circumstances. The estimated average time is:

Recordkeeping	7 min.
Learning about the law or the form	19 min.
Preparing the form	45 min.
Copying, assembling, and sending the form to the IRS . .	20 min.

If you have comments concerning the accuracy of these time estimates or suggestions for making this form simpler, we would be happy to hear from you. You can write to the Tax Forms Committee, Western Area Distribution Center, Rancho Cordova, CA 95743-0001. **Do not** send this form to this address. Instead, see **Where To Apply** on page 2.

Office of the County Clerk	Fees	FILING STAMP ONLY
Address _____ City _____ ☐ First Filing ☐ Renewal Filing	$ _____ for 1 FBN and registrant $ _____ for each additional FBN filed on same statement and doing business at same location $ _____ for each additional registrant	 **File Number:** _____

FICTITIOUS BUSINESS NAME STATEMENT

THE FOLLOWING PERSON(S) IS (ARE)

1 Fictitious Business Name(s)

1

3.

2

Articles of Incorporation Number (if applicable)
AL#

2 Street Address & City of Principal Place of Business in California (P.O. Box alone not acceptable) — Zip Code

3 Full Name of Registrant — if corporation—incorporated in what state

Residence Street Address — City — State — Zip Code

3a Full Name of Registrant — if corporation—incorporated in what state

Residence Street Address — City — State — Zip Code

3b Full Name of Registrant — if corporation—incorporated in what state

Residence Street Address — City — State — Zip Code

4 This Business is conducted by:
( ) an individual ( ) a general partnership ( ) joint venture ( ) a business trust
( ) co-partners ( ) husband and wife ( ) a corporation ( ) a limited partnership
( ) an unincorporated association other than a partnership ( ) other—please specify _____

5
( ) The registrant commenced to transact business under name or names listed on (date): _____
( ) Registrant has not yet begun to transact business under the fictitious business name or names listed herein.

6 If registrant is not a corporation or a limited liability company sign below:

SIGNATURE	TYPE OR PRINT NAME
SIGNATURE	TYPE OR PRINT NAME
SIGNATURE	TYPE OR PRINT NAME

6a If registrant is a corporation or a limited liability company sign below:

COMPANY NAME

SIGNATURE & TITLE

TYPE OR PRINT NAME AND TITLE

This statement was filed with the County Clerk of _____ County on date indicated by file stamp above.

NOTICE—THIS FICTITIOUS NAME STATEMENT EXPIRES FIVE YEARS FROM DATE IT WAS FILED IN THE OFFICE OF THE COUNTY CLERK.

A NEW FICTITIOUS BUSINESS NAME STATEMENT MUST BE FILED PRIOR TO THAT DATE. The filing of this statement does not of itself authorize the use in this state of a fictitious business name in violation of the rights of another under federal, state, or common law (SEE SECTION 14400 et seq., Business and Professional Code).

This form should be typed or printed legibly in black ink.

**APPLICATION FOR SELLER'S PERMIT AND
REGISTRATION AS A RETAILER
(INDIVIDUALS/PARTNERS)**

WHO MUST HAVE A PERMIT

If you sell taxable merchandise or provide a taxable service in California, such as renting merchandise or fabrication labor, you must have a seller's permit. Wholesalers as well as retailers **must have a separate permit for each place of business.**

This application includes information you need to obtain a permit as well as a brief description of your rights and responsibilities once the permit is obtained.

If you have specific questions about information contained in this application, please contact any Board of Equalization office listed on the back of this page.

HOW TO OBTAIN A PERMIT

To obtain a seller's permit, you must complete the attached application. Directions for completing the application follow.

1. **Type or print neatly in ink.** The application is organized into sections. To help us issue your permit quickly and accurately, be sure the information you include in each section is correct and legible. Your application will become a part of your permanent file with us, and the information you include on your application — except for your name, business name and address, permit number, and status (active or closed out) — is confidential and may not be furnished to the public.

2. **Complete only the unshaded portions of both sides of the application.**

3. **Be sure to indicate the type of ownership of your business.** If you check Partnership, please include a copy of the partnership agreement with your application. If you do not supply the necessary documents, your permit may be delayed.

4. **Be sure the Section I and Section IV information is completed and signed.** The application should be signed in the Certification Section IV by the owner, or in the case of a partnership each partner should sign.

5. **Return the completed application to the Board office closest to your business.** (Locations, mailing addresses, and telephone numbers of Board offices may be found on the back of this page.) Once your application is reviewed and found in order, you will be issued a permit without charge. In addition, copies of pertinent regulations, forms, and returns will be sent to you. Depending on the type of business and conditions surrounding ownership, you may be required to post a security deposit.

6. **Photocopies of your social security card and driver's license are required to ensure the accuracy of the information provided and to protect you against fraudulent use of your identification numbers.** Should your social security card not be readily available, copies of other documents with your social security number on them such as employer paycheck stubs, preprinted income tax labels, or withholding statements (W-2 forms) are suitable alternatives.

YOUR RIGHTS AND RESPONSIBILITIES AS A SELLER

When you obtain a seller's permit, you acquire valuable rights and privileges as well as responsibilities.

- **You may purchase property for resale without paying tax.** By providing the vendor with a completed resale certificate, you are not required to pay sales tax on tangible personal property you purchase for resale. However, you should not use a resale certificate if you intend to use the property prior to or instead of selling it. If you intend to use the property, you must pay sales tax.

- **You must keep records.** You must keep adequate records in order to substantiate your sales, deductions reported on your returns, and any purchases you have made for your business. Records must be kept for four years.

- **You must file returns.** Returns must be filed on or before the last day of the month following your reporting period. *You must file your return even if you did not sell any merchandise.*

- **You must pay taxes.** As a seller, you must pay taxes on gross receipts from retail sales. However, you are allowed by law to be reimbursed by collecting the tax from your customers.

- **You must notify the Board if you move, change ownership of, or sell your business.** Your permit is valid only at the address and for the type of ownership specified on the permit. You should notify the Board of any change in ownership. Failure to do so could result in your being held liable for the successor's operations. In addition, you should notify the Board immediately if you discontinue your business. Your notification will help us to close your account and return any security you may have on deposit.

- **You must provide your social security number.** See the notice (BOE-324-A) included in this application package regarding the disclosure of your social security number.

CALIFORNIA STATE BOARD OF EQUALIZATION OFFICES

BOARD MEMBERS

DISTRICT	MEMBER	OFFICE ADDRESS	AREA CODE	TELEPHONE NUMBER
First	Johan Klehs	22320 Foothill Boulevard, Suite 300, Hayward, 94541	510	247-2125
Second	Dean F. Andal	7540 Shoreline Drive, Suite D, Stockton, 95219	209	473-6579
Third	Ernest J. Dronenburg, Jr.	110 West C Street, Suite 1709, San Diego, 92101-3966	619	237-7844
Fourth	John Chiang (Acting)	15350 Sherman Way, Suite 110, Van Nuys, 91406	818	901-5733
Executive Director	E. L. Sorensen, Jr.	450 N Street, PO Box 942879, Sacramento, 94279-0001	916	445-6464

FOR GENERAL TAX INFORMATION CALL
1-800-400-7115
* For account specific information contact your local office

SACRAMENTO HEADQUARTERS
BUSINESS TAXES FIELD OFFICES

450 N Street, PO Box 942879, Sacramento 94279-0001   916   445-6464

CALIFORNIA CITIES	OFFICE ADDRESS	AREA CODE	TELEPHONE NUMBER
Bakersfield	1800 30th Street, Suite 380, PO Box 1728, 93302-1728	805	395-2880
City of Industry	12820 Crossroads Parkway, PO Box 90818, 91715-0818	562	908-5280
Concord	1001 Galaxy Way, Suite 212, 94520 (PO Box 5965, Concord, 94524)	925	687-6962
Culver City	5901 Green Valley Circle, PO Box 3652, 90231-3652	310	342-1000
El Centro	1550 W. Main Street, 92243-2832	760	352-3431
Eureka	134 D Street, Suite 301, PO Box 4884, 95502-4884 (hours 8-12 & 1-5 M-F)	707	445-6500
Fresno	5070 N. Sixth Street, Suite 110, PO Box 28580, 93729-8580	209	248-4219
Laguna Hills	23141 Moulton Parkway, Suite 100, PO Box 30890, 92654-0890	949	461-5711
Norwalk	12440 E. Imperial Highway, PO Box 409, 90651-0409	562	466-1694
Oakland	2101 Webster Street, Suite 200, No. 46, 94612-3027	510	286-0347
Rancho Mirage	42-700 Bob Hope Drive, Suite 301, 92270-4473	760	346-8096
Redding	391 Hemstead Drive, PO Box 492529, 96049-2529	530	224-4729
Riverside	3737 Main Street, Suite 1000, 92501-3395	909	680-6400
Sacramento	9823 Old Winery Place, Suite 1, 95827-1731	916	255-3350
Salinas	111 East Navajo Drive, Suite 100, 93906	408	443-3003
San Diego	1350 Front Street, Rm 5047, 92101-3612	619	525-4526
San Francisco	50 Fremont Street, Suite 1400, 94105-2234	415	396-9800
San Jose	250 South Second Street, 95113-2706	408	277-1231
San Marcos	334 Via Vera Cruz, Suite 107, 92069-2637	760	744-1330
Santa Ana	28 Civic Center Plaza, Rm 239, PO Box 12040, 92712-2040	714	558-4059
Santa Rosa	50 D Street, Rm 215, PO Box 730, 95402-0730	707	576-2100
Stockton	31 East Channel Street, Rm 264, PO Box 1890, 95201-1890	209	948-7720
Suisun City	333 Sunset Avenue, Suite 330, 94585	707	428-2041
Torrance	680 W. Knox Street, Suite 200, PO Box T, 90508-0270	310	516-4300
Van Nuys	15350 Sherman Way, Suite 250, 91406 (PO Box 7735, Van Nuys, 91409-7735)	818	904-2300
Ventura	4820 McGrath Street, Suite 260, Ventura, 93003-7778	805	677-2700

OUT-OF-STATE FIELD OFFICES

Sacramento	450 N Street, PO Box 188268, 95818-0268	916	322-2010
Chicago, Illinois	120 N. La Salle, Suite 1602, 60602	312	201-5300
New York, N.Y.	675 Third Avenue, Rm 520, 10017-4015	212	697-4680
Houston, Texas	1155 Dairy Ashford, Suite 550, 77079-3007	281	531-3450

TDD INFORMATION

California Relay Telephone Service for the Deaf and Hearing Impaired - From TDD telephones dial 1-800-735-2929. From voice operated telephones 1-800-735-2922.

Addresses and telephone numbers are current as of 5-1-98

APPLICATION FOR SELLER'S PERMIT AND REGISTRATION
AS A RETAILER (INDIVIDUALS/PARTNERS)

SECTION I: OWNERSHIP INFORMATION

FOR BOARD USE ONLY

1. PLEASE CHECK TYPE OF OWNERSHIP *(use additional sheet to include information about additional co-owners or partners)*

☐ Sole Owner   ☐ Husband/Wife Co-ownership

☐ Partnership (If partnership enter Federal Employer Indentification Number (FEIN) numbers)

Photocopy of Driver's License and Social Security Card is required
See instruction number 6

TAX	OFFICE	NUMBER
S		

BUSINESS CODE	AREA CODE
PREPARER	VERIFICATION: ☐ SSN ☐ DL ☐ Other

	OWNER OR PARTNER	CO-OWNER OR PARTNER
2. FULL NAME *(first, middle, last)*		
3. RESIDENCE ADDRESS *(enter full address including zip code)*		
4. RESIDENCE TELEPHONE NO.	( )	( )
5. SOCIAL SECURITY NO.		
6. DRIVER'S LICENSE NO. & DATE OF BIRTH		
7. PRESENT/PAST EMPLOYER *(enter full address including zip code & telephone no.)*		
8. NAME, ADDRESS & TELEPHONE NO. OF TWO PERSONAL REFERENCES	1. 2.	1. 2.
9. SPOUSE'S NAME		
10. SPOUSE'S SOCIAL SECURITY NO.		
11. SPOUSE'S DRIVER'S LICENSE NO. & DATE OF BIRTH		
12. SIGNATURE		

SECTION II: BUSINESS INFORMATION

1. BUSINESS NAME	BUSINESS TELEPHONE ( )

2. BUSINESS ADDRESS *(do not list P.O. Box or mailing service)*	CITY	STATE	ZIP CODE
3. MAILING ADDRESS *(if different from No. 2 above)*	CITY	STATE	ZIP CODE

4. DATE YOU WILL BEGIN SALES *(month, day & year)*	5. DAYS & HOURS OF OPERATION	SUNDAY	MONDAY	TUESDAY	WEDNESDAY	THURSDAY	FRIDAY	SATURDAY

6. TYPE OF BUSINESS *(check one)*

☐ Retail ☐ Wholesale ☐ Mfg. ☐ Repair ☐ Service ☐ Construction Contractor

CHECK ONE ☐ Full Time ☐ Part Time ☐ Mail Order

7. TYPE OF ITEMS SOLD

8. ARE YOU

☐ Starting a new business? ☐ Adding/dropping partner? ☐ Other? _____

☐ Buying a business? *(indicate name & account number in area at right)*

FORMER OWNER'S NAME

ACCOUNT NUMBER

9. PURCHASE PRICE $	10. VALUE OF FIXTURES & EQUIPMENT	11. NUMBER OF SELLING LOCATIONS *(if 2 or more attach list of all locations)*

12. IF AN ESCROW COMPANY IS REQUESTING A TAX CLEARANCE ON YOUR BEHALF, PLEASE LIST THEIR NAME, ADDRESS, TELEPHONE NUMBER AND THE ESCROW NUMBER

13. IF ALCOHOLIC BEVERAGES ARE SOLD, PLEASE LIST YOUR ALCOHOLIC BEVERAGE CONTROL LICENSE NO. AND TYPE

14. NAME, ADDRESS & TELEPHONE NUMBER OF ACCOUNTANT/BOOKKEEPER

15. NAME, ADDRESS & TELEPHONE NUMBER OF BUSINESS LANDLORD

16. NAME & LOCATION OF BANK OR OTHER FINANCIAL INSTITUTION *(Note whether business or personal)*	CHECKING AND SAVINGS ACCOUNT NUMBER
17. NAME & ADDRESS OF MAJOR SUPPLIERS	PRODUCTS PURCHASED

18. OTHER ACCOUNT NUMBERS ISSUED TO YOU BY THE BOARD

SECTION III: INCOME AND EXPENSES

1. PROJECTED MONTHLY BUSINESS EXPENSES	2. PROJECTED MONTHLY SALES	3. INFORMATION CONCERNING EMPLOYMENT DEVELOPMENT DEPARTMENT (EDD)
		a. Are you registered with EDD? ☐ Yes ☐ No
RENT $_____	TOTAL GROSS SALES $_____	b. If no, will your payroll exceed $100 per quarter? ☐ Yes ☐ No
PAYROLL $_____	NON-TAXABLE $_____	If yes, you must make application with EDD. Number of employees See pamphlet DE 44, "California Employer's Guide."
MISC. $_____	TAXABLE $_____	c. I have already received pamphlet DE 44,
TOTAL $_____	TAX $_____	"California Employer's Guide." ☐ Yes ☐ No

SECTION IV: CERTIFICATION

The statements contained herein are hereby certified to be correct to the best knowledge and belief of the undersigned who is duly authorized to sign this application. (If spouse co-ownership both signatures must appear below.)

SIGNATURE	TITLE	SIGNATURE	TITLE
NAME *(typed or printed)*		NAME *(typed or printed)*	DATE

FOR BOARD USE ONLY
Furnished to Taxpayer

REPORTING BASIS			REGULATIONS
	☐ BOE-8	☐ DE-44	
SECURITY REVIEW	☒ BOE-324A	☐ OTHER	
	☐ BT-400Y	_____	
☐ BT-598 $_____	☐ BOE-467	_____	PAMPHLETS
☐ BT-1009	☐ BOE-519	_____	
BY	☐ BT-1241-D	_____	
APPROVED BY	☐ REG. 1668	_____	
REMOTE INPUT DATE	☐ REG. 1698	_____	RETURNS
BY	☐ REG. 1700		
☐ Permit Issued Date _____			

NOTICE TO INDIVIDUALS REGARDING INFORMATION
FURNISHED TO THE BOARD OF EQUALIZATION

The Information Practices Act of 1977 and the Federal Privacy Act requires this agency to provide the following notice to individuals who are asked by the State Board of Equalization (Board) to supply information, including the disclosure of the individual's social security account number.

Individuals applying for permits, certificates, or licenses, or filing tax returns, statements, or other forms prescribed by this agency, are required to include their social security numbers for proper identification. [See Title 42 United States Code §405(c)(2)(C)(i)]. It is mandatory to furnish all the appropriate information requested by applications for registration, applications for permits or licenses, tax returns and other related data. Failure to provide all of the required information requested by an application for a permit or license could result in your not being issued a permit or license. In addition, the law provides penalties for failure to file a return, failure to furnish specific information required, failure to supply information required by law or regulations, or for furnishing fraudulent information.

Provisions contained in the following laws require persons meeting certain requirements to file applications for registration, applications for permits or licenses, and tax returns or reports in such form as prescribed by the State Board of Equalization: Alcoholic Beverage Tax, Sections[1] 32001-32556; Childhood Lead Poisoning Prevention Fee, Sections 43001-43651, Health & Safety Code, Sections 105275-105310; Cigarette and Tobacco Products Tax, Sections 30001-30481; Diesel Fuel Tax, Sections 60001-60709; Emergency Telephone Users Surcharge, Sections 41001-41176; Energy Resources Surcharge, Sections 40001-40216; Hazardous Substances Tax, Sections 43001-43651; Integrated Waste Management Fee, Sections 45001-45984; International Fuel Tax Agreement, Sections 9401-9433; Motor Vehicle Fuel License Tax, Sections 7301-8405; Occupational Lead Poisoning Prevention Fee, Sections 43001-43651, Health & Safety Code, Sections 105175-105197; Oil Spill Response, Prevention, and Administration Fees, Sections 46001-46751, Government Code, Sections 8670.1-8670.53; Publicly Owned Property, Sections 1840-1841; Sales and Use Tax, Sections 6001-7279.6; State Assessed Property, Sections 721-868, 4876-4880, 5011-5014; Tax on Insurers, Sections 12001-13170; Timber Yield Tax, Sections 38101-38908; Tire Recycling Fee, Sections 55001-55381, Public Resources Code, Sections 42860-42895; Underground Storage Tank Maintenance Fee, Sections 50101-50161, Health & Safety Code, Sections 25280-25299.96; Use Fuel Tax, Sections 8601-9355.

The principal purpose for which the requested information will be used is to administer the laws identified in the preceding paragraph. This includes the determination and collection of the correct amount of tax. Information you furnish to the Board may be used for the purpose of collecting any outstanding tax liability.

As authorized by law, information requested by an application for a permit or license could be disclosed to other agencies, including, but not limited to, the proper officials of the following: 1) United States governmental agencies: U.S. Attorney's Office; Bureau of Alcohol, Tobacco and Firearms; Depts. of Agriculture, Defense, Justice; Federal Bureau of Investigation; General Accounting Office; Internal Revenue Service; the Interstate Commerce Commission; 2) State of California governmental agencies and officials: Air Resources Board; Dept. of Alcoholic Beverage Control; Auctioneer Commission; Employment Development Department; Energy Commission; Exposition and Fairs; Food & Agriculture; Board of Forestry; Forest Products Commission; Franchise Tax Board; Dept. of Health Services; Highway Patrol; Dept. of Housing & Community Development; California Parent Locator Service; 3) State agencies outside of California for tax enforcement purposes; and 4) city attorneys and city prosecutors; county district attorneys, sheriff departments.

As an individual, you have the right to access personal information about you in records maintained by the State Board of Equalization. Please contact your local Board office listed in the white pages of your telephone directory for assistance. If the local Board office is unable to provide the information sought, you may also contact the Disclosure Office in Sacramento by telephone at (916) 445-2918. The Board officials responsible for maintaining this information, who can be contacted by telephone at (916) 445-6464, are: **Sales and Use Tax,** Deputy Director, Sales and Use Tax Department, 450 N Street, MIC:43, Sacramento, CA 95814; **Excise Taxes, Fuel Taxes and Environmental Fees,** Deputy Director, Special Taxes Department, 450 N Street, MIC:31, Sacramento, CA 95814; **Property Taxes,** Deputy Director, Property Taxes Department, 450 N Street, MIC:63, Sacramento, CA 95814.

---

[1] All references are to the California Revenue and Taxation Code unless otherwise indicated.

SALES AND USE TAX REGULATIONS

Regulation 1668.   RESALE CERTIFICATES.

References: Sections 6012.8, 6012.9, 6072, 6091-6095, 6241-6245, Revenue and Taxation Code.
Automobile Dealers, effect of accepting from nondealer retailer, see Regulation 1566.
Construction Contractors, use by, see Regulation 1521.
Demonstration and Display, use of property purchased under resale certificates for, see Regulation 1669.
Drapery hardware installers accepting, see Regulation 1521.
Newspapers and Periodicals, for component parts of, see Regulation 1590.
Salt used by food processors, giving for, see Regulation 1525.
Vending machine operators furnishing, see Regulation 1574.

(a) EFFECT OF CERTIFICATE.

(1) The burden of proving that a sale of tangible personal property is not at retail is upon the seller unless the seller timely takes a certificate from the purchaser that the property is purchased for resale. If timely taken in good faith from a person who is engaged in the business of selling tangible personal property and who holds a California seller's permit, the certificate relieves the seller from liability for the sales tax and the duty of collecting the use tax. A certificate will be considered timely if it is taken at any time before the seller bills the purchaser for the property, or any time within the seller's normal billing and payment cycle, or any time at or prior to delivery of the property to the purchaser.

(2) If a purchaser who gives a resale certificate for property makes any storage or use of the property other than retention, demonstration, or display while holding it for sale in the regular course of business, the storage or use is taxable as of the time the property is first so stored or used. The use tax must be reported and paid by the purchaser with the purchaser's tax return for the period in which the property is first so stored or used. The purchaser cannot retroactively rescind or revoke the resale certificate and thereby cause the transaction to be subject to sales tax rather than use tax.

(b) FORM OF CERTIFICATE.

(1) Any document, such as a letter or purchase order, timely provided by the purchaser to the seller will be regarded as a resale certificate with respect to the sale of the property described in the document if it contains all of the following essential elements:

(A) The signature of the purchaser or an agent or employee of the purchaser.

(B) The name and address of the purchaser.

(C) The number of the seller's permit held by the purchaser, or if the purchaser is not required to hold a permit because the purchaser sells only property of a kind the retail sale of which is not taxable, e.g., food products for human consumption, or because the purchaser makes no sales in this State, an appropriate notation to that effect in lieu of a seller's permit number.

(D) A statement that the property described in the document is purchased for resale. The document must contain the phrase "for resale". The use of phrases such as "nontaxable", "exempt", or similar terminology is not acceptable.

(E) Date of execution of document. (An otherwise valid resale certificate will not be considered invalid solely on the ground that it is undated.)

(2) A document containing the essential elements described in (1) above is the minimum form which will be regarded as a resale certificate. However, in order to preclude potential controversy, the seller should timely obtain from the purchaser a certificate substantially in the following form:

Regulation 1668.   RESALE CERTIFICATES. (Continued 1)

CALIFORNIA RESALE CERTIFICATE

....
(Name of Purchaser)

....
(Address of Purchaser)

I HEREBY CERTIFY: That I hold valid seller's permit No. .... issued pursuant to the Sales and Use Tax Law; That I am engaged in the business of selling ....
.... ;

that the tangible personal property described herein which I shall purchase from: ....

....

will be resold by me in the form of tangible personal property; provided, however, that in the event any of such property is used for any purpose other than retention, demonstration, or display while holding it for sale in the regular course of business, it is understood that I am required by the Sales and Use Tax Law to report and pay tax, measured by the purchase price of such property or other authorized amount. Description of property to be purchased: ....

....

Date: .... 19.........   ....
                                            (Signature of Purchaser or Authorized Agent)

....
(Title)

Under "Description of property to be purchased" there may appear:

(A) Either an itemized list of the particular property to be purchased for resale, or

(B) A general description of the kind of property to be purchased for resale. (A certificate, thus describing the property is good until revoked in writing.)

If the purchaser is not required to hold a permit because the purchaser sells only property of a kind the retail sale of which is not taxable, e.g., food products for human consumption, or because the purchaser makes no sales in this State, the purchaser should make an appropriate notation to that effect on the certificate in lieu of a seller's permit number.

(3) If a purchaser issues a general (blanket) resale certificate which provides a general description of the items to be purchased, and subsequently issues a purchase order which indicates that the transaction covered by the purchase order is taxable, the resale certificate does not apply with respect to that transaction. However, the purchaser will bear the burden of establishing either that the purchase order was sent to and received by the seller or that the tax or tax reimbursement was paid to the seller. The purchaser may avoid this burden by using the procedure described in subsection (b)(4) below.

(4) If a purchaser wishes to designate on each purchase order that the property is for resale, the seller should obtain a qualified resale certificate, i.e., one that states "see purchase order" in the space provided for a description of the property to be purchased. Each purchase order must then specify whether the property covered by the order is purchased for resale or whether tax applies to the order. If each purchase order does not so specify, it will be assumed that the property covered by that purchase order was purchased for use, and not for resale. If the purchase order includes both items to be resold and items to be used, the purchase order must specify which items are purchased for resale and which items are purchased for use. For example, a purchase order issued for produced parts for resale and also for tooling used to produce the parts should specify that the parts are purchased for resale and that the sale of the tooling is subject to tax.

(5) If the seller does not timely obtain a resale certificate, the fact that the purchaser deletes the tax or tax reimbursement from the seller's billing, provides a seller's permit number to the seller, or informs the seller that the transaction is "not taxable" does not relieve the seller from liability for the tax nor from the burden of proving the sale was for resale.

(c) OTHER EVIDENCE TO REBUT PRESUMPTION OF TAXABILITY. A sale for resale is not subject to sales tax. However, a resale certificate which is not timely taken is not retroactive and will not relieve the seller of the liability for the tax. Consequently, if the seller does not timely obtain a resale certificate, the seller will be relieved of liability for the tax only if the seller presents satisfactory evidence that the specific property sold:

(1) Was in fact resold by the purchaser and was not used by the purchaser for any purpose other than retention, demonstration, or display while holding it for sale in the regular course of business, or

(2) Is being held for resale by the purchaser and has not been used by the purchaser for any purpose other than retention, demonstration, or display while holding it for sale in the regular course of business, or

(3) Has been used or consumed by the purchaser and the purchaser has paid the use tax directly to this State.

(d) GOOD FAITH. A seller will be presumed to have taken a resale certificate in good faith in the absence of evidence to the contrary. If the purchaser insists that the purchaser is buying for resale property of a kind not normally resold in the purchaser's business, the seller should require a resale certificate containing a statement that the specific property is being purchased for resale in the regular course of business.

(e) MOBILEHOMES. A mobilehome retailer who purchases a new mobilehome for sale to a customer for installation for occupancy as a residence on a foundation system pursuant to Section 18551 of the Health and Safety Code, or for installation for occupancy as a residence pursuant to Section 18613 of the Health and Safety Code, and which mobilehome is thereafter subject to property taxation, may issue a resale certificate to the mobilehome vendor even though the retailer is classified as a consumer of the mobilehome by Sections 6012.8 and 6012.9 of the Revenue and Taxation Code. Also, effective September 19, 1985, a mobilehome retailer, licensed as a mobilehome dealer under Section 18002.6 of the Health and Safety Code, who purchases a new mobilehome for sale to a customer for installation for occupancy as a residence on a foundation system pursuant to Section 18551 of the Health and Safety Code, may issue a resale certificate to the mobilehome vendor even though the mobilehome retailer may have the mobilehome installed on a foundation system as an improvement to realty prior to the retailer's sale of the mobilehome to the customer for occupancy as a residence.

Where the mobilehome is acquired by a mobilehome retailer, who is not licensed as a dealer pursuant to Section 18002.6 of the Health and Safety Code, for affixation by the retailer to a permanent foundation, or for other use or consumption (except demonstration or display while holding for sale in the regular course of business), prior to sale, the mobilehome retailer may not issue a resale certificate. The mobilehome retailer shall notify the vendor that the purchase is for consumption and not for resale. When a mobilehome manufacturer or other vendor is informed or has knowledge that the purchaser will install the mobilehome on a permanent foundation prior to its resale, the manufacturer or other vendor is not making a sale for resale. Such vendor is making a taxable retail sale and cannot accept a resale certificate in good faith.

(f) MOBILE TRANSPORTATION EQUIPMENT. Any person, not exempt from use tax pursuant to Section 6352 of the Revenue and Taxation Code, who leases mobile transportation equipment and who is the consumer thereof, may issue a resale certificate to the equipment vendor for the limited purpose of reporting use tax on the fair rental value of the mobile transportation equipment.

(g) IMPROPER USE OF CERTIFICATE. Except when a resale certificate is issued in accordance with the terms of subdivisions (e) or (f):

(1) A purchaser, including any officer or employee of a corporation, is guilty of a misdemeanor if the purchaser gives a resale certificate for property which the purchaser knows at the time of purchase will be used rather than resold. Such improper use of a certificate also may cause the purchaser to become liable for penalties called for by Sections 6072, 6094.5, 6484, or 6485.

Regulation 1668.   RESALE CERTIFICATES.   (Continued 3)

(2) Any person, including any officer or employee of a corporation, who gives a resale certificate for property which he or she knows at the time of purchase is not to be resold by him or her or the corporation in the regular course of business is liable to the state for the amount of tax that would be due if he or she had not given such resale certificate.

History: Effective July 1, 1939.

Adopted as of January 1, 1945, as a restatement of previous rulings.

Amended June 20, 1967, effective July 1, 1967.

Amended and renumbered November 3, 1969, effective December 5, 1969.

Amended April 6,1977, effective July 1,1977. Added new method of proof for resale, detailed what is adequate proof for resale, and clarified effect of purchase for use on a resale certificate.

Amended December 7, 1977, effective January 19, 1978. In (e) added the tax that would be due.

Amended July 28,1982, effective June 26,1983. Added new (e) and (f), renumbered (g) and (h), and added reference to Section 6072 to (g).

Amended April 9, 1985, effective June 27, 1985. In subdivision (9), amended to specify that the penalty provisions are also applicable to any officer or employee of a corporation who gives a resale certificate for property which he or she knows at the time of purchase will be used rather than resold. Added a reference to Section 6094.5 of the Revenue and Taxation Code with respect to the type of penalties a purchaser may be liable for if the purchaser makes an improper use of a resale certificate. Deleted subdivision (h) since it pertained to the effective date of amendments to the regulation which occurred in 1977.

Amended April 9, 1986, effective July 5, 1986. In subdivision (e), amended explanation under which mobilehome retailers may issue resale certificates to mobilehome vendors.

CALIFORNIA RESALE CERTIFICATE

....
(Name of Purchaser)

....
(Address of Purchaser)

I HEREBY CERTIFY: That I hold valid seller's permit No. ....issued pursuant to the Sales and Use Tax Law; That I am engaged in the business of selling ....
................;

that the tangible personal property described herein which I shall purchase from: ....
....

will be resold by me in the form of tangible personal property; provided, however, that in the event any of such property is used for any purpose other than retention, demonstration, or display while holding it for sale in the regular course of business, it is understood that I am required by the Sales and Use Tax Law to report and pay tax, measured by the purchase price of such property or other authorized amount. Description of property to be purchased: ....

Date: .... 19........

....
(Signature of Purchaser or Authorized Agent)

....
(Title)

CALIFORNIA RESALE CERTIFICATE

....
(Name of Purchaser)

....
(Address of Purchaser)

I HEREBY CERTIFY: That I hold valid seller's permit No. ....issued pursuant to the Sales and Use Tax Law; That I am engaged in the business of selling ....
................;

that the tangible personal property described herein which I shall purchase from: ....
....

will be resold by me in the form of tangible personal property; provided, however, that in the event any of such property is used for any purpose other than retention, demonstration, or display while holding it for sale in the regular course of business, it is understood that I am required by the Sales and Use Tax Law to report and pay tax, measured by the purchase price of such property or other authorized amount. Description of property to be purchased: ....

Date: .... 19........

....
(Signature of Purchaser or Authorized Agent)

....
(Title)

CALIFORNIA RESALE CERTIFICATE

....
(Name of Purchaser)

....
(Address of Purchaser)

I HEREBY CERTIFY: That I hold valid seller's permit No. ....issued pursuant to the Sales and Use Tax Law; That I am engaged in the business of selling ....
................;

that the tangible personal property described herein which I shall purchase from: ....
....

will be resold by me in the form of tangible personal property; provided, however, that in the event any of such property is used for any purpose other than retention, demonstration, or display while holding it for sale in the regular course of business, it is understood that I am required by the Sales and Use Tax Law to report and pay tax, measured by the purchase price of such property or other authorized amount. Description of property to be purchased: ....

Date: .... 19........

....
(Signature of Purchaser or Authorized Agent)

....
(Title)

CALIFORNIA RESALE CERTIFICATE

....
(Name of Purchaser)

....
(Address of Purchaser)

I HEREBY CERTIFY: That I hold valid seller's permit No. ....issued pursuant to the Sales and Use Tax Law; That I am engaged in the business of selling ....
................;

that the tangible personal property described herein which I shall purchase from: ....
....

will be resold by me in the form of tangible personal property; provided, however, that in the event any of such property is used for any purpose other than retention, demonstration, or display while holding it for sale in the regular course of business, it is understood that I am required by the Sales and Use Tax Law to report and pay tax, measured by the purchase price of such property or other authorized amount. Description of property to be purchased: ....

Date: .... 19........

....
(Signature of Purchaser or Authorized Agent)

....
(Title)

PUBLICATIONS ORDER

Please enter the quantity of each publication you wish to order and send your completed order form to the State Board of Equalization, Supply Unit 920 West Capitol Avenue, West Sacramento, CA 95691 or FAX your order to (916) 372-6078.

NAME OF BUSINESS	FOR OFFICE USE ONLY	REQUEST IS FOR	☐ New ☐ One Time ☐ Replacement ☐ Distribution Change

ATTENTION	RECEIVED BY

MAILING ADDRESS	DATE REQUEST RECEIVED

CITY	STATE	ZIP	SHIPPED BY

TELEPHONE NUMBER ( )	DATE MATERIAL SHIPPED

PAMPHLETS *(No Charge)*

QTY.	NO.	TITLE
_____	1	Sales and Use Tax Law
_____	2	Uniform Local Sales & Use Tax Law and Transactions & Use Tax Law
_____	3	Use Fuel Tax Law
_____	4	Cigarette Tax Law
_____	5	Alcoholic Beverage Tax Law
_____	6	Motor Vehicle Fuel License Tax Law
_____	7	Tax on Insurers Law
_____	8	Private Railroad Car Tax Law
_____	9	Tax Tips for Construction and Building Contractors
_____	10	Energy Resources Surcharge Law
_____	11	Energy Resources Surcharge Regulations
_____	12	Use Fuel Tax for Vendors and Users
_____	12S	Use Fuel Tax for Vendors and Users (Spanish)
_____	14	Motor Vehicle Fuel License Tax Regulations
_____	15	Cigarette Tax Regulations
_____	16	Alcoholic Beverage Tax Regulations and Instructions
_____	17	Appeals Procedures
_____	18	Tax Tips for Nonprofit Organizations
_____	19	Diesel Fuel Tax Law
_____	20	California Emergency Telephone Users Surcharge Law
_____	21	State Board of Equalization
_____	22	Tax Tips for the Dining and Beverage Industry
_____	22C	Tax Tips for the Dining and Beverage Industry (Chinese)
_____	22K	Tax Tips for the Dining and Beverage Industry (Korean)
_____	22S	Tax Tips for the Dining and Beverage Industry (Spanish)
_____	22V	Tax Tips for the Dining and Beverage Industry (Vietnamese)
_____	23	Occasional Sales of Vehicles, Vessels and Aircraft
_____	24	Tax Tips for Liquor Stores
_____	24C	Tax Tips for Liquor Stores (Chinese)
_____	24K	Tax Tips for Liquor Stores (Korean)
_____	24S	Tax Tips for Liquor Stores (Spanish)
_____	24V	Tax Tips for Liquor Stores (Vietnamese)
_____	25	Tax Tips for Auto Repair Garages and Service Stations
_____	25C	Tax Tips for Auto Repair Garages and Service Stations (Chinese)

QTY.	NO.	TITLE
_____	25K	Tax Tips for Auto Repair Garages and Service Stations (Korean)
_____	25S	Tax Tips for Auto Repair Garages and Service Stations (Spanish)
_____	25V	Tax Tips for Auto Repair Garages and Service Stations (Vietnamese)
_____	26	Tax Information Bulletin Index
_____	27	Tax Tips for Drug Stores
_____	28	Business & Property Tax Information for City and County Officials
_____	29	Property Tax Facts for Policy Makers
_____	31	Tax Tips for Grocery Stores
_____	31S	Tax Tips for Grocery Stores (Spanish)
_____	32	Tax Tips for Purchasers from Mexico
_____	32S	Tax Tips for Purchasers from Mexico (Spanish)
_____	34	Tax Tips for Motor Vehicle Dealers (New & Used)
_____	35	Tax Tips for Interior Designers and Decorators
_____	36	Tax Tips for Veterinarians
_____	37	Tax Tips for the Graphic Arts Industry
_____	38	Tax Tips for Advertising Agencies
_____	39	Emergency Telephone Users Surcharge Regulations
_____	40	Tax Tips for the Watercraft Industry
_____	41	Taxes and Fees Administered by Board of Equalization
_____	43	Timber Yield Tax Law
_____	44	Tax Tips for District Taxes
_____	45	Tax Tips for Hospitals
_____	46	Tax Tips for Leasing of Tangible Personal Property in California
_____	47	Tax Tips for Mobilehomes and Factory-Built Housin
_____	48	Church Exemption; Religious Exemption; and Religious Aspects of the Welfare Exemption
_____	49	California Underground Storage Tank Maintenance Fee Law
_____	50	Guide to the International Fuel Tax Agreement
_____	50S	Guide to the International Fuel Tax Agreement (Spanish)
_____	50-A	Introduction to the International Fuel Tax Agreement
_____	50-A-S	Introduction to the International Fuel Tax Agreement (Spanish)
_____	51	Guide to Board of Equalization Services
_____	58-A	How to Inspect & Correct Your Records

QTY.	NO.	TITLE
_____	59	Local Motor Vehicle Fuel Taxation Law
_____	60	Hazardous Substances Tax Law
_____	61	Sales and Use Taxes: Exemptions and Exclusions
_____	62	Tax Tips for Locksmiths
_____	64	Tax Tips for Jewelry Stores
_____	66	Tax Tips for Retail Feed and Farm Supply Stores
_____	68	Tax Tips for Photographers, Photo Finishers and Film Processing Laboratories
_____	69	Solid Waste and Disposal Site Cleanup and Maintenance Fee Law
_____	70	The California Taxpayers' Bill of Rights
_____	70C	The California Taxpayers' Bill of Rights (Chinese)
_____	70K	The California Taxpayers' Bill of Rights (Korean)
_____	70S	The California Taxpayers' Bill of Rights (Spanish)
_____	70V	The California Taxpayers' Bill of Rights (Vietnamese)
_____	71	California City and County Sales and Use Tax Rates
_____	73	Your California Seller's Permit
_____	73C	Your California Seller's Permit (Chinese)
_____	73K	Your California Seller's Permit (Korean)
_____	73S	Your California Seller's Permit (Spanish)
_____	73V	Your California Seller's Permit (Vietnamese)
_____	74	Closing Out Your Seller's Permit
_____	74C	Closing Out Your Seller's Permit (Chinese)
_____	74K	Closing Out Your Seller's Permit (Korean)
_____	74S	Closing Out Your Seller's Permit (Spanish)
_____	74V	Closing Out Your Seller's Permit (Vietnamese)
_____	75	Interest and Penalty Payments
_____	76	Audits and Appeals
_____	76C	Audits and Appeals (Chinese)
_____	76K	Audits and Appeals (Korean)
_____	76S	Audits and Appeals (Spanish)
_____	79	Documented Vessels & California Tax
_____	80	Electronic Funds Transfer Program

QTY.	NO.	TITLE
_____	80A	EFT Program ACH Credit Information
_____	80B	ACH Debit Information
_____	81	Franchise and Income Tax Appeals
_____	82	Prepaid Sales Tax on Sales of Fuel
_____	83	Tire Recycling Fee Law
_____	84	Use Fuel Permit Requirements
_____	85	Oil Recycling Fee Law
_____	86	Timber Yield Tax (brochure)
_____	88	Underground Storage Tank Fee
_____	89	Oil Recycling Fee
_____	90	Environmental Fee
_____	91	Tire Recycling Fee
_____	92	Alcoholic Beverage Tax
_____	93	Cigarette Tax
_____	Other	_____
		_____
		_____
		_____
		_____
		_____
		_____
		_____
		_____
		_____

MISCELLANEOUS *(No Charge)*

_____ Annual Calendar of Board Meetings

_____ Annual Report of the State Board of Equalization

_____ State of California Sales Tax Reimbursement Schedules

_____ Tax Information Bulletin (published quarterly)
Issue _____

_____ Other _____

Form **1040-ES**

Department of the Treasury
Internal Revenue Service

Estimated Tax for Individuals

This package is primarily for first-time filers of estimated tax.

OMB No. 1545-0087

1998

Purpose of This Package

Use this package to figure and pay your estimated tax. Estimated tax is the method used to pay tax on income that is not subject to withholding (for example, earnings from self-employment, interest, dividends, rents, alimony, etc.). In addition, if you do not elect voluntary withholding, you should make estimated tax payments on unemployment compensation and the taxable part of your social security benefits. See the 1997 instructions for your tax return for more details on income that is taxable.

This package is primarily for first-time filers who are or may be subject to paying estimated tax. This package can also be used if you did not receive or have lost your preprinted 1040-ES package. The estimated tax worksheet on page 4 will help you figure the correct amount to pay. The payment vouchers in this package are for crediting your estimated tax payments to your account correctly. Use the **Record of Estimated Tax Payments** on page 6 to keep track of the payments you have made and the number and amount of your remaining payments.

After we receive your first payment voucher from this package, we will mail you a 1040-ES package with your name, address, and social security number preprinted on each payment voucher. Use the preprinted vouchers to make your **remaining** estimated tax payments for the year. This will speed processing, reduce processing costs, and reduce the chance of errors.

Do not use the vouchers in this package to notify the IRS of a **change of address.** If you have a new address, complete **Form 8822,** Change of Address, and send it to the Internal Revenue Service Center at the address shown in the Form 8822 instructions. The service center will update your record and send you new preprinted payment vouchers.

Note: *Continue to use your old preprinted payment vouchers to make payments of estimated tax until you receive the new vouchers.*

Who Must Make Estimated Tax Payments

In most cases, you must make estimated tax payments if you expect to owe at least $1,000 in tax for 1998 (after subtracting your withholding and credits) and you expect your withholding and credits to be less than the **smaller** of:

1. 90% of the tax shown on your 1998 tax return, **or**

2. The tax shown on your 1997 tax return.

However, if you did not file a 1997 tax return or that return did not cover all 12 months, item 2 above does not apply.

For this purpose, include household employment taxes when figuring the tax shown on your tax return, but **only** if **either** of the following is true:

c You will have Federal income tax withheld from wages, pensions, annuities, gambling winnings, or other income, **or**

c You would be required to make estimated tax payments to avoid a penalty even if you did not include household employment taxes when figuring your estimated tax.

Exception. You do not have to pay estimated tax if you were a U.S. citizen or resident alien for all of 1997 and you had no tax liability for the full 12-month 1997 tax year.

The estimated tax rules apply to:

c U.S. citizens and residents,

c Residents of Puerto Rico, the Virgin Islands, Guam, the Commonwealth of the Northern Mariana Islands, and American Samoa, and

c Nonresident aliens (use Form 1040-ES (NR)).

If you also receive salaries and wages, you may be able to avoid having to make estimated tax payments on your other income by asking your employer to take more tax out of your earnings. To do this, file a new **Form W-4,** Employee's Withholding Allowance Certificate, with your employer.

You can also choose to have Federal income tax withheld on certain government payments. For details, see **Form W-4V,** Voluntary Withholding Request.

Caution: *You may not make joint estimated tax payments if you or your spouse is a nonresident alien, you are separated under a decree of divorce or separate maintenance, or you and your spouse have different tax years.*

Additional Information You May Need

Most of the information you will need can be found in:

Pub. 505, Tax Withholding and Estimated Tax.

Other available information:

c **Pub. 553,** Highlights of 1997 Tax Changes.

c Instructions for the 1997 Form 1040 or 1040A.

c **What's Hot** at www.irs.ustreas.gov.

For details on how to get forms and publications, see page 4 of the instructions for Form 1040 or 1040A.

If you have tax questions, call 1-800-829-1040 for assistance.

Tax Law Changes Effective for 1998

Use your 1997 tax return as a guide in figuring your 1998 estimated tax, but be sure to consider the changes noted in this section. For more information on changes that may affect your 1998 estimated tax, see Pub. 553.

Estimated tax payments of household employment taxes. Beginning in 1998, you must **include** household employment taxes when figuring your estimated tax payments if **either** of the following applies for the year:

c You will have Federal income tax withheld from wages, pensions, annuities, gambling winnings, or other income, **or**

c You would be required to make estimated tax payments (to avoid a penalty) even if you **did not** include household employment taxes when figuring your estimated tax.

Increase in amount of tax exempt from estimated tax requirements. Beginning in 1998, the requirement to make estimated tax payments (to avoid a penalty) will not apply unless the tax you owe, after subtracting withholding and other credits, is at least $1,000.

Modification of estimated tax safe harbor for some taxpayers. For 1998, the estimated tax safe harbor that is based on the tax shown on the prior year tax return is the same for all taxpayers (except for farmers and fishermen), regardless of adjusted gross income (AGI). That safe harbor is 100% of the tax shown on the 1997 tax return.

Child tax credit. For 1998, you may be entitled to a $400 credit for each of your dependent children who is under age 17 on December 31, 1998. The credit is subject to limits based on your tax, and a phaseout, which begins when your modified AGI exceeds $75,000 ($110,000 if married filing jointly or qualifying widow(er); $55,000 if married filing separately). Above this level, the credit is reduced by $50 for each $1,000 (or fraction thereof) of modified AGI.

Credits for higher education expenses. You may be able to claim the *Hope Scholarship Credit* for tuition and related expenses you pay in 1998 for yourself, your spouse, or dependents to enroll at or attend an eligible educational institution. This credit applies only to the first 2 years of postsecondary education. The student must be enrolled in a degree, certificate, or other program leading to a recognized

Cat. No. 11340T

(Continued on page 2)

credential at an eligible educational institution and must carry at least one-half of a normal full-time work load. The maximum credit per student is $1,500 (100% of the first $1,000 of qualified tuition and related expenses, plus 50% of the next $1,000 of such expenses).

For qualified expenses paid after June 30, 1998, you may be able to claim the *Lifetime Learning Credit*. This credit does not require enrollment in a degree or other program and may be claimed for undergraduate, graduate, or professional degree expenses or for any course at an accredited institution of higher education that helps the student acquire or improve job skills. The credit is 20% of up to $5,000 of qualified tuition and related expenses (the maximum credit per tax return is $1,000).

These credits are available only for expenses paid during the tax year for an academic period beginning in that tax year and cannot be claimed for the cost of books, room and board, or similar expenses. You **cannot** claim either credit if you are married filing separately or you are claimed as a dependent on another person's 1998 tax return.

Each credit is subject to a limit based on your tax and is phased out ratably over a range that:
c Begins when your modified AGI exceeds $40,000 ($80,000 if married filing jointly or qualifying widow(er)), and
c Ends at $50,000 ($100,000 if married filing jointly or qualifying widow(er)).

Caution: *You may not claim both the Hope Scholarship Credit and the Lifetime Learning Credit on behalf of the same student in 1998. Also, you may not claim either of these credits for expenses incurred on behalf of a student in any year in which you also exclude distributions from an education IRA to pay higher education costs for that student.*

Student loan interest. You may be allowed to deduct up to $1,000 for interest due after 1997 that is paid during 1998 on a qualified higher education loan you used to pay for education expenses for yourself, your spouse, or a dependent. A loan made by a related person is not a qualified loan. The deduction is allowed in arriving at AGI (i.e., you do not have to itemize deductions to claim it). The student must have been enrolled in a degree, certificate, or other program leading to a recognized credential at an eligible educational institution and must have carried at least one-half of a normal full-time work load. The deduction is allowed only during the first 60 months in which interest payments are required.

The deduction is phased out ratably over a range that:
c Begins when your modified AGI exceeds $40,000 ($60,000 if married filing jointly or qualifying widow(er)), and
c Ends at $55,000 ($75,000 if married filing jointly or qualifying widow(er)).

You **cannot** take this deduction if you are claimed as a dependent on another person's 1998 tax return or you are married filing a separate return.

IRA deduction increased or restored for some people covered by retirement plans. The income limits for claiming an IRA deduction for 1998 have been increased if you are covered by a retirement plan. Under the new rules, the deduction is phased out ratably over a range that:
c Begins when your modified AGI exceeds $30,000 ($50,000 if married filing jointly or qualifying widow(er)), and
c Ends at $40,000 ($60,000 if married filing jointly or qualifying widow(er)).

Also, if your spouse is covered by a retirement plan but you are not, you are eligible beginning in 1998 to claim an IRA deduction (unless you are married filing a separate return). In this case, the maximum IRA deduction is phased out ratably over a range that begins at a modified AGI of $150,000 and ends at $160,000.

Distributions from IRAs to pay for qualified higher education expenses or "first-time homebuyer" expenses. Beginning with distributions made after 1997, the 10% tax on an early distribution from an IRA will not apply if you use the distribution to pay for either of the following:
c Qualified higher education expenses for academic periods beginning after 1997 for yourself, your spouse, child, grandchild, stepchild, or step-grandchild for attendance at an accredited institution of higher education.
c Certain expenses incurred to buy, build, or rebuild a "first" home that is your main home, your spouse's main home, or the main home of a child, grandchild, or ancestor of yours or your spouse's. Distributions used for this purpose are subject to a lifetime limit of $10,000. In most cases, a home is considered your "first" home if you had no present ownership in a main home during the 2-year period ending on the date you acquired your new home.

(Continued on page 3)

1998 Tax Rate Schedules

Caution: *Do not use these Tax Rate Schedules to figure your 1997 taxes. Use only to figure your 1998 estimated taxes.*

Single—Schedule X

If line 5 is: Over—	But not over—	The tax is:	of the amount over—
$0	$25,350	.........15%	$0
25,350	61,400	$3,802.50 + 28%	25,350
61,400	128,100	13,896.50 + 31%	61,400
128,100	278,450	34,573.50 + 36%	128,100
278,450	....	88,699.50 + 39.6%	278,450

Head of household—Schedule Z

If line 5 is: Over—	But not over—	The tax is:	of the amount over—
$0	$33,950	.........15%	$0
33,950	87,700	$5,092.50 + 28%	33,950
87,700	142,000	20,142.50 + 31%	87,700
142,000	278,450	36,975.50 + 36%	142,000
278,450	....	86,097.50 + 39.6%	278,450

Married filing jointly or Qualifying widow(er)—Schedule Y-1

If line 5 is: Over—	But not over—	The tax is:	of the amount over—
$0	$42,350	.........15%	$0
42,350	102,300	$6,352.50 + 28%	42,350
102,300	155,950	23,138.50 + 31%	102,300
155,950	278,450	39,770.00 + 36%	155,950
278,450	....	83,870.00 + 39.6%	278,450

Married filing separately—Schedule Y-2

If line 5 is: Over—	But not over—	The tax is:	of the amount over—
$0	$21,175	.........15%	$0
21,175	51,150	$3,176.25 + 28%	21,175
51,150	77,975	11,569.25 + 31%	51,150
77,975	139,225	19,885.00 + 36%	77,975
139,225	....	41,935.00 + 39.6%	139,225

Foreign earned income exclusion. For 1998, the maximum foreign earned income exclusion amount has been increased to $72,000.

Section 179 expense deduction increased. For 1998, the deduction to expense certain property under section 179 generally has been increased to $18,500.

Self-employed health insurance deduction increased. For 1998, the self-employed health insurance deduction is increased to 45% of health insurance expenses.

Matching contributions to 401(k) plans of self-employed individuals. Generally, matching contributions made for tax years after 1997 to 401(k) plans of self-employed persons are not treated as elective employer contributions and therefore are not subject to the $10,000 annual limit on elective contributions.

Welfare-to-work credit. Employers that pay wages to long-term family assistance recipients may qualify for the welfare-to-work credit. This new credit is based on wages paid to qualified individuals who begin work after December 31, 1997. For more details, see **Form 8861,** Welfare-to-Work Credit.

Income averaging for farmers. Starting in 1998, farmers may elect to average farm income over the 3 prior tax years. This election does not affect the computation of self-employment tax.

Standard deduction for 1998. If you do not itemize your deductions, you may take the 1998 standard deduction listed below:

Filing Status	Standard Deduction
Married filing jointly or Qualifying widow(er)	.$7,100
Head of household	.$6,250
Single	.$4,250
Married filing separately	.$3,550

However, if you can be claimed as a dependent on another person's 1998 return, your standard deduction is the greater of:

c $700, **or**

c Your earned income plus $250 (up to the standard deduction amount).

An additional amount is added to the standard deduction if:

1. You are an unmarried individual (single or head of household) and are:

65 or older or blind	$1,050
65 or older and blind	.$2,100

2. You are a married individual (filing jointly or separately) or a qualifying widow(er) and are:

65 or older or blind	$850
65 or older and blind	.$1,700
Both spouses 65 or older	$1,700 *
Both spouses 65 or older and blind	$3,400 *

* If married filing separately, these amounts apply only if you can claim an exemption for your spouse.

To Figure Your Estimated Tax Use:

c The **1998 Estimated Tax Worksheet** on page 4.

c The instructions on this page for the worksheet on page 4.

c The **1998 Tax Rate Schedules** on page 2.

c Your 1997 tax return and instructions as a guide to figuring your income, deductions, and credits (but be sure to consider the tax law changes noted earlier).

If you receive your income unevenly throughout the year (e.g., you operate your business on a seasonal basis), you may be able to lower or eliminate the amount of your required estimated tax payment for one or more periods by using the annualized income installment method. See Pub. 505 for details.

To amend or correct your estimated tax, see **Amending Estimated Tax Payments** on page 4.

Instructions for Worksheet on Page 4

Line 1—Use your 1997 tax return and instructions as a guide to figuring the adjusted gross income you expect in 1998 (but be sure to consider the tax law changes noted earlier). For more details on figuring your adjusted gross income, see **Expected Adjusted Gross Income** in Pub. 505. If you are self-employed, be sure to take into account the deduction for one-half of your self-employment tax.

Line 7—Additional Taxes. Enter the additional taxes from **Form 4972,** Tax on Lump-Sum Distributions, or **Form 8814,** Parents Election To Report Child's Interest and Dividends.

Line 9—Credits. See the 1997 Form 1040, lines 40 through 45, or Form 1040A, lines 24a, 24b, and 24c, and the related instructions.

Line 11—Self-Employment Tax. If you and your spouse make joint estimated tax payments and you both have self-employment income, figure the self-employment tax for each of you separately. Enter the total on line 11. When figuring your estimate of 1998 net earnings from self-employment, be sure to use only 92.35% of your total net profit from self-employment.

Line 12—Other Taxes. Except as noted below, enter any other taxes, such as alternative minimum tax, tax on accumulation distribution of trusts, tax on a distribution from an MSA, and the tax on early distributions from **(a)** a qualified retirement plan (including your IRA), **(b)** an annuity, or **(c)** a modified endowment contract entered into after June 20, 1988.

Include household employment taxes on line 12 if **either** of the following is true:

c You will have Federal income tax withheld from wages, pensions, annuities, gambling winnings, or other income, **or**

c You would be required to make estimated tax payments (to avoid a penalty) even if you did not include household employment taxes when figuring your estimated tax.

Do not include tax on recapture of a Federal mortgage subsidy, social security and Medicare tax on unreported tip income, or uncollected employee social security and Medicare or RRTA tax on tips or group-term life insurance. These taxes are not required to be paid until your income tax return is due (not including extensions).

Payment Due Dates

You may pay all of your estimated tax by April 15, 1998, or in four equal amounts by the dates shown below:

1st payment	April 15, 1998
2nd payment.	June 15, 1998
3rd payment	Sept. 15, 1998
4th payment	Jan. 15, 1999*

*You do not have to make the payment due January 15, 1999, if you file your 1998 tax return by February 1, 1999, **AND** pay the entire balance due with your return.

Note: *Payments are due by the dates indicated whether or not you are outside the United States and Puerto Rico.*

If, after March 31, 1998, you have a large change in income, deductions, additional taxes, or credits that requires you to start making estimated tax payments, you should figure the amount of your estimated tax payments by using the annualized income installment method, as explained in Pub. 505. Although your payment due dates will be the same as shown above, the payment amounts will vary based on your income, deductions, additional taxes, and credits for the months ending before each payment due date. As a result, this method may allow you to skip or lower the amount due for one or more payments. If you use the annualized income installment method, be sure to file **Form 2210,** Underpayment of Estimated Tax by Individuals, Estates, and Trusts, with your 1998 tax return, even if no penalty is owed.

(Continued on page 4)

Farmers and fishermen. If at least two-thirds of your gross income for 1997 or 1998 is from farming or fishing, you may do one of the following:

c Pay all of your estimated tax by January 15, 1999, or

c File your 1998 Form 1040 by March 1, 1999, and pay the total tax due. In this case, 1998 estimated payments are not required.

Fiscal year taxpayers. You are on a fiscal year if your 12-month tax period ends on any day except December 31. Due dates for fiscal year taxpayers are the 15th day of the 4th, 6th, and 9th months of your current fiscal year and the 1st month of the following fiscal year. If any payment date falls on a Saturday, Sunday, or legal holiday, use the next business day.

Amending Estimated Tax Payments

To change or amend your estimated payments, refigure your total estimated payments due (line 16 of the worksheet below). Then use the worksheets under **Amended estimated tax** in Chapter 2 of Pub. 505 to figure the payment due for each remaining payment period. If an estimated tax payment for a previous period is less than one-fourth of your amended estimated tax, you may owe a penalty when you file your return.

(Continued on page 5)

1998 Estimated Tax Worksheet (keep for your records)

1 Enter amount of adjusted gross income you expect in 1998 (see instructions)	**1**	
2 c If you plan to itemize deductions, enter the estimated total of your itemized deductions. **Caution:** If line 1 above is over $124,500 ($62,250 if married filing separately), your deduction may be reduced. See Pub. 505 for details.		
c If you do not plan to itemize deductions, see **Standard Deduction for 1998** on page 3, and enter your standard deduction here.	**2**	
3 Subtract line 2 from line 1	**3**	
4 Exemptions. Multiply $2,700 by the number of personal exemptions. If you can be claimed as a dependent on another person's 1998 return, your personal exemption is not allowed.**Caution:** If line 1 above is over $186,800 ($155,650 if head of household; $124,500 if single; $93,400 if married filing separately), see Pub. 505 to figure the amount to enter	**4**	
5 Subtract line 4 from line 3	**5**	
6 **Tax.** Figure your tax on the amount on line 5 by using the 1998 Tax Rate Schedules on page 2. DO NOT use the Tax Table or the Tax Rate Schedules in the 1997 Form 1040 or Form 1040A instructions. **Caution:** If you have a net capital gain, see Pub. 505 to figure the tax.	**6**	
7 Additional taxes (see instructions)	**7**	
8 Add lines 6 and 7	**8**	
9 Credits (see instructions). Do not include any income tax withholding on this line	**9**	
10 Subtract line 9 from line 8. Enter the result, but not less than zero	**10**	
11 Self-employment tax (see instructions). Estimate of 1998 net earnings from self-employment $......................... ; if **$68,400 or less,** multiply the amount by 15.3%; if **more than $68,400,** multiply the amount by 2.9%, add $8,481.60 to the result, and enter the total. **Caution:** If you also have wages subject to social security tax, see Pub. 505 to figure the amount to enter	**11**	
12 Other taxes (see instructions)	**12**	
13a Add lines 10 through 12	**13a**	
b Earned income credit and credit from **Form 4136**	**13b**	
c Subtract line 13b from line 13a. Enter the result, but not less than zero. **THIS IS YOUR TOTAL 1998 ESTIMATED TAX**	**13c**	
14a Multiply line 13c by 90% (66⅔% for farmers and fishermen) **14a**		
b Enter the tax shown on your 1997 tax return **14b**		
c Enter the **smaller** of line 14a or 14b. **THIS IS YOUR REQUIRED ANNUAL PAYMENT TO AVOID A PENALTY**	**14c**	
Caution: Generally, if you do not prepay (through income tax withholding and estimated tax payments) at least the amount on line 14c, you may owe a penalty for not paying enough estimated tax. To avoid a penalty, make sure your estimate on line 13c is as accurate as possible. Even if you pay the required annual payment, you may still owe tax when you file your return. If you prefer, you may pay the amount shown on line 13c. For more details, see Pub. 505.		
15 Income tax withheld and estimated to be withheld during 1998 (including income tax withholding on pensions, annuities, certain deferred income, etc.)	**15**	
16 Subtract line 15 from line 14c. **(Note:** If zero or less, or line 13c minus line 15 is less than $1,000, stop here. You are not required to make estimated tax payments.)	**16**	
17 If the first payment you are required to make is due April 15, 1998, enter ¼ of line 16 (minus any 1997 overpayment that you are applying to this installment) here and on your payment voucher(s)	**17**	

When a Penalty Is Applied

In some cases, you may owe a penalty when you file your return. The penalty is imposed on each underpayment for the number of days it remains unpaid. A penalty may be applied if you did not pay enough estimated tax for the year, or you did not make the payments on time or in the required amount. A penalty may apply even if you have an overpayment on your tax return.

The penalty may be waived under certain conditions. See Pub. 505 for details.

How To Complete and Use the Payment Voucher

There is a separate payment voucher for each due date. The due date is shown in the upper right corner. Please be sure you use the voucher with the correct due date for each payment you make. Complete and send in the voucher **only** if you are making a payment. To complete your voucher:

c Type or print your name, address, and social security number in the space provided on the voucher. If filing a joint voucher, also enter your spouse's name and social security number. List the names and social security numbers in the same order on the joint voucher as you will on your joint return. If you and your spouse plan to file separate returns, file separate vouchers instead of a joint voucher.

c Enter on the payment line of the voucher only the amount you are sending in. When making payments of estimated tax, be sure to take into account any 1997 overpayment that you choose to credit against your 1998 tax, but do not include the overpayment amount on this line.

c Enclose your payment, making the check or money order payable to: "Internal Revenue Service" (not "IRS").

c Write your social security number and "1998 Form 1040-ES" on your check or money order.

c Do not staple or attach your payment to the voucher.

c Mail your payment voucher to the address shown on page 6 for the place where you live.

c Fill in the **Record of Estimated Tax Payments** on page 6 for your files.

If you changed your name and made estimated tax payments using your old name, attach a statement to the front of your 1998 tax return. List all of the estimated tax payments you and your spouse made for 1998, the address where you made the payments, and the name(s) and social security number(s) under which you made the payments.

Paperwork Reduction Act Notice. We ask for the information on the payment vouchers to carry out the Internal Revenue laws of the United States. You are required to give us the information. We need it to ensure that you are complying with these laws and to allow us to figure and collect the right amount of tax.

You are not required to provide the information requested on a form that is subject to the Paperwork Reduction Act unless the form displays a valid OMB control number. Books or records relating to a form or its instructions must be retained as long as their contents may become material in the administration of any Internal Revenue law. Generally, tax returns and return information are confidential, as required by Internal Revenue Code section 6103.

The time needed to complete the worksheets and prepare and file the payment vouchers will vary depending on individual circumstances. The estimated average time is: **Recordkeeping,** 1 hr., 19 min.; **Learning about the law,** 22 min.; **Preparing the worksheets and payment vouchers,** 49 min.; **Copying, assembling, and sending the payment voucher to the IRS,** 10 min. If you have comments concerning the accuracy of these time estimates or suggestions for making this package simpler, we would be happy to hear from you. You can write to the Tax Forms Committee, Western Area Distribution Center, Rancho Cordova, CA 95743-0001. **DO NOT** send the payment vouchers to this address. Instead, see **Where To File Your Payment Voucher** on page 6.

--------------------------------- Tear off here ---------------------------------

Form **1040-ES**
Department of the Treasury
Internal Revenue Service

1998 Payment Voucher 4

OMB No. 1545-0087

Calendar year—Due Jan. 15, 1999

File only if you are making a payment of estimated tax. Return this voucher with check or money order payable to the "**Internal Revenue Service.**" Please write your social security number and "1998 Form 1040-ES" on your check or money order. Do not send cash. Enclose, but do not staple or attach, your payment with this voucher.

Amount of payment	Please type or print	Your first name and initial	Your last name	Your social security number
		If joint payment, complete for spouse		
		Spouse's first name and intitial	Spouse's last name	Spouse's social security number
		Address (number, street, and apt. no.)		
$		City, state, and ZIP code (If a foreign address, enter city, province or state, postal code, and country.)		

For Paperwork Reduction Act Notice, see instructions on page 5.

Page 5

Record of Estimated Tax Payments (see page 3 for payment due dates)

Payment number	(a) Date	(b) Check or money order number	(c) Amount paid	(d) 1997 overpayment credit applied	(e) Total amount paid and credited (add (c) and (d))
1					
2					
3					
4					
Total					

Where To File Your Payment Voucher

Mail your payment voucher to the Internal Revenue Service at the address shown below for the place where you live. **Do not** mail your tax return to this address. Also, do not mail your estimated tax payments to the address shown in the Form 1040 or 1040A instructions.

Note: *For proper delivery of your estimated tax payment to a P.O. box, you must include the box number in the address. Also, note that only the U.S. Postal Service can deliver to P.O. boxes.*

If you live in:	Use this address:
New Jersey, New York (New York City and counties of Nassau, Rockland, Suffolk, and Westchester)	P.O. Box 162 Newark, NJ 07101-0162
New York (all other counties), Connecticut, Maine, Massachusetts, New Hampshire, Rhode Island, Vermont	P.O. Box 371999 Pittsburgh, PA 15250-7999
Delaware, District of Columbia, Maryland, Pennsylvania, Virginia	P.O. Box 8318 Philadelphia, PA 19162-8318
Florida, Georgia, South Carolina	P.O. Box 105900 Atlanta, GA 30348-5900
Indiana, Kentucky, Michigan, Ohio, West Virginia	P.O. Box 7422 Chicago, IL 60680-7422
Alabama, Arkansas, Louisiana, Mississippi, North Carolina, Tennessee	P.O. Box 1219 Charlotte, NC 28201-1219

Illinois, Iowa, Minnesota, Missouri, Wisconsin	P.O. Box 970006 St. Louis, MO 63197-0006
Kansas, New Mexico, Oklahoma, Texas	P.O. Box 970001 St. Louis, MO 63197-0001
Alaska, Arizona, California (counties of Alpine, Amador, Butte, Calaveras, Colusa, Contra Costa, Del Norte, El Dorado, Glenn, Humboldt, Lake, Lassen, Marin, Mendocino, Modoc, Napa, Nevada, Placer, Plumas, Sacramento, San Joaquin, Shasta, Sierra, Siskiyou, Solano, Sonoma, Sutter, Tehama, Trinity, Yolo, and Yuba), Colorado, Idaho, Montana, Nebraska, Nevada, North Dakota, Oregon, South Dakota, Utah, Washington, Wyoming	P.O. Box 510000 San Francisco, CA 94151-5100
California (all other counties), Hawaii	P.O. Box 54030 Los Angeles, CA 90054-0030
American Samoa	P.O. Box 8318 Philadelphia, PA 19162-8318
The Commonwealth of the Northern Mariana Islands	P.O. Box 8318 Philadelphia, PA 19162-8318
Puerto Rico (or if excluding income under section 933)	P.O. Box 8318 Philadelphia, PA 19162-8318

Guam: Nonpermanent residents	P.O. Box 8318 Philadelphia, PA 19162-8318
Permanent residents*	Department of Revenue and Taxation Government of Guam P.O. Box 23607 GMF, GU 96921

* You must prepare separate vouchers for estimated income tax and self-employment tax payments. Send the income tax vouchers to the Guam address and the self-employment tax vouchers to the address for Guam nonpermanent residents shown above.

Virgin Islands: Nonpermanent residents	P.O. Box 8318 Philadelphia, PA 19162-8318
Permanent residents*	V.I. Bureau of Internal Revenue 9601 Estate Thomas Charlotte Amalie St. Thomas, VI 00802

* You must prepare separate vouchers for estimated income tax and self-employment tax payments. Send the income tax vouchers to the Virgin Islands address and the self-employment tax vouchers to the address for Virgin Islands nonpermanent residents shown above.

All APO and FPO addresses	P.O. Box 8318 Philadelphia, PA 19162-8318
Foreign country: U.S. citizens and those filing Form 2555, Form 2555-EZ, or Form 4563	P.O. Box 8318 Philadelphia, PA 19162-8318

Form **1040-ES**
Department of the Treasury
Internal Revenue Service

1998 Payment Voucher **3**

OMB No. 1545-0087

Calendar year—Due Sept. 15, 1998

File only if you are making a payment of estimated tax. Return this voucher with check or money order payable to the **"Internal Revenue Service."** Please write your social security number and "1998 Form 1040-ES" on your check or money order. Do not send cash. Enclose, but do not staple or attach, your payment with this voucher.

Amount of payment	Please type or print	Your first name and initial	Your last name	Your social security number
		If joint payment, complete for spouse		
		Spouse's first name and initial	Spouse's last name	Spouse's social security number
		Address (number, street, and apt. no.)		
$		City, state, and ZIP code (If a foreign address, enter city, province or state, postal code, and country.)		

For Paperwork Reduction Act Notice, see instructions on page 5.

- Tear off here -

Form **1040-ES**
Department of the Treasury
Internal Revenue Service

1998 Payment Voucher **2**

OMB No. 1545-0087

Calendar year—Due June 15, 1998

File only if you are making a payment of estimated tax. Return this voucher with check or money order payable to the **"Internal Revenue Service."** Please write your social security number and "1998 Form 1040-ES" on your check or money order. Do not send cash. Enclose, but do not staple or attach, your payment with this voucher.

Amount of payment	Please type or print	Your first name and initial	Your last name	Your social security number
		If joint payment, complete for spouse		
		Spouse's first name and initial	Spouse's last name	Spouse's social security number
		Address (number, street, and apt. no.)		
$		City, state, and ZIP code (If a foreign address, enter city, province or state, postal code, and country.)		

For Paperwork Reduction Act Notice, see instructions on page 5.

- Tear off here -

Form **1040-ES**
Department of the Treasury
Internal Revenue Service

1998 Payment Voucher **1**

OMB No. 1545-0087

Calendar year—Due April 15, 1998

File only if you are making a payment of estimated tax. Return this voucher with check or money order payable to the **"Internal Revenue Service."** Please write your social security number and "1998 Form 1040-ES" on your check or money order. Do not send cash. Enclose, but do not staple or attach, your payment with this voucher.

Amount of payment	Please type or print	Your first name and initial	Your last name	Your social security number
		If joint payment, complete for spouse		
		Spouse's first name and initial	Spouse's last name	Spouse's social security number
		Address (number, street, and apt. no.)		
$		City, state, and ZIP code (If a foreign address, enter city, province or state, postal code, and country.)		

For Paperwork Reduction Act Notice, see instructions on page 5.

1998 Instructions for Form 540-ES
Estimated Tax For Individuals

A Purpose

Use this form to make installment payments of estimated tax. Estimated tax is the tax you expect to owe for 1998 after subtracting the tax you expect to have withheld and any credits you plan to take. Use these instructions and the Estimated Tax Worksheet to determine if you owe estimated tax and to figure the required installment amount. The required installment amount is based on the lesser of 80% of the current year's tax or 100% of the prior year's tax.

B Who Must Make Estimated Tax Payments

Important note: California and federal estimated tax payment requirements are not the same.

Generally, you must make 1998 estimated tax payments unless:

- More than 80% of your 1997 tax was paid by withholding; or
- More than 80% of your 1998 California adjusted gross income (AGI) will be wages subject to withholding; or
- More than 80% of your 1998 tax will be paid by withholding; or
- Your tax for 1997 (after subtracting withholding and credits) was less than $100; or
- Your tax for 1998 (after subtracting withholding and credits) will be less than $100.

Generally, you and your spouse may file either joint or separate payment vouchers. However, you must make separate estimated tax payments if:

- You are separated under a decree of divorce or separate maintenance; or
- You and your spouse have different taxable years.

If you make joint estimated tax payments but you and your spouse do not file a joint return for the taxable year, you and your spouse must agree on how to divide the estimated tax payments. You and your spouse may agree to claim the entire estimated tax on either spouse's separate return or divide the payments in any manner.

C When To Make Your Estimated Tax Payments

For estimated tax purposes, the year is divided into four payment periods. Each period has a specific payment due date. If you do not pay enough tax by the due date of each of the payment periods, you may be charged a penalty even if you are due a refund when you file your income tax return. The chart below lists the payment periods and due dates.

For the period	The payment due date is
January 1 through March 31, 1998	April 15, 1998
April 1 through May 31, 1998	June 15, 1998
June 1 through August 31, 1998	September 15, 1998
Sept. 1 through Dec. 31, 1998	January 15, 1999

Filing An Early Return In Place of the 4th Installment. If you file your 1998 tax return by February 1, 1999, and pay the entire balance due, you do not have to make your last estimated tax payment.

Annualization Option. If you do not receive your taxable income evenly during the year, it may be to your advantage to annualize your income. This method allows you to match your estimated tax payments to the actual period when you earned the income. You may use the annualization schedule included with form FTB 5805, Underpayment of Estimated Tax by Individuals and Fiduciaries.

Farmers and Fishermen. If at least two-thirds of your gross income for 1997 or 1998 is from farming or fishing, you may:

- Pay all of your estimated tax by January 15, 1999; or
- File your tax return for 1998 on or before March 1, 1999 and pay the total tax due. In this case, you need not make estimated tax payments for 1998. Attach form FTB 5805F, Underpayment of Estimated Tax by Farmers and Fishermen to the front of your return.

Fiscal Year. If you file your return on a fiscal year basis, your due dates will be the 15th day of the 4th, 6th and 9th months of your fiscal year and the 1st month of the following fiscal year. If a due date falls on a Saturday, Sunday or legal holiday, the next regular workday is the due date.

D How To Use Form 540-ES Payment Voucher

Use the Estimated Tax Worksheet and your 1997 California income tax return as a guide for figuring your 1998 estimated tax. There is a separate payment voucher for each due date. Please be sure you use the voucher with the correct due date shown on the right side of the voucher.

Fill in Form 540-ES:

1. Print your name, address and social security number in the space provided on Form 540-ES. Use black or blue ballpoint pen. The scanning machines may not be able to read other colors of ink or pencil. Print all names and words in CAPITAL LETTERS. Print letters and numbers inside boxes. Fill in your name as in the following example:

Your first name	Initial	Last name
JOHN	A	DOE

If your name or address is too long to fit in the boxes provided do not shorten your name or address. Instead, ignore the boxes and fit the information in the space provided. Example:

Your first name	Initial	Last name
JONATHAN	A	ZIGGZEPHYRSTONE

2. Enter in the payment box of the voucher only the amount you are sending in. When making payments of estimated tax, be sure to take into account any 1997 overpayment that you chose to credit against your 1998 tax, but do not include the overpayment amount in the amount of your payment. Therefore, the amount shown on line 19 of the Estimated Tax Worksheet should be reduced by any overpaid tax on your 1997 return that you chose to apply toward your 1998 estimated tax payment.

3. Make your check or money order payable to **"Franchise Tax Board."** Write your social security number and "Form 540-ES 1998" on the check or money order. Mail your Form 540-ES and your check or money order to:

   540-ES UNIT
   FRANCHISE TAX BOARD
   PO BOX 942867
   SACRAMENTO CA   94267-0031

4. Fill in the Record of Estimated Tax Payments (located on the bottom of the Estimated Tax Worksheet) for your files.

5. **Fiscal year filers:** If you file your return on a fiscal year basis, be sure to fill in the month as in the following example:

   month | 0 | 6 |

E Failure To Make Estimated Tax Payments

If you are required to make estimated tax payments and do not, or if you underpay any installment, a penalty will be assessed (with certain exceptions) on the portion of estimated tax that was underpaid from the due date of the installment to the date of payment or the due date of your tax return, whichever is earlier. For more information, refer to form FTB 5805.

1998 Estimated Tax Worksheet   Keep this worksheet for your records.

Caution: If your adjusted gross income (AGI) is over $114,152, your itemized deductions and your exemption credits may be limited. See the instructions for Form 540 or Form 540NR for more information.

1 **Residents:** Enter your estimated 1998 California AGI . . . . **1** _____

  Nonresidents and part-year residents: Enter your estimated 1998 total AGI from all sources.

2 a If you plan to itemize deductions, enter the estimated total of your itemized deductions . . . . . . **2a** _____

  b If you do not plan to itemize deductions, enter the standard deduction for your filing status:

    $2,583 if you are single or married filing a separate return

    $5,166 if you are married filing a joint return, head of household or a qualifying widow(er) . . . **2b** _____

  c Enter the amount from line 2a or line 2b, whichever applies . . . . **2c** _____

3 Subtract line 2c from line 1 . . . . **3** _____

4 Tax. Figure your tax on the amount on line 3 using the 1997 tax table or tax rate schedule in the instructions for Form 540, Form 540A or Form 540NR; or form FTB 3800, Tax Computation for Children with Investment Income. Also include any tax from form FTB 3803, Parents' Election to Report Child's Interest and Dividends . . . . **4** _____

5 **Residents:** Skip to line 6.

  Nonresidents and part-year residents:

    a Compute this ratio: $\dfrac{\text{Estimated 1998 California AGI (using Form 540NR)}}{\text{Estimated 1998 AGI from all sources (using Form 540NR)}}$ = ... **5a** __ . __ __ __ __

    b Multiply the amount on line 4 by the ratio on line 5a. Enter the result on line 5b . . . . **5b** _____

6 **Residents:** Enter the exemption credit amount from the 1997 instructions for Form 540, or Form 540A . . . . **6** _____

  Nonresidents or part-year residents: Multiply the total exemption credit amount from the 1997 instructions for Form 540NR by the ratio on line 5a.

7 **Residents:** Subtract line 6 from line 4 . . . . **7** _____

  Nonresidents or part-year residents: Subtract line 6 from line 5b.

8 Tax on accumulation distribution of trusts. See instructions for form FTB 5870A . . . . **8** _____

9 Add line 7 and line 8 . . . . **9** _____

10 Credits for joint custody head of household, dependent parent and senior head of household (1997 amounts) . . . . **10** _____

  Nonresidents and part-year residents: Multiply the total 1997 credit amount by the ratio on line 5a.

11 Subtract line 10 from line 9 . . . . **11** _____

12 Other credits such as other state tax credit. See your 1997 instructions for Form 540, Form 540A or Form 540NR . . . . **12** _____

13 Subtract line 12 from line 11 . . . . **13** _____

14 Interest on deferred tax from installment obligations under IRC Section 453 or 453A . . . . **14** _____

15 1998 Estimated Tax. Add line 13 and line 14. Enter the result, but not less than zero . . . . **15** _____

16 a Enter 80% (66⅔% for farmers and fishermen) of line 15 . . . . **16a** _____

  b Enter 100% of the tax shown on your 1997 Form 540, line 34; Form 540A, line 23 or Form 540NR, line 43 . . . . **16b** _____

  c Required Annual Payment. Enter the lesser of line 16a or line 16b. . . . . **16c** _____

  Caution: Generally, if you do not prepay at least the amount on line 16c, you may owe a penalty for not paying enough estimated tax. To avoid a penalty, make sure your estimated tax on line 15 is as accurate as possible. If you prefer, you may pay 100% of your 1998 estimated tax (line 15).

17 California income tax withheld and estimated to be withheld during 1998 (include withholding on pensions, annuities, etc) . . **17** _____

18 Balance. Subtract line 17 from line 16c. If less than $100 (or less than $50, if married filing separate), you do not have to make a payment at this time. . . . . **18** _____

19 Installment amount. Divide the amount on line 18 by 4. Enter the result here and on each of your Forms 540-ES. If you will earn your income at an uneven rate during the year, see, Annualization Option, in the instructions under paragraph C . . **19** _____ .00

Record of Estimated Tax Payments

Payment voucher number	(a) Date	(b) Amount paid	(c) 1997 overpayment applied	(d) Total amount paid and credited (add (b) and (c))
1		$	$	
2				
3				
4				
Total. . . . . ▶		$		

Mail your Form 540-ES payment vouchers to: **540-ES UNIT, FRANCHISE TAX BOARD, PO BOX 942867, SACRAMENTO CA 94267-0031.**

Form 540-ES Instructions (REV. 1997)

1998 Estimated Tax for Individuals

540-ES

Fiscal year filers, enter year ending: month [ ][ ] year [1][9][9][9]

| Your first name | Initial | Last name | Your social security number |
| | | | [ ] - [ ] - [ ] |

| If joint payment, spouse's first name | Initial | Last name | Spouse's social security number |
| | | | [ ] - [ ] - [ ] |

Present home address — number and street including PO Box or rural route   Apt. no.

Payment Voucher
1
Due April 15, 1998

City, town or post office   State   ZIP Code

Make your check or money order payable to **"Franchise Tax Board."** Write your social security number and "Form 540-ES 1998" on it. **Do not combine this payment with payment of your tax due for 1997.** Mail this voucher and your check or money order to: **540-ES UNIT
FRANCHISE TAX BOARD
PO BOX 942867
SACRAMENTO CA   94267-0031**

Amount of payment

$ .0 0

For Privacy Act Notice, see form FTB 1131. File only if you are making a payment of estimated tax.

— - DETACH HERE — — — — — — — — — — — — — —

TAXABLE YEAR

1998 Estimated Tax for Individuals

CALIFORNIA FORM

540-ES

Fiscal year filers, enter year ending: month ☐☐ year 1 9 9 9

Your first name ☐ Initial ☐ Last name ☐

Your social security number ☐☐☐-☐☐-☐☐☐☐

If joint payment, spouse's first name ☐ Initial ☐ Last name ☐

Spouse's social security number ☐☐☐-☐☐-☐☐☐☐

Present home address — number and street including PO Box or rural route ☐ Apt. no. ☐

Payment Voucher 2
Due June 15, 1998

City, town or post office ☐ State ☐ ZIP Code ☐

Make your check or money order payable to **"Franchise Tax Board."** Write your social security number and "Form 540-ES 1998" on it. **Do not combine this payment with payment of your tax due for 1997.** Mail this voucher and your check or money order to: **540-ES UNIT**
FRANCHISE TAX BOARD
PO BOX 942867
SACRAMENTO CA 94267-0031

Amount of payment

$ _____ . 0 0

For Privacy Act Notice, see form FTB 1131. File only if you are making a payment of estimated tax.

— — — — — — — — — — — — — — — — — DETACH HERE — — — — — — — — — — — — — — — — —

TAXABLE YEAR

1998 Estimated Tax for Individuals

CALIFORNIA FORM

540-ES

Fiscal year filers, enter year ending: month ☐☐ year 1 9 9 9

Your first name ☐ Initial ☐ Last name ☐

Your social security number ☐☐☐-☐☐-☐☐☐☐

If joint payment, spouse's first name ☐ Initial ☐ Last name ☐

Spouse's social security number ☐☐☐-☐☐-☐☐☐☐

Present home address — number and street including PO Box or rural route ☐ Apt. no. ☐

Payment Voucher 3
Due Sept. 15, 1998

City, town or post office ☐ State ☐ ZIP Code ☐

Make your check or money order payable to **"Franchise Tax Board."** Write your social security number and "Form 540-ES 1998" on it. **Do not combine this payment with payment of your tax due for 1997.** Mail this voucher and your check or money order to: **540-ES UNIT**
FRANCHISE TAX BOARD
PO BOX 942867
SACRAMENTO CA 94267-0031

Amount of payment

$ _____ . 0 0

For Privacy Act Notice, see form FTB 1131. File only if you are making a payment of estimated tax.

— — — — — — — — — — — — — — — — — DETACH HERE — — — — — — — — — — — — — — — — —

TAXABLE YEAR

1998 Estimated Tax for Individuals

CALIFORNIA FORM

540-ES

Fiscal year filers, enter year ending: month ☐☐ year 1 9 9 9

Your first name ☐ Initial ☐ Last name ☐

Your social security number ☐☐☐-☐☐-☐☐☐☐

If joint payment, spouse's first name ☐ Initial ☐ Last name ☐

Spouse's social security number ☐☐☐-☐☐-☐☐☐☐

Present home address — number and street including PO Box or rural route ☐ Apt. no. ☐

Payment Voucher 4
Due Jan. 15, 1999

City, town or post office ☐ State ☐ ZIP Code ☐

Make your check or money order payable to **"Franchise Tax Board."** Write your social security number and "Form 540-ES 1998" on it. **Do not combine this payment with payment of your tax due for 1997.** Mail this voucher and your check or money order to: **540-ES UNIT**
FRANCHISE TAX BOARD
PO BOX 942867
SACRAMENTO CA 94267-0031

Amount of payment

$ _____ . 0 0

For Privacy Act Notice, see form FTB 1131. File only if you are making a payment of estimated tax.

— — — — — — — — — — — — — — — — — DETACH HERE — — — — — — — — — — — — — — — — —

Form **8832**
(December 1996)
Department of the Treasury
Internal Revenue Service

Entity Classification Election

OMB No. 1545-1516

Please Type or Print

Name of entity	Employer identification number (EIN)

Number, street, and room or suite no. If a P.O. box, see instructions.

City or town, state, and ZIP code. If a foreign address, enter city, province or state, postal code and country.

1   Type of election (see instructions):

a ☐ Initial classification by a newly-formed entity (or change in current classification of an existing entity to take effect on January 1, 1997)

b ☐ Change in current classification (to take effect later than January 1, 1997)

2   Form of entity (see instructions):

a ☐ A domestic eligible entity electing to be classified as an association taxable as a corporation.

b ☐ A domestic eligible entity electing to be classified as a partnership.

c ☐ A domestic eligible entity with a single owner electing to be disregarded as a separate entity.

d ☐ A foreign eligible entity electing to be classified as an association taxable as a corporation.

e ☐ A foreign eligible entity electing to be classified as a partnership.

f ☐ A foreign eligible entity with a single owner electing to be disregarded as a separate entity.

3   Election is to be effective beginning (month, day, year) (see instructions) . . . . ▶ __/__/__

4 Name and title of person whom the IRS may call for more information	**5** That person's telephone number

Consent Statement and Signature(s) (see instructions)

Under penalties of perjury, I (we) declare that I (we) consent to the election of the above-named entity to be classified as indicated above, and that I (we) have examined this consent statement, and to the best of my (our) knowledge and belief, it is true, correct, and complete. If I am an officer, manager, or member signing for all members of the entity, I further declare that I am authorized to execute this consent statement on their behalf.

Signature(s)	Date	Title

For Paperwork Reduction Act Notice, see page 2.   Cat. No. 22598R   Form **8832** (12-96)

General Instructions

Section references are to the Internal Revenue Code unless otherwise noted.

Paperwork Reduction Act Notice

We ask for the information on this form to carry out the Internal Revenue laws of the United States. You are required to give us the information. We need it to ensure that you are complying with these laws and to allow us to figure and collect the right amount of tax.

You are not required to provide the information requested on a form that is subject to the Paperwork Reduction Act unless the form displays a valid OMB control number. Books or records relating to a form or its instructions must be retained as long as their contents may become material in the administration of any Internal Revenue law. Generally, tax returns and return information are confidential, as required by section 6103.

The time needed to complete and file this form will vary depending on individual circumstances. The estimated average time is:

Recordkeeping . . .1 hr., 20 min.
Learning about the law or the form . . .1 hr., 41 min.
Preparing and sending the form to the IRS. . . .17 min.

If you have comments concerning the accuracy of these time estimates or suggestions for making this form simpler, we would be happy to hear from you. You can write to the Tax Forms Committee, Western Area Distribution Center, Rancho Cordova, CA 95743-0001. **DO NOT** send the form to this address. Instead, see **Where To File** on page 3.

Purpose of Form

For Federal tax purposes, certain business entities automatically are classified as corporations. See items **1** and **3** through **8** under the definition of corporation on this page. Other business entities may choose how they are classified for Federal tax purposes. Except for a business entity automatically classified as a corporation, a business entity with at least two members can choose to be classified as either an association taxable as a corporation or a partnership, and a business entity with a single member can choose to be classified as either an association taxable as a corporation or disregarded as an entity separate from its owner.

Generally, an eligible entity that does not file this form will be classified under the default rules described below. An eligible entity that chooses not to be classified under the default rules or that wishes to change its current classification must file Form 8832 to elect a classification. The IRS will use the information entered on this form to establish the entity's filing and reporting requirements for Federal tax purposes.

Default Rules

Existing entity default rule.— Certain domestic and foreign entities that are already in existence before January 1, 1997, and have an established Federal tax classification, generally do not need to make an election to continue that classification. However, for an eligible entity with a single owner that claimed to be a partnership under the law in effect before January 1, 1997, that entity will now be disregarded as an entity separate from its owner. If an existing entity decides to change its classification, it may do so subject to the rules in Regulations section 301.7701-3(c)(1)(iv). A foreign eligible entity is treated as being in existence prior to the effective date of this section only if the entity's classification is relevant at any time during the 60 months prior to January 1, 1997.

Domestic default rule.— Unless an election is made on Form 8832, a domestic eligible entity is:

1. A partnership if it has two or more members.

2. Disregarded as an entity separate from its owner if it has a single owner.

Foreign default rule.— Unless an election is made on Form 8832, a foreign eligible entity is:

1. A partnership if it has two or more members and at least one member does not have limited liability.

2. An association if all members have limited liability.

3. Disregarded as an entity separate from its owner if it has a single owner that does not have limited liability.

Definitions

Business entity.—A business entity is any entity recognized for Federal tax purposes that is not properly classified as a trust under Regulations section 301.7701-4 or otherwise subject to special treatment under the Code. See Regulations section 301.7701-2(a).

Corporation.—For Federal tax purposes, a corporation is any of the following:

1. A business entity organized under a Federal or state statute, or under a statute of a federally recognized Indian tribe, if the statute describes or refers to the entity as incorporated or as a corporation, body corporate, or body politic.

2. An association (as determined under Regulations section 301.7701-3).

3. A business entity organized under a state statute, if the statute describes or refers to the entity as a joint-stock company or joint-stock association.

4. An insurance company.

5. A state-chartered business entity conducting banking activities, if any of its deposits are insured under the Federal Deposit Insurance Act, as amended, 12 U.S.C. 1811 et seq., or a similar Federal statute.

6. A business entity wholly owned by a state or any political subdivision thereof.

7. A business entity that is taxable as a corporation under a provision of the Code other than section 7701(a)(3).

8. A foreign business entity listed in Regulations section 301.7701-2(b)(8). However, a foreign business entity listed in those regulations generally will not be treated as a corporation if all of the following apply:

a. The entity was in existence on May 8, 1996.

b. The entity's classification was relevant (as defined below) on May 8, 1996.

c. No person (including the entity) for whom the entity's classification was relevant on May 8, 1996, treats the entity as a corporation for purposes of filing that person's Federal income tax returns, information returns, and withholding documents for the tax year including May 8, 1996.

d. Any change in the entity's claimed classification within the 60 months prior to May 8, 1996, was a result of a change in the organizational documents of the entity, and the entity and all members of the entity recognized the Federal tax consequences of any change in the entity's classification within the 60 months prior to May 8, 1996.

e. The entity had a reasonable basis (within the meaning of section 6662) for treating the entity as other than a corporation on May 8, 1996.

f. Neither the entity nor any member was notified in writing on or before May 8, 1996, that the classification of the entity was under examination (in which case the entity's classification will be determined in the examination).

Binding contract rule.— If a foreign business entity described in Regulations section 301.7701-2(b)(8)(i) is formed after May 8, 1996, under a written binding contract (including an accepted bid to develop a project) in effect on May 8, 1996, and all times thereafter, in which the parties agreed to engage (directly or indirectly) in an active and substantial business operation in the jurisdiction in which the entity is formed, **8** on page 2 is applied by substituting the date of the entity's formation for May 8, 1996.

Eligible entity.— An eligible entity is a business entity that is not included in items **1** or **3** through **8** under the definition of corporation on page 2.

Limited liability.— A member of a foreign eligible entity has limited liability if the member has no personal liability for any debts of or claims against the entity by reason of being a member. This determination is based solely on the statute or law under which the entity is organized (and, if relevant, the entity's organizational documents). A member has personal liability if the creditors of the entity may seek satisfaction of all or any part of the debts or claims against the entity from the member as such. A member has personal liability even if the member makes an agreement under which another person (whether or not a member of the entity) assumes that liability or agrees to indemnify that member for that liability.

Partnership.— A partnership is a business entity that has **at least** two members and is not a corporation as defined on page 2.

Relevant.— A foreign eligible entity's classification is relevant when its classification affects the liability of any person for Federal tax or information purposes. The date the classification of a foreign eligible entity is relevant is the date an event occurs that creates an obligation to file a Federal tax return, information return, or statement for which the classification of the entity must be determined.

Effect of Election

The resulting tax consequences of a change in classification remain the same no matter how a change in entity classification is achieved. For example, if an organization classified as an association elects to be classified as a partnership, the organization and its owners must recognize gain, if any, under the rules applicable to liquidations of corporations.

Who Must File

File this form for an **eligible entity** that is one of the following:

c A domestic entity electing to be classified as an association taxable as a corporation.

c A domestic entity electing to change its current classification (even if it is currently classified under the default rule).

c A foreign entity that has more than one owner, all owners have limited liability, and it elects to be classified as a partnership.

c A foreign entity that has at least one owner without limited liability, and it elects to be classified as an association taxable as a corporation.

c A foreign entity with a single owner having limited liability, and it elects to have the entity disregarded as an entity separate from its owner.

c A foreign entity electing to change its current classification (even if it is currently classified under the default rule).

Do not file this form for an eligible entity that is:

c Tax-exempt under section 501(a), or

c A real estate investment trust (REIT), as defined in section 856.

When To File

See the instructions for line 3.

Where To File

File Form 8832 with the Internal Revenue Service Center, Philadelphia, PA 19255. Also attach a copy of Form 8832 to the entity's Federal income tax or information return for the tax year of the election. If the entity is not required to file a return for that year, a copy of its Form 8832 must be attached to the Federal income tax or information returns of all direct or indirect owners of the entity for the tax year of the owner that includes the date on which the election took effect. Although failure to attach a copy will not invalidate an otherwise valid election, each member of the entity is required to file returns that are consistent with the entity's election. In addition, penalties may be assessed against persons who are required to, but who do not, attach Form 8832 to their returns. Other penalties may apply for filing Federal income tax or information returns inconsistent with the entity's election.

Specific Instructions

Employer Identification Number (EIN)

Show the correct EIN on Form 8832. If the entity does not have an EIN, it generally must apply for one on **Form SS-4,** Application for Employer Identification Number. If the filing of Form 8832 is the only reason the entity is applying for an EIN, check the "Other" box on line 9 of Form SS-4 and write "Form 8832" to the right of that box. If the entity has not received an EIN by the time Form 8832 is due, write "Applied for" in the space for the EIN. **Do not** apply for a new EIN for an existing entity that is changing its classification. If you are electing to disregard an entity as separate from its owner, enter the owner's EIN.

Address

Include the suite, room, or other unit number after the street address. If the Post Office does not deliver mail to the street address and the entity has a P.O. box, show the box number instead of the street address.

Line 1

Check box 1a if the entity is choosing a classification for the first time **and** the entity does not want to be classified under the applicable default classification. **Do not** file this form if the entity wants to be classified under the default rules.

Check box 1b if the entity is changing its current classification to take effect later than January 1, 1997, whether or not the entity's current classification is the default classification. However, once an eligible entity makes an election to change its classification (other than an election made by an existing entity to change its classification as of January 1, 1997), the entity cannot change its classification by election again during the 60 months after the effective date of the election. However, the IRS may permit (by private letter ruling) the entity to change its classification by election within the 60-month period if more than 50% of the ownership interests in the entity as of the effective date of the election are owned by persons that did not own any interests in the entity on the effective date of the entity's prior election.

Line 2

Check the appropriate box if you are changing a current classification (no matter how achieved), or are electing out of a default classification. **Do not** file this form if you fall within a default classification that is the desired classification for the new entity.

Line 3

Generally, the election will take effect on the date you enter on line 3 of this form or on the date filed if no date is entered on line 3. However, an election specifying an entity's classification for Federal tax purposes can take effect no more than 75 days prior to the date the election is filed, nor can it take effect later than 12 months after the date on which the election is filed. If line 3 shows a date more than 75 days prior to the date on which the election is filed, the election will take effect 75 days before the date it is filed. If line 3 shows an effective date more than 12 months from the filing date, the election will take effect 12 months after the date the election was filed.

Regardless of the date filed, an election will in no event take effect before January 1, 1997.

Consent Statement and Signatures

Form 8832 must be signed by:

1. Each member of the electing entity who is an owner at the time the election is filed; or

2. Any officer, manager, or member of the electing entity who is authorized (under local law or the organizational documents) to make the election and who represents to having such authorization under penalties of perjury.

If an election is to be effective for any period prior to the time it is filed, each person who was an owner between the date the election is to be effective and the date the election is filed, and who is not an owner at the time the election is filed, must also sign.

If you need a continuation sheet or use a separate consent statement, attach it to Form 8832. The separate consent statement must contain the same information as shown on Form 8832.

Form **8716**
(Rev. July 1997)
Department of the Treasury
Internal Revenue Service

Election To Have a Tax Year Other Than a Required Tax Year

OMB No. 1545-1036

Please Type or Print

Name		Employer identification number
Number, street, and room or suite no. (or P.O. box number if mail is not delivered to street address)		
City or town, state, and ZIP code		

1 Check applicable box to show type of entity:
- ☐ Partnership
- ☐ S corporation (or C corporation electing to be an S corporation)
- ☐ Personal service corporation (PSC)

2 Name and telephone number (including area code) of person who may be called for information:

	Month	Day	Year
3 Enter ending date of the tax year for the entity's last filed return. A new entity should enter the ending date of the tax year it is adopting.			

	Month	Day	
4 Enter ending date of required tax year determined under section 441(i), 706(b), or 1378 . . .			

	Month	Day	Year
5 Section 444(a) Election.—Check the applicable box and enter the ending date of the first tax year for which the election will be effective that the entity is (see instructions):			
☐ Adopting ☐ Retaining ☐ Changing to			

Under penalties of perjury, I declare that the entity named above has authorized me to make this election under section 444(a), and that the statements made are, to the best of my knowledge and belief, true, correct, and complete.

_____
Signature and title (see instructions)

_____
Date

General Instructions

Section references are to the Internal Revenue Code unless otherwise noted.

Purpose of Form

Form 8716 is filed by partnerships, S corporations, and personal service corporations (as defined in section 441(i)(2)) to elect under section 444 to have a tax year other than a required tax year.

Attach a copy of the Form 8716 you file to Form 1065 or a Form 1120 series form (1120, 1120-A, 1120S, etc.), whichever is applicable, for the first tax year for which the election is made.

When To File

Form 8716 must be filed by the earlier of:

1. The 15th day of the 5th month following the month that includes the 1st day of the tax year the election will be effective, or

2. The due date (not including extensions) of the income tax return for the tax year resulting from the section 444 election.

Items **1** and **2** relate to the tax year, or the return for the tax year, for which the ending date is entered on line 5 above.

Under Temporary Regulations section 301.9100-2T, the entity is automatically granted a 12-month extension to make an election on Form 8716. To obtain an extension, type or legibly print "FILED PURSUANT TO SECTION 301.9100-2T" at the top of a properly prepared Form 8716, and file the form within 12 months of the original due date.

Where To File

File the election with the Internal Revenue Service Center where the entity will file its return. See the instructions for Form 1065 or a Form 1120 series form for service center addresses. For a foreign entity, file Form 8716 with the Internal Revenue Service Center, Philadelphia, PA 19255.

Effect of Section 444 Election

Partnerships and S corporations.—An electing partnership or S corporation must file **Form 8752**, Required Payment or Refund Under Section 7519, for each year the election is in effect. Form 8752 is used to figure and make the payment required under section 7519 or to obtain a refund of net prior year payments. Form 8752 must be filed by May 15 following the calendar year in which each applicable election year begins.

The section 444 election will end if the partnership or S corporation is penalized for willfully failing to make the required payments.

Personal service corporations.—An electing personal service corporation (PSC) should not file Form 8752. Instead, it must comply with the minimum distribution requirements of section 280H for each year the election is in effect. If the PSC does not meet these requirements, the applicable amounts it may deduct for payments made to its employee-owners may be limited.

Use **Schedule H (Form 1120),** Section 280H Limitations for a Personal Service Corporation (PSC), to figure the required minimum distribution and the maximum deductible amount. Attach Schedule H to the income tax return of the PSC for each tax year the PSC does not meet the minimum distribution requirements.

The section 444 election will end if the PSC is penalized for willfully failing to comply with the requirements of section 280H.

Members of Certain Tiered Structures May Not Make Election

No election may be made under section 444(a) by an entity that is part of a tiered structure other than a tiered structure that consists entirely of partnerships and/or S corporations all of which have the same tax year. An election previously made will be terminated if an entity later becomes part of a tiered structure that is not allowed to make the election. See Temporary Regulations section 1.444-2T for other details.

Acceptance of Election

After your election is received and accepted by the service center, the center will stamp it "ACCEPTED" and return a copy to you. Be sure to keep a copy of the form marked "ACCEPTED" for your records.

End of Election

The election is made only once. It remains in effect until the entity changes its accounting period to its required tax year or some other permitted year or it is penalized for willfully failing to comply with the requirements of section 280H or 7519. If the election is terminated, the entity may not make another section 444 election.

Signature

Form 8716 is not a valid election unless it is signed. For partnerships, a general partner or limited liability company member must sign and date the election.

For corporations, the election must be signed and dated by the president, vice president, treasurer, assistant treasurer, chief accounting officer, or any other corporate officer (such as tax officer) authorized to sign its tax return.

If a receiver, trustee in bankruptcy, or assignee controls the entity's property or business, that person must sign the election.

Specific Instructions

Line 1

Check the applicable box to indicate whether the entity is classified for Federal income tax purposes as a partnership, an S corporation (or a C corporation electing to be an S corporation), or a personal service corporation.

A corporation electing to be an S corporation that wants to make a section 444 election is not required to attach a copy of Form 8716 to its **Form 2553,** Election by a Small Business Corporation. However, the corporation is required to state on Form 2553 its intention to make a section 444 election (or a backup section 444 election). If a corporation is making a backup section 444 election (provided for in item Q, Part II, of Form 2553), it must type or print the words "BACKUP ELECTION" at the top of the Form 8716 it files. See Temporary Regulations section 1.444-3T for more details.

Line 2

Enter the name and telephone number (including the area code) of a person that the IRS may call for information needed to complete the processing of the election.

Line 4

For a definition of a required tax year and other details, see the instructions for Form 1065 or a Form 1120 series form, whichever is applicable, and section 441(i), 706(b), or 1378.

Line 5

The following limitations and special rules apply in determining the tax year an entity may elect.

New entity adopting a tax year.—An entity adopting a tax year may elect a tax year under section 444 only if the deferral period of the tax year is not longer than 3 months. See below for the definition of deferral period.

Existing entity retaining a tax year.—In certain cases, an entity may elect to retain its tax year if the deferral period is no longer than 3 months. If the entity does not want to elect to retain its tax year, it may elect to change its tax year as explained below.

Existing entity changing a tax year.—An existing entity may elect to change its tax year if the deferral period of the elected tax year is no longer than the shorter of 3 months or the deferral period of the tax year being changed.

Example. ABC, a C corporation that historically used a tax year ending October 31, elects S status and wants to make a section 444 election for its tax year beginning 11-1-97. ABC's required tax year under section 1378 is a calendar tax year. In this case, the deferral period of the tax year being changed is 2 months. Thus, ABC may elect to retain its tax year beginning 11-1-97 and ending 10-31-98, or change it to a short tax year beginning 11-1-97 and ending 11-30-97. However, it may not elect a short tax year beginning 11-1-97 and ending 9-30-98 because the deferral period for that elected tax year is 3 months (9-30 to 12-31), which is longer than the 2-month deferral period of the tax year being changed. After filing the short year return (11-1-97 to 11-30-97), and as long as the section 444 election remains in effect, the corporation's tax year will begin 12-1 and end 11-30.

Deferral period.—The term "deferral period" means the number of months that occur between the last day of the elected tax year and the last day of the required tax year. For example, if you elected a tax year that ends on September 30 and your required tax year is the calendar year, the deferral period would be 3 months (the number of months between September 30 and December 31).

Paperwork Reduction Act Notice.—We ask for the information on this form to carry out the Internal Revenue laws of the United States. You are required to give us the information. We need it to ensure that you are complying with these laws and to allow us to figure and collect the right amount of tax.

You are not required to provide the information requested on a form that is subject to the Paperwork Reduction Act unless the form displays a valid OMB control number. Books or records relating to a form or its instructions must be retained as long as their contents may become material in the administration of any Internal Revenue law. Generally, tax returns and return information are confidential, as required by section 6103.

The time needed to complete and file this form will vary depending on individual circumstances. The estimated average time is:

Recordkeeping . . . . 2 hr., 38 min.

Learning about the law or the form . . . . 1 hr., 5 min.

Preparing and sending the form to the IRS. . . 1 hr., 11 min.

If you have comments concerning the accuracy of these time estimates or suggestions for making this form simpler, we would be happy to hear from you. You can write to the Tax Forms Committee, Western Area Distribution Center, Rancho Cordova, CA 95743-0001. **DO NOT** send the form to this address. Instead, see **Where To File** on page 1.

Form **SS-8**

(Rev. June 1997)

Department of the Treasury
Internal Revenue Service

Determination of Employee Work Status
for Purposes of Federal Employment Taxes
and Income Tax Withholding

OMB No. 1545-0004

Paperwork Reduction Act Notice

We ask for the information on this form to carry out the Internal Revenue laws of the United States. You are required to give us the information. We need it to ensure that you are complying with these laws and to allow us to figure and collect the right amount of tax.

You are not required to provide the information requested on a form that is subject to the Paperwork Reduction Act unless the form displays a valid OMB control number. Books or records relating to a form or its instructions must be retained as long as their contents may become material in the administration of any Internal Revenue law. Generally, tax returns and return information are confidential, as required by Code section 6103.

The time needed to complete and file this form will vary depending on individual circumstances. The estimated average time is: **Recordkeeping, 34 hr., 55 min.; Learning about the law or the form,** 12 min.; and **Preparing and sending the form to the IRS,** 46 min. If you have comments concerning the accuracy of these time estimates or suggestions for making this form simpler, we would be happy to hear from you. You can write to the Tax Forms Committee, Western Area Distribution Center, Rancho Cordova, CA 95743-0001. **DO NOT** send the tax form to this address. Instead, see **General Information** for where to file.

Purpose

Employers and workers file Form SS-8 to get a determination as to whether a worker is an employee for purposes of Federal employment taxes and income tax withholding.

General Information

Complete this form carefully. If the firm is completing the form, complete it for **ONE** individual who is representative of the class of workers whose status is in question. If you want a written determination for more than one class of workers, complete a separate Form SS-8 for one worker

from each class whose status is typical of that class. A written determination for any worker will apply to other workers of the same class if the facts are not materially different from those of the worker whose status was ruled upon.

Caution: Form SS-8 is **not** a claim for refund of social security and Medicare taxes or Federal income tax withholding. Also, a determination that an individual is an employee does not necessarily reduce any current or prior tax liability. A worker must file his or her income tax return even if a determination has not been made by the due date of the return.

Where to file.—In the list below, find the state where your legal residence, principal place of business, office, or agency is located. Send Form SS-8 to the address listed for your location.

Location:	Send to:
Alaska, Arizona, Arkansas, California, Colorado, Hawaii, Idaho, Illinois, Iowa, Kansas, Minnesota, Missouri, Montana, Nebraska, Nevada, New Mexico, North Dakota, Oklahoma, Oregon, South Dakota, Texas, Utah, Washington, Wisconsin, Wyoming	Internal Revenue Service SS-8 Determinations P.O. Box 1231, Stop 4106 AUSC Austin, TX 78767
Alabama, Connecticut, Delaware, District of Columbia, Florida, Georgia, Indiana, Kentucky, Louisiana, Maine, Maryland, Massachusetts, Michigan, Mississippi, New Hampshire, New Jersey, New York, North Carolina, Ohio, Pennsylvania, Rhode Island, South Carolina, Tennessee, Vermont, Virginia, West Virginia, All other locations not listed	Internal Revenue Service SS-8 Determinations Two Lakemont Road Newport, VT 05855-1555
American Samoa, Guam, Puerto Rico, U.S. Virgin Islands	Internal Revenue Service Mercantile Plaza 2 Avenue Ponce de Leon San Juan, Puerto Rico 00918

Name of firm (or person) for whom the worker performed services	Name of worker	
Address of firm (include street address, apt. or suite no., city, state, and ZIP code)	Address of worker (include street address, apt. or suite no., city, state, and ZIP code)	
Trade name	Telephone number (include area code) ( )	Worker's social security number
Telephone number (include area code) ( )	Firm's employer identification number	

Check type of firm for which the work relationship is in question:

☐ **Individual** ☐ **Partnership** ☐ **Corporation** ☐ **Other** (specify) ▶ --

---

Important Information Needed To Process Your Request

This form is being completed by: ☐ Firm ☐ Worker

If this form is being completed by the worker, the IRS **must** have your permission to disclose your name to the firm.

Do you object to disclosing your name and the information on this form to the firm? . . . . ☐ Yes ☐ No

If you answer "Yes," the IRS cannot act on your request **Do not complete the rest of this form unless the IRS asks for it.**

Under section 6110 of the Internal Revenue Code, the information on this form and related file documents will be open to the public if any ruling or determination is made. However, names, addresses, and taxpayer identification numbers will be removed before the information is made public.

Is there any other information you want removed? . . . . ☐ Yes ☐ No

If you check "Yes," we cannot process your request unless you submit a copy of this form and copies of all supporting documents showing, in brackets, the information you want removed. Attach a separate statement showing which specific exemption of section 6110(c) applies to each bracketed part.

This form is designed to cover many work activities, so some of the questions may not apply to you. **You must answer ALL items or mark them** "**Unknown**" **or** "**Does not apply.**"   *If you need more space, attach another sheet.*

Total number of workers in this class. (Attach names and addresses. If more than 10 workers, list only 10.) ▶ _____

This information is about services performed by the worker from _____ to _____
                                          (month, day, year)   (month, day, year)

Is the worker still performing services for the firm? . . . . ☐ **Yes**   ☐ **No**

- If "No," what was the date of termination? _____
                                            (month, day, year)

1a Describe the firm's business ....

  b Describe the work done by the worker ....

....

2a If the work is done under a written agreement between the firm and the worker, attach a copy.

  b If the agreement is not in writing, describe the terms and conditions of the work arrangement ....

....

  c If the actual working arrangement differs in any way from the agreement, explain the differences and why they occur ....

....

3a Is the worker given training by the firm? . . . . ☐ **Yes**   ☐ **No**
- If "Yes," what kind?..
- How often? ....

  b Is the worker given instructions in the way the work is to be done (exclusive of actual training in 3a)? . ☐ **Yes**   ☐ **No**
- If "Yes," give specific examples..

  c Attach samples of any written instructions or procedures.

  d Does the firm have the right to change the methods used by the worker or direct that person on how to do the work? . . . . ☐ **Yes**   ☐ **No**
- Explain your answer ....

....

  e Does the operation of the firm's business require that the worker be supervised or controlled in the performance of the service? . . . . ☐ **Yes**   ☐ **No**
- Explain your answer ....

....

4a The firm engages the worker:
  ☐ To perform and complete a particular job only
  ☐ To work at a job for an indefinite period of time
  ☐ Other (explain) ....

  b Is the worker required to follow a routine or a schedule established by the firm? . . . . ☐ **Yes**   ☐ **No**
- If "Yes," what is the routine or schedule?..

....

  c Does the worker report to the firm or its representative?. . . . . ☐ **Yes**   ☐ **No**
- If "Yes," how often?..
- For what purpose? ....
- In what manner (in person, in writing, by telephone, etc.)? ....
- Attach copies of any report forms used in reporting to the firm.

  d Does the worker furnish a time record to the firm? . . . . ☐ **Yes**   ☐ **No**
- If "Yes," attach copies of time records.

5a State the kind and value of tools, equipment, supplies, and materials furnished by:
- The firm ....

....

- The worker ....

....

  b What expenses are incurred by the worker in the performance of services for the firm? ....

....

  c Does the firm reimburse the worker for any expenses? . . . . ☐ **Yes**   ☐ **No**
- If "Yes," specify the reimbursed expenses..

6a Will the worker perform the services personally? . . . . ☐ **Yes** ☐ **No**

  b Does the worker have helpers? . . . . ☐ **Yes** ☐ **No**

    • If "Yes," who hires the helpers? ☐ Firm ☐ Worker

    • If the helpers are hired by the worker, is the firm's approval necessary? . . . . ☐ **Yes** ☐ **No**

    • Who pays the helpers?   ☐ Firm ☐ Worker

    • If the worker pays the helpers, does the firm repay the worker? . . . . ☐ **Yes** ☐ **No**

    • Are social security and Medicare taxes and Federal income tax withheld from the helpersÕ pay? . . ☐ **Yes** ☐ **No**

    • If "Yes," who reports and pays these taxes?   ☐ Firm   ☐ Worker

    • Who reports the helpers' earnings to the Internal Revenue Service? ☐ Firm ☐ Worker

    • What services do the helpers perform? ....

7 At what location are the services performed? ☐ Firm's ☐ Worker's ☐ Other (specify) ....

8a Type of pay worker receives:

    ☐ Salary   ☐ Commission ☐ Hourly wage   ☐ Piecework ☐ Lump sum ☐ Other (specify) ....

  b Does the firm guarantee a minimum amount of pay to the worker? . . . . ☐ **Yes** ☐ **No**

  c Does the firm allow the worker a drawing account or advances against pay? . . . . ☐ **Yes** ☐ **No**

    • If "Yes," is the worker paid such advances on a regular basis? . . . . ☐ **Yes** ☐ **No**

  d How does the worker repay such advances? ....

9a Is the worker eligible for a pension, bonus, paid vacations, sick pay, etc.? . . . . ☐ **Yes** ☐ **No**

    • If "Yes," specify..

  b Does the firm carry worker   compensation insurance on the worker? . . . . ☐ **Yes** ☐ **No**

  c Does the firm withhold social security and Medicare taxes from amounts paid the worker? . . . . . ☐ **Yes** ☐ **No**

  d Does the firm withhold Federal income tax from amounts paid the worker? . . . . ☐ **Yes** ☐ **No**

  e How does the firm report the worker's   earnings to the Internal Revenue Service?

    ☐ Form W-2 ☐ Form 1099-MISC ☐ Does not report ☐ Other (specify) ....

    • Attach a copy.

  f Does the firm bond the worker? . . . . ☐ **Yes** ☐ **No**

10a Approximately how many hours a day does the worker perform services for the firm? ....

  b Does the firm set hours of work for the worker? . . . . ☐ **Yes** ☐ **No**

    • If "Yes," what are the worker's set hours? _____ a.m./p.m. to_____ a.m./p.m. (Circle whether a.m. or p.m.)

  c Does the worker perform similar services for others? . . . . ☐ **Yes** ☐ **No** ☐ **Unknown**

    • If "Yes," are these services performed on a daily basis for other firms? . . . . . ☐ **Yes** ☐ **No** ☐ **Unknown**

    • Percentage of time spent in performing these services for:

      This firm .... % Other firms .... % ☐ **Unknown**

    • Does the firm have priority on the worker's time?. . . . . ☐ **Yes** ☐ **No**

    • If "No," explain..

  d Is the worker prohibited from competing with the firm either while performing services or during any later

    period? . . . . ☐ **Yes** ☐ **No**

11a Can the firm discharge the worker at any time without incurring a liability? . . . . ☐ **Yes** ☐ **No**

    • If "No," explain..

  b Can the worker terminate the services at any time without incurring a liability? . . . . ☐ **Yes** ☐ **No**

    • If "No," explain..

12a Does the worker perform services for the firm under:

    ☐ The firm's business name ☐ The worker's own business name ☐ Other (specify)...........................

  b Does the worker advertise or maintain a business listing in the telephone directory, a trade

    journal, etc.? . . . . ☐ **Yes** ☐ **No** ☐ **Unknown**

    • If "Yes," specify..

  c Does the worker represent himself or herself to the public as being in business to perform

    the same or similar services? . . . . ☐ **Yes** ☐ **No** ☐ **Unknown**

    • If "Yes," how?..

  d Does the worker have his or her own shop or office? . . . . ☐ **Yes** ☐ **No** ☐ **Unknown**

    • If "Yes," where?..

  e Does the firm represent the worker as an employee of the firm to its customers? . . . . ☐ **Yes** ☐ **No**

    • If "No," how is the worker represented?..

  f How did the firm learn of the worker's services?..

13 Is a license necessary for the work? . . . . ☐ **Yes** ☐ **No** ☐ **Unknown**

    • If "Yes," what kind of license is required?..

    • Who issues the license? ....

    • Who pays the license fee?

14 Does the worker have a financial investment in a business related to the services
performed?. . . . . ☐ **Yes** ☐ **No** ☐ **Unknown**
  • If "Yes," specify and give amount of the investment

15 Can the worker incur a loss in the performance of the service for the firm? . . . . ☐ **Yes** ☐ **No**
  • If "Yes," how?

16a Has any other government agency ruled on the status of the firm's workers? . . . . ☐ **Yes** ☐ **No**
  • If "Yes," attach a copy of the ruling.

  b Is the same issue being considered by any IRS office in connection with the audit of the worker's tax
return or the firm's tax return, or has it been considered recently? . . . . ☐ **Yes** ☐ **No**
  • If "Yes," for which year(s)?

17 Does the worker assemble or process a product at home or away from the firm   place of business? ☐ **Yes** ☐ **No**
  • If "Yes," who furnishes materials or goods used by the worker? ☐ Firm   ☐ Worker   ☐ Other
  • Is the worker furnished a pattern or given instructions to follow in making the product? . . . . . ☐ **Yes** ☐ **No**
  • Is the worker required to return the finished product to the firm or to someone designated by the firm? ☐ **Yes** ☐ **No**

18 Attach a detailed explanation of any other reason why you believe the worker is an employee or an independent contractor.

Answer items 19a through o only if the worker is a salesperson or provides a service directly to customers.

19a Are leads to prospective customers furnished by the firm?. . . . . ☐ **Yes** ☐ **No** ☐ **Does not apply**
  b Is the worker required to pursue or report on leads? . . . . ☐ **Yes** ☐ **No** ☐ **Does not apply**
  c Is the worker required to adhere to prices, terms, and conditions of sale established by the firm? . . ☐ **Yes** ☐ **No**
  d Are orders submitted to and subject to approval by the firm? . . . . ☐ **Yes** ☐ **No**
  e Is the worker expected to attend sales meetings?. . . . . ☐ **Yes** ☐ **No**
  • If "Yes," is the worker subject to any kind of penalty for failing to attend? . . . . ☐ **Yes** ☐ **No**
  f Does the firm assign a specific territory to the worker? . . . . ☐ **Yes** ☐ **No**
  g Whom does the customer pay?   ☐ Firm   ☐ Worker
  • If worker, does the worker remit the total amount to the firm? . . . . ☐ **Yes** ☐ **No**
  h Does the worker sell a consumer product in a home or establishment other than a permanent retail
establishment? . . . . ☐ **Yes** ☐ **No**
  i List the products and/or services distributed by the worker, such as meat, vegetables, fruit, bakery products, beverages (other
than milk), or laundry or dry cleaning services. If more than one type of product and/or service is distributed, specify the
principal one
  j Did the firm or another person assign the route or territory and a list of customers to the worker? . . ☐ **Yes** ☐ **No**
  • If "Yes," enter the name and job title of the person who made the assignment
  k Did the worker pay the firm or person for the privilege of serving customers on the route or in the territory? ☐ **Yes** ☐ **No**
  • If "Yes," how much did the worker pay (not including any amount paid for a truck or racks, etc.)? $
  • What factors were considered in determining the value of the route or territory?
  l How are new customers obtained by the worker? Explain fully, showing whether the new customers called the firm for service,
were solicited by the worker, or both
  m Does the worker sell life insurance? . . . . ☐ **Yes** ☐ **No**
  • If "Yes," is the selling of life insurance or annuity contracts for the firm the worker's entire business
activity? . . . . ☐ **Yes** ☐ **No**
  • If "No," list the other business activities and the amount of time spent on them
  n Does the worker sell other types of insurance for the firm? . . . . ☐ **Yes** ☐ **No**
  • If "Yes," state the percentage of the worker's total working time spent in selling other types of insurance . . . . %
  • At the time the contract was entered into between the firm and the worker, was it their intention that the worker sell life
insurance for the firm: ☐ on a full-time basis   ☐ on a part-time basis
  • State the manner in which the intention was expressed
  o Is the worker a traveling or city salesperson? . . . . ☐ **Yes** ☐ **No**
  • If "Yes," from whom does the worker principally solicit orders for the firm?
  • If the worker solicits orders from wholesalers, retailers, contractors, or operators of hotels, restaurants, or other similar
establishments, specify the percentage of the worker's time spent in the solicitation . . . . %
  • Is the merchandise purchased by the customers for resale or for use in their business operations? If used by the customers
in their business operations, describe the merchandise and state whether it is equipment installed on their premises or a
consumable supply

Signature ▶   Title ▶   Date ▶

How to Use the Forms Disk

All of the forms in Appendix C are included on a "forms" CD-ROM disk in the back of the book. This CD-ROM, which can be used with Windows and Macintosh computers, installs files that can be opened, printed and edited using a word processor or other software. It is NOT a stand-alone software program. Please read this appendix and the README.TXT file included on the CD-ROM for instructions on using the forms disk.

How to View the README File

If you do not know how to view the file README.TXT, insert the forms disk into your computer's CD-ROM drive and follow these instructions:

- **Windows 95:** (1) On your PC's desktop, double-click the My Computer icon; (2) double-click the icon for the CD-ROM drive into which the forms disk was inserted; (3) double-click the file README.TXT.

- **Windows 3.1:** (1) Open File Manager; (2) double-click the icon for the CD-ROM drive into which the forms disk was inserted; (3) double-click the file README.TXT.

- **Macintosh:** (1) On your Mac desktop, double-click the icon for the CD-ROM that you inserted; (2) double-click on the file README.TXT.

While the README file is open, print it out by using the Print command in the File menu.

Most of the forms contained on the CD-ROM are federal and state forms in PDF format, which you can open and print out only with the Adobe Acrobat Reader program (see Section C, below). You will not be able to use your computer to fill in these forms.

In addition, there's a partnership agreement form that you can open and fill in with your word processor (see Section B, below).

A. Installing the Form Files Onto Your Computer

Before you can do anything else, you need to install the files from the CD-ROM onto your hard disk. In accordance with U.S. copyright laws, remember that copies of the disk and its files are for your personal use only.

Insert the forms disk and do the following:

1. Windows 95 Users

Follow the instructions that appear on screen.

By default, all of the files are installed in the C:\CA_BIZ directory.

2. Windows 3.1 Users

Step 1: In Program Manager, choose Run from the File menu.

Step 2: Enter D:\INSTALL.HLP (substitute the letter of your CD-ROM drive for "D").

Step 3: Follow the instructions that appear on screen.

By default, all of the files are installed in the C:\CA_BIZ directory.

3. Macintosh Users

Step 1: If the "CA Business Forms" CD window is not open, open it by double-clicking the "CA Business Forms" CD icon.

Step 2: Select the "CA Business Forms" folder icon.

Step 3: Drag and drop the folder icon onto the icon of your hard disk.

B. Creating a Partnership Agreement With Your Word Processor

This section concerns the partnership agreement file that can be opened and edited with your word processing program. (Other forms in PDF format are discussed in Section C, below.)

The form comes in two file types (or formats): 1) the standard ASCII text format (TXT), and 2) rich text format (RTF). The document can be created using PARTAGRE.RTF or PARTAGRE.TXT.

ASCII text files can be read by every word processor or text editor, including DOS Edit, all flavors of MS Word and WordPerfect (including Macintosh), Windows Notepad, Write and WordPad, and Macintosh SimpleText and TeachText.

RTF files have the same text as the ASCII files, but have additional formatting. They can be read by most recent word processing programs, including all versions of MS Word for Windows and Macintosh, WordPad for Windows 95, and recent versions of WordPerfect for Windows and Macintosh.

To use a form on the disk to create your documents, you must (1) open a file in your word processor or text editor; (2) edit the form by filling in the required information; (3) print it out; and (4) save your revised file.

The following are general instructions on how to do this. However, each word processor uses different commands to open, format, save and print documents. Please read your word processor's manual for specific instructions on performing these tasks.

DO NOT CALL NOLO'S TECHNICAL SUPPORT IF YOU HAVE QUESTIONS ON HOW TO USE YOUR WORD PROCESSOR.

1. Step 1: Opening a File

To open a file in your word processor, you need to start your word processing program and open the file from within the program. This process usually entails going to the File menu and choosing the Open command. This opens a dialog box where you will tell the program (1) the type of file you want to open (either *.TXT or *.RTF) and (2) the location and name of the file (you will need to navigate through the directory tree to get to the folder/ directory on your hard disk to which you installed or copied the CD's files). If these directions are unclear you will need to look through the manual for your word processing program—Nolo's technical support department will NOT be able to help you with the use of your word processing program.

Which File Format Should You Use?

If you are not sure which file format to use with your word processor, try opening the RTF file first. Most current Windows and Macintosh word processing programs, such as Microsoft Word or WordPerfect, can read RTF files.

If you are unable to open the RTF file in your word processor, or a bunch of "garbage" characters appear on screen when you do, then use the TXT files instead. All word processors and text editors can read TXT files, which contain only text, tabs and carriage returns; all other formatting and special characters have been stripped.

You can also open a file more directly by double-clicking on it. Use File Manager (Windows 3.1), My Computer or Windows Explorer (Windows 95 and 98), or the Finder (Macintosh) to go to the folder/directory to which you copied the disk's files, then double-click on the specific file that you want to open. If you click on an RTF file and you have a program installed that "understands" RTF, your word processor should launch and load that file. If the file doesn't load, or if it contains a bunch of "garbage" characters, use your word processor's Open command, as described above, to open the TXT file instead. If you double-click directly on a TXT file, it will load into a basic text editor like Notepad or SimpleText rather than your word processor.

2. Step 2: Editing Your Document

Fill in the appropriate information according to the instructions and sample agreements in the book. Underlines are used to indicate where you need to enter your information, frequently followed by instructions in brackets. Be sure to delete the underlines and instructions from your edited document and, if necessary, renumber the paragraphs. If you do not know how to use your word processor to edit a document, you will need to look through the manual for your word processing program—Nolo's technical support department will NOT be able to help you with the use of your word processing program.

Editing Forms That Have Optional or Alternative Text

Some of the forms have check boxes before text. The check boxes indicate

- optional text, which you choose whether to include or exclude, and

- alternative text, where you select one alternative to include and exclude the other alternatives.

If you are using the tear-out forms in the Appendix, simply mark the appropriate box to make your choice.

If you are using the forms disk, however, we recommend that instead of marking the check boxes you do the following:

Optional text

If you don't want to include optional text, just delete it from your document.

If you do want to include optional text, just leave it in your document.

In either case, delete the check box itself as well as the italicized instructions that the text is optional.

Alternative text

First delete all the alternatives that you do not want to include.

Then delete the remaining check box, as well as the italicized instructions that you need to select one of the alternatives provided.

3. Step 3: Printing Out the Document

Use your word processor's or text editor's Print command to print out your document. If you do not know how to use your word processor to print a document, you will need to look through the manual for your word processing program—Nolo's technical support department will NOT be able to help you with the use of your word processing program.

4. Step 4: Saving Your Document

After filling in the form, use the "Save As" command to save and rename the file. Because all the files are "read-only," you will not be able to use the "Save" command. This is for your protection. If you save the file without renaming it, the underlines that indicate where you need to enter your information will be lost and you will not be able to create a new document with this file without recopying the original file from the CD-ROM.

If you do not know how to use your word processor to save a document, you will need to look through the manual for your word processing program—Nolo's technical support department will NOT be able to help you with the use of your word processing program.

C. Using the Government Form Files

Electronic copies of useful federal and state forms are also included on the CD-ROM disk. These forms are in Adobe Acrobat PDF format; you must have the Adobe Acrobat Reader installed on your computer (see below) to view and print them. After printing them out, you'll need to fill them in manually—you cannot edit these forms using your computer.

To complete your document using these files, you must (1) start Acrobat Reader; (2) open a file; (3) print it out; and (4) complete them by hand or typewriter. You will not be able to complete these forms using your computer.

Installing Acrobat Reader

To install the Adobe Acrobat Reader, insert the CD into your computer's CD-ROM drive and follow these instructions:

- **Windows 95:** Follow the instructions that appear on screen.

- **Windows 3.1 Users:** (1) In Program Manager, choose Run from the File menu; (2) enter D:\INSTALL.HLP (substitute the letter of your CD-ROM drive for "D"); (3) follow the instructions that appear on screen.

- **Macintosh:** (1) If the "CA Business Forms" CD window is not open, open it by double-clicking the "CA Business Forms" CD icon; (2) double-click on the "Install Acrobat Reader 3.0" icon.

For instructions on how to use Adobe Acrobat to view and print the files, you will need to consult the online documentation in Acrobat Reader's Help menu program. Do NOT call Nolo technical support if you have questions on how to use Acrobat Reader.

Index